DATE DUE

DEMCO 38-296

Online Retrieval

DATABASE SEARCHING SERIES

Edited by Carol Tenopir

Online Retrieval

A Dialogue of Theory and Practice

Geraldene Walker
School of Information Science & Policy
State University of New York at Albany

Joseph Janes
School of Information & Library Studies
University of Michigan

1993
Libraries Unlimited, Inc.
Englewood, Colorado

Libraries Unlimited, Inc.
P.O. Box 6633
Englewood, CO 80155-6633

Library of Congress Cataloging-in-Publication Data

Walker, Geraldene.
　　Online retrieval : a dialogue of theory and practice / Geraldene
Walker, Joseph Janes.
　　　xi, 221 p. 22x28 cm. -- (Database searching series)
　　Includes bibliographical references and index.
　　ISBN 1-56308-157-1
　　　1. Online bibliographic searching--United States. 2. DIALOG
(Information retrieval system) I. Janes, Joseph. II. Title.
III. Series.
Z699.35.O55W35 1993
025.5'24--dc20
　　　　　　　　　　　　　　　　　　　　　　　　　　　93-4955
　　　　　　　　　　　　　　　　　　　　　　　　　　　CIP

Contents

The search for documents relevant to an individual's information needs, usually termed *information retrieval*, is the central objective of all library and information systems. The automation of parts of this process through remote access to computerized databases has speeded the search process and made it possible to perform searches of much greater depth and breadth. Searching these systems is a complex operation, drawing on many different skills and talents simultaneously and usually operating under constraints of both time and money. It is not surprising, therefore, that learning effective and efficient online searching is not trivial.

This book is designed to assist the beginning searcher of those online systems that primarily provide information in the form of bibliographic citations. These systems often also contain files in other formats that are designed to provide answers to reference-type questions.

Although other books have been written for use in training online searchers, we believe our approach in this book to be unique in terms of the alternative perspectives brought to the task by two authors with very different, yet complementary experiences. Geraldene has been conducting searches and teaching online searching for many years and has a great wealth of practical knowledge about the finer points of search strategy and online systems. In addition, her doctoral dissertation studied the performance and behavior of naive end-users, and she continues to conduct research involving the user interface. Joe, on the other hand, is more familiar with the broader setting for information retrieval and the research that has been conducted regarding the construction and design of information retrieval systems in general. His current research is concerned with the theory and design of information systems, information searching, and users' evaluation of information items.

A new textbook on online searching was suggested by the need to emphasize both research and practice and to link these twin aspects in the training of beginning searchers. In fact, it occurred to us that a dialogue between the two of us, not unlike conversations we have actually had, on the practice and theory of online searching would be an interesting and fruitful way to raise important issues about the process, while still giving beginners a solid background in search techniques.

We are directing this book to several audiences: students in library and information science programs for use as a textbook in an online retrieval course; practicing librarians and online searchers in library settings as a quick reference or for use in training sessions; and finally information seekers who want to perform their own searches for information using an online search system. It is intended not only to provide basic "how-to" information on the use of such systems but also to raise topics on which there is not an accepted paradigm and to provide discussion of alternative points of view in a framework of previous research.

The book is laid out in the following way: Chapter 1 gives a broad overview of the search for information in computerized settings. Chapter 2 traces the conceptual and technical history of online systems and investigates the advantages of their use, and chapter 3 describes the telecommunications connection. Background information on how databases are constructed and searched is introduced in chapter 4.

The actual practice of searching begins in chapter 5 with a discussion of search protocols, the use of a command language, and the design of a search. Search practice continues in chapters 6 and 7, which deal respectively with controlled vocabulary searching and the use of thesauri, and with free-text searching. The search interview is covered in chapter 8. More sophisticated search features and capabilities of online systems are discussed in chapter 9, and chapter 10 describes the complexities of multiple file searching. The searching component ends with an overview of other database types—citation indexes, full-text files, and reference databases—in chapter 11.

For the technique and search strategy sections and for sample searches, we have chosen to use the DIALOG system. We make this choice on two grounds: 1) it would be difficult to write a book such as this trying to work with several different systems at once, and 2) DIALOG is probably the best-known and most widely used of the search vendors. To be sure, there are many other vendors available, but we feel it is best to work with just one.

The last few chapters raise broader issues related to the search process. Chapter 12 deals with the evaluation of searches from a variety of perspectives, chapter 13 discusses management issues, and chapter 14 looks at the development and implementation of direct user access on online databases. Finally, in chapter 15, we present a brief but important discussion of a new and exciting domain: wide-area telecommunications such as the Internet and the National Research and Education Network (NREN). These networks are already providing access to an enormous variety of information sources, and it is likely that searching for information online will change dramatically as a result of their emergence.

We have divided up the responsibility for chapters based on our backgrounds, experiences, and research interests. But because we envisioned this book as a dialogue, we have made comments on each other's chapters (and sometimes our own) to illuminate points and even to disagree with each other.

This is a comment box. When you see this, you will know one of us is commenting on the other's text, or in some cases elaborating on our own.

Our hope is that this method of discussion, example, and dialogue will put the practice and theory of online searching into a helpful perspective and thus give searchers a sense of the larger environment in which searching takes place and the range of possible developments suggested by current research and development.

We would like to take this opportunity to acknowledge some people without whose help you would not now be holding this book in your hands.

First of all, thanks to the several generations of students in our respective online searching courses. We wrote this book primarily to help us make those classes and our teaching more effective, and we hope we've succeeded in that aim.

Jim Ottaviani and Janet Smith read and commented on sections of the book. Their advice was most helpful, and we thank them here.

Thanks also to the staff of the School of Information and Library Studies at Michigan, especially Dawn Nugent, who assisted with the preparation of sections of the manuscript and was a calming presence in an occasionally hectic process.

Carol Tenopir was our content editor and gave us a number of insightful observations and suggestions that made this a much better book. We owe her a real debt of gratitude.

Two people deserve special recognition: Lou Rosenfeld read many drafts of the Internet chapter and contributed several sections of the final work. His technical and content knowledge improved that chapter greatly. We believe this to be the first and only chapter on networked information resources in an online searching text, and Lou was an enormous help.

Finally, there is Laura Bost, who has been Joe's assistant for the past year. Not only did she supervise the preparation of the manuscript and figures, the final revisions, and the requests for reprint permissions, but her good humor and patience, both of which were sorely tested, made this book a reality.

1

THE SEARCH FOR INFORMATION IN THE ONLINE AGE

The organization and control of information is nothing new. As early as the seventh century B.C. there were collections of information-bearing artifacts, though at that time and for many centuries thereafter the emphasis was on collection rather than retrieval.[1] The aim was the preservation of society's cultural heritage in an uncertain world, rather than access to individual items of information. Today, the situation is very different. The pressures brought about by the explosion of published materials over the last 50 years have highlighted the problems involved in retrieving a single desired item from the proverbial haystack of available information. The focus has moved from collection and preservation to retrieval and selection.

It is all too easy to assume that modern technology can entirely solve this retrieval problem or at the very least make the process much easier. It is true that the use of computer and communications technologies has had an enormous influence on the way that information is produced, organized, stored, searched, and transmitted and has certainly made more information available. But these new technologies have decidedly not solved the problems of information retrieval, and in some ways they have made retrieval more difficult. On the one hand, there is much more information to choose from, and it is becoming increasingly important to learn to use a variety of search systems. On the other hand, technology has speeded the search process, increased the amounts of information that can be searched at one time, and enabled the searcher to use much more sophisticated search strategies. Technological developments have resulted in an increased need for user training if the searchers on these systems are to make the best use of the new powerful retrieval capabilities.

This book will introduce the reader to one of the most widely used applications of computer and telecommunications technologies that has been developed to assist with access to a wide variety of information sources—online search services. These systems are called "online" because the search is conducted interactively while the searcher is connected from a terminal, via a telecommunications link, to a file of information stored on a remote computer. The interaction progresses in the form of a "conversation" in which the searcher and the computer take turns "speaking," rather like a conversation on a CB radio. These systems were earlier known as "document retrieval" systems, because many of the first databases to become available provided only citations to other bibliographic items—journal articles, research reports, dissertations, and books or book chapters—rather than information per se.

What Information Can You Find Online?

The heart of an online retrieval system is the information that it contains—the *databases* that are available for searching. Databases come in all shapes and sizes, ranging from vast files such as *MEDLINE* or *CA Search* (each containing around 8 million records), to tiny specialized files such as *The Philosopher's Index* (165,000 records), *AIDSLINE* (60,000 records), or *Arthur D. Little/Online* (with less than 4,000 records). Although most of the early databases contained bibliographic citations that were machine-readable versions of a parallel printed index, today there is a great range of information, available for searching online. Different databases not only contain different types of information but are useful for a variety of purposes, so that it is possible to find answers to almost any type of reference query using online resources.

In this book we are going to concentrate on a single example of one of these online search services: the DIALOG system. The access language that you will learn will be the DIALOG command language, and most of our examples will be taken from the DIALOG system. The reason for this concentration on DIALOG is our belief that it is very difficult to learn more than one new language at the same time. One keeps mixing them up! It is better to become fluent in one new language before trying another. We also believe that, because most online systems have a very similar range of commands, once you are proficient on one system, it is not difficult to transfer to a new system with a slightly different command language.

Some search systems provide information in a single subject field. For example, *MEDLINE*, the database from the National Library of Medicine, covers only medical-related subjects, and *LEXIS* from Mead Data Central covers only legal case law. DIALOG, however, is a multisubject system, so that it is a particularly useful example to illustrate the diversity of information that is available online.

There are three basic types of databases currently available for searching on DIALOG:

- Bibliographic citations (sometimes with abstracts)
- Full-text or directory files
- Numeric data

It is not uncommon for a single search topic to be covered by several databases that may provide different kinds of information. The degree of overlap between files and the occurrence of unique items will vary considerably by both topic and database. In order to demonstrate the diversity of information available, let us look at how some different files may be used to answer a variety of information requests.

Bibliographic Citations

Although the original use of online systems was normally to produce a bibliography of *citations* in response to a subject search request, the same type of record is also useful as a quick source for checking an incomplete or misremembered reference. For example, a request for "that book about tough California writers" can be swiftly identified by using a database such as the Library of Congress *MARC* file or the online version of *Books in Print*. The resulting citation in *Books in Print* (fig. 1.1) contains information not unlike that in a standard catalog record. The same record in LC *MARC* (fig. 1.2) looks rather different.

Notice how the information provided in individual records varies enormously, even when both cover the same type of material (monographs) and even the same item. Similar differences apply in regard to journal articles. Compare, for example, the two records in figures 1.3 and 1.4 on the same topic—the effects of taking vitamin E supplements. *Magazine Index* provides popular-type information, while *BIOSIS Previews* covers the topic from the purely scientific angle.

Fig. 1.1. *Books In Print* citation.

```
00598185   1034311XX    STATUS: Out of print (06-92)
  TITLE: California Writers: Jack London, John Steinbeck, the Tough Guys
  AUTHOR: Martin, Stoddard
  PUBLISHER: St Martin   PUBLICATION DATE: 01/1984 (840101)
  NO. OF PAGES: 224p.
  LCCN: 82-020451
  BINDING: Trade - $22.50
  ISBN: 0-312-11420-6
  VOLUME(S): N/A
  ORDER NO.: N/A
  IMPRINT: N/A
  STATUS IN FILE: New (84-02)

  LIBRARY OF CONGRESS SUBJECT HEADINGS: LONDON, JACK, 1876-1916 (00280707)
```

Fig. 1.2. *Library of Congress MARC* citation.

```
1637993  LCCN:  82020451
  California writers  ;  Jack London,  John Steinbeck, the tough guys /
  Stoddard Martin
Martin, Stoddard, 1948-

New York : St. Martin's Press,   viii, 224 p. ; 23 cm.
PUBLICATION DATE(S) : 1983
PLACE OF PUBLICATION: New York
ISBN: 0312114206
LC CALL NO.: PS283.C2 M35 1983   DEWEY CALL NO.: 813/.54/099794
RECORD STATUS: Increase in encoding level from prepublication record
BIBLIOGRAPHIC LEVEL: Monograph
LANGUAGE:  English
GEOGRAPHIC LOCATION: California
NOTES:
  Includes bibliographical references and index.
DESCRIPTORS:
American fiction -- California -- History and criticism; American fiction --
  20th century -- History and criticism; California in literature
```

Fig. 1.3. *Magazine Index* citation.

```
12535757  DIALOG File 47:  MAGAZINE INDEX  *Use Format 9 for FULL TEXT*
'Hearty' vitamins;  sparing arteries with megadose supplements. (research
  using soybean-oil and vitamin E)
Raloff, Janet
Science News  v142 p76(1) August 1, 1992
SOURCE FILE:  MI File 47
CODEN: SCNEB  ISSN: 0036-8423
AVAILABILITY: FULL TEXT Online  LINE COUNT:  00092
ABSTRACT:  Scientists are conducting tests that boost LDL oxidant defensive
  benefits in order to discourage plaque buildup in the human body.  The
  study includes large doses of soybean-oil capsules and vitamin E.
  Researchers say that vitamin therapy will probably be used to ward off
  heart disease.
DESCRIPTORS: Atherosclerosis--Prevention;  Cholesterol,  LDL--Research;
  Oxidation--Research; Vitamin therapy--Research
```

Fig. 1.4. *BIOSIS Previews* citation.

```
9610212      BIOSIS Number: 94115212
  HEPATIC CYTOTOXICITY AND MUTAGENIC POTENTIAL OF SODIUM SELENITE VITAMIN E
ICCF BUCURESTI ON MOUSE BONE MARROW IN-VIVO
  SOCACIU C; PASCA I; LISOVSCHI C
  USACN, STR. MANASTUR NR. 3, CLUJ-NAPOCA 3400, ROMANIA.
  BUL INST AGRON CLUJ-NAPOCA SER ZOOTEH MED VET 46 (0). 1992.  121-127.
CODEN: BIAVD
  Full Journal Title: Buletinul Institutului Agronomic Cluj-Napoca Seria
Zootehnie si Medicina Veterinara
  Language: ROMANIAN
  Subfile: BA (Biological Abstracts)
  The  cytotoxic and mutagenic potential of a Natrium Selenite - vitamine E
mixture through "in vivo" treatment was investigated. Swiss-Albino male
mice were  orally administered with 0.7, 1.4 or 3.5 mg drug/kg body weight
and  sacrificed after  24 hrs.  The micronucleus test was applied on bone
marrow  cells  and  the  percentage  of  micronucleated  polychromatic
erythrocytes was  significantly  increased versus control only for 3.5 mg
drug/kg b. w.  This effect was comparable with 550 mg/kg cyclophosphamide
(positive  control)  treatment  in  the  same  conditions.  The  hepatic
cytotoxicity was  investigated in the same experimental and control groups
through  evaluation of some marker enzymes activities: Ca-ATPase. G-6-Pase,
lactatedehydrogenase (LDH)  sorbitolydehydrogenase (SDH), peroxidase (Px)
and  also  through  nucleotide  protein  ratio  (DO260/280). All  drug
concentrations  revealed  a  liver  metabolic  activation, significantly
increased versus control. The  experiment  revealed  a  mutagenic  and a
cytotoxic  potential  for  Natrium  Selenite--Vitamin  E mixture especially
around  3.5 mg/kg but for the practical significance of this result we must
consider  that  the  therapeutic  dose  is always much more inferior to the
toxicity limit.
Descriptors/Keywords: ERYTHROCYTE
Concept Codes:
  *02506  Cytology and Cytochemistry-Animal
  *03506  Genetics and Cytogenetics-Animal
  *10063  Biochemical Studies-Vitamins
  *10066  Biochemical Studies-Lipids
  *13016  Metabolism-Fat-Soluble Vitamins
  *14006  Digestive System-Pathology
  *15008  Blood, Blood-Forming Organs and Body Fluids-Lymphatic Tissue and
            Reticuloendothelial System
  *18004  Bones, Joints, Fasciae, Connective and Adipose Tissue-Physiology
            and Biochemistry
  *22504  Toxicology-Pharmacological Toxicology (1972- )
Biosystematic Codes:
  86375  Muridae
Super Taxa:
  Animals; Chordates; Vertebrates; Nonhuman Vertebrates; Mammals; Nonhuman
  Mammals; Rodents
```

The amount of information in the *records* differs vastly, with the *BIOSIS* record being much more detailed. Such differences in record content and length affect the ways in which you can search the files, given that any part, or field, of the record is usually searchable.

Full-Text Searching and Numeric Data

In some databases each record contains the entire text of a document, and online systems are able to search for the occurrence of any single word or phrase in these full-text documents. Many newspapers, legal cases, and reference sources, such as encyclopedias and directories, are now available in full-text format. Figures 1.5 and 1.6 provide two examples, one taken from the *ERIC* database and one from the Marquis *Who's Who* database.

These full-text records are often very long, so you have to employ special strategies when searching them in order to zero in on the exact information that you need and avoid wasting a lot of money.

Other databases containing numeric information of various types are also available for online searching. A file such as *Donnelley Demographics* can provide selected information from the most recent U.S. census, enhanced with estimates of the current situation and even offering five-year projections for certain categories of data.

Figure 1.7 (page 5) presents a very abbreviated section of one record, but it does give some idea of the wealth of data that can be found in numeric files.

(*Text continues on page 7.*)

Fig. 1.5. *ERIC* article.

```
EJ453381   PS519761
   Bush, Clinton, or Perot: Directors Speak Out--Opinions of the Exchange Panel of 200.
   Child Care Information Exchange; n87 p5,7-9 Sep-Oct 1992
   ISSN: 0164-8527
   Available from: UMI
   Language: English
   Document Type: JOURNAL ARTICLE (080), RESEARCH REPORT (143)
   Journal Announcement: CIJMAR93
   Presents the results of a survey of child care directors. Clinton and Perot were
the top vote getters among directors of nonprofit and for-profit centers, respectively.
Also includes directors' comments on Bush and Clinton, statements by Bush and Clinton
on education, and tables showing the results of the poll.  (SM)
   Descriptors: *Administrator Attitudes; Children; *Day Care Centers; Early Childhood
Education; Nonprofit Organizations; Opinions; *Political Candidates; *Presidential
Campaigns (United States); Proprietary Schools; Telephone Surveys
Identifiers: Bush (George); Clinton (William); Perot (Ross)
```

Fig. 1.6. Marquis *Who's Who* article.

```
00934100   Record provided by: Marquis
   Perot, H. Ross
   OCCUPATION(S): investments and real estate group executive; data
   BORN:  1930
   SEX: Male
   FAMILY:  married; 4 children.
   EDUCATION:
     Ed., U.S. Naval Acad.
   CAREER:
     founder, Perot Systems Corp., Washington, 1988-
     now with, The Perot Group, Dallas
     chmn., chief exec. officer, also dir., Electronic Data Systems Corp.,
        Dallas, to 1986
     founder, Electronic Data Systems Corp., Dallas, 1962-84
     data processing salesman, IBM Corp., 1957-62
   MILITARY:
     Served with USN, 1953-57
   AWARDS:
     Recipient Internat. Disting. Entrepreneur award, U. Man., 1988.

   Office: Dallas, TX
```

Fig. 1.7. *Donnelley Demographics* citation.

```
00007912
ST JOHNSVILLE (Zip Code 13452)

Level:          ZIP
State:          NY (New York)
County:         MONTGOMERY
SMSA:           ALBANY-SCHENECTADY-TROY NY (0160)
PMSA/MSA:       ALBANY-SCHENECTADY-TROY, NY MSA (0160)
ADI:            ALBANY-SCHENECTADY-TROY
DMA:            ALBANY-SCHENECTADY-TRO
SAMI:           ALBANY
Zip Code:       13452 (ST JOHNSVILLE, NY)
City or Place:  ST JOHNSVILLE
```

Totals & Medians

	1980 Census	1991 Estimate	% Change 80 to 91	1996 Projection
Total Population	4,766	4,494	-5.7	4,358
Total Households	1,647	1,570	-4.7	1,529
Household Population	4,763	4,487	-5.8	4,351
Average Household Size	2.9	2.9	-1.2	2.8
Average Household Inc.	$14,254	$28,152	97.5	$34,720
Median Household Income	$13,019	$23,833	83.1	$29,070

Population by Age and Sex

	1980 Census Number	Pct.	1991 Estimate Number	Pct.	1996 Projection Number	Pct.
Population by Age						
Total	4,766	100.0%	4,494	100.0%	4,358	100.0%
0 - 4	362	7.6%	374	8.3%	356	8.2%
5 - 9	414	8.7%	352	7.8%	351	8.1%
10 - 14	421	8.8%	321	7.1%	331	7.6%
15 - 19	454	9.5%	347	7.7%	302	6.9%
20 - 24	326	6.8%	367	8.2%	324	7.4%
25 - 29	334	7.0%	390	8.7%	344	7.9%
30 - 34	299	6.3%	297	6.6%	363	8.3%
35 - 39	285	6.0%	287	6.4%	278	6.4%
40 - 44	216	4.5%	266	5.9%	267	6.1%
45 - 49	206	4.3%	237	5.3%	246	5.6%
50 - 54	259	5.4%	189	4.2%	219	5.0%
55 - 59	300	6.3%	169	3.8%	168	3.9%
60 - 64	270	5.7%	196	4.4%	150	3.4%
65 - 69	225	4.7%	221	4.9%	168	3.9%
70 - 74	146	3.1%	191	4.3%	178	4.1%
75 - 79	102	2.1%	142	3.2%	144	3.3%
80 - 84	73	1.5%	79	1.8%	97	2.2%
85 +	73	1.5%	69	1.5%	74	1.7%
< 15	1,197	25.1%	1,047	23.3%	1,038	23.8%
65 +	619	13.0%	702	15.6%	661	15.2%
75 +	248	5.2%	290	6.5%	315	7.2%
Median Age	31.2		31.6		32.4	
Median Age Adult Pop.	45.1		42.6		42.6	

Female Population by Age

(Continues on page 6.)

Fig. 1.7. *Donnelley Demographics* citation—*cont.*

Total	2,464	100.0%	2,322	100.0%	2,253	100.0%
0 - 4	171	6.9%	182	7.8%	174	7.7%
5 - 9	223	9.1%	172	7.4%	171	7.6%
10 - 14	200	8.1%	152	6.5%	162	7.2%
15 - 19	239	9.7%	183	7.9%	143	6.3%
20 - 24	170	6.9%	178	7.7%	172	7.6%
25 - 29	161	6.5%	202	8.7%	167	7.4%
30 - 34	166	6.7%	156	6.7%	189	8.4%
35 - 39	136	5.5%	142	6.1%	146	6.5%
40 - 44	108	4.4%	142	6.1%	132	5.9%
45 - 49	110	4.5%	119	5.1%	132	5.9%
50 - 54	128	5.2%	95	4.1%	110	4.9%
55 - 59	165	6.7%	91	3.9%	85	3.8%
60 - 64	137	5.6%	101	4.3%	82	3.6%
65 - 69	116	4.7%	124	5.3%	89	4.0%
70 - 74	74	3.0%	105	4.5%	104	4.6%
75 - 79	66	2.7%	83	3.6%	84	3.7%
80 - 84	48	1.9%	46	2.0%	61	2.7%
85 +	46	1.9%	49	2.1%	50	2.2%
< 15	594	24.1%	506	21.8%	507	22.5%
65 +	350	14.2%	407	.17.5%	388	17.2%
75 +	160	6.5%	178	7.7%	195	8.7%
Median Age	32.0		32.9		33.6	
Median Age Adult Pop.	46.2		43.6		43.7	

Male Population by Age

Total	2,301	100.0%	2,172	100.0%	2,107	100.0%
0 - 4	191	8.3%	192	8.8%	182	8.6%
5 - 9	191	8.3%	180	8.3%	180	8.5%
10 - 14	221	9.6%	169	7.8%	169	8.0%
15 - 19	215	9.3%	164	7.6%	159	7.5%
20 - 24	156	6.8%	189	8.7%	152	7.2%
25 - 29	173	7.5%	188	8.7%	177	8.4%
30 - 34	133	5.8%	141	6.5%	174	8.3%
35 - 39	149	6.5%	145	6.7%	132	6.3%
40 - 44	108	4.7%	124	5.7%	135	6.4%
45 - 49	96	4.2%	118	5.4%	114	5.4%
50 - 54	131	5.7%	94	4.3%	109	5.2%
55 - 59	135	5.9%	78	3.6%	83	3.9%
60 - 64	133	5.8%	95	4.4%	68	3.2%
65 - 69	109	4.7%	97	4.5%	79	3.7%
70 - 74	72	3.1%	86	4.0%	74	3.5%
75 - 79	36	1.6%	59	2.7%	60	2.8%
80 - 84	25	1.1%	33	1.5%	36	1.7%
85 +	27	1.2%	20	0.9%	24	1.1%
< 15	603	26.2%	541	24.9%	531	25.2%
65 +	269	11.7%	295	13.6%	273	13.0%
75 +	88	3.8%	112	5.2%	120	5.7%
Median Age	30.1		30.1		31.0	
Median Age Adult Pop.	44.0		41.5		41.5	

Population by Race

Fig. 1.7. *Donnelley Demographics* citation—*cont.*

Total	4,766	100.0%	4,494	100.0%	4,358	100.0%
White	4,739	99.4%	4,449	99.0%	4,304	98.8%
Black	2	0.0%	7	0.2%	8	0.2%
Other	24	0.5%	38	0.8%	46	1.1%
Hispanic	20	0.4%	21	0.5%	22	0.5%

	1980 Census		1991 Estimate		1996 Projection	
	Number	Pct.	Number	Pct.	Number	Pct.
Household Income						
$ 0- 7,499	399	24.2%	181	11.5%	145	9.5%
$ 7,500-14,999	569	34.5%	270	17.2%	197	12.9%
$15,000-24,999	507	30.8%	377	24.0%	306	20.0%
$25,000-34,999	120	7.3%	319	20.3%	285	18.6%
$35,000-49,999	38	2.3%	256	16.3%	292	19.1%
$50,000-74,999	13	0.8%	123	7.8%	200	13.1%
$75,000 +	1	0.1%	44	2.8%	104	6.8%

	1991 Estimate
Neighborhood Mobility	
Household Moved In:	
Most Recent Year	179
Last 5 Years	539
6 - 9 Years Ago	221
10 - 14 Years Ago	226
15+ Years Ago	528
SocioEconomic Status:	
Socioeconomic Status Score	27
Private Sector Employment	1,295

It is particularly useful to be able to retrieve this type of information in machine-readable form, because it can then be uploaded to a statistical or database program for further analysis and manipulation.

Other numeric-type databases of particular interest in the business environment are the various financial and company files. Information regarding U.S. import and export figures, for example, is available in a file such as *Piers Exports* (see fig. 1.8).

It is also easy to collect data on the financial status of a particular U.S. or international corporation using one of the Moody files. For example, figure 1.9 (page 8) provides the record for the IBM Corporation from *Moody's Corporate Profiles*.

Fig. 1.8. *Piers Exports* citations.

```
08532492
Product Exported: VOLKSWAGEN 85 JETTA
Product Code: 6921000 (AUTOMOBILES,MOTOR VEHICLES,TRAILERS)
     Weight of Cargo:              1900 POUNDS
     Number of Units of Cargo:        1 UNITS

Date of Shipment (YY/MM/DD): 920831

U.S.-Based Exporter: A & M INTL SERVICE
     Company Location: MIAMI, FL

U.S. Port of Loading: PT EVERGLADES (5203)

Destination Point: CALLAO (33303), PERU (333)
```

Fig. 1.9. *Moody's Corporate Profiles—U.S.* citation.

```
0004427
INTERNATIONAL BUSINESS MACHINES CORP.

MOODY'S NUMBER: 00004427
DUNS NUMBER: 00-136-8083
```

STATISTICAL RECORD

	12/31/91	12/31/90	12/31/89	12/31/88	12/31/87
Operating profit margin%	1.5	16.0	11.0	14.7	14.3
Book value	56.96	67.79	61.28	62.23	60.09
Return on equity%	NIL	14.1	9.8	13.9	13.7
Return on assets%	NIL	6.9	4.8	7.5	8.3
Average yield%	4.3	4.4	4.2	3.8	3.2
P/E ratio-high	NIL	11.7	20.2	14.0	20.2
P/E ratio-low	NIL	9.0	14.4	11.2	11.7
Price range-high	139 3/4	123 1/8	130 7/8	129 1/2	175 7/8
Price range-low	83 1/2	94 1/2	93 3/8	104 1/4	102

```
7-YEAR PRICE SCORE: 54.40   12-MONTH PRICE SCORE: 64.61
                              NYSE COMPOSITE INDEX=100
```

CAPITALIZATION (12/31/91):

	($000)	(%)
Long Term Debt	13,231,000	25.4
Deferred Income Tax	1,927,000	3.7
Common & Surplus	37,006,000	70.9
Total	52,164,000	100.0

```
INSTITUTIONAL SHARES: 262,516,211
INSTITUTIONAL HOLDERS: 1,197
NUMBER OF COMMON STOCKHOLDERS: 772,047
```

Examples such as these could be almost endless. They are included here to give you a feeling for the depth and breadth of information that is available in online databases. They should help to convince you that online searching skills are vital to the provision of an effective and efficient information service in today's fast-changing information environment.

How Does Information Retrieval Work?

Any formal search for information involves some interaction with an information retrieval (IR) system. The word *system* is used in general to describe a wide variety of phenomena that we encounter in our daily lives, such as the educational system or the political system, but may best be seen as some set of components that interact to provide a desired result. (See fig. 1.10) These components consist of a group of interlinked entities (organizations, people, documents, and so on) that participate in a group of interlinked processes (transmitting, updating, searching, and so on).

Outside the system, separated from it by a boundary but influencing its operation, lies the system environment. The dynamic nature of the system and the relationships between the elements in it are represented by the information flowing through the system. That is why we often speak of the information retrieval "cycle." The transfer of information across the boundary between the system and its environment is known as "input" and "output." The nature of these inputs, processes, and outputs is governed by the objectives that the system is aiming to fulfill and the external environment within which it operates.

Thus, the typical elements of a document-based IR system consist of inputs and outputs, the matching mechanism, and a series of activities, including the

selection of documents,

conceptual analysis of documents,

organization of document representations,

storage of documents,

conceptual analysis of queries,

matching of documents and queries, and

delivery of documents.

Let us elaborate on these different elements. The inputs to the system are

- new documents selected on the basis of user needs,
- ad hoc queries posed by the system users, and
- the indexing language used by both the indexer and the searcher.

The outputs are

- documents retrieved in response to queries, and
- factual answers to queries.

The relationships among the elements of such an IR system are illustrated in simplified form in figure 1.11 (page 10).

This structure is generalized in that it makes no assumptions about how any activity will be carried out and is equally applicable to either a manual or a computerized system. In practice a range of other activities are necessary in order to link the system inputs and outputs. For example, once the documents have been acquired (A) they need to be

Fig. 1.10. A system.

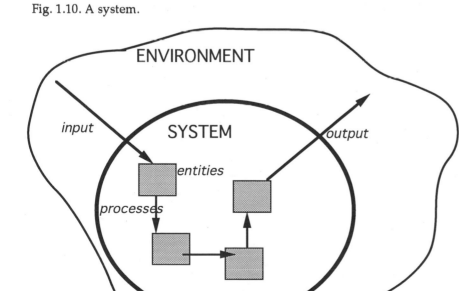

Fig. 1.11. The IR cycle (adapted form Lancaster[2]).

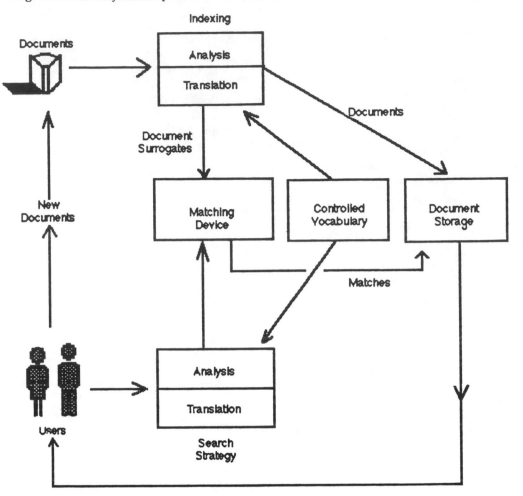

organized in some way so that they can be identified and located in response to a search request. This involves cataloging (i.e., description), subject indexing, and sometimes abstracting. The indexing consists of two separate stages—the determination of subject content (conceptual analysis) (B) and then the translation (C) of that concept into the *controlled vocabulary* (D) of the system. Such a system vocabulary may consist of a list of subject headings, a subject thesaurus, or a classification scheme, and its

role is to represent the subject matter of the documents within the system for purposes of searching. Most computer systems also make use of keywords, or uncontrolled natural language terms that occur in the documents themselves, and these, too, will be searchable. In these systems terms from both the controlled vocabulary and the keywords may thus be considered as subject terms, which are searched as representing the documents themselves.

Indexing is a simple term that sometimes causes confusion. The reason for this is probably that it is used in two rather different ways. We use it to talk of assigning index terms from a controlled vocabulary, but we know that one can also draw index terms—keywords—from natural language. Further confusion can be added by the fact that classification numbers are also often considered to be a kind of indexing. Perhaps we can best summarize by saying that indexing involves any type of subject specification assigned to documents in order to assist with their retrieval. - GW

Other pieces of information about documents (author's name, date of publication, language, etc.) may also be incorporated into the document representation and thus become available for searching. These document representations (or *surrogates*) are in fact little summaries of the basic characteristics of the documents being input to the system. They are, of course, much easier to search than the documents themselves because of their condensed nature and their ability to be searched in a variety of ways.

Once the indexing process has been completed, the documents are put into storage (E), and the document representations (F) are entered into the matching mechanism (G). This file of document surrogates may be as simple as a card file or a printed index, but for the purposes of online retrieval it is a machine-readable file (database) stored on a computer system. The aim is to make the file conveniently searchable on any search keys that are deemed to be potentially useful as access points to the document. In the case of the traditional library card catalog, the available search keys are normally limited to the author, the title, and a single subject heading. Thus, one of the major advantages of computerized IR systems is their ability to permit searching on a much wider range of document keys—by date, by keyword, by language, and so on.

The input from the other end of the system, the user's query (1), is treated in a fashion as similar as possible to that used for inputting the documents. Queries are analyzed (2) for conceptual content, which is then translated into the vocabulary of the system (3). This translated version of the query (often with natural language keywords or other desired document attributes added) becomes the "search strategy," to be used for matching against the document surrogates in the database.

The output from a document-based IR system will consist of a set of records (4) that the computer has found to match the search strategy. These records are deemed by the system to be relevant to the user's information need. The success of the retrieval process is usually judged by this attribute of *relevance*, which is generally accepted to be qualitative in nature and uncertain in definition. (For more on relevance, see chapter 12.) The search process, which may be iterative, is finally completed when the user is satisfied with the results of the search, or when it becomes clear that there are no more relevant documents to be found.

Relevance happens to be my current area of research interest, and we will cover it in more detail later, but for the moment let me just point out that many researchers believe relevance to be a **quantitative,** continuous entity, which can be measured in subtle ways. Geraldene is quite right that we really don't have a good definition for relevance beyond its primitive intuitive notions—your idea of relevance is probably just as good as mine. It is an individual thing, and that makes it all the more difficult to study. - JWJ

Information Seeking

It is widely believed that user requests for information usually fall into one of two broad categories:

1. The need to locate and obtain a particular document for which the author or title is known, usually called a "known item" search.

2. The need to locate material dealing with a particular subject or to answer a particular question, known as a subject search.

Most information services need to be able to provide answers to both types of information need. The bibliographic networks (such as OCLC and RLIN[3]) are excellent examples of known item search systems, because they are normally used to provide cataloging data for items that are already in hand. Their use is fairly straightforward, because they can be searched on accurate and relatively stable elements, such as the ISBN (International Standard Book Number) or an author's name. Subject searching is far more difficult, because one is in effect searching for what is not known and which may not even exist. In such cases users are looking for information that will fill a gap in their personal conceptual frameworks, which are probably entirely unique and individual.

A couple of different research approaches have been tried on users and gaps in their knowledge states. Belkin, Oddy, and Brooks[4] in a project now known as ASK, studied the "anomalous states of knowledge" exhibited by users when approaching information systems.

Their contention is that because users have perceived a gap in their knowledge state, they will be "unable to state precisely what is needed to resolve that anomaly." Instead, users were asked to give a "problem statement" describing their current knowledge state and the researchers attempted to derive a structural representation of that state to assist in retrieval.

Dervin[5] has developed a similiar "sense-making" model, which states that people are constantly trying to make sense of their world as they move through time and space. When they find they are unable to continue moving due to a gap in their sense of the world, they express that gap as an information need, which must be fulfilled for the gap to be resolved and the person to continue on. Both of these theories have been very useful in thinking about and designing information systems.
- JWJ

The problems involved in trying to answer this type of subject search stem not only from the difficulty in defining the question but also from the intangible nature of information itself. *Information* is very difficult to define accurately, it is perceived differently by different individuals, and their perceptions are likely to change over time. Although information can reasonably be regarded as anything that helps to answer an information need and may be presented in any way—oral, written, graphic, and so on—or in any format—print, microform, computer data, and so on—it should be recognized that the mere provision of information-bearing documents does not necessarily mean that information has been effectively transferred.

The growth of funded research and the escalation of publication rates in recent years have posed enormous problems for those whose task it is to acquire and organize the files of published information that have resulted. The organization and processing of this information is far from simple, and increased amounts of it have merely served to exacerbate a long-standing conceptual problem. As early as 1960 Maron and Kuhns[6] had highlighted the difficulties involved in identifying the subject content of either documents or queries, because such decisions not only are restricted by the nature of the controlled vocabulary in use but also are bound to contain an element of subjectivity. This was confirmed by Lancaster's early research on the MEDLARS search system,[7] which suggested that search vocabulary and human errors were the major causes of retrieval failure. The move to computerized systems has undoubtedly speeded up the more mechanical aspects of IR but has done little to help with the conceptual problems involving subject description.

In fact, the term *information retrieval* itself is something of a misnomer, because what is retrieved by an IR system is usually either a set of documents or citations to documents that are believed to contain the required information. For example, a library catalog can be searched by subject terms to retrieve records related to the subject required. But the documents identified must then be tracked to the shelves and searched for particular items of information. The catalog entries are used for the purpose of identifying relevant items, because they are easier to search than the shelves themselves, but they do not necessarily provide the requested information.

Notice that what we are doing in this situation is matching the terms that represent our required subject with the terms that represent the contents of the documents. Thus, the IR system, in this case the library catalog, is essentially a matching device for comparing individual words or phrases between documents and queries. Crucial to the success of this type of retrieval is the vocabulary used to index the documents and to search the document surrogates. It is clear that the same vocabulary has to be used by both the indexer and the searcher, or no match will be found. This standardization is the role of a controlled vocabulary. For example, if we are searching a file for the term "motor cars" when the indexer has entered documents on this subject under the heading "automobiles," we will retrieve nothing, although relevant material is in fact available in the collection. Notice also that, although an IR system does not usually retrieve information, this is the term commonly used to describe the types of literature-searching activities with which this volume is concerned.

As we shall see in chapter 2, the growing problems faced by these traditional search systems (the card catalog and printed indexes) as they attempted to cope with escalating publication rates led to the early experiments with automated and semiautomated IR systems during the 1950s.

[1]Peter Briscoe, et al. (March 1986), "Ashurbanipal's Enduring Archetype: Thoughts on the Library's Role in the Future," *College & Research Libraries* 46(2):121-26.

[2]F. Wilfred Lancaster (1979), *Information Retrieval Systems: Characteristics, Testing and Evaluation*, 2nd ed. (New York: Wiley), 8.

[3]Here's our first example of the rampant acronyms in this profession. OCLC and RLIN are large-scale (many millions of records) bibliographic systems used by many libraries to assist in cataloging and interlibrary loan functions. OCLC is produced by the Online Computer Library Center in Ohio; RLIN stands for Research Library Information Network and is produced by the Research Libraries Group.

[4]N. J. Belkin, R. N. Oddy, and H. M. Brooks (1982), "ASK for Information Retrieval: Part I. Background and Theory," *Journal of Documentation* 38(2):61-71; and N. J. Belkin, R. N. Oddy, and H. M. Brooks (1982), "ASK for Information Retrieval: Part II. Results of a Design Study," *Journal of Documentation* 38(3):145-64.

[5]B. Dervin (1983), "An Overview of Sense-Making Research: Concepts, Methods and Results to Date." Paper presented at the International Communication Association Annual Meeting, Dallas, TX; and B. Dervin and P. Dewdney (1986), "Neutral Questioning: A New Approach to the Reference Interview," *RQ* 25:506-13.

[6]M. E. Maron and J. L. Kuhns (1960), "On Relevance, Probabilistic Indexing and Information Retrieval," *Journal of Association of Computing Machinery* 7(3):216-44.

[7]F. W. Lancaster (1968), Evaluation of the MEDLARS Demand Search Service (Bethesda, MD: National Library of Medicine).

This chapter looks at the way that information retrieval (IR) systems have developed over the years. It explains how dissatisfaction with the performance of manual systems led to experiments with alternative methods and gradually to the use of computer systems for the storage and searching of information records. All early IR systems were what is now called *pre-coordinate*

2

DEVELOPMENTS IN INFORMATION RETRIEVAL

systems, and many of these traditional systems are still in use for library catalogs and printed indexes. In order to allow documents to be searched and retrieved on the basis of subject, the vocabulary of the system must permit the subject matter to be adequately described, and both the indexer and the searcher must be aware of the appropriate terminology.

Problems with Pre-Coordinate Systems

Do we use MEDIEVAL ARCHITECTURE or ARCHITECTURE, MEDIEVAL, or even ARCHITECTURE—MEDIEVAL as our preferred subject entry for a document on that topic? And supposing the topic to be indexed is "Medieval church architecture." How do we structure a heading to cover all three aspects of this subject? Should it be CHURCH ARCHITECTURE, MEDIEVAL or MEDIEVAL ARCHITECTURE—CHURCHES, or any other of a variety of possibilities? The term "pre-coordinate" is used to indicate that a group of different search terms are to be coordinated (put together) in some prescribed order. This method of indexing is called precoordinate because the total coordinated heading is constructed at the *input* or *indexing* stage (i.e., *before* the document surrogates are entered into the system). The development of such an index "string" is an attempt to specify a multifaceted subject with a single standardized index entry. Terms are linked in a designated order using standardized punctuation,

so that documents on the same subject will not be entered into the system under variant combinations of the subject terms. You can imagine the problems involved if the order is not standardized and also the difficulties in trying to specify a compound subject with a single, all-encompassing index entry if there are no rules.

The most obvious answer to this problem would appear to be to make multiple entries, one under each of the selected headings. In the above example, this would require three separate entries—one under MEDIEVAL, one under ARCHITECTURE, and one under CHURCHES—so that whichever term the searcher used, the relevant document or documents would eventually be retrieved. This raises another problem, in that none of the entries is *specific*. That is, none of them completely specifies the document; they are not *coextensive* with the subject of the document.

"Specificity" is a term used in relation to how accurately the document or query is represented in the system. It refers to how completely the terms in the system vocabulary fit with the subject of the document to be indexed. It can also refer to how accurately a search statement represents a particular information need. Specificity is not an inherent, predetermined value for a given term but varies in relation to a particular document or a particular query. - GW

In real life this means that one might expend a great deal of time searching a very large section of the file under any one of these individual headings. In this case we are having to search much too broadly, because we have lost specificity when we search under only one part of the subject involved. The basic aim of any IR system must be to limit the search for a given query to a manageable subset of the collection. In this sense dividing a compound heading into its individual parts appears to be counterproductive. As we lose topic specificity, we increase search time.

Another possible way to improve retrieval performance would be to retain specificity by using the entire pre-coordinated string but making *multiple entries* under each of the rotated combinations. We would thus have three entries for the previous example:

CHURCHES : ARCHITECTURE : MEDIEVAL

ARCHITECTURE : MEDIEVAL : CHURCHES

MEDIEVAL : CHURCHES : ARCHITECTURE

Notice that not every reasonable possibility is covered even now. For example, there is no entry under MEDIEVAL ARCHITECTURE (with or without punctuation), although it is a very likely search string. The problem is that the number of entries required to cover all possible combinations of multiple terms grows exponentially with the number of individual terms, and most system managers are not prepared to allow for more than two or three entries per document. As the content of documents has become more detailed and specialized the limitations of the pre-coordinate systems have become increasingly evident, and we have seen a move away from a total reliance on controlled subject headings such as the *Library of Congress Subject Headings (LCSH)*, even in traditional library catalogs.

Post-Coordinate Retrieval Systems

Not only is there more information to be processed, but that information is more specialized and therefore needs more detailed indexing. In response to this problem, a series of experimental systems was developed during the 1950s that was intended to provide greater specificity in indexing and more flexibility in searching. These new systems became known as *post-coordinate* systems, based on the fact that they relied on the coordination of multiple subject terms at the *search* rather than the input stage. Index terms were assigned *individually*, with one entry made for each term, as we suggested earlier, but provision was made for searching them *in combination* rather than by single terms only.

This was a totally new approach that required new matching mechanisms and was based on the idea of storing document surrogates in a document-term matrix rather than in a single alphabetic sequence. The original post-coordinate search systems were card-based manual systems that permitted the combination of search terms without the restrictions of linear order. This was accomplished by having the search file used for matching consist of records for subjects, rather than records for documents. Document numbers were entered on the subject cards for the selected index terms at the input (indexing) stage. They were then filed in alphabetical order by subject term, and the subject cards appropriate to the search topic were retrieved and compared at the search stage, looking for document numbers that matched on each subject card (see fig. 2.1).

These systems were enthusiastically adopted in a number of special libraries, whose users were facing the most serious problems with subject retrieval.

Fig. 2.1. Post-coordinate Uniterm cards, showing document number 15 is on the topic of medieval church architecture.

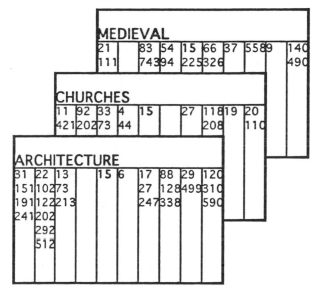

Unfortunately, the new systems also had their limitations in the numbers of index terms or records they could accommodate or both, and in their complicated and unwieldy matching processes. Nevertheless, they did enable searching of multiple terms in combination. They also had another major advantage not realized at the time, in that they turned out to be easily convertible to computer operation when the appropriate technology eventually became available.

The terms **pre-coordinate** and **post-coordinate** tend to confuse some people, so let's recap what we have said about them. Coordination refers to the combining of separate index terms in order to specify a compound subject. Pre- and post- refer to the time at which the terms are combined, with pre- meaning the input (indexing) stage and post- meaning the output (searching) stage.

This means that indexers in pre-coordinate search systems will construct a single compound subject heading for each document input, resulting in an index entry such as FRANCE : HISTORY : REVOLUTION or similar entries with these terms rotated.

> Notice that none of the entries conforms to natural language, where the user may decide to search under FRENCH REVOLUTION and thus will fail to retrieve relevant material unless the controlled vocabulary provides a structure of linkages (references) leading from unused to used terms. In a post-coordinate system the indexer would probably select the same individual terms but make three separate entries—one under FRANCE, one under HISTORY, and one under REVOLUTION—that will be filed separately and not coordinated unless a searcher selects all three terms. The problem of combination order is thus eliminated. - GW

Computer Retrieval Systems

The theories behind these manual post-coordinate systems formed the basis for the *offline batch processed* computer retrieval systems that started appearing in the early 1960s. Most of these early systems were developed using U.S. government funding and were initially justified on the basis of being multipurpose. Although computer systems were originally developed to speed the production of printed indexes, they could also be used for retrospective searching and current awareness services. They used magnetic tape as their storage medium, were usually updated on a periodic basis, and were searched somewhat inefficiently in serial fashion (i.e., searching one document at a time). Almost all of them were based on human indexing and searching, using controlled vocabularies with terms selected from *thesauri*.

These early computer retrieval systems offered a number of advantages over their manual predecessors, including the ability to

- provide multiple access points to a document,
- handle complex search strategies,
- generate printed output,

- collect operating data automatically, and
- produce a variety of services from a single input.

But they also had a number of basic drawbacks, of which the biggest was undoubtedly their lack of interaction. This meant that a search was essentially a one-shot affair with no browsing capability. This process was very different from the traditional manual search process. It frequently meant that the search was delegated to a specialist searcher, known as the *intermediary*, who often had minimal or no contact with the individual who made the original information request. The other big disadvantage was the delayed response time, largely a result of the way in which searches were processed. Because they were collected and saved to be processed in batches, the user might have to wait several days or weeks for the results, despite the fact that the actual searching process had been enormously speeded up. This was particularly unsatisfactory in view of the lack of interaction during the search, because it often meant that the complete search cycle had to be repeated if the results proved unsatisfactory to the user.

Online Retrieval Systems

Online systems differ in two fundamental ways from the pre- and post-coordinate systems that we have been discussing so far. First, when the search is conducted online it progresses in an *interactive*, conversational fashion, making it not unlike the manual search process, where the searcher selects and discards items based on what is found while the search is being conducted. Online searches are thus conducted in *real time*—the computer is searching and comparing while the searcher is connected to the system. This means that search results are available almost immediately, because the computer is capable of searching very quickly despite the great size of the files involved. It is this speed of response that is particularly attractive in many IR situations—airline reservations or bank balance queries, for example. It

also means that users can take advantage of new information as they find it in order to adapt and refine their search strategies. This process is known as *feedback* and has been found to have a major effect on the relevance of the material retrieved.

Second, an online system provides remote access, which means that the searcher and the file of documents are not necessarily in the same place. The user terminal and the search system are linked by a telecommunication network, so that their geographical locations are irrelevant. Although the majority of the search systems in most frequent use are in the United States, they can be accessed from almost anywhere in the world. All that is needed is a reliable telephone system, a computer terminal, and, of course, a password and knowledge of the system protocols. This means that not only bibliographic information but bank, insurance, tax, and even security information is potentially available to users with sufficient expertise. In recent years several serious cases of illegal access by hackers have heightened recognition of the importance of adequate security measures for computer-held data.

The whole notion of hacking has changed in the last few years. When I was first learning computing in the late 1970s, hacking was a fun and harmless thing—trying to get the machine to do what you wanted it to do and learning about how it worked in the process. A group of us hacked on a couple of different systems (I remember the MULTICS system at MIT fondly), annoyed people enough until they gave us guest accounts, then played around. We did no damage and learned a lot.

Recently, though, the hacker as criminal has arisen. Individuals and groups with charming but ominous names like the Legion of Doom have appropriated hacking and feel it is their right or even their duty to break into otherwise secure systems (especially governmental and corporate systems but also universities and hospitals) to demonstrate that it can be done and in some cases to damage or destroy data. These people are foolish at best, felons at worst.

If you're interested in this transition, I can recommend a few excellent books: Sherry Turkle's **The Second Self** (New York: Simon & Schuster, 1984) examines the effect of computers on our self-image, and her chapter 6 is devoted to the innocent days of hacking. Theodore Roszak's **The Cult of Information** (New York: Pantheon, 1986) also looks at the effects of computing but from a broader societal perspective. His chapter 7 on "The Computer and the Counterculture" should not be missed. Finally, a superb and very readable book on the evils of hacking is Clifford Stoll's **The Cuckoo's Egg** (New York: Pocket, 1990). - JWJ

This ability to provide access from remote locations and the additional ability of present-day computers to handle multiple tasks in parallel have led to the development of a mass market for online information.

This remote access provided by online systems has had another very important by-product. It means that almost all information seeking is now on a much wider scale than it ever was in the old days of manual systems. Users are no longer limited in their information gathering to the materials available in their own library or group of local libraries. The question is no longer "What have we got on XYZ?" but "What has been published anywhere on XYZ?" This has led to great increases in the use of journal literature and has escalated interlibrary loan requests over recent years.

Growth of Online Systems

The widespread use of online computer search systems has thus been a relatively recent phenomenon, dating back only to the early 1970s. During the 1960s, experimental systems were being developed by organizations that were facing problems with the storage and retrieval of their own in-house information. In 1964, the U.S. National Library of Medicine offered on-demand batch searching of their MEDLARS system to the medical profession, and by the following year Lockheed Missiles Corporation, the Systems Development Corporation (SDC), and the Chemical Abstracts Service were all developing computer search services with funding from the federal government. In 1968 the first online access was accomplished from the State University of New York Biomedical Network in Albany to the MEDLARS database in Bethesda, Maryland, using dedicated lines. By 1969, the first packet-switched data communications network (ARPAnet) had begun test operation, and the necessary components for online access were gradually falling into place.

The first major online dial-up service was MEDLINE, the online version of MEDLARS, which was swiftly followed in 1972 by the offer of commercial online services to the general public from DIALOG (Lockheed) and ORBIT (SDC). From that date, systems have proliferated; LEXIS from Mead Data Central, *The New York Times* Information Bank, and the Dow Jones News/Retrieval Service arrived in swift succession. By 1975 over 300 public access databases were available from a range of different vendors, and online was finally established in both North America and western Europe. Using these early systems required considerable training, and most of their use became delegated to professional searchers in library settings. But gradually the idea of direct user access developed, and by 1979 two systems were initiated that directly targeted the home user—The

Source and CompuServe. (See more on this in chapter 14.)

Since the early seventies the rate of growth of all aspects of online has been truly extraordinary (see fig. 2.2), and the impact of online systems on information seeking and worldwide information use has been profound. By 1992 the number of different search services available worldwide had grown to 933, offering 7,367 databases from 2,372 different database producers.

Although the United States has retained the largest share of this online market, both as a supplier and as a user, Europe has been making considerable strides since national monopolies over telephone and communications networks (PTTs) have been deregulated.

Like all really good inventions, the development of economical access to online information required input from a range of seemingly unrelated technologies and the coming together of a group of unconnected developments in order to flourish:

- The first of these developments was a growing recognition of the importance of information and information products as a vital national resource. A major impact on the attitude of the U.S. government was the Soviet Union's 1957 launching of the Sputnik satellite. This event, widely regarded in the United States as heralding a major loss of technological superiority, prompted the investment of large amounts of federal money for the development of computer systems for the storage and processing of information and for the collection of data in machine-readable files. The most important of these early systems were initiated by the Armed Services Technical Information Agency (later Defence Documen-

tation Center [DDC]) and the National Aeronautics and Space Administration (NASA), which were soon followed by the National Library of Medicine (MEDLARS) and the Educational Resources Information Center (ERIC). Although these early services were initially in-house batch-processed systems and were not generally available to the public, the file structures and search features designed at that time have influenced the way in which most other computer IR systems have since developed. SDC and Lockheed were among the nongovernmental agencies that received federal funding to develop search software and to mount additional databases provided through contracts with outside database-producing agencies, such as the National Agricultural Library and the Chemical Abstracts Service. Both organizations quickly developed into commercial vendors of online information.

- The second area to influence the development of online systems was more directly concerned with the provision of information products—the production of printed indexes and abstracts. During the 1960s it became economically advantageous for the publishers of these secondary services to have their indexes produced by computer-assisted phototypesetting. One of the prime requirements for any current awareness product is speed of production, and the computer proved to be ideal for the swift duplication, reformatting, sorting, and printing of the multiple entries required by this type of information product. In addition to saving time and money for the index publishers, computerized typesetting

Fig. 2.2 Growth in Online Services.[1]

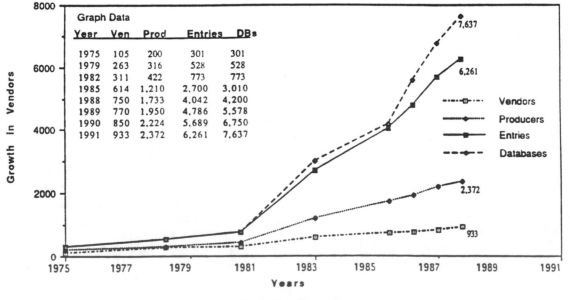

Database Records

does another important thing—it creates databases. As a by-product of the typesetting operation, the information contained in the printed publication (initially bibliographic citations) becomes available in machine-readable form at no extra cost to the producer. The database producers became aware that there was a potential market for the sale of these databases to organizations that could mount them on their own computers for in-house searching. A number of information centers started buying the index tapes and using them as sources for current awareness and the selective dissemination of information (SDI) services to their clients. As the numbers of available databases grew, it also became possible to provide access to a whole sequence of the same file for comprehensive retrospective searching. Eventually this became recognized as a commercially viable operation, and organizations such as DIALOG and SDC began to buy tapes from a variety of database producers and, via their own search interface, to offer remote searching for information as a product for sale.

- The third area to influence developments and to hasten the move from batch to online was the computer field itself. Not only were computers becoming faster and more powerful, but storage costs were going down—an important consideration when dealing with the massive bibliographic files involved in this type of operation. Another vital computer development was the facility for timesharing, which led the way to the commercial possibilities of a mass market. Once multiple searchers were able to use the system at the same time, there was a large enough user base for economic operation.

- The final piece of the jigsaw puzzle that was needed to enable the birth of viable online IR systems was the ability to provide remote access in an efficient and economical fashion. This required the development of telecommunications networks designed especially to link two computers (or a computer and a terminal) and to transmit data in digitized form. Early online access to databases was usually through the ordinary telephone network, which was, of course, widely available but insufficiently reliable for the transmission of digitized data and also too expensive when longer distances were involved. Telecommunication networks such as TYMNET and TELENET were thus developed during the 1970s to cover most of North America and now are linked by satellite to networks like Euronet in other countries to provide worldwide access. Users enter one of the network nodes via a local telephone call and are routed through the most convenient path of the network to the service of their choice. These communications networks have proved to be cheaper and more reliable than telephone lines and are used today for almost all computer communication that is not hard-wired.

Putting It All Together

The online industry is thus composed of three basic elements:

1. *Database producers*, who select the documents for input, sometimes index them using a controlled vocabulary, and input the resulting records to machine-readable form. Many of them produce print products as well as machine-readable databases. Producers fall into one of three very different groups:
   a. government agencies, such as the National Library of Medicine, producers of the MEDLINE database;
   b. professional and academic organizations, such as the American Psychological Association, producers of the PsycINFO database; and
   c. commercial organizations, such as the Institute for Scientific Information, producers of the SCISEARCH database.

   Their differing levels of subject expertise and different motivations for the production of a database mean that these agencies operate to their own highly variable standards and that, despite some subject overlap, almost every database has its own vocabulary and individual record structure.

2. *Online vendors* (search services), most of which lease a variety of databases, mount them on timesharing computers, and provide an interface and command language with which they can be searched. A few vendors are also database producers, selling only their own products. The vendor situation has been extremely volatile in recent years, with mergers and takeovers as the norm. The original commercial online systems, SDC and Lockheed, are still in business, though not under the same names, but there is also a plethora of other operators offering a wide range of services from popular-type bulletin boards (Prodigy, CompuServe) to highly specialized legal or stock-market information (LEXIS, Dow Jones).

3. *The information searchers*, who may be the information seekers themselves but are often professional search specialists in libraries and information agencies. Because the first users of

online search services were technical information centers and specialized scientific libraries, the role of the librarian in these organizations came to include that of professional search intermediary. The specialized contribution made by these intermediaries was familiarity with the protocols and search features of a range of online services and knowledge of the availability and idiosyncrasies of the different databases. Early attempts to encourage users to search for themselves and later the development of simplified systems aimed at the end-user market have not so far proved very successful. (See more on this in chapter 14.) However, the recent availability of databases for searching on CD-ROM (compact disk read-only memory) has been greeted with enthusiasm by users, who now appear keen to do their own searching. More people are becoming aware of the advantages of using online IR search systems, though they seem to expect them to be not only simple to use, but also available free of charge.

Note

[1]*Directory of Online Databases.* 8th ed. New York: Cuadra/Elsevier, 1992.

Getting access to an online search system is largely a question of compatibility between your own machine and the vendor's mainframe. Attention to the nitty-gritty of telecommunications is essential, so this chapter goes over the various aspects in considerable detail. Together with the manual for your computer and the vendor's documentation, it should get you started with a reasonable understanding of what is going

3
GOING ONLINE

on. The most basic requirement for online searching is to be able to communicate with the host system where the files of information are stored. This involves the use of a terminal, usually a microcomputer, connected via a modem, a telephone line, and a packet-switched telecommunication network to the large timesharing computer on which the databases available for searching are stored.

Getting Connected

Although the networks take care of the long-distance communications, they rely on the local telephone system to provide the initial link between the searcher and the nearest node of the network. (*Nodes*

are available in most major U.S. cities, but rural areas may require a long-distance call to connect.) The total picture looks something like the setup displayed in figure 3.1.

Fig. 3.1. The online connection.

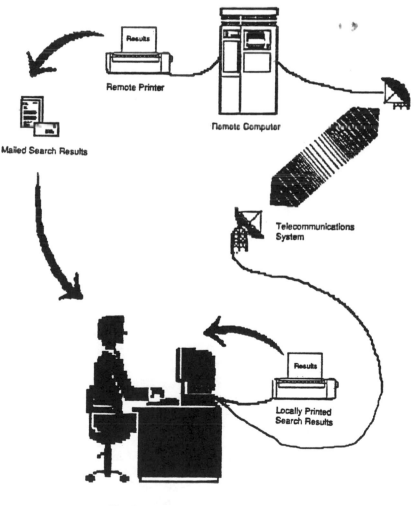

Remote Printer

Remote Computer

Mailed Search Results

Telecommunications System

Locally Printed Search Results

User Inputs Search

To enable your microcomputer to link into this system, four basic items are necessary:

- a plug-in communications card,

- a modem,

- access to a telecommunication network, and

- a communications software package.

Let's look at how these components fit together to get your connection and the role that each of them plays.

Communications Card

We all know that computers communicate in terms of *binary digits*—bits. These bits are grouped together to form bytes, just as letters of the alphabet are grouped to form words. Unfortunately, microcomputers think of these grouped bits as "words," though to you and me they are merely single characters, which can lead to some terminological confusion. These computer words usually consist of eight bits, and because they are passed along together, each word requires eight wires. This works fine within your own machine, but remote access to another machine requires the use of telephone lines that do not have sufficient wires, so that the bits have to travel one at a time along them. It is thus necessary to change things so that your computer will talk in single bits.

This is the job of the communications card, which is a printed circuit board slotted into the inside of your machine. It is responsible for converting the computer's internal parallel communications into a serial output for transmission over the telephone lines. For this reason it is sometimes called a serial card. The port at the rear of the card is called an RS-232 interface and is one of the few standardized components in the microcomputer world. It enables you to connect almost any brand of modem to your computer.

Modems

If computers and telephones spoke the same "language," you would not need a modem. Unfortunately, they do not. Virtually everything in your computer happens electronically, using digital signals to indicate either an on or off condition. This is referred to as binary format, where there are only two options—either a one or a zero, with no in-between. It is rather like Morse code, where everything has to be encoded as either a dot or a dash. If you could hear digital information, it would sound like a series of clicks and clacks, and we might imagine it looking something like figure 3.2.

Fig. 3.2. Digital pattern.

A telephone, on the other hand, is an analog device, meaning it uses sound waves to function. Sound can rise or fall to cover all levels, rather like an air-raid siren in old movies. It might look something like figure 3.3, where we can see a gradual transition from top to bottom.

As you can imagine, digital and analog devices are essentially incompatible. A modem is necessary to translate from one language to the other—digital signals to analog tones and vice versa—during an online session.

Fig. 3.3. Analog pattern.

The word modem is an abbreviation for modulator/demodulator. During a telecommunications session the modem performs two essential operations:

1. When you are transmitting information, it converts or modulates the digital signals from your PC into sound signals compatible with today's analog telephone systems.

2. When you are receiving information, the modem converts or demodulates the analog signals coming over the phone line back into the digital format required by your PC.

There are two types of modems—internal modems and external modems. As a rule, installing an internal modem is like adding any other expansion board to your system. It must be inserted directly into an unoccupied expansion slot in the back of your machine. External modems, on the other hand, require an RS-232 cable so that they can be connected to the outside of a serial port on the back of your machine. In either case, once the modem is in place, you use a standard telephone cord to connect it to a phone jack or wall plug. In certain locations you may want to add a telephone line surge protector to your modem setup to protect your hardware from damage by voltage spikes on the phone lines.

Most modems today are directly connected from the computer to a modular telephone jack. The major option with regard to modems is their transmission speed, which is measured in baud. The number of bits that are transmitted over the communication line each second is the *baud rate*, which can vary from 1,200 to 2,400 to 9,600 bits per second (bps), depending on the choice of modem. Speeds have been increasing over the years, and even higher speeds are now becoming available. It might appear self-evident that faster would necessarily be better, but it is difficult to read text that is scrolling up the screen at even 120 baud,[1] and no one can type fast enough to take advantage of the higher speeds for input. However, if one intends to capture and download large amounts of data, the faster speeds will be more economical.

The speeds Geraldene talks about above are quite acceptable for online searching, but if you have heard about some of the very-large-scale networks in use, these speeds may sound quite slow. They are. Networks such as the BITNET, the Internet, NSFNet, and the NREN (National Research and Educational Network, in the planning stages as I write this) may have telecommunications capacities in excess of billions of characters per second. These will be used for high-speed transfer of data, especially very dense data such as video and audio information. Certainly they could be utilized in IR situations, but as long as most libraries still have 1200 or 2400 baud modems on their PCs and Macs, these speeds won't do us a whole lot of good. - JWJ

Two other concerns regarding terminal compatibility with the system are parity and duplex. *Parity*, used for checking whether data has been corrupted in transit, operates by the computer adding an additional bit (the parity bit) to each character at the time it is being input. The system and the terminal need to be operating on the same parity—either even or odd, and the computer will automatically check every character as it is transmitted. *Duplex* refers to the mode of transmission of data down the line.

Half-duplex is very similar to how people communicate on walkie-talkies or CB radios—one person speaks at a time, and communication switches back and forth. Using full-duplex, however, both terminals can send and receive simultaneously, so information transfer is faster and more efficient. Both parity and duplex are settings that you will need to program into the configuration of the communications software (see page 24).

Telecommunications

The database systems that we want to access may be anywhere in the United States or even in Europe. DIALOG's computers are in California, SDC's are in Virginia, MEDLINE's are outside Washington, D.C., and the European Space Agency's files are at Frascati, outside Rome. Other databases are scattered all over the world. If we had to pay regular long-distance telephone charges every time we wished to access them, online searching would be very expensive indeed! Fortunately, in most locations you can gain access to online systems through a local telephone call. The technology that makes this possible is provided through packet-switched networks, which divide the data traffic into discrete "packets" before routing them. Each packet contains a set number of computer bits, and when the data are too small to fill a complete packet, they are combined with fillers. Each packet is stamped with an electronic address that tells the system its destination and is then sent along the most efficient route available on the network. Luckily, this complex process is transparent to the user, who needs to know only the telephone number that provides the gateway into the network. Once the connection to the host system has been made, the network can, thankfully, be ignored.

The major telecommunication networks have nodes in most large metropolitan centers, so that it is usually possible to link into them via a local (i.e., free) telephone call. Because they are designed especially for the transfer of data, as opposed to voice traffic, they are faster and less prone to interference than the telephone network. The complete connection is represented by figure 3.4.

The two largest networks in North America are TELENET (now SPRINTNET) and TYMNET, though some search services also have their own telecommunications networks, such as DIALOG's DIALNET. Prices vary only slightly among networks, and costs are usually incorporated into your system costs, so that you are not billed directly for telecommunications. Europe also has a number of different networks, such as SCANNET and BLAISE, which are

Fig. 3.4. The telecommunications link.

terminal   modem/   node   telecommunications
                phone   link

linked into EURONET-Diane. Communications between the two continents is by satellite links between two of the networks. It is thus possible to use an online search service from almost any place in the world with reliable telephone service. This is an important factor for some countries, because most database systems are in either the United States or western Europe.

Each network has slightly different sign-on procedures, or protocols, but this is not a major problem because they are explained in the system instruction manuals that you receive when you become a

subscriber. You will also receive a complete listing of TYMNET, SPRINTNET, and DIALNET telephone numbers, where you must identify the number of your local node. This is the telephone number that you must call to connect to the system. You will be connected to a computer (hear that funny whine?), and you need to give it the correct protocols in order to establish your link to the system of your choice. Establishing this connection can be vastly simplified by your communications software, so let's look next at how that operates.

Communications Software

Perhaps the most important component of the whole setup is the communications software package—the programs that tell your microcomputer how to send and receive information as though it were a dumb terminal with no memory, no storage, and no "intelligence" at all. Once you have installed the software on your machine, you must use the configuration program to make your computer and modem compatible with the online system. This initial customizing of your software is a tedious task but will save endless effort in the long run. The configuration program will walk you through a series of steps that will tell the system about your equipment and set the correct parameters (such as baud rate, parity, etc.) to make your machine compatible with the computer of the online service. Figure 3.5 gives you an idea of the type of information you will need to enter, but of course each software package is slightly different.

Because noise on the line can cause the receiving computer to misunderstand the message that has been sent, a number of techniques have been developed to help minimize interference with the transmission of data. Probably the most important of these is parity checking. Each character in computer code is made up of eight bits, or binary digits, of which only seven are used to denote the character. The remaining eighth bit is the parity bit. It is used as a kind of check digit, to check that the other seven bits have been correctly transmitted. Parity can be even or odd, and the two systems that want to communicate have to agree on which they are using. It works like this: For each individual character, the "spare" bit is used as a parity bit. At the time when data are sent, the computer totals the value of all the bits and adds a zero or a one to make the total an even or an odd number, depending on the parity in use. At the time of receipt, the receiving computer will check that the total is

Fig. 3.5. Customizing menu.[2]

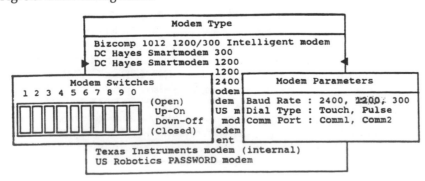

correct (i.e., odd or even) and issue a message to say that there is noise on the line if it is not. In any case, once the parity bit has served its function, the receiving machine discards it.

Parity checking is based on the possibility that one of the bits in a character may get transformed, but that it is unlikely that two bits in the same character will get changed. Notice that if two bits in a character do get changed, the resulting character will have the correct parity and there is no way for the receiving machine to detect the error. That is why you sometimes get strange characters that you did not type, or the machine does not understand a perfectly correct command. Parity checking, a relatively simple checking device, is not foolproof.

Normally things like parity and duplex are customized into your communications software package, so that they are performed only once, when you are installing your software, and you do not need to worry about them thereafter. It is usually a case of making sure that everything "matches," so that if anything on your system changes (you might be lucky enough to acquire a new high-speed modem), you will need to revise the configuration program in order to reconfigure your system.

Choosing your communications software package is particularly important, because you will be living with it for a long time to come. For a review of different types of software, see chapter 14. In general,

the more expensive the package, the more sophisticated its capabilities. Three important capabilities to look for in a communications package are

- upload and download capability,
- ability to access a range of different systems, and
- automatic log-on and autodial.

The ability to type in complete searches before going online (uploading them) and to download results for post-processing is particularly important, because it saves online time and thus reduces costs. When this feature is available, downloaded data is saved to a buffer (an area of temporary storage space) and can be transferred offline either to memory or a printer, or to disk for input to a word-processing package. Using a word processor in this way makes it possible to customize your search results to produce a professional-looking, value-added end product.

The ease of customizing system parameters and protocols depends on the ability of the communications software to allow different settings to be predefined so as to simplify access to a variety of search services. It is then possible to select a system from an initial menu and have the computer automatically adjust to the appropriate configuration without the need for further searcher input.

A personal note: Setting up modems and communications software can be a real pain in the neck. These protocols (baud rate, parity, duplex, stop bits) have to **exactly** match what your network or vendor requires or it's not going to work. Things have gotten a bit easier over the years as more and more people are connecting up, but it still can be a nuisance. On one level, it really doesn't matter what these settings are, so long as they match. Find out what they are, configure your software and modem accordingly, and hope for the best. The nice part is that in most cases, once you get these set, you'll never have to worry about them again. Good luck!

Furthermore, the whole telecommunications business is changing with the increasing use of wide-area networks. We'll see more about this in chapter 15 on the Internet. - JWJ

Search Databases

The files available for searching are stored on magnetic disks, which are direct-access storage devices that permit almost instantaneous response. The range of subject information available is one of the great advantages of online searching, as no library can afford to purchase all the texts or printed indexes that are currently being published. For the historical reasons discussed earlier, most of the earliest databases to become available were in the scientific and technical fields. Biological, physical, chemical, and medical sciences were all well represented from the early days, as were engineering and agriculture. Also, a number of multidisciplinary scientific subjects, such as energy and the environment, have been

added since. Most of these files provide retrospective coverage back to the late 1960s or early 1970s, usually depending on when their producers started computer typesetting, because retrospective conversion is not regarded as an economic option. The next group of files to become available online were those covering business and the social sciences—education, law, psychology, and economics—most going back to the early to mid-1970s. Last to be converted were the humanities files, many of which cover a much briefer time span. This is particularly unfortunate in view of the historical nature of many of the humanities disciplines. A number of more popular information resources, such as newspapers and magazines, have now become available for online searching, and more full-text files are being mounted almost every month.

In fact, nearly all index and abstract publications are now being produced by computer typesetting, so that most available online databases mirror their hard-copy reference counterparts, and many are also available on compact disk (CD-ROM) or to be leased for in-house mounting. Libraries are increasingly faced with acquisition choices between different versions of the same databases, with decisions being based on their levels of usage and the types of searches they most commonly perform. Many of the more popular databases are available from more than one vendor, often in slightly different forms and at different prices, so that it pays to do some comparison shopping and to analyze library use patterns over the years.

What Will Happen in the Future?

If online has so many advantages, why then are the printed indexing services still in business? Surely searching them must be much slower? It is, but although several writers have forecast the demise of all printed materials,[3] most libraries still regard electronic (online and CD-ROM) resources as useful adjuncts to their traditional print resources. Why is that? Possibly because libraries are very traditional places, and change comes slowly. Maybe because users and some librarians have been slow to realize the potential and variety of online resources. It is beginning to look as if the availability of databases on CD-ROM may well bring about big changes in the perceptions of users. Initially, the introduction of databases on CD-ROM led to a big fall in the number of online searches being performed in most libraries, but this may well be a short-term effect. People may start to ask about subjects that are not available on CD-ROM. Will they then want an online search? Will they want to do it themselves? How will they feel about paying for it? People are not used to the idea of paying for information. Should they have to pay for it? (See more on that in chapter 14.)

What about costs for online searching? Is it cheaper than a manual search? It is difficult to price a manual search in a realistic fashion, but it is clear that online searches save a lot of time, because a single search covers the entire retrospective file. Is it cheaper than it was at first? Originally, it was feared that many libraries would cancel subscriptions to printed index publications as a result of having online access, and that search costs would increase to compensate for lost print revenues. In general, that has not happened, and over the years online costs have risen less quickly than prices in general. What will happen if CD-ROM causes a serious decline in online income? We can only hazard some guesses. It is no wonder that the major online service providers are also heavily involved with the compact disk market. Will print, leased databases, online access, and in-house compact disks continue to share the market, or will some entirely new format arrive to take over? Information is a very volatile product, and the products and the players continue to change almost weekly.

Notes

[1]"Baud rate" is another term used to describe the speed of a telecommunications transmission; it is strictly bps divided by 10, but the terms are widely used interchangeably.

[2]*Pro-Search Manual* (Santa Clara, CA: Menlo, 1984), 2–5.

[3]For example, F. W. Lancaster in *Towards Paperless Information Systems* (New York: Academic Press), as far back as 1978.

In this chapter, we will discuss the ways in which databases and search systems are constructed, and how they are accessed in searching. Knowing this can assist searchers in building and executing search strategies and performing better searches.

A database is an organized collection of records in machine-readable form.

4

DATABASE CONSTRUCTION

Each record in the database will be in a standardized format, though the individual records will, of course, contain unique data representing different documents. We begin by examining the structure of a sample record from an online database to see what information it contains and how it is organized.

Record Structures

The following is a sample record from the *ERIC* database:

AN	EJ355024 TM511910
TI	An Experimental, Exploratory Study of Causes of Bias in Test Items
AU	Scheuneman, Janice Dowd
JO	Journal of Educational Measurement, v24 n2 p97-118 Sum 1987
AV	Available from: UMI
LA	Language: English
DT	Document Type: JOURNAL ARTICLE (080); RESEARCH REPORT (143)
JA	Journal Announcement: CIJSEP87
AB	This study evaluated 16 hypotheses concerning possible sources of bias in test items on the Graduate Record Examination General Test. Ten of the hypotheses showed interactions between group membership and the item performance of Black and White examinees. (Author/LMO)
DE	Descriptors: *Blacks; *College Entrance Examinations; Higher Education; Hypothesis Testing; *Racial Differences; Sex Differences; Statistical Bias; *Test Bias; *Test Items; *Whites
ID	Identifiers: *Graduate Record Examinations; Log

The two-letter codes point to the different *fields* of the *record*. A *field* is an individual piece of information about a document, and the collection of these fields about the same document is called a *record*. The fields shown above are described in the following:

AN - *accession number*; a number assigned by the database producer when a document is entered into the database. This number uniquely identifies each record in the file. Documents in the *ERIC* database have two

accession numbers: one assigned by the individual ERIC clearinghouse where the document was produced (here TM 511 910), and one by the overall ERIC system (here EJ 355 024).

TI - *title*; the title of the original document.

AU - *author*; the author of the original document. There may be more than one author; if so, all may or may not be listed. An agency or organization may also be credited with authorship. This is referred to as a *corporate author*.

JO - *journal name and citation*; the name of the journal where the original document appeared, if it is a journal article; if not, identifying information about the original source is given. In addition, the journal's volume, number, pages, and year of publication are given.

AV - *availability*; where the document may be obtained, in addition to the source journal. In this case, the document is available from University Microfilms International (UMI).

LA - *language*; the language in which the original document is written.

DT - *document type*; *ERIC* assigns a code to each document to describe its type: journal article, guidebook, manual, dissertation, report, and so on. Other databases have similar information, although the specific types involved will differ.

JA - *journal announcement*; all documents in the ERIC database are also listed in the two *ERIC* print indexes: *CIJE* (*Current Index to Journals in Education*) for journal articles and *RIE* (*Resources in Education*) for all other documents. This field shows that this document appeared in *CIJE* in September 1987.

AB - *abstract*; a brief summary of the document, typically a paragraph, which may have been written by the original author or by the indexers.

DE - *descriptors*; index terms assigned, generally

from a predetermined list, by a professional indexer to represent this document and assist searchers in looking for it. This list is known as a controlled vocabulary, and we will discuss this further in chapter 6. The descriptors in this record are taken from the *ERIC Thesaurus*. The starred descriptors are referred to as *major descriptors*; they have been identified by the indexer as the terms that best describe what the document is about and are the only descriptors that appear in the printed version of the file.

ID - *identifiers*; terms assigned by the indexer that are similar in form to descriptors but are freely assigned and are not from a predetermined list. Often, identifiers are terms so new in an area that they are not yet widely used or known and have not yet been added to the accepted vocabularies. In *ERIC* this field is also used for proper names (i.e., names of places and people).

Different databases have different record structures, as we shall see: different fields, different codes for the same fields, and different orderings of the fields. But this *ERIC* record is a good example of the type of bibliographic record stored in an online database.

All the records in a database are stored in one large file, organized numerically by accession number. But that file, known as the *linear file*, is not used for searching. To search through the linear file for a particular search key (i.e., subject term or author's name, for example) would be very time-consuming and extremely inefficient. Instead, database designers have developed a shortcut for searching such files.

Inverted Files

This shortcut to speed search time is known as the *inverted file* and is constructed from the linear file by the computer at the time the database is mounted on the system. The major inverted file on DIALOG is the subject file, which is known as the *Basic Index*.

It is simply an alphabetical list of all words in the title, abstract, descriptor, and identifier fields, with pointers to the documents that contain those words.

The following is a sample database showing the subject fields of four documents:

101
Cats and Dogs: Mortal Enemies or Simply Misunderstood?
Examines the traditional antipathy between dogs and cats and attempts to discern the sources and causes of their mutual distrust.
DE: Cats; Dogs; Cross Cultural Studies
ID: Enemies; Hatred

102
New Methods of Feeding Pigs and Cows
Surveys several recent studies of feeding behaviour among pigs and cows and attempts to provide new insight for farmers.
DE: Pigs; Cows; Feeding Behavior
ID: Corn; Hay

103

Canine Mandibular Structure

Analyzes the muscular and skeletal aspects of the mandible of the common canine.

DE: Dogs; Anatomy; Musculature; Skeleton

ID: Mandible

104

Farm Animals as House Pets

A study conducted to determine the usefulness and desirability of keeping common farm animals (cows, pigs, horses) as family pets. Findings included: a pig is smarter than a dog, and a cow is bigger than a cat.

DE: Cows; Pigs; Horses; Farm Animals; Cross Cultural Studies

ID: House Pets

We will use this sample database to demonstrate the process of constructing an inverted file. That process consists of the following three steps:

Step 1. Number all the words in each field of the record.

101

Cats and Dogs: Mortal Enemies or Simply Misunderstood?

  1   3   4   5   6   7   8

Examines the traditional antipathy between dogs and cats and attempts to discern the

  1   3   4   5   6   8   10   12

sources and causes of their mutual distrust.

 14   16   18   19   20

DE: Cats; Dogs; Cross Cultural Studies

       1   2   3   4   5

ID: Enemies; Hatred

     1   2

102

New Methods of Feeding Pigs and Cows

 1   2   4   5   7

Surveys several recent studies of feeding behaviour among pigs and cows and attempts to

 1   2   3   4   6   7   8 9   11   13

provide new insight for farmers.

 15   16   17   19

DE: Pigs; Cows; Feeding Behavior

      1   2   3   4

ID: Corn; Hay

    1   2

103

Canine Mandibular Structure

  1   2   3

Analyzes the muscular and skeletal aspects of the mandible of the common canine.

  1   3   5   6   9   12   13

DE: Dogs; Anatomy; Musculature; Skeleton

      1   2   3   4

ID: Mandible

     1

104

Farm Animals as House Pets

  1   2   3   4   5

A study conducted to determine the usefulness and desirability of keeping common

1 2   3   5   7   9   11   12

farm animals (cows, pigs, horses) as family pets. Findings included: a pig is smarter than a

 13   14   15   16   17   18 19   20   21   22   23 24 25 26   27 28

dog, and a cow is bigger than a cat.

 29   31 32 33 34   35 36 37

—continued

DE: Cows; Pigs; Horses; Farm Animals; Cross Cultural Studies
      1   2   3   4   5   6   7   8
ID: House Pets
     1   2

Note that some words are not numbered, but their positions are preserved, and succeeding words are numbered as if the excluded words also had been. Research in information retrieval has shown that some words are so common that they are of little or no use in searching for documents. These words are known as *stop words*, or *noise words*, and they are neither included in the inverted file nor available for searching. In DIALOG, there are nine stop words:

AN AND BY FOR FROM OF THE TO WITH

Two words that might be expected to be stop words because of their frequency in English are not on the DIALOG system: a and in. They are not stop words because they are sometimes used as content words in phrases such as *vitamin A* and *in vitro fertilization*. Thus, they are included in DIALOG's inverted file and may be used for searching.

The positions of the stop words are preserved, because the inverted file can be used to search for words that are next to each other or within a given number of words of each other. Therefore, absolute position within the original document must be maintained.

Step 2. Make a list of each word with a pointer to its document number, its field, and its position number.

Word	Pointer	Word	Pointer
CATS	101TI1	PIGS	102AB9
DOGS	101TI3	COWS	102AB11
MORTAL	101T14	ATTEMPTS	102AB13
ENEMIES	101T15	PROVIDE	102AB15
OR	101TI6	NEW	102AB16
SIMPLY	101TI7	INSIGHT	102AB17
MISUNDERSTOOD	101TI8	FARMERS	102AB19
EXAMINES	101AB1	*PIGS*	102DE1
TRADITIONAL	101AB3	*COWS*	102DE2
ANTIPATHY	101AB4	FEEDING	102DE3
BETWEEN	101AB5	BEHAVIOR	102DE4
DOGS	101AB6	*FEEDING BEHAVIOR*	102DE3, DE4
CATS	101AB8	CORN	102ID1
ATTEMPTS	101AB10	HAY	102ID2
DISCERN	101AB12	CANINE	103TI1
SOURCES	101AB14	MANDIBULAR	103TI2
CAUSES	101AB16	STRUCTURE	103TI3
THEIR	101AB18	ANALYZES	103AB1
MUTUAL	101AB19	MUSCULAR	103AB3
DISTRUST	101AB20	SKELETAL	103AB5
CATS	101DE1	ASPECTS	103AB6
DOGS	101DE2	MANDIBLE	103AB9
CROSS	101DE3	COMMON	103AB12
CULTURAL	101DE4	CANINE	103AB13
STUDIES	101DE5	*DOGS*	103DE1
CROSS CULTURAL STUDIES	101DE3, DE4, DE5	*ANATOMY*	103DE2
ENEMIES	101ID1	*MUSCULATURE*	103DE3
HATRED	101ID2	*SKELETON*	103DE4
NEW	102TI1	MANDIBLE	103ID1
METHODS	102TI2	FARM	104TI1
FEEDING	102TI4	ANIMALS	104TI2
PIGS	102TI5	AS	104TI3
COWS	102TI7	HOUSE	104TI4
SURVEYS	102AB1	PETS	104TI5
SEVERAL	102AB2	A	104AB1
RECENT	102AB3	STUDY	104AB2
STUDIES	102AB4	CONDUCTED	104AB3
FEEDING	102AB6	DETERMINE	104AB5
BEHAVIOUR	102AB7	USEFULNESS	104AB7
AMONG	102AB8	DESIRABILITY	104AB9

KEEPING	104AB11	*PIGS*	104DE2
COMMON	104AB12	*HORSES*	104DE3
FARM	104AB13	FARM	104DE4
ANIMALS	104AB14	ANIMALS	104DE5
COWS	104AB15	*FARM ANIMALS*	104DE4, DE5
PIGS	104AB16	CROSS	104DE6
HORSES	104AB17	CULTURAL	104DE7
AS	104AB18	STUDIES	104DE8
FAMILY	104AB19	*CROSS CULTURAL STUDIES*	104DE6, DE7, DE8
PETS	104AB20	HOUSE	104ID1
FINDINGS	104AB21	PETS	104ID2
INCLUDED	104AB22	HOUSE PETS	104ID1, ID2
A	104AB23		
PIG	104AB24		
IS	104AB25		
SMARTER	104AB26		
THAN	104AB27		
A	104AB28		
DOG	104AB29		
A	104AB31		
COW	104AB32		
IS	104AB33		
BIGGER	104AB34		
THAN	104AB35		
A	104AB36		
CAT	104AB37		
COWS	104DE1		

You will notice that in addition to the individual words from the linear file, the descriptors and identifiers that are phrases are also included *as phrases*. This is done so that these can be searched as phrases. Remember, the search is really conducted in the inverted file, so to enable phrase searching of the descriptors and identifiers, they must be included in the inverted file in the same way. We say that the title and abstract are *word indexed* because only individual words are included in the inverted file, and that the descriptor and identifier fields are both *word* and *phrase indexed* because both the individual words and the phrases are included.

Step 3. Alphabetize the list to finish the inverted file.

The final step in constructing an inverted file is to alphabetize the list derived in the previous step, thus inverting the data in the original record. This alphabetized list will be searched when a search request is presented to the system.

A	104AB1	CATS	101AB8
A	104AB23	CATS	101DE1
A	104AB28	CAUSES	101AB16
A	104AB31	COMMON	103AB12
A	104AB36	COMMON	104AB12
AMONG	102AB8	CONDUCTED	104AB3
ANALYZES	103AB1	CORN	102ID1
ANATOMY	103DE2	COW	104AB32
ANIMALS	104TI2	COWS	102TI7
ANIMALS	104AB14	COWS	102AB11
ANIMALS	104DE5	COWS	102DE2
ANTIPATHY	101AB4	COWS	104AB15
AS	104TI3	COWS	104DE1
AS	104AB18	CROSS	101DE3
ASPECTS	103AB6	CROSS	104DE6
ATTEMPTS	101AB10	CROSS CULTURAL STUDIES	101DE3, DE4, DE5
ATTEMPTS	102AB13	CROSS CULTURAL STUDIES	104DE6, DE7, DE8
BEHAVIOR	102DE4	CULTURAL	101DE4
BEHAVIOUR	102AB7	CULTURAL	104DE7
BETWEEN	101AB5	DESIRABILITY	104AB9
BIGGER	104AB34	DETERMINE	104AB5
CANINE	103TI1	DISCERN	101AB12
CANINE	103AB13	DISTRUST	101AB20
CAT	104AB37	DOG	104AB29
CATS	101TI1	DOGS	101TI3
		DOGS	101AB6
		DOGS	101DE2
		DOGS	103DE1
		ENEMIES	101TI5
		ENEMIES	101ID1
		EXAMINES	101AB1

FAMILY	104AB19
FARM	104TI1
FARM	104AB13
FARM	104DE4
FARM ANIMALS	104DE4, DE5
FARMERS	102AB19
FEEDING	102TI4
FEEDING	102AB6
FEEDING	102DE3
FEEDING BEHAVIOR	102DE3, DE4
FINDINGS	104AB21
HATRED	101ID2
HAY	102ID2
HORSES	104AB17
HORSES	104DE3
HOUSE	104TI4
HOUSE	104ID1
HOUSE PETS	104ID1, ID2
INCLUDED	104AB22
INSIGHT	102AB17
IS	104AB25
IS	104AB33
KEEPING	104AB11
MANDIBLE	103AB9
MANDIBLE	103ID1
MANDIBULAR	103TI2
METHODS	102TI2
MISUNDERSTOOD	101TI8
MORTAL	101T14
MUSCULAR	103AB3
MUSCULATURE	103DE3
MUTUAL	101AB19
NEW	102TI1
NEW	102AB16
OR	101TI6
PETS	104TI5
PETS	104AB20
PETS	104ID2
PIG	104AB24
PIGS	102TI5
PIGS	102AB9
PIGS	102DE1

PIGS	104AB16
PIGS	104DE2
PROVIDE	102AB15
RECENT	102AB3
SEVERAL	102AB2
SIMPLY	101TI7
SKELETAL	103AB5
SKELETON	103DE4
SMARTER	104AB26
SOURCES	101AB14
STRUCTURE	103TI3
STUDIES	101DE5
STUDIES	102AB4
STUDIES	104DE8
STUDY	104AB2
SURVEYS	102AB1
THAN	104AB27
THAN	104AB35
THEIR	101AB18
TRADITIONAL	101AB3
USEFULNESS	104AB7

We will use this example of an inverted file for some sample searching. Assume a person wants documents about cows. The searcher enters the system and asks for documents that contain the word COWS. The system searches through the inverted file, finds the word COWS, and reports that two documents are found. The searcher then may ask for the documents to be displayed, and the system will retrieve documents 102 and 104 from the linear file and display them.

This is a simple example, and searching is rarely this straightforward. Suppose the user wants documents that are about both cows and horses or about either cows or dogs. These individual sets could be searched for and retrieved and then compared or combined manually, but there is a better way. Online retrieval systems have a powerful capacity that can be used for searches that require the combination of a number of search terms.

In fact, it is probably fair to say that the more terms to be searched and the more complicated the search strategy involved, the greater the advantage of using an online search system. This is because a manual search in such a case is particularly slow and frustrating. Straightforward searches on a single topic are normally not too difficult in a printed index. - GW

Boolean Logic and Boolean Searching

Boolean logic is a set of techniques used in mathematics for manipulating sets in a rigorous, logical fashion. It is named for the English mathematician George Boole, who developed the framework on which it is based. Boolean logic provides three ways in which sets can be combined, and online systems use all three.

When a search term is entered, a set of documents that contain that term is created. Boolean search techniques allow the searcher to manipulate and combine these sets to provide the user with a set that corresponds to the logic of the initial query. We will discuss each of the three techniques in turn.

OR

To illustrate the use of the Boolean operators, let's look at a sample query with our toy database. A user asks for documents about keeping cats and dogs together.

We could simply retrieve a set of documents that contain the word DOGS and another that contain the word CATS, and then compare the two to see which documents are in both sets. Indeed, if we were performing the search manually, that is probably what we would do. But using Boolean logic with inverted files, we can do it much more easily.

First, we need to build a set of documents that deal with dogs. We could search on that word, DOGS, and get a set like this:

DOGS   101, 103

But there are other words we could use. DOG, for example:

DOG   103, 104
Or:
CANINE   103

OR is used primarily to combine two or more terms that are synonyms, equivalent, or variant terms. You may have noticed in the inverted file that some terms are very close in meaning but slightly different in form or spelling. Look at COWS and COW, DOGS and DOG, BEHAVIOR and BEHAVIOUR, and EXAMINES, STUDIES, and SURVEYS. OR can be used to make a set of all spellings and forms of a word for use in further searching:

DOG OR DOGS   101, 103, 104
OR CANINE

This is necessary for a variety of reasons. If the terms are from different documents, authors may use different forms of the words or variant spellings. It may also be that words in titles or abstracts may be slightly different from terms used as descriptors or identifiers. Finally, there simply may be more than one term or word used to represent a single concept or idea. We want the concept to be present in the documents we retrieve ("dogness," "catness," "Europe"), but because human languages are ambiguous and because retrieval systems can only match patterns of letters and numbers, we are forced to search for words (DOG, DOGS, CANINE, etc.) and hope that the presence of a word is a good indicator of the presence of a concept. That is by no means always the case, as we shall see many times.

For example, suppose a patron asked for documents about the single European market of 1992. To represent Europe, the searcher might look for EUROPE, but also might use EC (an abbreviation for the European Community) and EEC (European Economic Community) or even the names of individual European countries. In the *ABI/INFORM* database,

which covers periodicals in business, we find the following postings figures:

EUROPE	14,561 documents
EC	1,061 documents
EEC	2,033 documents
EUROPE OR EC OR EEC	14,813 documents

The final number (14,813) is less than the sum of the individual sets (14,561 + 1,061 + 2,033 = 17,655) due to overlap between the sets. Clearly, almost all of the EUROPE documents also contain either EC or EEC. OR will produce a set at least as large as the largest component set.

A tool known as a Venn diagram, named after John Venn, is often used to represent sets and Boolean operations; figure 4.1 is is a Venn diagram that represents this example:

Fig. 4.1. Venn diagram.

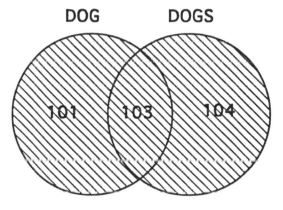

OR, then, is used for the following:

- synonyms or equivalent terms
    GARBANZOS OR CHICK-PEAS
- spelling variants
    HONOR OR HONOUR
- related terms
    GIFTED OR TALENTED

We use it to build up concept blocks; it makes sets *bigger* and retrieves *more* documents.

Be careful, though, of individual terms that dominate a concept set. In the Europe example above, most of those documents are probably about Europe in general and not the EC, because the EUROPE set is so much larger than the others. This is not necessarily a problem, but if your results are not specific enough, you might want to think about reformulating that set or dropping the big dominating term.

We will talk about how to do truncation in DIALOG in chapter 5, but we introduce it here because it is an implicit kind of OR. If we wanted documents about "learning," we could search on terms like LEARN, LEARNING, LEARNED, and so on, and OR them all together. It would be easier, though, to truncate and search on LEARN? (this example uses the DIALOG truncation operator; other systems use $ or # or *) and retrieve all documents that contain any word starting with the five characters L E A R N. Again, we will discuss this more fully later.

AND

The user above has asked for documents about both dogs and cats. These two sets could be individually retrieved thus:

    DOGS   102, 104
    CATS   101

The Boolean operator AND is used to combine two sets. The set that is produced as a result contains only those things that are in both sets. Thus, using AND here produces the following:

    DOGS AND CATS   —nothing—

But this is clearly not the case. What we need to do is build up concept sets for both "dogs" and "cats" and AND them together. So we try the following:

    (a): DOG OR DOGS OR CANINE   101, 103, 104
    (b): CAT OR CATS OR FELINE   101, 104
    (c): (a) AND (b)   101, 104

As a result we get the set of documents that refers to both cats and dogs.

AND is used in online searching to make a connection between two terms and will produce a set that is *no larger* than the *smaller* of the component sets.

When you are using AND, beware of small component sets. If one of the sets you are working with has very few or no documents, you may not want to AND it. If it contains only 15 or 25 items, try inspecting it before going on, even if it means omitting one concept from the query. Chances are if you AND in another set, your result will be very small, if not zero.

NOT

The third Boolean operator is also the least often used, for a couple of reasons. Many searchers do not fully appreciate NOT and its uses, and it is also a very powerful, sometimes too powerful, tool. NOT is used to exclude from a set items that contain a certain term or terms.

Our patron wants documents about dogs and cats but finds one that refers to farm animals in our first set. He does not want it and wants to be rid of the document. We can develop a farm-animal concept set:

    (d): PIG OR PIGS OR COW OR COWS OR
         HORSE OR HORSES   102, 104

and then NOT it out of our result (pets) set above:

    (e): set (c) not set (d)   101

to get one good document, 101, which does satisfy the request. This of course is a trivial example, because we are dealing with so few documents; the ability to do this becomes much more important as databases and sets get bigger and bigger.

NOT produces *smaller* sets; the result can be no larger than the first set. Figure 4.2 presents a Venn diagram for NOT:

NOT must be used with care. If the term being NOTted out is relatively unspecific, many relevant documents may be erroneously excluded. As we proceed, we will point out situations that could take advantage of NOT.

Fig. 4.2. Venn diagram for NOT.

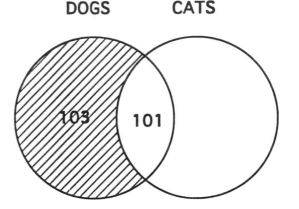

Several terms may often be specified in a single Boolean statement. The order in which they are executed by the computer in most but not all online systems, including DIALOG, is based on a priority of NOT first, then AND, and finally OR, though parentheses can be used to override this prescribed order. A statement such as

    (ORATORIO OR OPERA) AND HANDEL

would thus be different from

    ORATORIO OR OPERA AND HANDEL

The first statement would be interpreted this way: First, the operation inside the parentheses would be performed, so the system would create a set of documents that contain either the word ORATORIO or OPERA. Then, that set would be ANDed with the set of documents that contain the word HANDEL. This produces a set that, we hope, contains documents about vocal works of Handel.

The second statement, though, would be interpreted quite differently. Because there are no parentheses, AND is performed first, so a set of OPERA AND HANDEL would be created—documents that contain both words. This set would then be ORed with the ORATORIO set. The resulting set would consist of all documents about Handel's operas and all documents that mention oratorios. In figures 4.3 and 4.4, the Venn diagrams for these two situations illustrate the difference. This will be more fully described in chapter 5.

Fig. 4.3. Venn diagram for (ORATORIO OR OPERA) AND HANDEL.

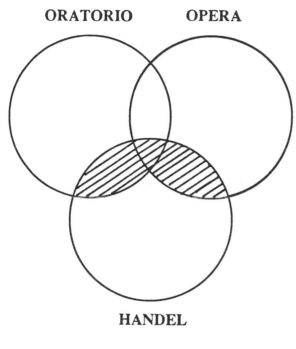

Fig. 4.4. Venn diagram for ORATORIO OR OPERA AND HANDEL.

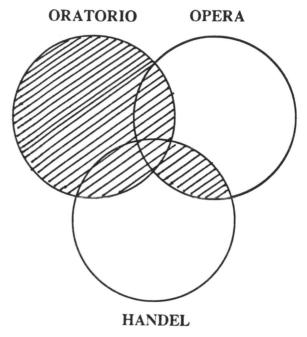

Query Indexing

We have been referring, throughout this chapter, to words in the document title and abstract as well as descriptors and identifiers as "words" or "search terms" that can be used to search for documents in response to a user's query. That is a rather simplistic view of the process. There is rarely a one-to-one match between search terms and concepts in documents. Just because a document contains the word "spy" in its abstract, it is not necessarily about spies, spying, or espionage. Rather, it may refer to *Spy* magazine, for example, Spy apples, or spy novels, or the abstract may even explicitly state, "This study is not about spy novels." The problem grows even worse when truncation is used. Searching for documents about inventing or inventors by using INVENT? as a search term (i.e., looking for all documents that contain words beginning with IN-VENT) will get INVENTOR and INVENTING and INVENTIONS, but also INVENTORY and INVEN-TIVE, which will probably retrieve a good deal of irrelevant material, depending on the database being searched.

We do not necessarily want these individual words in documents, we want the concepts they represent, but the only way we have of searching for those concepts is by searching for words that relate to them. Therefore, when analyzing a query to determine exactly what the user wants and then translating that into search statements for the online system, we essentially have to "index" the query in the same way documents are indexed before they enter the database. (We talked about this similarity in chapter 1.) It is assumed that these processes of "indexing" queries and indexing documents are inverse—that they will provide exact matches between documents and queries. This does happen, on occasion, but such an exact and perfect match is rare.

The vagaries and ambiguities of language are responsible for this lack of precision. Searchers deal with this problem in many different ways. In some situations, truncation, despite the pitfalls described above, can be quite effective. In others, it may be more appropriate to OR together a number of synonymous terms to try to capture all possible terms or senses of a word.

Discussion

An information retrieval (IR) system, such as those we are discussing here, is essentially the coming together of a variety of technologies and ideas having to do with information, its storage, and retrieval.

The technologies come straight from the world of computer science. IR systems have typically been mounted on mainframe computers, the direct descendants of the behemoth computer systems developed in the 1940s and commercially available in the 1960s. To be sure, the mainframe computers in use today are light years beyond the ENIAC, UNIVAC, and IBM System/360 in terms of capacity and speed, but the basic concept is essentially the same. Data are represented and manipulated in binary form (1's and 0's) as before, and the fundamental mode of operation of the machines is unchanged.

The computer on which the system runs may be hundreds or thousands of miles away from any given user, and therefore must be accessed via a telecommunications network. This access often takes place over a traditional telephone line. New telecommunication technologies have emerged over the years (use of microwave and satellite transmission, fiber-optic cables, etc.), and transmission is now much faster than previously possible, but again, the basic arrangement is the same as that of the 1970s.

The ideas underlying storage and retrieval of information also are not new. Record structures and file structures, much as presented in this chapter, inverted files, and Boolean logic all date from the late 1960s and were originally used in the manual post-coordinate systems.[1]

So, all the pieces for an IR system were in place quite a number of years ago. Has nothing changed since then? Well, of course—the computers and communications systems are faster, and the database vendors have added a few bells and whistles to their systems over the years. (We will be looking at these in more detail in chapters 9 and 10. However, free-text searching and other techniques were not available in manual systems. There are many more files available (more almost every day, in fact) and more variety in types of files: numeric, directory, full-text, reference, and so on. The files themselves are bigger, too; some now have millions of records.

But although the fundamentals remain unchanged, research on information retrieval has resulted in some interesting and potentially useful enhancements to these "traditional" systems.

One of the best known and earliest such enhancements is known as *relevance feedback*. The idea is quite simple: After an initial search is conducted, a retrieval set is presented to the user, who then makes judgments as to which documents are relevant and which are not. A relevance feedback system would make use of these relevance judgments to refine the search strategy and run the search again, looking for documents that resemble the relevant ones and rejecting those that do not. The idea is simple, but the implementation is more complex.

The most widely known test system using relevance feedback is SMART, developed at Cornell University by Salton and his colleagues,[2] which uses a vector space model to represent documents and queries. Other related approaches have been the use of relevance weighting[3] and probabilistic information retrieval.[4]

Yet none of these approaches has ever been incorporated into a large-scale, commercial database. Why not? Two reasons, I believe. First, there is the inertia of systems design. Systems such as DIALOG, used to organize and search databases of millions of records, are enormous, highly complex computer programs, which have been developed and refined over a period of many years. It is unlikely that any one person comprehends the entire package of software, and to introduce a new factor such as relevance feedback would be an undertaking of Herculean proportions. It is simply far easier to make small additions and enhancements and not try to change the world.

The second reason is the inertia of success. DIALOG, BRS, and the other major vendors generate millions of dollars of income for their parent corporations, and there is very little pressure on them to make such a dramatic change in their systems. It would take another large system using such features and in direct competition with these vendors to motivate change.

This might appear to suggest that these systems will never change, but I believe they will. We have seen amazing improvements in computing power, storage capacity, and telecommunications speed in the past few years, all of which permit the sort of experimentation and improvement discussed here. We have also seen users become more sophisticated as their experience with computing and its possibilities has grown. It is hoped that their needs and wishes, even more than the technological advancements, will drive the systems to change. So it may be only a question of time before a new idea will take hold and move information retrieval systems to a new level of sophistication.

[1]In fact, these systems gave us some terms we still use today. We still speak of nonrelevant documents we retrieve as "false drops" (cards bearing document representations that would falsely drop out of the pile being searched), and the proportion of such documents retrieved as "fallout."

[2]G. Salton (1971), "Relevance Feedback and the Optimization of Retrieval Effort," chapter 15 in *The SMART Retrieval System—Experiments in Automatic Document Processing* (Englewood Cliffs, NJ: Prentice-Hall), 324-36.

[3]S. Robertson, and K. Sparck Jones (1976), "Relevance Weighting of Search Terms," *Journal of the American Society for Information Science* 27:129-46.

[4]C. van Rijsbergen (1979), "Probabilistic Retrieval," chapter 6 in *Information Retrieval* (London: Butterworths) 111-43.

In this chapter we introduce the fundamental concepts of online searching: logging on (gaining access to the system), choosing a file or database in which to perform the search, analyzing the query statement and extracting the main concepts, formulating search strategies, creating retrieval sets, viewing these sets, and leaving the system. In addition, special techniques of search strategy development and execution are discussed, such as the use of building blocks, the "most specific first" rule, pearl growing, more on the use of Boolean logic, and truncation.

These are the most basic and the most often used online searching procedures. The techniques discussed

5

SEARCH TECHNIQUE

here will be used throughout the rest of the book, and later skills will build on these, so it is particularly important that the beginning searcher feel comfortable with these basic strategies before proceeding further.

To assist the reader, a sample search will be used to illustrate the concepts of this chapter. Suppose a patron contacts the library and asks for information on the effects of alcohol consumption on memory—both chronic abuse and acute intoxication but not alcoholism, which the patron feels is a quite different area. Figure 5.1 presents an example of a search request form that some libraries use.

Concept Analysis, Choice of Search Terms

Before beginning a search, a good searcher will spend some time in the analysis of the query, trying to understand exactly what the person requesting the search is looking for and in what format the answers are desired. It may be that at this stage the searcher decides that an online search is inappropriate, that instead a search of the library catalog, a

printed index, or some other source would better respond to the query.

When an online search is called for, the first step is to examine the query and determine the major concepts involved. This process is called *concept analysis*.

Concept means the abstract idea of a thing, regardless of what it may be called in a given instance. This is because very often a single concept (e.g., teacher) will have more than one recognizable name (instructor, tutor, professor, lecturer, master, coach).

The controlled vocabulary in an information retrieval (IR) system is an attempt to standardize to one preferred term that will always be used to represent a single concept, so that we will not find the same subject entered under different headings. A golden rule for most retrieval systems is to try to gather together all the material on one subject. - GW

Our searcher decides that an online search would help to answer this query and so begins to analyze the concepts it contains. Two concepts are found: alcohol use and abuse and effects on memory.

After the concepts are identified, the searcher starts to generate possible search terms that could be used to find documents that are "about" the concepts in the query. These terms could come from the patron or the original query statement, especially if it is in written form. Often a patron will be well acquainted with the literature of the field of the query and will know the specific terminology to be used. In such a case, that expertise can be a rich source of possible search terms.

In other cases, a relatively unsophisticated user may not have such detailed knowledge, and it is up

to the searcher to generate possible terms. Sources of terms would include the searcher's own knowledge in the subject area, familiarity with the databases and print indexes in the field, or just common sense.

We will discuss an important source of search terms—database thesauri and controlled vocabulary—in chapter 6. For now, however, our searcher generates these terms in cooperation with the patron and the thesaurus, as follows:

for *alcohol use and abuse*:
alcohol abuse
alcohol intoxication
alcohol

(Text continues on page 40.)

Fig. 5.1. Simple search request form.

Search Request Form

Please give a brief narrative description of your topic (use back if necessary):

Do you know of any index terms, vocabulary terms, or search terms that would be useful in searching for documents on this topic? Please list them here, or underline them in the above description.

Do you know of any authors or documents relevant to this topic? Please specify them here.

Type of materials of interest to you (circle):

Journal Articles	Y	N	Conference Papers	Y	N
Reports	Y	N	Dissertation	Y	N

Other (specify): _____

Years to be covered: _____

Languages of interest (list):_____

Please give any other information you think might be helpful in formulating a search strategy on the back.

for *memory*:
memory
long term memory
short term memory
memory disorders
amnesia

There are certainly other terms that could be used here, but we will begin with these. In the actual search, we may not need all of these terms; using only a few may get us a good set of documents, but it is advisable to generate a number of alternative possibilities in case the first search is not successful.

Building Blocks, Most Specific First

Most searchers use two techniques for constructing search strategies: building blocks, or concept blocks, and the "most specific first" rule.

Think of the search strategy as a structure, built up from individual pieces, each of which corresponds to a concept derived from the analysis of the query. This way of thinking about constructing a search strategy is called using *building blocks* and is the most common technique used in searching.

In our sample search, there will be two concept blocks: one on alcohol use and abuse and one on memory. Each block will be represented by at least one search term. As our search strategies become more sophisticated, there may be more than one search term per block. Figure 5.2 presents the search form submitted by the patron.

Another important and widely used technique is that of *most specific first*, which relates to the efficiency with which a search is conducted while online. Imagine you were doing a search on high schools in Nigeria in the *ERIC* database, which covers documents in the field of education. Here there would be two

concept blocks: high schools and Nigeria. But think about the nature of the database. If it covers education, how many documents about high schools will it have, as opposed to the number of documents about Nigeria? These terms obviously vary in level of specificity, and the system will take considerably longer to search for "high schools." So it makes sense to begin by looking for documents about Nigeria, and then searching within that set for documents also about high schools. The Nigeria block is far more specific and thus should be entered first. "Most specific first" uses characteristics of the documents in different databases to improve the efficiency of the search.

In our sample search, the more specific concept is probably that of alcohol; it is likely that in the *PsycINFO* database, which we are using for this search, there are many more documents about memory than about alcohol. So, when executing the search, we will search for alcohol first.

Having selected search terms and determined our search strategy, we are now ready to begin the search itself, by logging on.

Logging-On Protocols and Choosing a File (BEGIN)

The major online search services, such as DIALOG, BRS, or LEXIS/NEXIS, are accessed via telecommunications networks, as discussed in chapter 3. Typically, only a local phone call will be required to get on the nearest node of the network and gain access to the search service.

When the call is placed, and the service computer is reached, the searcher must log on to the system in order to perform the search. This is done by entering

the user number and password at the appropriate prompts. This is to prevent unauthorized access to the system and for accounting purposes. If the user number and password are correct (i.e., match a valid user number and password for that system), the searcher is logged on to the system and receives a greeting. An example of a DIALOG log-on is on page 42.

Fig. 5.2. Filled-in search form.

School of Information & Library Studies
Relevance Study
Search Request Form

Please give a brief narrative description of your topic (use back if necessary):

I am interested in the effects of alcohol consumption on memory. I am interested in the effects of acute intoxication as well as chronic abuse on memory.

Do you know of any index terms, vocabulary terms, or search terms that would be useful in searching for documents on this topic? Please list them here, or underline them in the above description.

encoding, storage, retrieval, ethanol, repitition priming, drinking.

Do you know of any authors or documents relevant to this topic? Please specify them here.

Type of materials of interest to you (circle):

Journal Articles	(Y) N	Conference Papers	(Y) N	
Reports	(Y) N	Dissertation	(Y) N	

Other (specify): *book chapters*

Years to be covered: *1920 - present*

Languages of interest (list): *english*

Please give any other information you think might be helpful in formulating a search strategy on the back.

```
%Call connected
DIALOG INFORMATION SERVICES
PLEASE LOGON:
   ********
ENTER PASSWORD:
   ********

Welcome to DIALOG
Dialog level 29.01.05B

Last logoff:  26jun92 12:59:09
Logon file001 26jun92 12:59:27
* * *  TEXTLINE is now available. Begin TXTLN or TEXTLINE * * *

File  1:ERIC  66-92/JUN.
FILE 1: Price changes will go into effect June 1, 1992.
Please see HOMEBASE Announcements for more details.

       Set  Items  Description
       ---  -----  -----------
?
```

You will notice that in the above, only the system's responses are shown. The searcher has typed in the password, but the system first types a blot (********) to mask the printing, so that no one can read the printout and gain access to the password illegally.

This greeting tells us that the last use of the system by this user number was earlier on June 26, 1992, and that we are in the *ERIC* database, DIALOG file 1. This is the default database selected by the user, meaning that unless told otherwise, all searches will be executed in the *ERIC* database. We will discuss *ERIC* in more detail in chapter 6; for now, you should know that it is a database of documents in the field of education.

Typically, at this stage, important system news will be given—new databases that have just become available, files that are not working at present, new services being offered by the system, and so on.

After the system news comes the file header. This tells us what file we are currently searching (in this case file 1, *ERIC*), the dates of coverage of that file (here 1966 to June 1992), and any other file-specific news. Then the headings Set, Items, and Description are printed (we will get back to these on page 00), and finally we get the system prompt, which tells us that the system is ready and waiting for us to begin searching. In DIALOG, that prompt is a question mark.

Professional searchers often prefer to use DIALOG and like systems in "command mode" (sometimes called "native mode"). When searching this way, you are confronted by a prompt character or characters (here a question mark) and you type your command at that prompt. Many of the online vendors have introduced alternative interfaces, often using menus, to make searching easier and attract less experienced end-users. These menu-driven systems often are less powerful and less flexible than command systems and may also provide access to only certain databases. - JWJ

Let's illustrate these fundamental techniques of searching by walking through our sample search on a command-driven system. We have selected several search terms; now we can start to put them to use.

First, however, we must enter the database we wish to search. As shown above, our default database is file 1, *ERIC*. It is possible that documents on this topic might be found in *ERIC*, but unlikely. A better option would be *PsycINFO*, DIALOG file 11. *Psyc-INFO* is the online version of *Psychological Abstracts* and is usually the database of choice for searches in the realm of psychology. The process of database selection will be covered in more detail in chapter 10.

To enter the *PsycINFO* database, use the BEGIN command. BEGIN is used to change between files in DIALOG. The form of the command is

BEGIN file-no

where file-no is the number of the file to enter. This command can also be abbreviated, as in:

B file-no

PsycINFO is DIALOG file number 11, so to start this search, at the DIALOG prompt, type the following:

```
         Set   Items   Description
         ---   -----   -----------
?b 11


File  11:PSYCINFO   67-92/JULY
         (COPR. AM. PSYCH. ASSOC.)

         Set   Items   Description
         ---   -----   -----------
?
```

Choosing Search Terms (SELECT)

The command used to search for a given term is SELECT. The form of the command is
SELECT search term
and can be abbreviated and often is, as in:
S search term

When the SELECT command is given, the system searches through the Basic Index for all the documents that contain that term.

SELECT may be used to search phrases as well as individual words. (Recall the inverted file example.) The descriptor and identifier fields are phrase indexed, which means that the intact phrases are available to be searched. So search statements like the following are possible:

```
?s attention span or attention deficit
   disorder or distraction
      196   ATTENTION SPAN
      493   ATTENTION DEFICIT DISORDER
     1133   DISTRACTION
  S1  1807   ATTENTION SPAN OR
             ATTENTION DEFICIT DISORDER
             OR DISTRACTION
```

Note that phrases may only be searched in fields that are phrase indexed. Fields such as titles and abstracts may not be phrase searched in this way. There are other techniques for searching for word combinations in word indexed fields, as we shall see in chapter 7.

You also see here the format in which DIALOG presents the results of a search. The *set number* (in this case S1) is given in the left column; each succeeding set will be numbered S2, S3, and so on. The *description*, in the right column, tells you what that set corresponds to—what terms or other strategies were used to create it. In the middle, we see the number of *items* (records) in that set (here 1807).

There is another form of the SELECT command that is useful if you are searching for several terms at once. It is known as SELECT STEPS and is abbreviated SS. The form of SELECT STEPS is
SELECT STEPS search statement
and its abbreviated form is
SS search statement

When SELECT STEPS is used, it performs the same operations as SELECT. The terms requested are searched for in the inverted file, and a set is produced.

The difference between this and SELECT is that when SELECT STEPS is used, sets are created for the individual terms in the statement as well as the entire Boolean expression.

Using SELECT, the following result is obtained:

```
?s freeware or shareware
         10   FREEWARE
         61   SHAREWARE
  S1    68   FREEWARE OR SHAREWARE
```

Using SELECT STEPS, this is the result:

```
?ss freeware or shareware
  S1    10   FREEWARE
  S2    61   SHAREWARE
  S3    68   FREEWARE OR SHAREWARE
```

Note that the postings are the same, but individual sets have been created for FREEWARE and SHAREWARE in the SELECT STEPS example.

These intermediate sets can be useful if, as the search continues, the searcher decides to use these terms in other combinations. The sets have already been created, so if the searcher wished to look for FREEWARE OR VAPORWARE, connect time and processing time, as well as typing, could be saved by using:

```
?ss s1 or vaporware
```

instead of

```
?s freeware or vaporware
```

SELECT STEPS can be used anywhere SELECT can be used, but it is not necessary when searching for single terms or phrases (e.g., *SS FREEWARE*), because in that context it is exactly the same as using SELECT. Also, if you do use SELECT STEPS, take advantage of it. Use the intermediate set rather than retyping the same terms. This is a common problem among beginning searchers, but as you gain experience, you will find it easier to use previously created sets for later searches.

The Boolean operators AND, OR, and NOT, discussed in chapter 4, can be used in SELECT statements in several ways. As we have seen, two or more terms may be joined by a Boolean operator, as in:

`?s altruism or assistance`

Set numbers may be used in place of terms, for example:

`?s s6 or drugs`
`?s s9 and s12`

Also, more than two components may be searched for, as in:

`?s s8 and s9 and s14`

A few cautionary words about SELECT: Always be sure to put a space after SELECT or S or SS. The system expects it, and if you omit it, you may get

unexpected results, such as:

`?ssystem`
`   S1    0   YSTEM`

Here the system saw SS and searched for the remainder of the statement (YSTEM).

A searcher must also be careful to watch for spelling and typing mistakes. Computers are very literal beasts, and a spelling or typing mistake will, more than likely, result in a zero-result set. For example:

`?s infomation`
`   S1    0   INFOMATION`

Beginning searchers often either fail to notice such an error or become flustered when it happens. If you do make such a mistake, simply type the offending search statement again and proceed from that point.

> One of the golden rules of online searching is stated thus: Always be suspicious when you get a set with zero postings. Have you spelled the term or terms correctly? Have you entered the command correctly? Notice the computer responds by repeating your requested term or terms, so see that it received what you intended. When using set numbers, check that the postings look consistent with what you had previously seen. - GW

Another common mistake among new searchers occurs during searches involving previously created sets. Sometimes, instead of the statement:

`?s s5 and france`

the searcher enters

`?s 5 and france`

In this instance, it is not set S5 that is ANDed with France, it is the numeral 5, and only documents

containing that number somewhere in the indexed fields will be retrieved. For example:

```
      407   5
     2076   FRANCE
S9     51   5 AND FRANCE
```

Again, if this should happen, simply reenter the statement. These errors are especially pernicious and hard to catch, because they create sets that may look right. However, if an error like this is carried through an entire search, it will probably result in an almost useless set of citations.

Our sample search begins thus:

```
    Set  Items  Description
    ---  -----  -----------
?ss alcohol abuse or alcohol intoxication
    S1    1149  ALCOHOL ABUSE
    S2     907  ALCOHOL INTOXICATION
    S3    2052  ALCOHOL ABUSE OR ALCOHOL INTOXICATION
?ss memory/df or long term memory or short term memory or memory disorders
    S4   12678  MEMORY/DF
    S5    1046  LONG TERM MEMORY
    S6    3626  SHORT TERM MEMORY
    S7     502  MEMORY DISORDERS
    S8   17209  MEMORY/DF OR LONG TERM MEMORY OR SHORT TERM MEMORY OR
               MEMORY DISORDERS
```

Because we want both of these concept blocks in the final set, we must AND them together. This can be accomplished using the SELECT command and the numbers of the previously selected sets:

```
?s s3 and s8
      2052  S3
     17209  S8
  S9   37  S3 AND S8
```

This tells us that there are 37 documents in the *PsycINFO* database that satisfy this search strategy.

Viewing Results, TYPE, and Formats

After a set is retrieved in response to a search statement, its contents may be viewed to determine the specific documents it contains. Online systems provide several different formats to display records, and they are typically used at different stages of the search.

The DIALOG command used to display records in a set is TYPE, which can be abbreviated as T. The format of the TYPE command is

TYPE n/f/b-e

or

T n/f/b-e

where n is the set number to be displayed, f is the number of the format to be used (there are several, which differ by file), b is the number of the first document to be displayed, and e is the number of the last document to be displayed. Thus,

```
?t s5/8/1-5
```

would display the first through the fifth documents from set S5, using format 8. The documents in retrieval sets are normally organized in reverse order by date, so the documents that have been most recently entered into the database will be the first output in any retrieved set.

Different databases have different formats, but there are some common formats across many databases. Let us return to our sample search. We had retrieved a set S9, containing 37 documents. Let's look at that set. We enter the command

```
?t s9/6/1-6
```

to view the first six documents of S9, using format 6. Format 6 in this database and in most others is accession number and title. Here are the results of that command:

```
?t 9/6/1-6

  9/6/1
00845989          29-74072
  Effects of post-trial ethanol treatment on memory.

  9/6/2
00820520          28-58069
  Gender differences in prose memory after acute intoxication with ethanol.

  9/6/3
00800010          78-18809
  Cue-exposure  interventions  for  alcohol  relapse prevention: Need for a
memory modification component.

  9/6/4
00797330          28-54252
  The effects of alcohol on semantic memory.

  9/6/5
00781282          51-02626
  Short-term memory function in alcohol addicts during intoxication.

  9/6/6
00778752          77-24881
  Some effects of alcohol on eyewitness memory.
```

You can see that the result of this search is quite good. The documents that have been retrieved seem to be relevant to the patron's query.

There are other formats that can be used to display retrieval sets. Format 8 is often called the "searcher's format," because it displays the title, descriptors, and identifiers, among other fields. In many cases, displaying retrieved documents in this format can be helpful for refining or extending a search as it progresses, as the searcher can select additional index terms from relevant documents. This technique is known as *pearl-growing*. We will discuss this on page 00, so watch for good terms in documents we look at. The following are the first six documents of this set in format 8:

```
?t 9/8/1-8

 9/8/1
00845989          29-74072
  Effects of post-trial ethanol treatment on memory.
  Major Descriptors:  *MEMORY;  *ETHANOL
  Minor Descriptors:  ALCOHOL INTOXICATION;  ADULTHOOD
  Descriptor Codes:  30570;  18040;  01700;  01150
  Identifiers:  alcohol intoxication, memory tasks, adults
  Section Headings:  2580 -PSYCHOPHARMACOLOGY

 9/8/2
00820520          28-58069
  Gender differences in prose memory after acute intoxication with ethanol.
  Major  Descriptors:    *MEMORY;    *ALCOHOL  INTOXICATION;    *HUMAN  SEX
    DIFFERENCES;  *ORAL CONTRACEPTIVES;  *HUMAN INFORMATION STORAGE
  Minor Descriptors:  RECALL (LEARNING);  ADULTHOOD
  Descriptor Codes:  30570;  01700;  23510;  35620;  23480;  43290;  01150
  Identifiers:  acute alcohol intoxication,  encoding  speed for prose &
    recall, male vs females taking vs not taking oral contraceptives
  Section Headings:  2660 -DRUG STIMULATION & PSYCHOPHARMACOLOGY

 9/8/3
00800010          78-18809
  Cue-exposure  interventions  for  alcohol  relapse  prevention: Need for a
memory modification component.
  Major Descriptors:  *CUES;  *CONDITIONED RESPONSES;  *RELAPSE (DISORDERS)
    ;  *ALCOHOL ABUSE
  Minor Descriptors:  MEMORY
  Descriptor Codes:  12680;  11090;  43660;  01660;  30570
  Identifiers:  cue CR, relapse prediction, problem drinkers
  Section Headings:  3233 -SUBSTANCE ABUSE

 9/8/4
00797330          28-54252
  The effects of alcohol on semantic memory.
  Major Descriptors:  *ALCOHOL INTOXICATION;  *MEMORY;  *SEMANTICS
  Minor Descriptors:  ADULTHOOD
  Descriptor Codes:  01700;  30570;  46390;  01150
  Identifiers:  alcohol intoxication, semantic memory, 21-29 yr old males
  Section Headings:  2660 -DRUG STIMULATION & PSYCHOPHARMACOLOGY

 9/8/5
00781282          51-02626
  Short-term memory function in alcohol addicts during intoxication.
  Major Descriptors:  *ALCOHOLISM;  *ALCOHOL  INTOXICATION;  *SHORT TERM
    MEMORY;  *DRUG EFFECTS
  Descriptor Codes:  01750;  01700;  47260;  15300
  Identifiers:  alcohol  intoxication vs  sobriety,  short-term  memory
    function, alcoholics with vs without history of blackouts
  Section  Headings:  2600 -PHYSIOLOGICAL  INTERVENTION;  3233 -SUBSTANCE
    ABUSE
```

```
9/8/6
00778752          77-24881
  Some effects of alcohol on eyewitness memory.
  Major Descriptors: *ALCOHOL INTOXICATION; *WITNESSES;  *MEMORY
  Minor Descriptors:  LEGAL PROCESSES;  ADULTHOOD
  Descriptor Codes:  01700;  56885;  30570;  28110;  01150
  Identifiers:  alcohol,  immediate  vs  delayed  eyewitness  memory, male
     college students, legal implications
Section Headings:  2660 -DRUG STIMULATION & PSYCHOPHARMACOLOGY
```

Another commonly used format is format 5 or 9, known as full format. In most databases, displaying documents in full format will show all fields in the record. This format should be used with care for these reasons: Long records take quite a while to be displayed, especially in full-text databases, which will use up connect time; and some databases charge hefty fees to type out records in full format.

Another useful format, often used at the conclusion of a search when a good set has been obtained, is format 3, which displays title and bibliographic citation so that the original document may be located.

Now that we have seen a couple of good documents, we can attempt some pearl-growing, which we mentioned earlier. If we look at the documents already retrieved that appear to be relevant, we see that there are some interesting new descriptors. We can perhaps use some of these terms to reformulate the search and try to get new good documents.

The descriptor that looks most promising here is

HUMAN INFORMATION STORAGE, which corresponds to our "memory" concept block. Let's search on this descriptor and see what we get:

```
?s human information storage
   S10 4670 HUMAN INFORMATION STORAGE

?s s3 and s10
     2052   3
     4670   10
   S11   10   S3 AND S10
```

We retrieve 10 documents, some of which we might already have seen. We can use NOT to get rid of those in the following manner:

```
?s s11 not s9
        10  S11
        37  S9
   S12    5  S11 NOT S9
```

We can now look at the five new documents:

```
?t 12/8/all

 12/8/1
00721181          77-09995
  Priming  and  cued  recall  in  elderly,  alcohol  intoxicated  and sleep
deprived subjects: A case of functionally similar memory deficits.
  Major  Descriptors:  *AGE  DIFFERENCES;  *PRIMING;  *RECALL (LEARNING);
     *ALCOHOL INTOXICATION;  *SLEEP DEPRIVATION
  Minor  Descriptors:  AGED;  VERY  OLD;  LEXICAL  DECISION;  HUMAN
     INFORMATION STORAGE;  ADULTHOOD
  Descriptor Codes:  01360;  40385;  43290;  01700;  47830;  01370;  55650
     ;  29296;  23480;  01150
  Identifiers:  lexical decision priming & cued recall, alcohol intoxicated
     or sleep deprived 20-30 yr olds vs healthy 61-85 yr olds
  Section Headings:  3233 -SUBSTANCE ABUSE

 12/8/2
00593443          74-24375
  Is  event  frequency  encoded  automatically? The  case  of  alcohol
intoxication.
  Major Descriptors:  *ALCOHOL INTOXICATION;  *COGNITIVE PROCESSES;  *HUMAN
     INFORMATION STORAGE;  *STIMULUS FREQUENCY
  Minor Descriptors:  ADULTHOOD
  Descriptor Codes:  01700;  10130;  23480;  49980;  01150
  Identifiers:  alcohol  intoxication,  sensitivity  to  event  frequency,
     college students
  Section Headings:  2660 -DRUG STIMULATION & PSYCHOPHARMACOLOGY
```

(Continues on page 48.)

```
12/8/3
00493030            72-00805
 Effect  of  alcohol  on recall and recognition as functions of processing
levels.
   Major Descriptors:  *ALCOHOLS;  *VERBAL LEARNING;  *ALCOHOL INTOXICATION;
    *HUMAN INFORMATION STORAGE;  *FREE RECALL;  *RECOGNITION (LEARNING)
   Minor Descriptors:  ADULTHOOD
   Descriptor Codes:   01760;  55550;  01700;  23480;  20350;  43350;  01150
   Identifiers:  alcohol intoxication,  effects of semantic vs phonemic vs
    graphemic  processing levels on verbal free recall & recognition, 21-32
    yr old male students
   Section Headings:  2660 -DRUG STIMULATION & PSYCHOPHARMACOLOGY


 12/8/4
00452496            71-00850
 Alcohol-induced  state-dependent  learning:  Differentiating stimulus and
storage hypotheses.
   Major Descriptors:  *ALCOHOL INTOXICATION;  *RECALL (LEARNING);  *HUMAN
    INFORMATION STORAGE;  *STATE DEPENDENT LEARNING
   Minor Descriptors:  ADULTHOOD
   Descriptor Codes:   01700;  43290;  23480;  49525;  01150
   Identifiers:  alcohol following initial learning,  subsequent recall,
    22-28 yr olds, implications for impaired storage & retrieval in state
    dependent learning
   Section Headings:  2660 -DRUG STIMULATION & PSYCHOPHARMACOLOGY


 12/8/5
00210492            56-02093
 Encoding-imagery specificity in alcohol state-dependent learning.
   Minor Descriptors:  HUMAN INFORMATION STORAGE;  IMAGERY;  DRUG EFFECTS;
    ALCOHOL INTOXICATION;  FREE RECALL;  ADULTS;  VERBAL LEARNING
   Descriptor Codes:   23480;  24470;  15300;  01700;  20350;  01160;  55550
   Identifiers:  storage during alcohol intoxication  vs sobriety & word
    imagery  level, free recall in intoxicated vs sober state, 21-35 yr old
    females
   Section Headings:  2660 -DRUG STIMULATION & PSYCHOPHARMACOLOGY
```

This new set appears to be good, thus we can add it to the previously retrieved good set by using the OR command, as follows:

```
?s s9 or s12
        37  S9
         5  S12
   S13  42  S9 OR S12
```

This new set, S13, contains all the documents in either S9 or S12 or both.

Let's try one more potential term and demonstrate the use of the truncation operator.

Truncation

The truncation operator in DIALOG is the question mark (?), which can be used several ways. The most common is also the simplest. To search for the alternatives LIBRARY, LIBRARIES, LIBRARIAN, and LIBRARIANSHIP, for example, you might use the search statement :

```
?s librar?
```

This statement directs the system to look through the inverted file for all documents containing words that begin with the characters LIBRAR. These will be collected in a single set by ORing them together. Care

needs to be taken to choose a sufficiently specific word stem, or some confusing results can occur. (Recall INVENT? from chapter 4.)

There are other forms of truncation. Instead of accepting any form of the word, the searcher can increase specificity by limiting the number of characters that may follow the stem. The statement:

```
?s statistic? ?
```

will search for STATISTIC itself and any word that begins with STATISTIC and has at most one character following. Thus, it will retrieve STATISTIC and

STATISTICS, but not STATISTICAL, STATISTI-
CALLY, or STATISTICIAN.

If more than one extra character is desired but
still a limited number, use as many question marks as
extra characters required. Thus,

?s retriev??

will get RETRIEVE, RETRIEVAL, RETRIEVED, and
RETRIEVER, each of which has two or fewer characters after the stem (allowed by the two question
marks), but will not get RETRIEVING, which has
three.

The question mark may also be useful inside a
word, to retrieve variant spellings. Perhaps the most
common example of this use of truncation is:

?s wom?n,

which will retrieve WOMAN and WOMEN. Such a
use of truncation would not work for most British
variants, seen in such words as COLOUR or HON-
OUR. These must be searched for using OR, as in

?s behavior or behaviour

Returning to the sample search, let's see how
searching for forms of the word AMNESIA may help:

```
?s amnesia?
    S14    1439   AMNESIA?
?s s3 and s14
           2052   S3
           1439   S14
    S15       9   S3 AND S14
?s s15 not s13
              9   S15
             42   S13
    S16       6   S15 NOT S13
?t 16/8/1-4

 16/8/1
00690845        76-29740
  Regional cerebral blood flow during alcoholic blackout.
  Major  Descriptors:   *BRAIN;  *BLOOD FLOW;  *ALCOHOLISM;  *ALCOHOL
    INTOXICATION;  *AMNESIA
  Minor Descriptors:  ADULTHOOD
  Descriptor Codes:  06750;  06270;  01750;  01700;  02120;  01150
  Identifiers:  regional  cerebral  blood  flow during alcoholic blackout,
    alcoholic 61 yr old male
  Section Headings:  3233 -SUBSTANCE ABUSE

 16/8/2
00630067        75-13758
  Alcoholic blackouts: Phenomenology and legal relevance.
  Major  Descriptors:   *COMPETENCY  TO  STAND  TRIAL;  *AMNESIA;  *ALCOHOL
    INTOXICATION;  *ADJUDICATION
  Minor Descriptors:  ALCOHOLISM
  Descriptor Codes:  10749;  02120;  01700;  00840;  01750
  Identifiers:  phenomenology  of  alcohol induced amnesia & competence to
    stand trial & mitigation of criminal responsibility
  Section  Headings:  2960  -POLITICAL & LEGAL PROCESSES;  3233 -SUBSTANCE
    ABUSE

 16/8/3
00432282        70-01262
  Blackouts   increase   with  age,  social  class  and  the  frequency  of
intoxication.
  Minor Descriptors:  AGE DIFFERENCES;  ALCOHOL DRINKING PATTERNS;  ALCOHOL
    INTOXICATION;  SOCIAL CLASS;  AMNESIA;  FOLLOWUP STUDIES
  Descriptor Codes:  01360;  01690;  01700;  48120;  02120;  20040
  Identifiers:  social  class  &  age & intoxication frequency, blackouts,
    males  originally  interviewed in 1953 at age 20 yrs or older & followed
    up in 1975
  Section  Headings:  3230 -BEHAVIOR DISORDERS & ANTISOCIAL BEHAVIOR;  3233
    -SUBSTANCE ABUSE
```

(*Continues on page 50.*)

```
16/8/4
00421954            69-10498
/ Alcoholic blackout and malingering.
Minor     Descriptors:    DIFFERENTIAL    DIAGNOSIS;    AMNESIA;    ALCOHOL
     INTOXICATION;   MALINGERING
Descriptor Codes:    14160;   02120;   01700;   29290
Identifiers:    analyses   of   psychopathic   personality   &   consciousness
     disturbance   during   drunkenness   &   patterns   of   amnesia,   differential
     diagnosis of blackout vs malingering vs hysterical amnesia
Section Headings:   3200 -PHYSICAL AND PSYCHOLOGICAL DISORDERS
```

Set S16 does relate, but these documents do not seem to be as good as our previous sets. At this point, if the user is present, you might want to ask her if these would be interesting, or if there are any other avenues she thinks might be worth pursuing. If the user is not present, you might choose to present S13 and S16 separately for her consideration, because you think S16's documents might be more marginal to the query.

Display Sets

This search is now over, but two basic commands remain to be discussed. First is the DISPLAY SETS command, usually abbreviated as DS. It is entered exactly like this: ?*ds* and it will show all the previously created sets and the number of documents in each. The following is the result:

```
S1  1149   ALCOHOL ABUSE
S2   907   ALCOHOL INTOXICATION
S3  2052   ALCOHOL ABUSEOR ALCOHOL
            INTOXICATION
S4 12678   MEMORY/DF
S5  1046   LONG TERM MEMORY
S6  3626   SHORT TERM MEMORY
S7   502   MEMORY DISORDERS
```

```
S8 17209   MEMORY/DF OR LONG TERM
            MEMORY OR SHORT TERM
            MEMORY OR MEMORY DISORDERS
S9    37   S3 AND S8
S10 4670   HUMAN INFORMATION STORAGE
S11   10   S3 AND S10
S12    5   S11 NOT S9
S13   42   S9 OR S12
S14 1439   AMNESIA?
S15    9   S3 AND S14
S16    6   S15 NOT S13
```

This is particularly useful when using a video terminal. It can be used during a search to review the strategy to that point, or at the end of a search so that the searcher or patron can maintain a copy of the strategy for later reference.

The DS provides an opportunity to review our search strategy and may indeed suggest a few new strategies. For instance, a combination such as ?*s s4 and s8* might produce some additional relevant material. - GW

Leaving the System (LOGOFF)

The final command to be discussed in this chapter is the final command of any search: LOGOFF, which can abbreviated as LOG. Several other "exit" words may also be used, such as BYE, QUIT, EXIT, OFF, and so on. The word is entered alone, as in ?*logoff*. At this point the searcher will be disconnected from the system, after accounting and timing data are presented, as in the following example:

```
?logoff
     26jun92 13:06:34 User007659 Session B840.2
       $5.38    0.116 Hrs File11
```

```
            $0.00   1 Type(s) in Format  3
            $3.15   9 Type(s) in Format  5
            $0.00   1 Type(s) in Format  6
            $0.00  25 Type(s) in Format  8
          $3.15   78 Types
    $8.53  Estimated cost File11
    $8.53  Estimated cost this search
    $8.56  Estimated total session cost   0.116 Hrs.
Logoff: level 29.01.05 B  13:06:40
```

When this message is received, the searcher is off the system, and the search is over. If the searcher were to reconnect at this point, the strategy and sets created during this search would be gone. There are ways to save a search strategy for use days or even weeks later, which we will discuss in chapter 10, but if a searcher wanted to log-off and save the search very

briefly (perhaps for consultation with the user or some printed documentation), the command LOGOFF HOLD could be used. It will disconnect the searcher from the system and preserve the strategy in the computer's memory for 30 minutes. After that, it will be gone.

Conclusion and Chapter Review

In this chapter we have begun the actual practice of searching and presented the basic online commands. We have covered SELECT; BEGIN; the use of the Boolean operators AND, OR, and NOT; SELECT STEPS; TYPE; the use of the truncation operator ?; DISPLAY SETS; and LOGOFF. In addition, some fundamental concepts of search strategy have been explored, including the notions of building blocks and most specific first, as well as general ideas of concept

analysis and the generation of search terms. As stated at the beginning of the chapter, these are the most basic ideas in online searching, and a searcher's success will depend in large part on mastery of these skills and techniques. All of the commands and techniques yet to be presented will build on these basics.

For your reference, the complete *transaction log* of the search we have just conducted is reprinted here:

```
%Call connected
DIALOG INFORMATION SERVICES
PLEASE LOGON:
  ********

ENTER PASSWORD:
  ********

Welcome to DIALOG
Dialog level 29.01.05B

Last logoff:  26jun92 12:59:09
Logon file001 26jun92 12:59:27
* * *   TEXTLINE is now available. Begin TXTLN or TEXTLINE * * *

File   1:ERIC    66-92/JUN.
FILE 1: Price changes will go into effect June 1, 1992.
Please see HOMEBASE Announcements for more details.

    Set  Items  Description
    ---  -----  -----------
?b 11
    26jun92 12:59:36 User007659 Session B840.1
          $0.03    0.002 Hrs File1
    $0.03  Estimated cost File1
    $0.03  Estimated cost this search
    $0.03  Estimated total session cost   0.002 Hrs.

File  11:PSYCINFO    67-92/JULY
    (COPR. AM. PSYCH. ASSOC.)
```

(Continues on page 52.)

```
     Set   Items   Description
     ---   -----   -----------
?ss alcohol abuse or alcohol intoxication
     S1    1149    ALCOHOL ABUSE
     S2     907    ALCOHOL INTOXICATION
     S3    2052    ALCOHOL ABUSE OR ALCOHOL INTOXICATION
?ss memory/df or long term memory or short term memory or memory disorders
     S4   12678    MEMORY/DF
     S5    1046    LONG TERM MEMORY
     S6    3626    SHORT TERM MEMORY
     S7     502    MEMORY DISORDERS
     S8   17209    MEMORY/DF OR LONG TERM MEMORY OR SHORT TERM MEMORY OR
                   MEMORY DISORDERS
?s s3 and s8
           2052    S3
          17209    S8
     S9      37    S3 AND S8
?t 9/6/1-6

  9/6/1
00845989           29-74072
  Effects of post-trial ethanol treatment on memory.


  9/6/2
00820520           28-58069
  Gender differences in prose memory after acute intoxication with ethanol.


  9/6/3
00800010           78-18809
  Cue-exposure  interventions  for  alcohol  relapse prevention: Need for a
memory modification component.


  9/6/4
00797330           28-54252
  The effects of alcohol on semantic memory.


  9/6/5
00781282           51-02626
  Short-term memory function in alcohol addicts during intoxication.


  9/6/6
00778752           77-24881
  Some effects of alcohol on eyewitness memory.
?t 9/8/1-8


  9/8/1
00845989           29-74072
  Effects of post-trial ethanol treatment on memory.
  Major Descriptors:  *MEMORY;  *ETHANOL
  Minor Descriptors:  ALCOHOL INTOXICATION;  ADULTHOOD
  Descriptor Codes:  30570;  18040;  01700;  01150
  Identifiers: alcohol intoxication, memory tasks, adults
  Section Headings:  2580 -PSYCHOPHARMACOLOGY


  9/8/2
00820520           28-58069
  Gender differences in prose memory after acute intoxication with ethanol.
  Major  Descriptors:   *MEMORY;   *ALCOHOL  INTOXICATION;  *HUMAN  SEX
    DIFFERENCES;  *ORAL CONTRACEPTIVES;  *HUMAN INFORMATION STORAGE
  Minor Descriptors:  RECALL (LEARNING);  ADULTHOOD
  Descriptor Codes:  30570;  01700;  23510;  35620;  23480;  43290;  01150
  Identifiers:  acute alcohol  intoxication,  encoding  speed for prose &
```

```
     recall, male vs females taking vs not taking oral contraceptives
   Section Headings:  2660 -DRUG STIMULATION & PSYCHOPHARMACOLOGY


   9/8/3
   00800010          78-18809
   Cue-exposure  interventions  for  alcohol  relapse prevention: Need for a
memory modification component.
   Major Descriptors:  *CUES;  *CONDITIONED RESPONSES;  *RELAPSE (DISORDERS)
     ;  *ALCOHOL ABUSE
   Minor Descriptors:  MEMORY
   Descriptor Codes:   12680;  11090;  43660;  01660;  30570
   Identifiers:  cue CR, relapse prediction, problem drinkers
   Section Headings:  3233 -SUBSTANCE ABUSE


   9/8/4
   00797330          28-54252
   The effects of alcohol on semantic memory.
   Major Descriptors:  *ALCOHOL INTOXICATION;  *MEMORY;  *SEMANTICS
   Minor Descriptors:  ADULTHOOD
   Descriptor Codes:   01700;  30570;  46390;  01150
   Identifiers:  alcohol intoxication, semantic memory, 21-29 yr old males
   Section Headings:  2660 -DRUG STIMULATION & PSYCHOPHARMACOLOGY


   9/8/5
   00781282          51-02626
   Short-term memory function in alcohol addicts during intoxication.
   Major  Descriptors:  *ALCOHOLISM;  *ALCOHOL  INTOXICATION;  *SHORT TERM
     MEMORY;  *DRUG EFFECTS
   Descriptor Codes:   01750;  01700;  47260;  15300
   Identifiers:   alcohol  intoxication  vs  sobriety,  short-term memory
     function, alcoholics with vs without history of blackouts
   Section  Headings:  2600  -PHYSIOLOGICAL  INTERVENTION;  3233 -SUBSTANCE
     ABUSE


   9/8/6
   00778752          77-24881
   Some effects of alcohol on eyewitness memory.
   Major Descriptors:  *ALCOHOL INTOXICATION;  *WITNESSES;  *MEMORY
   Minor Descriptors:  LEGAL PROCESSES;  ADULTHOOD
   Descriptor Codes:   01700;  56885;  30570;  28110;  01150
   Identifiers:  alcohol,  immediate  vs  delayed  eyewitness  memory, male
     college students, legal implications
   Section Headings:  2660 -DRUG STIMULATION & PSYCHOPHARMACOLOGY


?s human information storage
     S10    4670   HUMAN INFORMATION STORAGE
?s s3 and s10
           2052 S3
           4670 S10
     S11      10 S3 AND S10
?s s11 not s9
             10 S11
             37 S9
     S12       5 S11 NOT S9
?t 12/8/all


   12/8/1
   00721181          77-09995
   Priming  and  cued  recall  in  elderly,  alcohol  intoxicated  and sleep
deprived subjects: A case of functionally similar memory deficits.
   Major  Descriptors:  *AGE  DIFFERENCES;  *PRIMING;  *RECALL (LEARNING);
     *ALCOHOL INTOXICATION;  *SLEEP DEPRIVATION
```

(Continues on page 54.)

    Minor   Descriptors: AGED;   VERY   OLD;   LEXICAL   DECISION;   HUMAN
       INFORMATION STORAGE;   ADULTHOOD
    Descriptor Codes: 01360;   40385;   43290;   01700;   47830;   01370;   55650
       ;   29296;   23480;   01150
    Identifiers: lexical decision priming & cued recall, alcohol intoxicated
       or sleep deprived 20-30 yr olds vs healthy 61-85 yr olds
    Section Headings: 3233 -SUBSTANCE ABUSE

  12/8/2
  00593443   74-24375
  Is   event   frequency   encoded   automatically?   The   case   of   alcohol
  intoxication.
    Major Descriptors: *ALCOHOL INTOXICATION;   *COGNITIVE PROCESSES;   *HUMAN
       INFORMATION STORAGE;   *STIMULUS FREQUENCY
    Minor Descriptors: ADULTHOOD
    Descriptor Codes: 01700;   10130;   23480;   49980;   01150
    Identifiers: alcohol intoxication,   sensitivity   to event   frequency,
       college students
    Section Headings: 2660 -DRUG STIMULATION & PSYCHOPHARMACOLOGY

  12/8/3
  00493030   72-00805
  Effect   of   alcohol   on recall and recognition as functions of processing
  levels.
    Major Descriptors: *ALCOHOLS;   *VERBAL LEARNING;   *ALCOHOL INTOXICATION;
     *HUMAN INFORMATION STORAGE;   *FREE RECALL;   *RECOGNITION (LEARNING)
    Minor Descriptors: ADULTHOOD
    Descriptor Codes: 01760;   55550;   01700;   23480;   20350;   43350;   01150
    Identifiers: alcohol intoxication,   effects of semantic vs phonemic vs
       graphemic processing levels on verbal free recall & recognition, 21-32
       yr old male students
    Section Headings: 2660 -DRUG STIMULATION & PSYCHOPHARMACOLOGY

  12/8/4
  00452496   71-00850
  Alcohol-induced   state-dependent   learning: Differentiating stimulus and
  storage hypotheses.
    Major Descriptors: *ALCOHOL INTOXICATION;   *RECALL (LEARNING);   *HUMAN
       INFORMATION STORAGE;   *STATE DEPENDENT LEARNING
    Minor Descriptors: ADULTHOOD
    Descriptor Codes: 01700;   43290;   23480;   49525;   01150
    Identifiers: alcohol following initial learning,   subsequent recall,
       22-28 yr olds, implications for impaired storage & retrieval in state
       dependent learning
    Section Headings: 2660 -DRUG STIMULATION & PSYCHOPHARMACOLOGY

  12/8/5
  00210492   56-02093
   Encoding-imagery specificity in alcohol state-dependent learning.
    Minor Descriptors: HUMAN INFORMATION STORAGE;   IMAGERY;   DRUG EFFECTS;
       ALCOHOL INTOXICATION;   FREE RECALL;   ADULTS;   VERBAL LEARNING
    Descriptor Codes: 23480;   24470;   15300;   01700;   20350;   01160;   55550
    Identifiers: storage during alcohol intoxication vs sobriety & word
       imagery level, free recall in intoxicated vs sober state, 21-35 yr old
       females
    Section Headings: 2660 -DRUG STIMULATION & PSYCHOPHARMACOLOGY
  ?s s9 or s12
                   37   S9
                    5   S12
       S13   42   S9 OR S12
  ?s amnesia?
       S14   1439   AMNESIA?

```
?s s3 and s14
              2052   S3
              1439   S14
       S15       9   S3 AND S14
?s s15 not s13
                9   S15
               42   S13
       S16       6   S15 NOT S13
?t 16/8/1-4
```

```
  16/8/1
00690845          76-29740
 Regional cerebral blood flow during alcoholic blackout.
 Major  Descriptors:   *BRAIN;  *BLOOD  FLOW;   *ALCOHOLISM;   *ALCOHOL
    INTOXICATION;  *AMNESIA
 Minor Descriptors:  ADULTHOOD
 Descriptor Codes:   06750;  06270;  01750;  01700;  02120;  01150
 Identifiers:  regional  cerebral  blood  flow during alcoholic blackout,
    alcoholic 61 yr old male
 Section Headings:  3233 -SUBSTANCE ABUSE
```

```
  16/8/2
00630067          75-13758
 Alcoholic blackouts: Phenomenology and legal relevance.
 Major  Descriptors:   *COMPETENCY  TO  STAND  TRIAL;  *AMNESIA;  *ALCOHOL
    INTOXICATION;   *ADJUDICATION
 Minor Descriptors:  ALCOHOLISM
 Descriptor Codes:   10749;  02120;  01700;  00840;  01750
 Identifiers:  phenomenology  of  alcohol induced amnesia & competence to
    stand trial & mitigation of criminal responsibility
 Section  Headings:  2960  -POLITICAL & LEGAL PROCESSES;  3233 -SUBSTANCE
    ABUSE
```

```
  16/8/3
00432282          70-01262
 Blackouts   increase   with   age,  social  class  and  the  frequency  of
intoxication.
 Minor Descriptors:  AGE DIFFERENCES;  ALCOHOL DRINKING PATTERNS;  ALCOHOL
    INTOXICATION;  SOCIAL CLASS;  AMNESIA;  FOLLOWUP STUDIES
 Descriptor Codes:   01360;  01690;  01700;  48120;  02120;  20040
 Identifiers:  social  class  &  age  &  intoxication frequency, blackouts,
    males  originally interviewed in 1953 at age 20 yrs or older & followed
    up in 1975
 Section  Headings:  3230 -BEHAVIOR DISORDERS & ANTISOCIAL BEHAVIOR;  3233
    -SUBSTANCE ABUSE
```

```
  16/8/4
00421954          69-10498
 / Alcoholic blackout and malingering.
 Minor   Descriptors:   DIFFERENTIAL   DIAGNOSIS;   AMNESIA;   ALCOHOL
    INTOXICATION;  MALINGERING
 Descriptor Codes:   14160;  02120;  01700;  29290
 Identifiers:   analyses  of  psychopathic  personality  &  consciousness
    disturbance  during  drunkenness  &  patterns  of  amnesia, differential
    diagnosis of blackout vs malingering vs hysterical amnesia
 Section Headings:  3200 -PHYSICAL AND PSYCHOLOGICAL DISORDERS
?ds
       S1    1149   ALCOHOL ABUSE
       S2     907   ALCOHOL INTOXICATION
       S3    2052   ALCOHOL ABUSE OR ALCOHOL INTOXICATION
       S4   12678   MEMORY/DF
       S5    1046   LONG TERM MEMORY
```

(Continues on page 56.)

```
        S6      3626   SHORT TERM MEMORY
        S7       502   MEMORY DISORDERS
        S8     17209   MEMORY/DF OR LONG TERM MEMORY OR SHORT TERM MEMORY OR
                       MEMORY DISORDERS
        S9        37   S3 AND S8
        S10     4670   HUMAN INFORMATION STORAGE
        S11       10   S3 AND S10
        S12        5   S11 NOT S9
        S13       42   S9 OR S12
        S14     1439   AMNESIA?
        S15        9   S3 AND S14
        S16        6   S15 NOT S13
?logoff
        26jun92 13:06:34 User007659 Session B840.2
            $5.38    0.116 Hrs File11
                $0.00   1 Type(s) in Format   3
                $3.15   9 Type(s) in Format   5
                $0.00   1 Type(s) in Format   6
                $0.00  25 Type(s) in Format   8
            $3.15  78 Types
        $8.53  Estimated cost File11
        $8.53  Estimated cost this search
        $8.56  Estimated total session cost   0.116 Hrs.
Logoff: level 29.01.05 B  13:06:40
```

Now that we have seen the basic mechanical aspects of online searching, we can begin to tackle its cognitive aspects. There are two primary methods that we use to search for documents: controlled vocabulary searching and free-text searching. Each is effective in many circumstances, and in fact they are often used together. We will introduce them separately, though, pointing out the strengths and weaknesses of each and giving some tips on when each might best be used. Free-text searching will be covered in chapter 7.

6
CONTROLLED
VOCABULARY
SEARCHING

Before going into a fuller explanation of controlled vocabulary searching, we first need two new search techniques: qualifiers and the EXPAND command. Recall that the sample document record in chapter 4 was divided into fields: title, author, abstract, and so on. When we searched for a term, we were searching in the fields included in the primary inverted file (or Basic Index); title, abstract, descriptor, identifier. There is a way, however, to specify which field or fields will be searched. The use of *qualifiers* gives us that ability.

Qualifiers (Suffix Searching)

The search statement

```
?s alcohol
        S1    3228   ALCOHOL
```

searches for ALCOHOL in all the Basic Index fields. When the resulting postings are numerous, however, we may wish to search for the word only in the title field. We could use the statement

```
?s alcohol/ti
        S2    1139   ALCOHOL/TI
```

to increase specificity. We *qualify* a search statement with a suffix, using the slash and the field codes of the field or fields we wish to search in, such as:

S TERM/field code(s)

The most often used codes for *ERIC* are AB (abstract), DE (descriptor), ID (identifier), and TI (title). Other databases may have other fields and codes in their Basic Indexes, so you will need to check the bluesheets carefully. A further example is

```
?s computer?/ab
        S3   32375   COMPUTER?/AB
```

This statement searches for the word stem COMPUTER in the abstract field only and will retrieve COMPUTER, COMPUTERS, COMPUTERIZATION, and so on, in that field only.

We can specify more than one field to search in, as in this example:

```
?s frog/ti,ab
        S4     72   FROG/TI,AB
```

This statement searches for the word FROG in either the title or the abstract. It is the logical equivalent of

```
?s frog/ti or frog/ab
               25   FROG/TI
               54   FROG/AB
        S5     72   FROG/TI OR
FROG/AB
```

This technique will only work on Basic Index fields. To search in other fields, such as author, journal name, publication year, and so on, we use prefix searching, which will be described in chapter 9.

Qualifiers may be used also with sets that have already been created, as in the following example:

```
?s newspaper
        S6   3940   NEWSPAPER

?s s6/ti
        S7    940   S6/TI
```

The first statement produces S6, which contains all documents with the word NEWSPAPER in any Basic Index field and has 3,940 documents. Using *post-qualification* (as it is called in this instance of qualifying a previously existing set), we limit the search to the title field only and so create a new set S7, with only 940 documents.

This illustrates one of the primary uses of qualifying—to improve the quality of sets by focusing them. Often a document is more likely to be about a subject if that term is in the title or descriptor fields rather than in the abstract, a longer and often less specific indicator of content. Probably your most frequently used qualifiers will be DESCRIPTOR or TITLE, as in:

```
?s cats/ti,de
```

because these two fields will provide the most relevant retrievals. Using qualifiers is a good way to narrow searches, because you can check retrieval at each step. We will be using qualifiers again on pages 112 and 115 as part of controlled vocabulary searching.

EXPAND

The EXPAND command allows you to view an alphabetical display of a portion of the Basic Index. (We will use it with prefix searching in chapter 9 and citation searching in chapter 11.) It can be very useful when you are not sure of the spelling of a word, or when you think there may be variant spellings or misspellings in the database. The format of the command is

EXPAND term

which may be abbreviated as

E term

The result is a display like the following:

```
?e bias
```

```
Ref     Items   RT   Index-term
E1        1          BIARD
E2        1          BIARTS
E3      9929     8  *BIAS (AN INCLINATION, OR A LACK OF BALANCE (NOTE: ...)
E4        2          BIAS (LEONARD)
E5        1          BIAS ELIMINATION PROCEDURES
E6        1          BIAS IN ATTITUDE SURVEY
E7        2          BIAS IN ATTITUDES SURVEY
E8        1          BIASE
E9      986          BIASED
E10       2          BIASEDNESS
E11     821          BIASES
E12      99          BIASING
```

```
            Enter P or E for more
```

The display has four columns. The first gives reference numbers that we can use later to select terms from the display. The second gives the number of *postings*, which is the number of documents that contain each term. The third, RT, shows the number of related terms in the thesaurus; an entry in this column indicates that this term is a descriptor. Finally, we see the list of terms themselves. Notice that E3 is BIAS, the term we began with, and it has an asterisk in front of it. This is your indication that this is in fact the term you expanded. Also notice that there is a parenthetical expression after BIAS in E3. This is not part of the descriptor; rather, it is the very beginning of the scope note from the thesaurus. It should be reasonably clear to you when using an EXPAND display which of these parentheticals are scope notes and which are parts of descriptors. Another point of interest is E4, BIAS (LEONARD). This is an identifier (proper nouns cannot be descriptors in *ERIC*, but this is not true of other files) and refers to Leonard Bias, the college basketball star who died of a drug overdose in 1986. E5, E6, and E7 are also identifiers; we know this because they are multiword phrases but have no related terms. E8, BIASE, is probably a spelling or typing error in one of the documents.

If you wish to see the next "page" of the display (the next 12 entries), just type

P   (for PAGE)

or

E   (for more EXPAND)

The following is the result:

```
?p
```

```
Ref     Items   Index-term
E13       1     BIASING EFFECTS
E14       1     BIASNESS
E15       3     BIATHLON
E16       1     BIAZHUN
E17      20     BIB
E18      10     BIBB
E19       1     BIBB COUNTY INSTRUC-
TIONAL MATERIALS CENTER GA
E20       1     BIBBIDIBOBBIDIBOO
E21       1     BIBBINS
E22       1     BIBBITS
E23       1     BIBCON
E24       2     BIBDATA
```

Here we see more of the same. Because none of these are descriptors, there is no RT column (E19 is an identifier).

The reference numbers of these terms are now available for us to use in searching. We have as yet created no sets, but we can do this by selecting terms from the display using the E numbers:

?s e3, e8-e14

This command will create a set containing documents with the terms specified. As you can see, you can select more than one term at a time, separating them with commas or using a hyphen. The selected terms are then ORed together. The command above is equivalent to

?s e3 or e8 or e9 or e10 or e11 or e12 or e13 or e14

If you use several EXPAND statements, they are, in effect, overwritten in the same computer space. This means that you may only SELECT from that most recent display. The others have been lost to you.

Why Controlled Vocabulary Searching?

We've already seen that online searching is not perfect. In the previous chapter, the search for documents on the effect of alcohol on memory yielded documents not only on that topic but also on alcoholic blackouts and on memory modification techniques to prevent alcohol abuse relapses. We call these *false drops*; the retrieved documents contain the correct terms but in the wrong relationship to each other.

Why do we use controlled vocabulary searching?

Because of the infinite variety of the English language. Some of us call people who teach "teachers," some call them "faculty," some call them "instructors." Which term do we use if we want to search for articles about these people? We could use them all and OR them together, but what about "professors," "coaches," "tutors," "docents," "educators," "lecturers," and on and on? There are so many possibilities that it almost looks as if searching is a guessing game.

Thesaurus Structure and Use

There is an easier way. Many database producers compile and distribute lists in book form of subject terms that they use for indexing the documents in their files and that we can use for searching. These lists are often called *controlled vocabularies* or *thesauri*. Thesauri like *Roget's* variety are collections of synonyms and antonyms for words in the English language. Thesauri for databases are somewhat similar but much richer. They contain not only synonyms (in a way) but also relationships between terms and aids to help in selecting terms best used to search for a given concept.

As an example, let's look at one such controlled vocabulary—the *Thesaurus of ERIC Descriptors*, produced by the federally funded Educational Resources Information Center (ERIC). ERIC is the producer of the most comprehensive and most often used database, also called *ERIC*, in the field of education, although it covers a number of other areas, including information and library studies. Much of the discussion that follows is very specific to this thesaurus. Thesauri can differ greatly. For comparison's sake, we'll look at another one briefly before we leave the issue, but if you really want to know how a thesaurus (and, thus, a database) is put together and used, your best bet is to read the explanatory material included with a thesaurus. Experience doesn't hurt either—use

a few thesauri and you become skilled at figuring out how new ones work!

A look through the *ERIC Thesaurus* gives some examples of how a controlled vocabulary could be useful in searching. If you're looking for information about drunken driving, for example, you find that the term used to index this concept in ERIC documents is DRIVING WHILE INTOXICATED. A search for documents about discontinuation of programs would use the term PROGRAM TERMINATION (as opposed to PROGRAM DISCONTINUANCE, PROGRAM ELIMINATION, PROGRAM PHASEOUT, or TERMINATION OF PROGRAMS). If you were looking for the preferred term to refer to materials that are used in programmed instruction, you would find that from 1966 to 1980, the term was PROGRAMED MATERIALS (note the spelling difference), but that it was changed to PROGRAMED INSTRUCTIONAL MATERIALS in March 1980. In each of these instances, searching on the preferred term from the controlled vocabulary will give you an increased chance of retrieving documents that are on the topic of interest.

Let's look at a specific example of a search term from *ERIC* and examine its entry in the thesaurus. The term we choose is INFORMATION SCIENTISTS, and this is what the entry looks like:

INFORMATION SCIENTISTS

     CIJE: 170   RIE: 162   GC: 710

SN   Individuals who observe, measure, and describe the behavior of information, as
      well as those who organize information and provide services for its use.

UF   Information Brokers
      Information Professionals
      Information Specialists

NT   Librarians

BT   Professional Personnel

RT   Information Science
      Information Science Education
      Library Associations

Let's take this piece by piece and find out what it means, beginning with

INFORMATION SCIENTISTS

This first line gives the term name (INFORMATION SCIENTISTS) and the date it was added to the thesaurus (July 1971). The *ERIC* file dates back to July 1966, so that is the earliest possible date.

Some terms are ambiguous because they could be used in more than one way, and so they have a parenthetical component. An example is INEQUALITY. The term INEQUALITY could refer to the generic notion of inequality, specific inequalities (educational, social, economic), or even the mathematical concept of inequality. The descriptor INEQUALITIES was added in 1970 but was used inconsistently and was therefore removed in 1980. Alternatives are proposed, such as EQUAL EDUCATION, DISADVANTAGED, or a series of descriptors referring to social, ethnic, sexual, or racial bias and discrimination. But what about mathematical inequality? When INEQUALITIES was

removed in 1980, a new descriptor was added for just that concept: INEQUALITY (MATHEMATICS). The parenthetical part of the descriptor is used to remove the ambiguity about what kind of inequality is being referred to. The point of this seemingly elaborate discussion is this: When you want to use a term such as this in searching, you must remember that the parenthetical is an essential part of the descriptor. If you search just on

```
?s inequality
     S8     972   INEQUALITY
```

you will get each occurrence of the word "inequality" in all four Basic Index fields. But if you wish to use the much more specific descriptor, you must search with

```
?s inequality (mathematics)

     S9      11   INEQUALITY (MATHEMATICS) (MATHEMATICAL EXPRESSION OR PROPOSITION C
```

which will get you only documents indexed with that term. You must also be sure to include a space before

the first parenthesis—the system is very picky. If you do not you will get

```
?s inequality(mathematics)
S10      0   INEQUALITY(MATHEMATICS)
```

Let's go back to the next line on our entry for INFORMATION SCIENTISTS:

    CIJE: 170   RIE: 162   GC: 710

This line gives you the number of postings and group code information. *ERIC* is really two databases: a collection of citations to journal articles in the educational area (called the *Current Index to Journals in Education* in the printed version and identified by EJ accession numbers in the database), and a collection of citations to other kinds of documents, such as doctoral dissertations, technical reports, test banks, conference papers, bibliographies, guides, and so on.

(The printed version of the second database is called *Resources in Education*, and the records are identified with EJ accession numbers in the database.) This line in the thesaurus tells you how many documents in each of these two collections had been indexed using the given term at the time of publication of this edition. This can be of help in deciding whether or not to use a term—if it has significantly more or fewer "hits" or "postings," you may want to rethink using it. For INFORMATION SCIENTISTS, we see that as of April 1990 (for the 12th edition of the thesaurus), it had been used for 170 journal articles and 162 "other" documents.

The "group code" gives you the very broadest category to which that term belongs. INFORMATION

SCIENTISTS is in Group 710, INFORMATION/COMMUNICATION SYSTEMS. This piece of information is not particularly helpful in searching; don't worry about it.

> **SN** Individuals who observe, measure, and describe the behavior of information, as well as those who organize information and provide services for its use.

SN stands for *scope note* and gives a brief description of the term as it is used in *ERIC*. Not all terms have scope notes, but such notes can be very useful, especially if you are not familiar with the subject field or if you are trying to choose between two terms that appear to be very similar. This is perhaps the major fault with the *ERIC* thesaurus. There frequently is a multitude of terms with overlapping or similar connotations. Without scope notes it is difficult for the beginning searcher (and often the experienced searcher too!) to choose the most appropriate term to search. Personal experience suggests that *ERIC* is particularly frustrating in this respect. The scope notes are really aimed at the indexers, but we can use them, too. They often include notes about the interpretation of terms, warnings against the use of terms in certain ways, and recommendations regarding other potential terms.

> **UF** Information Brokers
> Information Professionals
> Information Specialists

UF stands for *Use For*. This indicates that INFORMATION SCIENTISTS is the preferred term for this concept and that these other three are not to be used. In fact, if you were to look in the thesaurus under any of these, you would see

Information Brokers
use INFORMATION SCIENTISTS

This is a reciprocal reference, rather like a "see" reference in a library catalog. You have looked up the nonpreferred term and are referred to the correct form of entry. In some cases, these are old terms that have been replaced by newer ones. For example,:

College Teachers (1967 1980)
use COLLEGE FACULTY

This means that from 1967 to 1980, the descriptor was COLLEGE TEACHERS; in 1980 it was changed to COLLEGE FACULTY.

> **NT** Librarians

Here's where we get to the interesting stuff. NT stands for *Narrower Term*. Terms in the *ERIC* thesaurus (and many others) are organized in hierarchies of specificity. Just as documents vary in how much detail they give on a particular topic, so do descriptors

vary. In this instance, we are told that LIBRARIANS is a narrower term than INFORMATION SCIENTISTS. If a document is strictly about "librarians," it will be indexed using that term. If it is broader, though, and talks about "information professionals," for example, it will probably be indexed with INFORMATION SCIENTISTS. In searching, you should be aware of how narrowly your client's search is focused and what kinds of terms best reflect that level of specificity. Also, you may find in perusing the thesaurus that you enter a hierarchy at too high or too low a level; the listing of hierarchies will give you a better idea of where you should be. It may be that the best search strategy encompasses many different levels of the hierarchy, as in:

```
?s librarians or information scientists
```

> **BT** Professional Personnel

BT stands for *Broader Term* and is the opposite of NT. In this particular case, I doubt PROFESSIONAL PERSONNEL is going to be much help for our search.

> **RT** Information Science
> Information Science Education
> Library Associations

The final part of the display is RT, the *Related Terms*. These are terms that are not part of the hierarchy for this particular descriptor but are related (at least in somebody's opinion) and may be of use in searching. When constructing a search strategy, you may find that some of the terms in the RT grouping look useful and you may then decide to use them. Notice that BTs, NTs, and RTs are all types of the familiar "see also" reference from the library catalog. They are suggestions of other terms that may be useful for your search. If you decide that one of them is a better term than your original choice, turn to the entry for it and start all over.

A caveat: After a while, all terms start to look good to you. Do not spend more than a few minutes looking through the thesaurus for descriptors, or you will wind up with too many terms, including some real losers, and you will have poor retrieval. Find two or three, or maybe only one, that look good, and see if there are maybe a couple of others that look possible and hold them in reserve. But the longer you look, the more you will find, and that is typically counterproductive. Do not be cavalier about term selection, but too much of a good thing is undesirable here, especially if some of the terms you pick have lots of postings—just a word to the wise.

Using these print thesauri can be a big help in planning searches. There may be another aid, though. In DIALOG, many databases have online versions of their controlled vocabularies that you can consult while conducting searches. We access the online thesaurus by using the EXPAND command with a couple of twists.

As we have said, all databases and all thesauri are different. Let's look at a couple of extracts from the *Thesaurus of Psychological Index Terms*, the controlled vocabulary for *Psychological Abstracts* and its online counterpart, *PsycINFO*. First, how would we go about searching for information scientists? There's no listing under that term, but there is the following:

```
Information Specialists  88
PN  2                                     SC   25338
  N    Librarians 88
  R    Professional Personnel/ 78
```

This looks familiar. The first line shows the descriptor name and the year in which it was added to the thesaurus (1988). The second line gives postings information (PN for postings notes) showing that two documents had been indexed with this term by June 1990, for the Sixth Edition. The second line also shows the unique code number (SC for subject code) assigned to this descriptor, which may also be used as a search term. LIBRARIANS is a narrower term, and PROFESSIONAL PERSONNEL is a related term. The slash after this last term indicates that it is an "array term," which "represents conceptually broad areas" and is "used in indexing and searching when a more specific term is not available."[1]

Because this database covers a different, although often related, subject area from *ERIC*, the terms it uses and the level of detail explored are different. Take, as an example, the term SCHIZOPHRENIA. This is a descriptor in both databases, but the entries are quite different. First, in *ERIC*:

```
SCHIZOPHRENIA                           Jul. 1966
       CIJE: 421    RIE: 115    GC: 230
UF   Dementia Praecox
BT   Psychosis
RT   Autism
       Echolalia
       Emotional Disturbances
       Paranoid Behavior
```

Compare this with the *PsycINFO* entry:

```
Schizophrenia  67
PN  13140 SC   45440
  UF   Chronic Schizophrenia
       Dementia Praecox
       Process Schizophrenia
       Pseudopsychopathic Schizophrenia
       Reactive Schizophrenia
       Schizophrenia (Residual Type)
       Simple Schizophrenia
  B    Psychosis  67
  N    Acute Schizophrenia 73
       Catatonic Schizophrenia 73
       Childhood Schizophrenia 67
       Hebephrenic Schizophrenia 73
       Paranoid Schizophrenia 67
       Undifferentiated Schizophrenia 73
  R    Anhedonia 85
       Catalepsy 73
       Expressed Emotion 91
       Fragmentation (Schizophrenia) 73
       Schizoid Personality 73
       Schizotypal Personality 91
```

This display contains more postings and many more detailed terms and possible alternative terms. It could be quite helpful in refining the search, especially through specifying exactly what type or form of schizophrenic disorder is desired. Of course, a search on schizophrenia *per se* would be much more productive in *PsycINFO* than in *ERIC*, but a search on the impact of schizophrenia on the learning process might yield equally good results in each. This gives you a glimpse of the challenges involved in database selection, which we will return to in chapter 10.

Every document, upon entering the *ERIC* database, is analyzed by an indexer. Using the thesaurus, the indexer assigns a series of these terms to that document, following the rules and structures set down. Therefore, if you are using controlled vocabulary techniques in searching, you have at least a reasonable assurance that a document that has been assigned the term HOME SCHOOLING has something to do with the "provision of compulsory education in the home as an alternative to traditional public/private schooling," as the scope note for that term indicates.

Almost all printed information retrieval tools make use of their own controlled vocabularies, and their use in searching can be quite a powerful technique, but it is not perfect. In the next chapter, we will discuss when it is best to use other, free-text, techniques either in place of or in combination with controlled vocabulary searching.

You should also be aware of the following:

1. Not all databases have controlled vocabularies. Some database producers do not have the resources or inclination to produce thesauri, and thus none exist. Other types of databases (numeric, financial, reference) have no controlled vocabulary because it would really make no sense.

2. Not all controlled vocabularies are useful. Some, such as the *Thesaurus of ERIC Descriptors* and the *Thesaurus of Psychological Index Terms*, are quite thorough and helpful in searching. Others are barely more than word lists (e.g., the thesaurus for *The Philosopher's Index*). Quite a number of databases use the *Library of Congress List of Subject Headings* (*LCSH*) in place of a thesaurus (e.g., *Magazine Index* or *Books in Print*). This suggests that both indexing languages and indexing standards vary greatly among different databases.

3. Not all indexing is done perfectly. In your experience in searching, you will undoubtedly find index terms that will confuse, amuse, or infuriate you.

However, a good controlled vocabulary can help you with more than just finding a useful term or two. If you are searching in an area with which you are not familiar, searching through the thesaurus for good terms can help you to better understand the topic. This process can show you the relationships among terms that you are thinking of using, may refine your thoughts, and may even give you some new ideas.

Mechanics of Controlled Vocabulary Searching

How does one actually search using controlled vocabulary? This section will present specific techniques, the next section will deal more generally with the process of constructing a search strategy, and the final section will walk you through a sample search.

We will present three ways of searching using controlled vocabulary: searching bound descriptors, searching for an individual word in the descriptor field, and searching for a single-word descriptor.

Searching Bound Descriptors

If, after rummaging through the thesaurus, you have found one or more terms you wish to search, you simply enter them as a search statement. For example:

```
?s choral music or rock music or vocal music
        117   CHORAL MUSIC  (MUSIC INTENDED FOR GROUP SINGING)
         73   ROCK MUSIC
        276   VOCAL MUSIC  (MUSICAL COMPOSITIONS WRITTEN FOR VOICES, EIT...
S11     430   CHORAL MUSIC OR ROCK
    MUSIC OR VOCAL MUSIC
```

Why don't we use field qualifiers to ensure that these terms are only searched in the descriptor field? Let's see what happens if we do:

```
?s choral music/de or rock music/de or vocal music/de
        117   CHORAL MUSIC/DE (MUSIC INTENDED FOR GROUP SINGING)
          9   ROCK MUSIC/DE
        276   VOCAL MUSIC/DE (MUSICAL COMPOSITIONS WRITTEN FOR VOICES, EIT...
S12     368   CHORAL MUSIC/DE OR ROCK MUSIC/DE OR VOCAL MUSIC/DE
```

What happened? Recall the discussion on word versus phrase indexing from chapter 4. In ERIC (most other databases are similar), the descriptor and identifier fields are phrase indexed. That means that both individual words (CHORAL, MUSIC, ROCK, VOCAL) and complete phrases (CHORAL MUSIC, ROCK MUSIC) are incorporated in the Basic Index.

The title and abstract fields, on the other hand, are word indexed. That means that only individual words are entered into the Basic Index. Thus, if we search for the pattern CHORAL MUSIC, the only place it can be found is in the descriptor or identifier fields.

For CHORAL MUSIC and VOCAL MUSIC, the results are the same, because both are terms from the thesaurus. But ROCK MUSIC retrieved 73 documents as is and only nine when qualified to the descriptor field. ROCK MUSIC used to be an identifier, but after several years it was promoted to the status of a descriptor. In the following example, we can see the remaining 64 documents were retrieved under its previous field:

```
?s rock music/id
        S13     64   ROCK MUSIC/ID
```

This is a relatively infrequent occurrence, but it is something you need to keep in mind.

Thus, for bound descriptors, we merely search on the phrase as given in the thesaurus. If the descriptor is a single word, it is a little different, as we will see shortly.

Searching Individual Words in the Descriptor Field

We already know how to search for individual words in the descriptor field. Using the field qualifiers we discussed earlier, we can specify that we wish to search any term in any given field, so the search

```
?s music/de
        S14    5537   MUSIC/DE
```

will retrieve any document with the word MUSIC anywhere in the descriptor field. That would include all the documents from the previous search statements above and also any indexed with MUSIC ACTIVITIES, APPLIED MUSIC, MUSIC EDUCATION, or even just MUSIC.

Why would you want to do this? Sometimes, you may wish to search on a broad concept that has many descriptors associated with it, all of which have a certain word in common. If you were interested in documents that discussed the use of music in foreign language education, you may want to be very broad in your search on the music concept. There are many good descriptors—perhaps too many. MUSIC itself is only used for documents generically about music but not for a document about, say, Japanese music, which would be indexed with ORIENTAL MUSIC. (Of course, this would be entered in the Basic Index under both ORIENTAL and MUSIC. This is called "double posting.") You may decide, then, that you will provisionally accept any document with any descriptor that includes the word MUSIC. This is a good initial strategy but will produce some false drops.

Searching One-Word Descriptors

Not all terms are phrases. Many are single words. As we just saw, the descriptor MUSIC is used when the document is generically about music but not any particular kind of music or for any particular purpose. Another example is a term such as SLEEP in *Psyc-*

INFO. This is a descriptor unto itself, but there are also descriptors such as SLEEP DISORDERS, SLEEP APNEA, REM SLEEP, SLEEP WAKE CYCLE, and so on, which incorporate the word SLEEP. Furthermore, it's a word that is relatively frequently used in abstracts but that is not as good an indicator of document content.

For example, searching on

```
?s sleep
        S1    9706   SLEEP
```

will retrieve all documents with the word SLEEP in any of the Basic Index fields.

Searching

```
?s sleep/de
        S2    6729   SLEEP/DE
```

will retrieve all documents with the word SLEEP in the descriptor field. But that is not the same thing as retrieving documents that have the one-word descriptor SLEEP. To get those, you must search

```
?s sleep/df
        S3    3945   SLEEP/DF
```

where the suffix /df ("descriptor full") qualifies the search to one-word descriptors only. This is an important and subtle distinction and is not always easily grasped initially. A tip: If you want to search a one-word descriptor as a one-word descriptor, /DF!

There are a couple of other techniques we can use to make controlled vocabulary searching more efficient or more precise: restricting to major descriptors and exploding.

Major Descriptors

You'll recall in chapter 4, when we discussed record structures, we saw that some descriptors were starred. (If you look at some search examples, you'll see many instances of this.) We called these "major descriptors" and said that the indexer had decided that these terms best described the document. We can use these decisions to try to improve the quality and precision of our search results.

If we wish to restrict our searching to major descriptors, we can give the command

```
?s music education/maj
```

and retrieve those documents that were assigned MUSIC EDUCATION as a major descriptor. If, as often happens, we had already gotten a set for MUSIC EDUCATION, say S6, and now wish to improve the specificity of that set, we can give the command

```
?s s6/maj
```

and the set will be so restricted.

A couple of comments here: First, this command looks a lot like the suffixes we called qualifiers earlier. It is very similar, but note that there we were restricting to a particular field (title or abstract), and here we are reducing within a field. A slight difference. Technically, /MAJ is not a qualifier but a limit, which we will discuss in chapter 9, but it makes sense to introduce it here. Second, there is a companion limit, /MIN, which, as you might have guessed, limits to minor descriptors (the unstarred ones). It escapes me why you would want to do that, but it is there if you want it.

Major descriptors are those that are also used in the printed indexes (RIE and CIJE) of **ERIC.** *They are obviously regarded as the most important index terms and are identified on your printout by having an asterisk beside them. They provide a useful and simple way of making your search more specific. But check your bluesheets for suffix codes, because they are not available on many files.*
- GW

Explode

Exploding is a nice technique that can save you a lot of typing and improve the breadth and recall of your searching. If you explode on a controlled vocabulary term, you will search on it and all its narrower terms, all ORed together. In some files (e.g., *ERIC*), you will get only the terms that are directly narrower (one level down) in the hierarchy. In other files (e.g., *PsycINFO*), you will get narrower terms of narrower terms, all the way down. Check documentation and thesauri to see what a particular file does. This feature is available only in files that have online thesauri.

The technique is very simple:

```
?s music!
```

is the equivalent of

```
?s music/df or applied music or
    jazz/df or oriental music or rock
    music or vocal music.
```

Very handy. However, there are some terms in the MUSIC hierarchy you will not get. CHORAL MUSIC, for example, is a narrower term under VOCAL MUSIC, but because *ERIC*'s explode only goes down one level, it will not get searched. Again, this can save you a lot of typing and possibly retrieve documents you might otherwise overlook. Beware of overuse, though—sometimes there are undesirable narrower terms, and it pays to examine the print or online thesaurus before trying an explode.

There are two ways to enter the online thesaurus. If you have a descriptor in an alphabetical EXPAND display (such as BIAS above), you can look at its online thesaurus entry to display the related terms by expanding on its E number, as in the following example:

```
?e e3
Ref    Items  Type  RT   Index-term
R1     9929         8   *BIAS  (AN   INCLINATION,   OR  A  LACK  OF  BALANCE  (NOTE:...)
R2     1069   U     1    PREJUDICE
R3     1449   N     20   SOCIAL BIAS
R4     376    N     10   STATISTICAL BIAS
R5     1557   N     19   TEST BIAS
R6     653    N     8    TEXTBOOK BIAS
R7     82045  R     52   ATTITUDES
R8     316    R     14   EGOCENTRISM
R9     60     R     3    MENTAL RIGIDITY
```

Now you see a new display, similar to the other but slightly different. Instead of the reference numbers beginning with E, they begin with R. This tells you that you are in an online thesaurus display rather than an alphabetical one. The Items column is the same, but now we see an additional column, Type, which indicates whether the listed term is a Use For (U), Narrower (N), Broader (B), or Related (R) Term

in the thesaurus. The final two columns are the same as before. You are not able to see the full entry as you would in the print version of the thesaurus, including scope notes, but the relationships and hierarchies are preserved and available for online consultation.

This process can continue indefinitely, as you can now expand on any terms in the display by EXPANDing on R numbers, as in this example:

```
?e r5

Ref    Items Type  RT   Index-term
R1     1557        19  *TEST BIAS   (UNFAIRNESS IN THE CONSTRUCTION, CONTENT,
                            ADM...)
R2     9929   B     8   BIAS
R3      420   R    10   CULTURE FAIR TESTS
R4     1379   R     9   ERROR PATTERNS
R5      581   R    15   OBJECTIVE TESTS
R6     1449   R    20   SOCIAL BIAS
R7     1277   R    23   SOCIAL DISCRIMINATION
R8      376   R    10   STATISTICAL BIAS
R9      302   R    11   TEST COACHING
R10    6052   R    29   TEST CONSTRUCTION
R11    2786   R    24   TEST INTERPRETATION
R12    2100   R    23   TEST ITEMS

           Enter P or E for more
```

The other way to enter the online thesaurus does not depend on having a previous E-display in hand. If you already know that a certain term is a descriptor, you may just EXPAND directly on it by using parentheses, as shown in this example:

```
?e (graduate students)

Ref    Items Type  RT   Index-term
R1     3052        12  *GRADUATE STUDENTS
R2      140   N     5   DENTAL STUDENTS
R3      169   N     5   LAW STUDENTS
R4     1680   N     8   MEDICAL STUDENTS
R5    22586   B    26   COLLEGE STUDENTS
R6     1936   R    13   COLLEGE GRADUATES
R7     1154   R    12   DOCTORAL PROGRAMS
R8     5313   R    22   GRADUATE STUDY
R9     9385   R     7   GRADUATES
R10  126309   R    29   HIGHER EDUCATION
R11     442   R     9   MASTERS PROGRAMS
R12      30   R    14   RESEARCH ASSISTANTS

           Enter P or E for more
```

These R numbers can now be SELECTed in groups in exactly the same way as before. (Remember, we do not create sets using EXPAND; we have to SELECT from the R-display.) For example:

```
?s r1-r4
             3052  GRADUATE STUDENTS
              140  DENTAL STUDENTS
              169  LAW STUDENTS
             1680  MEDICAL STUDENTS
        S2   4985  R1-R4
```

There are advantages and disadvantages to using the online version of the thesaurus. Its major disadvantage is that you are paying online time to work with the thesaurus. It is not a substitute for thorough preparation.

However, if you use the online controlled vocabulary cleverly, it can save you time, money, and effort. You can SELECT from the R-display directly, which will allow you to avoid typing long descriptors and possibly making typing or spelling errors. Because the online thesaurus is sometimes updated more frequently that the print version, there may be new descriptors or relationships online to help you, and certainly the postings information will be more up to date, so you can gauge the potential size of your retrieval.

Practice: The Eight-Step Procedure

All the techniques for controlled vocabulary searching are now at our disposal. This section describes an eight-step process that we hope will help you to formulate effective search strategies and conduct successful searches. There is nothing magical about this; it is mostly common sense, and it is really just an elaboration of the procedure we used in chapter 5. But we think you will find it useful to have a full version here, as follows:

1. Read the query.

1a. Listen to the query.

1b. Understand the query.

This is only slightly flippant. Whatever you receive to trigger the search—a phone call from a patron, a written search request on a form, a panicky visit to the reference desk—this is your first, best resource. The person requesting the search may know quite a bit about the search topic, particularly if he or she is a member of a college faculty, a graduate student, or a researcher. Or the person may be just starting out and clueless (e.g., high school students writing term papers). Any information you can get from the user about the search topic, could be useful, such as potential search terms, known authors or titles on the topic (watch out—these could do more harm than good!), previous search attempts made and results obtained, and so on. Many search services use forms to elicit this sort of information.

By the way, it is entirely possible that a query that is presented to an online search service has no business being there, and that a manual search or traditional reference transaction would provide the best results. Do not be seduced by the siren song of online. There are situations in which going online would be faster and cheaper, but this is not always the case.

2. Break the query into concept blocks.

We've already seen this process in the search on alcohol and memory in chapter 5. Many requests for information that can be searched effectively online involve more than one concept. One-concept searches can certainly be searched online, but often there is a second concept lurking in the user's mind. For example, a patron seeking information on bilingual education may actually be interested in bilingual education in elementary schools, or materials used in bilingual education, or the controversial nature of bilingual education.

It is not always easy or straightforward to identify these concept blocks, also called facets. Different people will find different blocks, and there is often no one "right" analysis.

3. Identify potential terms to correspond to concept blocks.

In chapter 5, we could only make up terms, either from personal knowledge or the user's statement. Now, though, we have the resources of a controlled vocabulary at our disposal. A look through the *PsycINFO* thesaurus yields descriptors like ALCOHOL ABUSE, MEMORY, and LONG TERM MEMORY, all of which were used to index good documents we found in the early search. Nevertheless, but we would have had a more efficient search strategy if we had been able to begin with these terms. As we will see in chapter 7, controlled vocabulary is not always the best source of search terms, but it is often a good start.

The form presented in figure 6.1 may help you in thinking about and constructing search strategies. There is a lot here, but for the moment just look at the three boxes marked "Concept 1, 2, and 3." On the top line of each box the searcher may write a brief description of a concept present in the search request, such as "parenting strategies," "Eastern Europe," or "high-speed computer networks."

Under the top line of each box are spaces marked "S#" and "Terms." These are provided to record a variety of potential search terms, often synonyms or near-synonyms. Be careful to keep your concepts separate at this stage. You don't want overlapping terms. Once the search commences, you can also enter the actual set numbers to help you keep track of sets as you go. There are a number of other spaces at the bottom of the form; we will cover these in chapters 9.

4. Determine logical (Boolean) relationships between terms.

OR is used to join synonyms, spelling variants, and related terms; AND is used to combine different concept blocks. NOT is used to remove concepts, if necessary.

Return to the strategy grid and notice how its construction reinforces the logical relationships we typically use: The terms in each individual concept box are all ORed together, as the brace at right indicates; then these concept blocks are ANDed together to produce the final search strategy.

5. Select alternative (often narrower, broader, or related) terms to use if the original strategy is unsatisfactory.

When working through the thesaurus, you may come across terms that you think are possibly or marginally useful but do not immediately appeal to you. These may be good (remember the warning about everything looking good, though!), but if your initial instinct is ambivalent, hold the term out as a reserve or alternative. Although you may find this hard to believe, your initial, beautifully honed and

Fig. 6.1. Search strategy grid.

File # 11

Concept 1 alcohol consumption

S#	S#	Terms	S#	Terms
___ ___	___	ALCOHOL ABUSE	___	___
___ ___	___	ALCOHOL INTOXICATION	___	___
___ ___	___	___	___	___
___ ___	___	___	___	___
___ ___	___	___	___	___

} OR

AND

Concept 2 memory

S#	S#	Terms	S#	Terms
___ ___	___	MEMORY/DF	___	MEMORY TRACE
___ ___	___	LONG TERM MEMORY	___	___
___ ___	___	SHORT TERM MEMORY	___	___
___ ___	___	MEMORY DISORDERS	___	___
___ ___	___	MEMORY DECAY	___	___

} OR

AND

Concept 3

S#	S#	Terms	S#	Terms
___ ___	___	___	___	___
___ ___	___	___	___	___
___ ___	___	___	___	___
___ ___	___	___	___	___
___ ___	___	___	___	___

} OR

S#	ADDITIONAL INDEXES	S#	LIMITS	OTHER FEATURES (NOT, etc.)
				S# command
___	LA = _____	___ ___ /ENG		___ _____
___	PY = _____	___ ___ /		___ _____
___	AU = _____	___ ___ /		**GOOD SETS**
___ __ = _____		___ ___ /		
___ __ = _____		___ ___ /		

crafted search strategy might not be perfect. You may find that you need more terms, narrower terms, broader terms, different terms, or even fewer terms. Thus, it is a good idea to have a few additional terms in your back pocket—just in case.

6. Begin the search.

Here is where you find out if your well-planned strategy will work or not. Remember to enter separate concept blocks and use the most specific first. Do not try to enter your entire strategy at once; there are too many opportunities to make errors. You will probably find it most effective to enter all the terms (ORed together) for the most specific concept block first, then each subsequent concept block in turn. This will yield you two or more concept sets. Finally, AND these concept sets together to get a set for your final result.

In many cases, that result set will be a good one and will contain useful documents for the patron. Often, it could be improved (more about that in the discussion of Step 8). Sometimes, though, it will be very poor: far too many documents, far too few or none at all, or documents that bear no resemblance to the query.

If you have no documents at all, it may be a mechanical or technical error. Check your concept sets. Does each of them contain documents? Are there spelling errors? Have you used the right set numbers? Have you forgotten to use some terms you intended to? If you find no such obvious error, it is possible that you have been overspecific in your strategy. Do you have too many concepts? You may want to eliminate some concept sets, removing the least specific one first. Or you may drop the least specific terms from each block and recombine them. Are your concept sets too small? If you're ANDing together three sets of 150, 68, and 200 documents, you are likely to get a very small, if not empty, result set.

However small your initial set, use it to check relevance and to discover new search terms.

7. Type out a few documents.

8. Refine the search based on your results.

The best way to know what you've got is to look at it. This first result set, provided it has something in it, is definitely worth looking at. Many searchers find it helpful to examine the first few documents in a potentially good set to see the type of documents it contains and to get clues on how the set might be improved. Format 8, in most DIALOG databases, is sometimes called the "searcher's format," as it usually displays title and indexing, as well as descriptors and identifiers, if the database has them. These can be very useful in evaluating the set and refining your strategy. You may also wish to try format 5 or 9 (full format—all available fields).

If you have very few documents, some of the advice from above also applies. Check the size and composition of your result sets, determine whether they are all strictly necessary, and check for errors in technique. If all looks correct, you may decide to use more terms and broader terms in your concept sets. Some of these new terms may come from the alternatives you prepared, and some may come from good documents you retrieved. This will increase the size and breadth of your concept sets and therefore most likely increase the size of result sets.

If you have many more hits than you expected (i.e., hundreds or even thousands), you may have too few or too large concept blocks, or you may be using terms that are too numerous or too broad. Consider either adding another concept, if you think it will help, or reformulating your concept sets by using fewer terms or more specific terms. Either of these tactics will produce a smaller or more focused result set.

All of this advice is fine, but it needs to be more concrete. Let's work through a sample search that demonstrates what we are talking about. Also bear in mind that the best way to become a good searcher is to *search*. You can read all you like, but you must practice to get good at it.

Search Example

For practice, search the following request:

"I'm looking for information about distance learning in library and information science education in the United States. There's been a lot of discussion about this lately in the field, and I'd like to know how and where it's being done, the kind of impact it's had, and how it's different from traditional methods."

1. Read the query.

1a. Listen to the query.

1b. Understand the query.

2. Break the query into concept blocks.

There are clearly three concept blocks in this request: "distance learning," "library and information science education," and "United States."

There are also some other ideas, such as how and where it goes on, impact, differences from traditional methods. These are probably subsidiary concepts and will be used only if the initial retrieval is very large. That would, at first glance, appear unlikely given the nature of the query, but it is a good thing to tuck away in the back of your mind.

3. Identify potential terms to correspond to concept blocks.

Going through the *ERIC* thesaurus, we find a few interesting terms. For *distance learning*, the descriptor is DISTANCE EDUCATION. If we examine its related terms (the broader and narrow terms do not look so promising), we see a few potential ones: EDUCATIONAL TELEVISION, EXTENSION EDUCATION, EXTERNAL DEGREE PROGRAMS, NONTRADITIONAL EDUCATION, OUTREACH PROGRAMS, and TELECOURSES. Looking at the entries for these terms, we find EDUCATIONAL TELEVISION to be a bit broad. The scope note suggests a more specific term such as TELECOURSES, which looks better. EXTENSION EDUCATION looks

pretty good, EXTERNAL DEGREE PROGRAMS is OK but refers to complete programs as opposed to individual course offerings, and both NONTRADITIONAL EDUCATION and OUTREACH PROGRAMS seem marginal.

For *library and information science education*, we find LIBRARY EDUCATION in the thesaurus, which looks right on the mark. A broader term is INFORMATION SCIENCE EDUCATION, which also looks good, and the related term LIBRARY SCHOOLS is also potentially useful. There really do not seem to be any other possible terms.

For *United States*, we find no good terms. "United States" is a proper noun and therefore cannot be a descriptor in *ERIC* (proper nouns are identifiers). We may find, after beginning the search, that there are few documents that do not refer to the United States, so this may not be a problem.

4. Determine logical (Boolean) relationships between terms.

We lay out the terms we intend to use and our alternatives in the grid represented in figure 6.2.

5. Select alternative (often narrower, broader, or related) terms to use if original strategy is unsatisfactory.

Some of the terms we have chosen above are probably not as good as others; let's retain the following as our alternatives: EDUCATIONAL TELEVISION, EXTERNAL DEGREE PROGRAMS, NONTRADITIONAL EDUCATION, OUTREACH PROGRAMS. We may use some of these later, if necessary.

6. Begin the search.

Steps 6, 7, and 8, along with the results, are presented as follows: see page 78 for the discussion.

Fig. 6.2. Strategy grid.

File #_____

Concept 1			
distance learning			

S#	S#	Terms	S#	Terms
___ ___	___	DISTANCE EDUCATION	___	EDUCATIONAL TELEVISION
___ ___	___	TELECOURSES	___	NONTRADITIONAL EDUCATION
___ ___	___	EXTENSION EDUCATION	___	
___ ___	___	EXTERNAL DEGREE PROGRAMS	___	
___ ___	___		___	

} OR

AND

Concept 2			
library and information science education			

S#	S#	Terms	S#	Terms
___ ___	___	LIBRARY EDUCATION	___	
___ ___	___	INFORMATION SCIENCE EDUCATION	___	
___ ___	___	LIBRARY SCHOOLS	___	
___ ___	___		___	
___ ___	___		___	

} OR

AND

Concept 3			
United States			

S#	S#	Terms	S#	Terms
___ ___	___		___	
___ ___	___		___	
___ ___	___		___	
___ ___	___		___	
___ ___	___		___	

} OR

S#	ADDITIONAL INDEXES	S#	LIMITS	OTHER FEATURES (NOT,etc.)
				S# command
___	LA = _____	___ ___	/ENG	___ _____
___	PY = _____	___ ___	/	___ _____
___	AU = _____	___ ___	/	**GOOD SETS**
___ __ = _____		___ ___	/	
___ __ = _____		___ ___	/	

```
DIALOG INFORMATION SERVICES
PLEASE LOGON:
 ********
ENTER PASSWORD:
 ********

Welcome to DIALOG
Dialog level 28.11.10B

Last logoff:  06jan92 14:08:56
Logon file001 06jan92 14:09:35

File   1:ERIC _ 66-91/NOV.

        Set  Items  Description
        --   ---   ------
?ss library education or library schools or information science education
        S1    2053  LIBRARY EDUCATION  (EDUCATION OR TRAINING OF LIBRARY
                      PERSONNEL,
        S2     871  LIBRARY SCHOOLS  (PROFESSIONAL SCHOOLS, DEPARTMENTS, OR
                      DIVISI.
        S3      85  INFORMATION SCIENCE EDUCATION  (EDUCATION CONCERNED WITH
                      THE HANDLING OF IN
        S4    2335  LIBRARY EDUCATION OR LIBRARY SCHOOLS OR INFORMATION
                      SCIENCE EDUCATION
?ss distance education or extension education or telecourses/df
        S5    1775  DISTANCE EDUCATION  (EDUCATION VIA THE COMMUNICATIONS
                      MEDIA (COR
        S6    2616  EXTENSION EDUCATION  (INSTRUCTIONAL ACTIVITIES OFFERED
                      BEYOND THE
        S7     597  TELECOURSES/DF  (SEQUENCES OF LESSONS OFFERED OVER
                      TELEVISION...)
        S8    4659  DISTANCE EDUCATION OR EXTENSION EDUCATION OR
                      TELECOURSES/DF
?s s4 and s8
              2335  S4
              4659  S8
        S9      40  S4 AND S8
```

7. Type out a few documents.

```
?t 9/8/1-6

 9/8/1
EJ424818   IR522876
  Aberystwyth—At a Distance.
  Descriptors:  *Curriculum  Development;  *Distance Education;  *Educational
Planning;  Educational  Strategies;  Foreign  Countries;  Higher Education;
Library Administration; *Library Education; Program Descriptions
  Identifiers: *Wales


 9/8/2
EJ424817   IR522875
  The  Use  of  Distance Education in United States Library and Information
Science: History and Current Perspectives.
  Descriptors:  *Administrative  Problems;  *Distance Education; Educational
Technology;  *Extension  Education;  Higher  Education;  Institutional
Cooperation;  *Library  Education;  *Library  Research; Literature Reviews;
*Program Effectiveness; Telecommunications; United States History
```

```
   9/8/3
EJ417029    IR522270
   Recent  Trends  in Education for Library and Information Science in South
India.
   Descriptors:  Degrees (Academic); Developing Nations; Distance Education;
Educational  Trends;  Employment  Opportunities;  Foreign Countries; Higher
Education; *Information  Science  Education; Inservice Education; *Library
Schools
   Identifiers: *India (South); Information Science Research


   9/8/4
EJ413713    IR522068
   Distance  Education: A Report of a Survey of Off-Campus/Extension Courses
in  Graduate  Library Education Programs Accredited by the American Library
Association.
   Descriptors: *Distance  Education;  Extension Education; Graduate Study;
*Information  Science  Education;  *Library  Schools;  Literature  Reviews;
Questionnaires; Research Needs; School Surveys
   Identifiers: *University of Missouri Columbia


   9/8/5
EJ413590    IR521895
   On-Campus  and  Off-Campus  Programs  of  Accredited  Library  Schools: A
Comparison of Graduates.
   Descriptors:  *Alumni;  *Career  Development;  Comparative  Analysis;
Extension Education; Graduate Surveys; Higher Education; *Library Education
;  Library  Schools;  *Off  Campus  Facilities;  *Professional Development;
*Status; Tables (Data)


   9/8/6
EJ407221    IR521420
   Teaching  Reference Work by the Distance Education Mode: Reality or False
Hope?
   Descriptors: *Distance Education; Foreign Countries; Futures (of Society)
;  Higher  Education;  *Library  Education;  *Library  Services;  *Reference
Services
   Identifiers: Riverina Murray Inst of Higher Educ (Australia)
```

8. Refine the search based on your results.

We note immediately that several of these records refer to countries other than the United States. In order to refine the search we type

```
?ss s9 not foreign countries
            40  S9
   S10    39891  FOREIGN COUNTRIES   (COUNTRIES OTHER THAN THE U.S. (NOTE:
                  COORDIN...)
   S11      28  S9 NOT FOREIGN COUNTRIES
?t 11/8/1-7


   11/8/1
EJ424817    IR522875
   The  Use  of  Distance Education in United States Library and Information
Science: History and Current Perspectives.
   Descriptors: *Administrative  Problems; *Distance Education; Educational
Technology;  *Extension  Education;  Higher  Education;  Institutional
Cooperation;  *Library  Education;  *Library  Research; Literature Reviews;
*Program Effectiveness; Telecommunications; United States History
```

(*Text continues on page 78.*)

11/8/2
EJ413713   IR522068
  Distance Education: A Report of a Survey of Off-Campus/Extension Courses
in Graduate Library Education Programs Accredited by the American Library
Association.
  Descriptors: *Distance Education; Extension Education; Graduate Study;
*Information Science Education; *Library Schools; Literature Reviews;
Questionnaires; Research Needs; School Surveys
  Identifiers: *University of Missouri Columbia

11/8/3
EJ413590   IR521895
  On-Campus and Off-Campus Programs of Accredited Library Schools: A
Comparison of Graduates.
  Descriptors: *Alumni; *Career Development; Comparative Analysis;
Extension Education; Graduate Surveys; Higher Education; *Library Education
; Library Schools; *Off Campus Facilities; *Professional Development;
*Status; Tables (Data)

11/8/4
EJ357088   IR517117
  The Use and Perceived Barriers to Use of Telecommunications Technology.
  Descriptors: *Audiovisual Communications; *Delivery Systems; *Distance
Education; Educational Technology; Higher Education; *Information
Technology; *Library Education; School Surveys; *Telecommunications; Use
Studies
  Identifiers: Information Science Education

11/8/5
EJ357087   IR517116
  Academic Advisement for Distance Education Students.
  Descriptors: *Academic Advising; *Delivery Systems; *Distance Education;
Geographic Location; Graduate Study; Higher Education; *Job Placement;
*Library Schools; School Surveys

11/8/6
EJ357086   IR517115
  The Impact of a Distance Education Program on Enrollment Patterns.
  Descriptors: *Class Size; College Environment; *Distance Education;
Enrollment Influences; *Enrollment Trends; Graduate Students; Higher
Education; *Institutional Characteristics; *Library Schools; *Part Time
Students; Tables (Data); Trend Analysis
  Identifiers: University of South Carolina

11/8/7
EJ357085   IR517114
  Faculty and Student Perceptions of Distance Education Using Television.
  Descriptors: Case Studies; Comparative Analysis; *Distance Education;
Higher Education; Library Education; Literature Reviews; *Outreach Programs
; *Program Evaluation; Surveys; *Telecourses
  Identifiers: Information Science Education; *Interactive Television;
University of South Carolina Columbia
?s external degree programs
      S12   908   EXTERNAL DEGREE PROGRAMS   (HIGHER EDUCATION PROGRAMS
                      OFFERING VALI
?s s12 and s4
              908   S12
             2335   S4
      S13   4   S12 AND S4
?s s13 not s9
                4   S13
               40   S9

```
      S14          3   S13 NOT S9
?t 14/8/all


   14/8/1
EJ122955    IR502163
   Implications of the Open University for Changes in Library Education
   Descriptors: Adult  Education;  *External  Degree  Programs;  Independent
Study;   Individualized  Instruction;  *Library  Education;  Library  Role;
Library    Services;    *Nontraditional   Education;   Professional   Continuing
Education; *Public Libraries
   Identifiers: Library Independent Study And Guidance Projects


   14/8/2
ED160124    IR006573
   Going   Beyond   the   Rigidities   of   Formal,   Traditional   Education:
Independent, Self-Paced University Study.
   Descriptors:   *Experimental   Curriculum;   *External   Degree   Programs;
Independent Study; *Library Education; Library Schools; *Lifelong Learning;
*Nontraditional Education; Program Descriptions


   14/8/3
ED093361    IR000848
   Continuing Education.
   Descriptors: Annotated Bibliographies; Cooperative Programs; Coordination
; External  Degree  Programs;  *Inservice  Education;  *Librarians;  Library
Associations;  *Library  Education;  Nonprofessional Personnel; *Professional
Continuing   Education;   Program   Descriptions;   State   Libraries;   *State
Programs
   Identifiers: Illinois; Michigan; Missouri; Ohio; Wisconsin
?s delivery systems
      S15       5483   DELIVERY SYSTEMS   (ORGANIZATIONAL AND ADMINISTRATIVE
                        ASPECTS OF.
?s s15 and s4
                5483   S15
                2335   S4
      S16          7   S15 AND S4
?s s16 not s9
                   7   S16
                  40   S9
      S17          5   S16 NOT S9
?t 17/8/all


   17/8/1
EJ260054    IR509812
   A  School  Library  Media  Research Program for Today and Tomorrow: What,
Why, How.
   Descriptors: Delivery Systems; Educational Technology; Evaluation Needs;
*Information Dissemination; *Learning Resources Centers; Library Education;
Library  Research;  Media  Specialists;  *Program Development; Publications;
*Research; *Research Needs; *School Libraries
   Identifiers: Locally Based Research


   17/8/2
ED326226    IR053253
   IFLA  General  Conference,  1989. Pre-Session Seminar on Interlending and
Document Supply. Papers.
   Descriptors: Administrative Policy; Delivery Systems; Developing Nations;
Foreign   Countries;   Information   Retrieval;   *Interlibrary   Loans;
International  Cooperation;  Library  Administration; *Library Cooperation;
*Library  Education;  Library  Expenditures;  National  Libraries;  *Shared
Resources and Services; *Training Methods
```

(Continues on page 76.)

```
  17/8/3
ED232663    IR050298
  Needs Assessment for Oklahoma Academic Librarians: Summary Report.
  Descriptors: *Academic Libraries; Delivery Systems; Higher Education;
*Librarians; Library Associations; Library Education; Library Networks;
*Needs Assessment; *Professional Associations; *Professional Development;
Surveys
  Identifiers: *Oklahoma


  17/8/4
ED126953    IR003870
  Evaluation and Distribution Study of Videotapes Prepared for Training of
Library Personnel (The ACCESS Videotape Project). Final Report.
  Descriptors: Delivery Systems; Educational Television; Information
Dissemination; *Inservice Education; Librarians; *Library Education;
*Library Personnel; *Professional Continuing Education; Program Evaluation;
Publicize; Video Equipment; Videotape Cassettes; *Videotape Recordings
  Identifiers: Project ACCESS Videotape


  17/8/5
ED098991    IR001379
  The Public Library and Advocacy; Information for Survival. Commissioned
Papers Project, Teachers College, No. 5.
  Descriptors: Citizen Participation; Community Information Services; Daily
Living Skills; *Delivery Systems; *Disadvantaged; Information Dissemination
; *Information Needs; Information Networks; Information Services; Inner
City; Librarians; Library Education; Library Role; *Library Services;
Models; Outreach Programs; *Public Libraries; Systems Approach
  Identifiers: *Advocacy
?ss educational television or nontraditional education
      S18    5428   EDUCATIONAL TELEVISION  (TRANSMISSION OF EDUCATIONAL OR
                          INFORMATIONAL..
      S19    4574   NONTRADITIONAL EDUCATION  (EDUCATIONAL PROGRAMS THAT ARE
                          OFFERED AS AL
      S20    9897   EDUCATIONAL TELEVISION OR NONTRADITIONAL EDUCATION
?s s20 and s4
             9897   S20
             2335   S4
      S21      15   S20 AND S4
?s s21 not s9
               15   S21
               40   S9
      S22      12   S21 NOT S9
?t 22/8/1-5


  22/8/1
EJ187179    IR505977
  An Alternative to Library School
  Descriptors: *Apprenticeships; Librarians; *Library Education; Library
Schools; *Nontraditional Education; Work Experience


  22/8/2
EJ145153    IR503841
  Decisions for Library School Curricula
  Descriptors: *Educational Change; Employment Patterns; *Library Education
; Library Schools; Nontraditional Education


  22/8/3
EJ122955    IR502163
  Implications of the Open University for Changes in Library Education
  Descriptors: Adult Education; *External Degree Programs; Independent
Study; Individualized Instruction; *Library Education; Library Role;
```

Library   Services;   *Nontraditional   Education;   Professional   Continuing
Education; *Public Libraries
   Identifiers: Library Independent Study And Guidance Projects

   22/8/4
EJ094909   IR500282
   Use of Televised Role Playing in Special Library Education
   Descriptors: Curriculum   Evaluation;   Educational   Media;   Educational
Research; *Educational   Television;   Interpersonal   Relationship;   *Library
Education; *Role Playing; Special Libraries; Videotape Recordings

   22/8/5
ED330352   IR053515
   Sing   a   New   Song: A New Approach to Public Library Management in Rural
Snowflake, Arizona.
   Descriptors: Administrator   Attitudes;   *Advisory   Committees;   Curriculum
Design; *Library   Administration;   *Library Education;   Library Technicians;
*Nontraditional   Education;   Organizational   Change;   *Public Libraries;   Two
Year Colleges
   Identifiers: *Northland Pioneer College AZ
?t 22/8/6-10

   22/8/6
ED302266   IR052603
   Library School Educational Program without Walls. Final Report, September
1975-August 1976 and Final Report, September 1976-August 1977.
   Descriptors: Academic   Libraries;   Educational   Opportunities;   Higher
Education;   *Individualized   Instruction;   *Information   Dissemination;
*Library Schools; *Library Science; *Nontraditional Education; *Pacing;
Pilot Projects; Public Relations
   Identifiers: *Schools Without Walls

   22/8/7
ED281522   IR012643
   Media Specialist Handbook: You Are the Key.
   Descriptors: Board of Education Policy; *Certification; Educational Media
;   Educational   Television;   Elementary   Secondary   Education;   Facility
Guidelines;   Facility   Planning;   *Learning   Resources   Centers;   Library
Associations;   Library   Education;   Library   Networks;   *Media   Specialists;
Professional   Associations;   School   Libraries;   State   Programs;   *State
Standards
   Identifiers: Georgia Educational Television Network; Georgia Library
Information Network; *Georgia State Department of Education

   22/8/8
ED269020   IR051497
   Continuing Education of Library Science in the New China.
   Descriptors: *Continuing   Education;   *Correspondence   Study;   Foreign
Countries; Higher Education; History; *Library Education; Library Personnel
; *Library Science; Nontraditional   Education; Position Papers; Teaching
Methods
   Identifiers: *China

   22/8/9
ED160124   IR006573
   Going   Beyond   the   Rigidities   of   Formal,   Traditional   Education:
Independent, Self-Paced University Study.
   Descriptors: *Experimental   Curriculum;   *External   Degree   Programs;
Independent Study; *Library Education; Library Schools; *Lifelong Learning;
*Nontraditional Education; Program Descriptions

(Continues on page 78.)

```
 22/8/10
ED126953   IR003870
 Evaluation  and Distribution Study of Videotapes Prepared for Training of
Library Personnel (The ACCESS Videotape Project). Final Report.
  Descriptors:  Delivery   Systems;  Educational  Television;  Information
Dissemination;   *Inservice   Education;  Librarians;  *Library  Education;
*Library Personnel; *Professional Continuing Education; Program Evaluation;
Publicize; Video Equipment; Videotape Cassettes; *Videotape Recordings
  Identifiers: Project ACCESS Videotape
?s s11 or s14
              28  S11
               3  S14
     S23      31  S11 OR S14
?ds

Set    Items   Description
S1     2053   LIBRARY EDUCATION   (EDUCATION OR TRAINING OF LIBRARY PERSO-
                NNEL,
S2      871   LIBRARY SCHOOLS   (PROFESSIONAL SCHOOLS, DEPARTMENTS, OR DI-
                VISI.
S3       85   INFORMATION SCIENCE EDUCATION   (EDUCATION CONCERNED WITH T-
                HE HANDLING OF IN
S4     2335   LIBRARY EDUCATION OR LIBRARY SCHOOLS OR INFORMATION SCIENCE
                EDUCATION
S5     1775   DISTANCE EDUCATION   (EDUCATION VIA THE COMMUNICATIONS MEDIA
                (COR
S6     2616   EXTENSION EDUCATION   (INSTRUCTIONAL ACTIVITIES OFFERED BEY-
                OND THE
S7      597   TELECOURSES/DF   (SEQUENCES OF LESSONS OFFERED OVER TELEVIS-
                ION...)
S8     4659   DISTANCE EDUCATION OR EXTENSION EDUCATION OR TELECOURSES/DF
S9       40   S4 AND S8
S10   39891   FOREIGN COUNTRIES   (COUNTRIES OTHER THAN THE U.S. (NOTE: C-
                OORDIN...)
S11      28   S9 NOT FOREIGN COUNTRIES
S12     908   EXTERNAL DEGREE PROGRAMS   (HIGHER EDUCATION PROGRAMS OFFER-
                ING VALI
S13       4   S12 AND S4
S14       3   S13 NOT S9
S15    5483   DELIVERY SYSTEMS   (ORGANIZATIONAL AND ADMINISTRATIVE ASPEC-
                TS OF.
S16       7   S15 AND S4
S17       5   S16 NOT S9
S18    5428   EDUCATIONAL TELEVISION   (TRANSMISSION OF EDUCATIONAL OR IN-
                FORMATIONAL..
S19    4574   NONTRADITIONAL EDUCATION   (EDUCATIONAL PROGRAMS THAT ARE O-
                FFERED AS AL
S20    9897   EDUCATIONAL TELEVISION OR NONTRADITIONAL EDUCATION
S21      15   S20 AND S4
S22      12   S21 NOT S9
S23      31   S11 OR S14
```

The first concept block is "information and library science education," and the three terms chosen, LIBRARY EDUCATION, LIBRARY SCHOOLS, and INFORMATION SCIENCE EDUCATION, are ORed together to produce the first concept set, S4, with 2,335 documents. The same process is followed for the second concept block, "distance learning," and the three terms DISTANCE EDUCATION, EXTENSION EDUCATION, and TELECOURSES produce S8 with 4,659 documents. These two concept sets are then ANDed together to produce the first result set, S9, with 40 documents.

Examining the first six of those in format 8, we see that many of them look quite good, especially the second, fourth, fifth, and sixth ones. The first and third look good, too, except that they are not about programs in the United States. You may recall that we were concerned about this but found no good descriptor to use. If you look closely at documents one, three, and six, though, you will notice they all have been indexed with the descriptor FOREIGN COUNTRIES. This is an ideal example of when to use NOT to remove an unwanted concept, which we do to obtain S11 with 28 documents.

Looking at S11, we see some repeats from S10 (minus the documents about Wales, India, and Australia), and a few new ones that might be good. Overall, this set looks to be on target. There might be more, though, so we try a few of our reserve terms. Searching on EXTERNAL DEGREE PROGRAMS, an alternative in the "distance learning" concept block, produces 908 documents. If we AND this with S4, the "ILS education" concept set, we get four documents. Some of these may be documents we have already retrieved in S9; to remove those and see only "new" documents, we NOT out S9 to produce S14 with three documents, which means that one of the documents in S13 was a repeat. S14 looks OK; not as good as S11, but these documents are possibilities, so we will remember it.

A couple of the good documents in S11 had the term DELIVERY SYSTEMS; it might be worth entering the term to see if it nets more useful documents. Searching on it produces 5,483 documents. We AND it with S4 to produce seven, and NOT out S9 to yield

S17 with five hits. S17 does not look so good; the documents are marginal to poor, and we decide to discard it.

There were two other alternative terms in the "distance learning" set: EDUCATIONAL TELEVISION and NONTRADITIONAL EDUCATION. We search on them, ORed together, and get 9,897 hits. ANDed with S4, we get 15, and NOTing out S9 produces 12. Again, these are marginal. The fourth document is a possibility, as is the sixth, but it is from 1977 and probably too old to be useful. We also decide to discard S22.

Our best results, then, were in sets S11 and S14. To create one final good result set, we can OR them together, which produces S23 with 31 documents, most of which seem to be at least potentially relevant to the query.

This search demonstrates that controlled vocabulary searching can be a very powerful tool; when it works, it can produce high-quality results and give you confidence that you have found most of the good documents in a database. However, there are a number of situations in which controlled vocabulary searching cannot be used, does not work well, or is just a bad idea. In those instances, we use our other primary technique: free-text searching, which we discuss in chapter 7.

Note

[1] Alvin Walker, Jr., ed. *Thesaurus of Psychological Index Terms*, 6th ed. (Arlington, VA: American Psychological Association, 1991), vii.

In chapter 6, we saw that searching using controlled vocabulary techniques can be effective and efficient. In many cases, we prefer to search using controlled vocabulary terms, because we often get higher-quality, more specific results. Sometimes, though, controlled vocabulary searching is either not good enough or not even possible. In these situations, we must rely on another set of techniques described in this chapter: searching free-text.

You may have run across or even used free-text searching before. It is sometimes called *keyword searching* and is used in many online library catalogs and other computerized information retrieval systems.

7

FREE-TEXT SEARCHING

Essentially, searching with free-text techniques involves using terms from everyday or specialized language rather than controlled vocabulary terms.

You might want to take a peek at the search example at the end of the chapter now, just to get a feel for what we are describing and to see how different it is from what we have done so far.

In this chapter, we shall explore online search techniques used with free-text, the situations in which this searching works best, where free-text terms come from, some problems with free-text searching, and how to refine searches to broaden or narrow results. As always, we conclude with a search example.

Proximity Operators

Recall once again how the inverted file is constructed. Each word (excluding stop words) that occurs in a document is marked with its position, and then an alphabetical list of all such words is created. Index terms that are intact phrases, such as descriptors and identifiers, are often included both as individual words and as full phrases (we said these fields are both word indexed and phrase indexed). We do not know yet how to search for phrases in other, word indexed fields, such as titles or abstracts.

We can, at this point, search for such phrases, but in a very crude way, using single words joined by the AND operator. If we were looking for documents about the Graduate Record Examinations, for example, we could simply search GRADUATE AND RECORD AND EXAM? and see what comes up. But there would be no guarantee that documents we retrieved would have anything to do with the Graduate Record Examinations. We could get documents that talk about examinations of record buying habits of gradu-

ate students. Or we might retrieve a paper about record keeping of graduate schools for foreign language examinations. AND does not allow us to specify relationships between concepts; we can only say that terms occur in the same record.

There are techniques, however, that allow us to do just that. These are called *proximity operators*, and they are used to specify how close you wish two or more words to be in the documents that are retrieved. There are several proximity operators, but they all work in essentially the same way.

The simplest of these allows you to retrieve documents that have two or more words in direct proximity, that is, right next to each other. In this way, you can search for a phrase in word indexed fields. For example, if you wanted to search for the phrase "information industry" in titles (a rather specific tactic, by the way), you would use the (W) operator, as in the following example from ERIC:

```
      Set   Items   Description
      ---   -----   -----------
?s information(w)industry/ti
            13082   INFORMATION/TI
             2152   INDUSTRY/TI   (PRODUCTIVE ENTERPRISES, ESPECIALLY
                    MANUFACTU...)
      S1      12    INFORMATION(W)INDUSTRY/TI
```

This command tells DIALOG to retrieve all documents that have the word "information" directly followed by the word "industry" in the title field.

```
?s  management(w)information(w)systems
           41955   MANAGEMENT
          125433   INFORMATION
           53499   SYSTEMS
      S2    2173   MANAGEMENT(W)INFORMATION(W)SYSTEMS
```

More than two words can be chained together, as in the following example:

This expression will retrieve documents with these three words in this order, in any Basic Index field.

The general form of the command is

S term(W)term

S term(W)term(W)term

. . . etc.

Compare the following three expressions, again in ERIC:

```
?s day care
        S3    3515   DAY CARE  (CARE
OF CHILDREN BY PERSONS OTHER THAN
THEIR...)
```

```
?s day(w)care/de
              5602   DAY/DE
              8391   CARE/DE
        S4    4950   DAY(W)CARE/DE
```

```
?s day()care
             17723   DAY
             20189   CARE
        S5    5837   DAY()CARE
```

The first of these searches for the bound descriptor DAY CARE. The second searches for the word DAY followed by the word CARE in the descriptor

field and retrieves almost 1,500 more documents. Why? Because there are several descriptors that incorporate those two words in that order, including ADULT DAY CARE, DAY CARE CENTERS, FAMILY DAY CARE, SCHOOL AGE DAY CARE, and so on. S4 includes all of these. Finally, S5 includes all documents that have these two words in this order in any field and retrieves almost 1,000 more records than S4. You begin to see the power and some of the potential problems of free-text searching.

Also note that there is no W between the parentheses in the search expression for S5. That is not a mistake—in this situation *only*, you can leave out the W. (W) and () work in exactly the same way, and the W can be either upper or lower case.

You may also specify that you would like two words together, but allow for words, especially stop words, to intervene. Remember that although stop words are not included in the inverted file, their positions were preserved, so you must take account of them in free-text searching. You can do this by indicating how many words, at most, you will allow to intervene, as in the following example:

S term(nW)term

where n is any number one or greater.[1] To search for documents containing the phrase "University of Michigan" in the abstract (remember OF is a stop word), we would search the following:

```
?s university(1w)michigan
            66777   UNIVERSITY
             6678   MICHIGAN
        S6    890   UNIVERSITY(1W)MICHIGAN
```

This command retrieves all documents with the word UNIVERSITY followed by the word MICHIGAN, with at most one word in between.

In practice, a number higher than (3W) or (4W) tends to be counterproductive, as the farther apart terms get, the more we revert to the simple Boolean AND. - GW

This tactic can also be used when you want two words close together but not necessarily next to each other, as in the following example:

```
?s (online or information)(2w)retrieval
          5646   ONLINE
        125433   INFORMATION
          7013   RETRIEVAL
     S7   5555   (ONLINE OR INFORMATION)(2W)RETRIEVAL
```

You could be interested in documents that have the phrase "information retrieval," "online retrieval," "online bibliographic retrieval," "online systems for retrieval of information," and so on, so you broaden the search a bit. This set contains all documents with either ONLINE or INFORMATION

followed by the word RETRIEVAL with zero, one, or two words in between.

The search statement would be

```
s(online information) (2w) retrieval.
```

Notice that we have a Boolean expression on the left
side of the (2W). You can also have set numbers here,
truncations, or anything legal, as in the following:

```
?s s7(W)system?
             5555   S7
           110345   SYSTEM?
      S8      662   S7(W)SYSTEM?
?t 8/5/1
```

```
  8/5/1
EJ438017   IR523849
  Sense-Making in a Database Environment.
  Jacobson, Thomas L.
  Information Processing and Management; v27 n6 p647-57 1991
  ISSN: 0306-4573
  Available from: UMI
  Language: English
  Document Type: JOURNAL ARTICLE (080); RESEARCH REPORT (143)
  Journal Announcement: CIJMAY92
  Describes a study of undergraduate students' search sessions on a
full-text information retrieval system, NEXIS, that was conducted (1) to
evaluate a novice user's ability to use such an information retrieval
system, and (2) to analyze users' information seeking behavior.
Sense-making theory and timeline interviews are discussed. (38 references)
(LRW)
  Descriptors: Evaluation Methods; *Full Text Databases; Higher Education;
*Information Seeking; Interviews; *Online Searching; Undergraduate Students;
*Users (Information)
  Identifiers: *Sense Making Approach; Timelines
```

English grammar being what it is, the words you
want may not always be in the same order. An author
writing a document about relativity theory might use
that phrase, but she might also use "theory of relativity,"
"theory of general relativity," "relativity theories," or
"theory of special relativity." If you were looking for
these documents, you might be tempted to use a
command like the following:

```
?s relativity(w)theory
             384   RELATIVITY
           38845   THEORY
      S9      13   RELATIVITY(W)THEORY
?t 9/5/1
```

```
  9/5/1
EJ398251   SE545258
  Reference Frames and Relativity.
  Swartz, Clifford
  Physics Teacher; v27 n6 p437-46 Sep 1989
  Available from: UMI
  Language: English
  Document Type: JOURNAL ARTICLE (080); PROJECT DESCRIPTION (141)
  Journal Announcement: CIJMAR90
  Target Audience: Teachers; Practitioners
  Stresses the importance of a reference frame in mechanics. Shows the
Galilean transformation in terms of relativity theory. Discusses
accelerated reference frames and noninertial reference frames. Provides
examples of reference frames with diagrams. (YP)
  Descriptors: College Science; *Force; Higher Education; *Mechanics
(Physics); *Motion; *Physics; *Relativity; Scientific Concepts; *Secondary
Education; Secondary School Science; Vectors (Mathematics)
```

You might also want documents that contain the other phrases, so perhaps you could try the following:

```
?s relativity(2n)theor?
          384   RELATIVITY
        63161   THEOR?
   S10    49    RELATIVITY(2N)THEOR?
```

```
?t 10/5/1
```

```
10/5/1
EJ426340   SE547463
  Maximum Possible Transverse Velocity in Special Relativity.
  Medhekar, Sarang
  Physics Education; v7 n4 p320-22 Jan-Mar 1991
  Journal availability: see SE 547 456.
  ISSN: 0970-5953
  Language: English
  Document Type: JOURNAL ARTICLE (080); TEACHING GUIDE (052)
  Journal Announcement: CIJSEP91
  Target Audience: Teachers; Practitioners
  Using  a  physical  picture,  an  expression  for  the  maximum  possible
transverse  velocity  and orientation required for that by a linear emitter
in  special  theory of relativity has been derived. A differential calculus
method is also used to derive the expression. (Author/KR)
  Descriptors: Calculus; Computation; Higher Education; *Motion; *Physics;
Problem Solving; *Relativity; *Science Activities; Science Education; Space;
Time
```

This command uses the (N) proximity operator, which retrieves documents that have the two terms near each other (hence the "N") with the possibility of intervening words, in this case as many as two. The general form

S term(nN)term

is similar to that of (W), and the same guidelines apply about using set numbers, Boolean expressions, truncation, and so on. In many cases, (nN) is more useful than (nW) because of this tendency in English to invert phrases and insert words.

A couple more examples further illustrate the use of (nN): If a patron requests documents on hypothesis testing (a technique from statistics), the concept might be referred to in documents as "hypothesis testing," but you might also see by "testing the hypothesis," or "a test of two null hypotheses." So instead of HYPOTHESIS(W)TESTING, you might prefer HYPOTHES?S(3N)TEST??? to get many variant forms of the phrase.

Also, you can use (nN) to save typing. If you were looking for documents about public universities in Michigan, you could try a strategy such as UNIVERSIT?(1N)MICHIGAN, which would retrieve documents with "University of Michigan" and also "Eastern Michigan University," "Michigan Technological University," and even "Michigan State University." Of course, you would miss some things (notably Wayne State University), but these could be ORed in, and you have still saved yourself quite a bit of typing.

The use of proximity operators is available on most of the major online systems, though their exact formats vary. On BRS, for example, the (w) operator is replaced by ADJ (adjacent to). So we may have a command in search mode, such as DAY ADJ CARE, that will be equivalent to DAY()CARE on DIALOG - GW

There are other, broader proximity operators in DIALOG. The (F) operator will seek documents that have two words in the same field (i.e., both in the title, both in the abstract, etc.). You can specify which field you want to search in or leave it unqualified. See the following examples:

S term(F)term
S term(F)term/field code

A search in LISA for documents about the use of
CD-ROM in school libraries might go something like
the following:

```
? s cdrom? or cd()rom?
                8  CDROM?
             3143  CD
             2198  ROM?
             2185  CD(W)ROM?
     S1      2186  CDROM OR CD()ROM?
?s school (w) (librar? or media)
Processing
Processing
             9247  SCHOOL
            84831  LIBRAR?
             5634  MEDIA
     S2      5131  SCHOOL(W)(LIBRAR? OR MEDIA)
?s s1(F)s2
             2186  S4
             5131  S2
     S3        43  S4(F)S2
? t 3/5/1-3
 3/5/1
0216776   92-1716   Library and Information Science Abstracts   (LISA)
    TITLE: Information skills in the school curriculum.
    AUTHOR(S): Williams, Dorothy A.
    JOURNAL: In: Computers in Libraries International 91. Proceedings of the
5th Annual Conference on Computers in Libraries, London, February 1991
    SOURCE: 108-112. 7 refs
    LANGUAGES: English
    ABSTRACT: Discusses  the potential for teaching the use of computerised
      information  retrieval  (on-line,  CD-ROM)  in  schools  with specific
      reference  to MISLIP (Microcomputer in the School Library Project).
      N.L.M.
    NOTE: MISLIPP (Microcomputer in the School Library Project)
    DESCRIPTORS: Information  storage and retrieval; Information retrieval;
Subject    indexing;  Computerised  information    retrieval; Computerised
information  storage and retrieval; Searching; Subject indexing;
Computerised    subject    indexing;  School  libraries; Computer  assisted
      instruction; Use instructions
    SECTION HEADINGS: COMPUTERISED SUBJECT INDEXING
    SECTION HEADING CODES: ZkRmi&HykGp


 3/5/2
0216736   92-1705   Library and Information Science Abstracts   (LISA)
     TITLE: End  user  training  for CD-ROM MEDLINE: a survey of UK medical
      school libraries.
    AUTHOR(S): Steele, Alena; Tseng, Gwyneth
    JOURNAL: Program
    SOURCE: 26 (1) Jan 92, 55-61. 9 refs
    LANGUAGES: English
    ABSTRACT: Reports  on  a  questionnaire  survey of 31 UK medical school
      libraries  to  determine  the  end  user training methods used for the
      CD-ROM  MEDLINE  data  base. 27  medical  school  libraries replied and
      provided  information  concerning:  medical  librarians' attitudes to
      training  needs  of  CD-ROM  searchers; the extent to which training is
      considered  necessary;  whether  training  is a common prerequisite of
      access  to CD-ROM MEDLINE; availability, objectives, format, frequency
      and  contest  of  training  services; and number of libraries producing
      in-house  documentation. Medical  libraries  were  faced  to consider
      training  to be a important  element in the provision of CD-ROM MEDLINE.
      The  most  common  objective  was  to  give users the skill to search
```

efficiently rather than on all-encompassing programme of advanced
search techniques. N.L.M.
NOTE: MEDLINE
DESCRIPTORS: Information storage and retrieval; Information retrieval;
Subject indexing; Computerised information storage and retrieval;
Computerised subject indexing; Subject indexing; Discs; Optical discs;
Storage media; CD-ROMs; Compact discs; Data bases; Information services;
  Surveys; U.K.; Medical school libraries; End users; Use instructions;
  Medicine
SECTION HEADINGS: CD-ROMS
SECTION HEADING CODES: ZjjcRnM(61)Rmi

3/5/3
0215824   92-1022   Library and Information Science Abstracts   (LISA)
  TITLE: A system for statewide sharing of resources: a case study of
  ACCESS PENNSYLVANIA.
AUTHOR(S): Epler, Doris M.; Tuzinski, Jean H.
JOURNAL: School Library Media Quarterly
SOURCE: 20 (1) Fall 91, 19-23. illus. table. 1 ref
LANGUAGES: English
ABSTRACT: ACCESS PENNSYLVANIA is a statewide data base on CD-ROM
  combining the resources of over 500 academic, public, special, and
  school libraries in Pennsylvania. Discusses the programmes background
  and stresses the commitment its members must make to service the
  state's population through resource sharing. Focuses in particular on
  the incentive the programme provides for school library media centres
  to automate and its benefits in terms of interlibrary loans and
  collaborative collection development. Original abstract—amended
NOTE: ACCESS PENNSYLVANIA
DESCRIPTORS: Technical processes and services; Catalogues by special
characteristics; Union catalogues; Cooperation; Computerised union
catalogues; CD-ROMs; Storage media
  SECTION HEADINGS: UNION CATALOGUES
  SECTION HEADING CODES: UzhOqjc

The first document in S3 looks promising, but the other two are off the track because the strategy is so broad. However, we notice the good descriptor SCHOOL LIBRARIES in document 1, so we use the following instead:


```
?s school libraries
     S4    2774   SCHOOL LIBRARIES
?s s1 and s4
           2186   S1
           2774   S4
     S5      20   S4 AND S6
?t 5/6/1-4
```

 5/6/1
0216776   92-1716
  TITLE: Information skills in the school curriculum.

 5/6/2
0213796   91-5573
  TITLE: MultiPlatter goes to school.

 5/6/3
0211940   91-3849
  TITLE: TOM welcomed by students.

```
5/6/4
0206460    90-6382
   TITLE: Report  on the 17th annual 'International Association of School
   Librarianship'  Conference,  held at the Western Michigan, University,
   Michigan USA from 24 to 29 July, 1988.
```

With this strategy, we get much improved results. There are other proximity operators; we will see how to use some in chapter 11.

Why Free-Text Searching?

As we have seen, controlled vocabulary searching is often an excellent way to go. But that is not always the case. The following examples illustrate several situations in which searching using terms selected from a thesaurus or controlled vocabulary is not the best method:

- *There is no thesaurus.* Obviously, if there is no controlled vocabulary, you cannot use it. Some databases have no thesaurus at all. Others use one, but it is unavailable because it is not published or your particular institution does not have access to it. If there is no indexing at all (often the case with newspaper databases, for example), all you have left are free-text techniques. If documents in the database have been indexed in some way, but you do not know how, you can begin with free-text searching and then use pearl-growing techniques to weave in controlled vocabulary searching. This is an often used and successful approach.

- *There are no good terms.* In some cases, the vocabulary simply may not cover the subject area of the query very well. There may be several related, marginal terms, but no single good term.

- *The term is new.* It may also be the case that the subject area or terminology of the query is new, and so no term or terms have yet been accepted into the thesaurus. In general, it will take some time, probably years rather than months, for a new term to become widely used and incorporated into the printed controlled vocabulary. Some disciplines and databases move faster than others, but if you are searching for swiftly developing areas or very new terms, controlled vocabulary may not work. Further, when the term is included in the thesaurus, typically older documents will not be reindexed, so they will be accessible only using free-text searching. We will see an example of this in the sample search on pages 100-110.

- *There is only one good term, and it is not an index term.* This is particularly the case when there is a good term that is outside of a subject area. For example, if you were searching for documents about the role of school libraries in assisting with information literacy, you might decide to search in ERIC, but ERIC, as of this writing, has no good descriptor for the concept "information literacy." There are several possibilities: LIBRARY SKILLS, COMPUTER LITERACY, COURSE INTEGRATED LIBRARY INSTRUCTION, LIBRARY INSTRUCTION, TECHNOLOGICAL LITERACY, and even LITERACY itself, but no term "INFORMATION LITERACY." In this case, we might choose to search for this phrase as a free-text expression like the following:

```
?s information()literacy
        125433   INFORMATION
         14705   LITERACY  (ABILITY TO READ AND WRITE — ALSO,
                  COMMUNICA...)
    S11       78   INFORMATION()LITERACY

?s  s11 and school libraries
          78   S11
        2618   SCHOOL LIBRARIES
    S12       14   S11 AND SCHOOL LIBRARIES
?t 12/5/1
```

```
12/5/1
EJ436215   IR523691
  Library Orientation and Instruction—1990.
  Rader, Hannelore B.
  Reference Services Review; v19 n4 p71-83 Win 1991
  ISSN: 0090-7324
  Language: English
  Document Type: JOURNAL  ARTICLE  (080);  REVIEW  LITERATURE  (070);
BIBLIOGRAPHY (131)
  Journal Announcement: CIJAPR92
  This  annotated  bibliography  includes  materials  in  English  published  in
1990  that  deal  with  information  literacy,  including  instruction  in  the  use
of  information  resources;  research;  and  computer  skills  related  to
retrieving,  using,  and  evaluating  information. Publications  on  user
instruction  are  included  for  all  types  of  libraries  and  for  all  levels  of
users. (132 references) (LRW)
  Descriptors: Academic  Libraries;  Annotated  Bibliographies;  Computer
Assisted  Instruction;  Elementary  Secondary  Education;  Higher  Education;
Information  Retrieval;  Information  Utilization;  *Library  Instruction;
*Library  Skills;  Literature  Reviews;  Public  Libraries;  Research  Skills;
School  Libraries;  Special  Libraries;  Users  (Information)
  Identifiers: *Information  Literacy;  User  Training
```

- *There are not many hits, either in the database or using controlled vocabulary.* Free-text strategies are inherently broader than controlled vocabulary and thus will generally retrieve more documents. If an initial controlled vocabulary search pulls up very few or no good hits, or if you have some prior knowledge that there will be little good material in the database, you might decide to try a free-text strategy to widen the net and pull in more records. There is no guarantee that these will be desirable, but at least you will have a starting point. Always keep in mind that the file may not contain what you seek, no matter how good your strategy.

- *You are looking for a known item.* Known-item searches are a special case. If you know the document's title (to provide a bibliographic verification, for example) or a portion of it, there is no need to do an elaborate controlled vocabulary search. Just do a reasonable free-text attempt. Be careful, though, not to over-specify—your user's memory may not be perfect. In looking for Marcia Bates's well-known article on "the perfect thirty-item search," you might search in Library & Information Science Abstracts for the following:

```
?s perfect()thirty()item()search/ti
            90   PERFECT
            62   THIRTY
           463   ITEM
          4890   SEARCH/TI
    S1       0   PER-
FECT()THIRTY()ITEM()SEARCH/TI
```

You would get nothing, but then try a broader strategy like the following:

```
?s thirty()item
            62   THIRTY
           463   ITEM
    S2       1   THIRTY()ITEM
```

This approach retrieves one item, which is correct:[2]

```
?t 2/6/1

 2/6/1
168472   85-2684
   TITLE: The fallacy of the perfect thirty-item online search
?t 2/3/1

 2/3/1
168472   85-2684   Library and Information Science Abstracts   (LISA)
   TITLE: The fallacy of the perfect thirty-item online search
   AUTHOR(S): Bates, Marcia J.
   JOURNAL: RQ
   SOURCE: 24 (1) Fall 84, 43-50. 11 refs
```

- *You do not want to deal with a new controlled vocalulary.* As we have seen, thesauri and vocabulary differ, sometimes widely, from database to database. If you are confronted with a search in an unfamiliar database, you might decide that it is not really worth learning an entirely new vocabulary for one search. If you are under time pressure, you might try an initial free-text strategy and see what happens, perhaps pearl-growing from good things as they come up. This can work, but clearly it is not a preferred method. Some people, though, are good at this sort of thing.

If you find that your style works in this setting, more power to you.

It should be pointed out early and often that neither technique—controlled vocabulary nor free-text searching—is superior to the other. In some cases, one will be preferable, but often they work in tandem: You begin with a free-text search and pearl grow using index terms from good documents; or you begin with a good index term or two, discover a useful free-text expression, and use it. The blending of these two sets of techniques to produce high-quality searches is part of the real art of searching.

Choosing Free-Text Terms

Once you have made the decision to use free-text techniques, how do you generate your terms? You may have no controlled vocabulary from which to draw. Or, if you do, you may have decided to use a controlled vocabulary term or two, but in free-text fashion. This is not done frequently, though, so where do these terms come from?

Your first and potentially best source of free-text terms is your user. He or she may have quite a good idea about the vocabulary of the subject area you will be searching and will be able to give you helpful clues for further searching. This is particularly true with university faculty, researchers, and other specialists looking for new or new-to-them documents in their fields. In this situation, use the information they provide on search request forms and through interviews.

However, many users do not have much background or experience in the areas of their topics and may not be reliable sources of terms. They are cer-

tainly worth exploring, and if they know of any good documents, titles, or authors, these are often sources of good terms.

You can also try pearl-growing with free-text terms from good documents, in addition to index terms, if any. As you proceed through the search and find good documents, look for additional good terms in abstracts and especially in titles. If a word or phrase is used in the title, it is often an indication that the document is really about that concept.

You need to strike a balance between generality and specificity. If you use a very general, single-word term free-text, you may retrieve thousands of documents, only a few of which are of interest to the user. On the other hand, if your expression is too specific, you may retrieve very little, miss good things, and perhaps get nothing at all. This balancing act can be very tricky, but it gets easier with experience.

Problems with Free-Text Searching: False Drops

Free-text searching is certainly not a panacea, although it can be a helpful complement to controlled vocabulary techniques. However, there are situations in which free-text searching can be very problematic. The major difficulty we encounter in searching free-text is false drops: retrieved documents that are not germane to the topic. Because there is no control over the vocabulary in title and abstract fields, when you search for words in those fields the author or abstracter may or may not be using them in the same way as the searcher.

The following are a few examples of common sources of false drops and a few pieces of advice to help you to avoid them:[3]

Problem: Reverse concepts. If you were doing a search on school libraries and used the expression LIBRAR? AND SCHOOL?, you would get not only "school library" material but also "library school" material, which is not what you want.

Solution: Use proximity operators to more closely tie concepts together. A search on SCHOOL(W)LIBRAR? would not retrieve "library schools," but neither would it retrieve "libraries in schools" nor "libraries in elementary schools." You would be tempted to try SCHOOL?(2N)LIBRAR?, but you would be right back where you started. In many cases, you can avoid reverse concepts by using (W), but in some instances you might have to go to controlled vocabulary.

Problem: Homographs/conflation. These are two terms for the same problem: two or more concepts that use the same word or words. Examples include words like CRACK (cocaine or seismic fault?), FIELD (part of a bibliographic record or a meadow?), and SDI (Strategic Defense Initiative or selective dissemination of information?). We say that these terms are "conflated."

Solution: Qualify or focus your expression. If you are interested in crack cocaine, you might try something like CRACK AND (DRUG? OR COCAINE). This will focus your results and eliminate seismic and other extraneous material. Alternatively, you might try CRACK/TI and qualify the term down to the title field. You will still retrieve some nonrelevant records, but you will eliminate marginal or offhand mentions of the word in the abstract field.

Problem: Excessive truncation. Truncation is a wonderful thing, but too much of any good thing is too much. It would not be a good idea, for example, to search on BOOK? in *ABI/Inform* (you will also get BOOKKEEPING), or to search on INTERN? in *ERIC*, which would get INTERN and INTERNS but also INTERNAL and INTERNATIONAL.

Solution: Do not truncate too far to the left. Try to imagine all the variant forms that your word can take (e.g., COMPUTER, COMPUTING, COMPUTERS, COMPUTE, etc.) and either truncate further to the right (COMPUT?—still pretty bad), or restrict the length of your truncation (COMPUT??? will only get up to three more characters; COMPUTER? ? will only get up to one more), or do not truncate at all (COMPUTER OR COMPUTING OR COMPUTERS OR COMPUTE), depending on the database and the vocabulary.

Problem: Acronyms. Many acronyms (CBS, USA, NASA) are not a problem because they have essentially entered the language as words in their own right. Some, however, will conflate with other common words. Acronyms such as ADD (attention deficit disorder, from psychology), SAD (seasonal affective disorder), AIDS (acquired immune deficiency syndrome), and so on will retrieve many more documents than you intend, because they will also retrieve based on the words "add," "sad," and "aids."

Solution: There are several things you can try: Focus or qualify your set (ADD AND ATTENTION). Use the full expression (SEASONAL()AFFECTIVE()DISORDER?). Search in the descriptor field and see if the expression or acronym is an index term (ACQUIRED()IMMUN?/DE).

Problem: Negation. Suppose you are searching for documents about programs to teach older people how to use computers. A strategy like COMPUTER? ? AND (OLDER OR ELDERLY) might seem like a good start, but it retrieves documents that contain sentences like, "We had hoped to include elderly people in our program, but our funding wouldn't allow us to." Grrr!

Although many databases instruct their indexers and abstracters not to incorporate negative phrases, it is not a universal instruction, and the instructions do not always do a lot of good.

Solution: Shy of completely reworking abstracts and the way they are written, there is not a lot you can do about this. It is not a major problem, but it is particularly frustrating when it happens.

Good Places to Use Free-Text Searching

There are several situations in which free-text techniques are especially useful, situations in which controlled vocabulary simply will not work or cannot be used. The following are a few examples:[4]

- *Geography.* Some databases have geographical descriptors (*ABI/Inform, PAIS*) or identifiers (*ERIC*), but many do not. If you are searching for documents that mention a particular geographic name, free-text techniques may be your only option: ANN()ARBOR, NEW()YORK. Keep in mind, though, that there may be several geographic names that refer to the same area. For a search on New England, you might want to do the following:

(NEW()ENGLAND OR MAINE OR VERMONT OR NEW()HAMPSHIRE OR CONNECTICUT OR RHODE()ISLAND OR MASSACHUSETTS)

and even then you might miss records that refer to Boston or Providence or the White Mountains or the Berkshires.

- *Other proper names.* Again, some databases have personal name fields or include names as descriptors or identifiers, but if these are not available or if you are looking for other proper names, use free-text: GROUCHO(W) MARX, HOUSE (1W)REPRESENTATIVES, MICROSOFT ()WORD.

- *Concepts marginal to the database.* Say you are looking for documents about virtual reality systems and their potential impact on teaching. Searching in *ERIC*, you discover a number of descriptors on "teaching" but none on virtual reality, so you might use VIRTUAL()REALITY as a free-text expression.

The Ladder of Specificity: Broadening and Narrowing Searches

You will have noticed, as we have discussed searching techniques using controlled vocabulary and free-text, that the idea of broadening and narrowing search statements has come up more than once. It is possible to think of these methods of searching as falling on a continuum, or ladder, of specificity.

We have already seen that controlled vocabulary searching is a very specific technique. The fact that an indexer, after evaluating a document, has assigned it a particular term, gives us a reasonably good idea that that document is about that concept. With free-text techniques, because you are dealing with parts of the document that are in natural language (titles and abstracts), you do not have that kind of confidence about the topic covered based on the simple presence of a word or phrase.

Consider the diagram in figure 7.1:

If you find that you have too many documents or that those you have are too broad, you might decide to narrow your strategy by moving up the ladder, say from (5N) to (2N), or from (2N) to (2W), or from (W) to a controlled vocabulary term. You might also decide to add a field qualifier like /TI or /DE, or to limit the search to documents that have the controlled vocabulary terms you have chosen as major descriptors only (/MAJ). You will probably find that you will get fewer documents (you cannot get more), and that they will be more focused.

Fig. 7.1. The ladder of specificity.

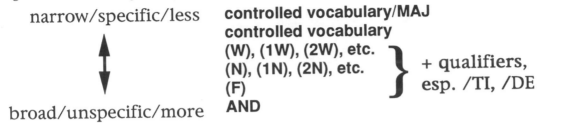

As you move from the bottom of this ladder toward the top, you will see that your strategies become more specific and narrower and will retrieve fewer documents. Conversely, as you move down, your strategies become less specific and broader and retrieve more documents. The /MAJ limit moves you up the ladder, as do field qualifiers, especially /TI to qualify to titles and /DE to limit to the descriptor field.

This may be intellectually interesting, but it is also of considerable use in searching. Depending on the nature of the topic, the user, and the database, you can choose to begin your search with a strategy or set of strategies at a selected level on the ladder. After reviewing initial results, you may decide that your documents are too broad, or that you have too many or too few. One of the ways in which you can cope with this is to move up or down on the ladder.

Similarly, if you are finding fewer documents than you would expect or none, or if you think they are maybe a bit too narrow, you might want to move down the ladder. You can move from controlled vocabulary to free-text, drop /MAJ or field qualifiers, or move to a broader free-text strategy: (W) to (1W) or (2W) or (N), (N) to (1N) or (2N) or (F), and so on.

These are not the only ways in which you can broaden or narrow searches, though. You can broaden a search by using more terms (ORing them together), using broader controlled vocabulary terms as they are marked in the thesaurus, or dropping a marginal concept altogether. You can narrow a search by using fewer terms, using narrower controlled vocabulary terms, adding another concept, or NOTting out a concept.

I am not a big fan of NOT—it is a seductively easy way of reducing the size of sets, but I think that it is often a bad idea. It is really easy to lose good documents that way. If you NOT a term out, especially using free-text, any good documents that happen to have that term will also go away. If you are **positive** that **any** document that contains that term is bad, under **all** circumstances, you might **think** about trying NOT, but I would be very careful about it. - JWJ

The following is a brief example showing this "ladder" at work in *ERIC* on the two-word phrase "test bias." We begin with the broadest strategy, by

searching for the two words in the same document, using AND:

```
     Set   Items   Description
     ---   -----   -----------
?s test and bias
           60274   TEST
           11176   BIAS   (AN INCLINATION, OR A LACK OF BALANCE (NOTE: ...)
     S1     2560   TEST AND BIAS
```

There are over 2,500 documents in *ERIC* that contain both the word TEST and the word BIAS. Now we move to a slightly narrower strategy, (F), and look for those words in the same field:

```
?s test(f)bias
          60274   TEST
          11176   BIAS  (AN INCLINATION, OR A LACK OF BALANCE (NOTE: ...)
    S2     2264   TEST(F)BIAS
```

We get fewer documents. Let us use NOT to see what we lost when we went to a narrower strategy:

```
?s s1 not s2
           2560   S1
           2264   S2
    S3      296   S1 NOT S2
?t 3/5/1
```

```
 3/5/1
EJ438240   PS519256
   The Representation of Females in Computer Education Text for Grades K-12.
   Brownell, Gregg
   Journal of Computing in Childhood Education; v3 n1 p43-54 1992
   ISSN: 1043-1055
   Language: English
   Document Type: JOURNAL ARTICLE (080); RESEARCH REPORT (143)
   Journal Announcement: CIJMAY92
   Investigated representation of females in computer education texts for
grades K-12 published within last decade. Females were found to be under
represented in positions of power and as active computer users although
overrepresented as passive in relation to the computer. In general, females
were well represented in the test, but the roles in which they were
represented were problematical. (Author/GLR)
   Descriptors: Attitudes; *Computers; Computer Science; *Elementary
Secondary Education; *Females; Males; Power Structure; *Sex Stereotypes;
*Textbook Bias; *Textbook Content; Textbook Selection
```

The above is one of those documents. You see that the words TEST and BIAS appear, but they are unrelated and not in the same field. The document has nothing to do with "test bias," and the extremely broad strategy using AND did not serve us well. We will continue to use narrower strategies like the following and view documents we exclude to demonstrate how moving up the ladder focuses searching more closely at each step.

```
?s test(10w)bias
          60274   TEST
          11176   BIAS  (AN INCLINATION, OR A LACK OF BALANCE (NOTE: ...)
    S4     1818   TEST(10W)BIAS
?s s2 not s4
           2264   S2
           1818   S4
    S5      446   S2 NOT S4
?t 5/5/1-3
```

```
 5/5/1
EJ435191   TM516021
   Differential Testlet Functioning: Definitions and Detection.
   Wainer, Howard; And Others
   Journal of Educational Measurement; v28 n3 p197-219 Fall 1991
   ISSN: 0022-0655
   Language: English
   Document Type: JOURNAL ARTICLE (080); EVALUATIVE REPORT (142)
```

Journal Announcement: CIJMAR92
A testlet is an integrated group of test items presented as a unit. The concept of testlet differential item functioning (testlet DIF) is defined, and a statistical method is presented to detect testlet DIF. Data from a testlet-based experimental version of the Scholastic Aptitude Test illustrate the methodology. (SLD)
  Descriptors: College Entrance Examinations; *Definitions; Graphs; *Item Bias; Item Response Theory; *Mathematical Models; *Scores; *Test Construction; Test Items
  Identifiers: Anchor Tests; Scholastic Aptitude Test; *Testlets

  5/5/2
EJ435180   TM516010
  Influence of Prior Distributions on Detection of DIF.
  Cohen, Allan S.; And Others
  Journal of Educational Measurement; v28 n1 p49-59 Spr 1991
  ISSN: 0022-0655
  Language: English
  Document Type: JOURNAL ARTICLE (080); RESEARCH REPORT (143)
  Journal Announcement: CIJMAR92
  Detecting differential item functioning (DIF) on test items constructed to favor 1 group over another was investigated on parameter estimates from 2 item response theory-based computer programs—BILOG and LOGIST—using data for 1,000 White and 1,000 Black college students. Use of prior distributions and marginal-maximum a posteriori estimation is discussed. (SLD)
  Descriptors: Black Students; College Students; *Computer Assisted Testing; Equations (Mathematics); *Estimation (Mathematics); Higher Education; *Item Bias; Item Response Theory; Mathematical Models; Maximum Likelihood Statistics; Multiple Choice Tests; *Racial Bias; Statistical Distributions; Test Items; Vocabulary Skills; White Students
  Identifiers: BILOG Computer Program; LOGIST Computer Program; *Prior Distributions

  5/5/3
EJ434122   CG539987
  Curriculum Bias and Reading Achievement Test Performance.
  Webster, Raymond E.; Braswell, Louise A.
  Psychology in the Schools; v28 n3 p193-99 Jul 1991
  ISSN: 0033-3085
  Available from: UMI
  Language: English
  Document Type: JOURNAL ARTICLE (080); RESEARCH REPORT (143)
  Journal Announcement: CIJMAR92
  Compared standardized achievement test performance of 62 second graders receiving instruction in 2 different reading curricula (Open Court and Houghton-Mifflin) to determine whether either curriculum generates different quantitative estimates of reading achievement. Found significant Curriculum X Test interaction, suggesting differences among tests in estimates of reading ability as function of reading program. (Author/NB)
  Descriptors: Achievement Tests; *Bias; *Curriculum; Elementary School Students; *Grade 2; Primary Education; *Reading Achievement; *Reading Tests

   The above are documents that have TEST and BIAS in the same field but not within 10 words of each other in that order. A couple of these are close, referring to item bias in tests, but they are still not quite on the mark. Another attempt yields the following:

?s test(3n)bias
            60274   TEST
            11176   BIAS (AN INCLINATION, OR A LACK OF BALANCE (NOTE: ...)

```
     S6     1786    TEST(3N)BIAS
?s s4 not s6
            1818    S4
            1786    S6
     S7       57    S4 NOT S6
?t 7/5/1-3
```

7/5/1
EJ369920   CG533825
  Personal Hypothesis Testing: The Role of Consistency and Self-Schema.
  Strohmer, Douglas C.; And Others
  Journal of Counseling Psychology; v35 n1 p56-65 Jan 1988
  Available from: UMI
  Language: English
  Document Type: JOURNAL ARTICLE (080); RESEARCH REPORT (143)
  Journal Announcement: CIJSEP88
  Studied how individuals test hypotheses about themselves. Examined extent
to which Snyder's bias toward confirmation persists when negative or
nonconsistent personal hypothesis is tested. Found negativity or positivity
did not affect hypothesis testing directly, though hypothesis consistency
did. Found cognitive schematic variable (vulnerability for depression),
related to confirmatory or nonconfirmatory personal hypothesis testing
about depression. (Author/KS)
  Descriptors: *Attitudes; *Bias; College Students; Depression (Psychology);
  Higher Education; *Hypothesis Testing; Personality Measures; *Reliability;
  *Schemata (Cognition); Self Concept; *Self Evaluation (Individuals);
Social Cognition

7/5/2
EJ348476   TM511742
  Positional Response Bias in Multiple-Choice Tests of Learning: Its
Relation to Testwiseness and Guessing Strategy
  Fagley, N. S.
  Journal of Educational Psychology; v79 n1 p95-97 Mar 1987
  Available from: UMI
  Language: English
  Document Type: JOURNAL ARTICLE (080); RESEARCH REPORT (143)
  Journal Announcement: CIJMAY87
  This article investigates positional response bias, testwiseness, and
guessing strategy as components of variance in test responses on
multiple-choice tests. University students responded to two content exams,
a testwiseness measure, and a guessing strategy measure. The proportion of
variance in test scores accounted for by positional response bias,
testwiseness, and guessing strategy was .18. (Author/JAZ)
  Descriptors: Achievement Tests; *Guessing (Tests); Higher Education;
*Multiple Choice Tests; *Response Style (Tests); *Test Theory; Test
Validity; *Test Wiseness

7/5/3
EJ324707   TM510829
  Children's Casual Attributions for Success and Failure in Achievement
Settings: A Meta-Analysis.
  Whitley, Bernard E., Jr.; Frieze, Irene Hanson
  Journal of Educational Psychology; v77 n5 p608-16 Oct 1985
  Available from: UMI
  Language: English
  Document Type: JOURNAL ARTICLE (080); RESEARCH REPORT (143)
  Journal Announcement: CIJJAN86
  A meta analysis of research on children's attributions for success and
failure was conducted to test the adequacy of the egotistic bias hypothesis
for children in grades one to seven. Results supported the egotism
hypothesis and indicated that both question wording and research context

are important determinants of children's attributions. (Author/BS)
   Descriptors: Academic Achievement; *Attribution Theory; Children;
Elementary Education; *Locus of Control; Measurement Techniques; Meta
Analysis; Models; *Research Design; *Self Concept; Student Motivation

   Again, the above are marginal at best, documents that have the two words within 10 words of each other but not within three. Narrowing still further, we get the following:


```
?s test(n)bias
          60274   TEST
          11176   BIAS  (AN INCLINATION, OR A LACK OF BALANCE (NOTE: ...)
     S8    1744   TEST(N)BIAS
?s s6 not s8
           1786   S6
           1744   S8
     S9      42   S6 NOT S8
?t 9/5/1-3
```

```
  9/5/1
EJ434122   CG539987
  Curriculum Bias and Reading Achievement Test Performance.
  Webster, Raymond E.; Braswell, Louise A.
  Psychology in the Schools; v28 n3 p193-99 Jul 1991
     ISSN: 0033-3085
  Available from: UMI
  Language: English
  Document Type: JOURNAL ARTICLE (080); RESEARCH REPORT (143)
  Journal Announcement: CIJMAR92
  Compared standardized achievement test performance of 62 second graders
receiving instruction in 2 different reading curricula (Open Court and
Houghton-Mifflin) to determine whether either curriculum generates
different quantitative estimates of reading achievement. Found significant
Curriculum X Test interaction, suggesting differences among tests in
estimates of reading ability as function of reading program. (Author/NB)
  Descriptors: Achievement Tests; *Bias; *Curriculum; Elementary School
Students; *Grade 2; Primary Education; *Reading Achievement; *Reading Tests
```

```
  9/5/2
EJ412458   SP519739
  An Empirical Comparison of Mantel-Haenszel and Rasch Procedures for
Studying Differential Item Functioning on Teacher Certification Tests.
  Engelhard, George, Jr.; And Others
  Journal of Research and Development in Education; v23 n3 p172-79 Spr 1990
  An earlier draft of this paper was presented at the Annual Meeting of the
American Educational Research Association (Anneheim, CA, March 1989).
  Available from: UMI
  Language: English
  Document Type: JOURNAL ARTICLE (080); RESEARCH REPORT (143)
  Journal Announcement: CIJDEC90
  Results are reported from a study that investigated the correspondence
between two methods used to assess differential item functioning (test item
bias). The study also explored the influence of sample size on the two
procedures. Although agreement between the two procedures was generally
good, the Rasch procedure was more reliable. (IAH)
  Descriptors: *Comparative Analysis; Elementary Secondary Education; *Item
Bias; Racial Differences; Teacher Certification; Testing; Test Items; *Test
Reliability
  Identifiers: Georgia Teacher Certification Testing Program; *Mantel
Haenszel Procedure; Rasch Model; Teacher Testing
```

```
9/5/3
EJ388894    EC212618
  Sources of Assessment Errors.
  Lowenthal, Barbara
  Academic Therapy; v24 n3 p285-88 Jan 1989
  Language: English
  Document Type: JOURNAL ARTICLE (080); NON-CLASSROOM MATERIAL (055)
  Journal Announcement: CIJSEP89
  The special educator must be aware of possible sources of error in
assessment of children with learning problems. Sources of error can be
attributed to unconscious examiner bias, ambiguous test responses,
linguistic and cultural differences of the examiner and examinee, previous
test-taking experience, and problems with test reliability and validity.
(JDD)
  Descriptors: *Disabilities; Elementary Secondary Education; *Evaluation
Problems; Experimenter Characteristics; *Student Evaluation; *Testing
Problems; Test Reliability; Test Validity; Test Wiseness
```

The above documents are getting closer. The words are now within three words of each other but not directly adjacent. There are probably some good retrievals there. But we can go still further with the following:

```
?s test(w)bias
          60274   TEST
          11176   BIAS   (AN INCLINATION, OR A LACK OF BALANCE (NOTE: ...)
    S10    1738   TEST(W)BIAS
?s s8 not s10
           1744   S8
           1738   S11
    S11       6   S8 NOT S10
?t 11/5/1

  11/5/1
EJ213055    RC503536
  In North Carolina: Overlooked Causes and Implications of School Finance
Disparities.
  Nord, Stephen; Ledford, Manfred H.
  Growth and Change; v10 n4 p16-19 Oct 1979
  Available from: Reprint: UMI
  Language: ENGLISH
  Document Type: JOURNAL ARTICLE (080); RESEARCH REPORT (143)
  Journal Announcement: CIJAPR80
  Describes model, data, results, and implications of a study attempting to
clarify two issues previously overlooked in studies of financing public
education with local property taxes: (1) that regionally aggregated data
may bias test results, and (2) that local fiscal response to grant programs
may vary with the wealth of school districts. (SB)
  Descriptors: Assessed Valuation; *Educational Finance; *Equalization Aid;
Federal Aid; *Financial Policy; *Government School Relationship; Grants;
Models; Policy Formation; *Property Taxes; Public Education; *School Taxes;
State Aid; State School District Relationship; Tax Allocation
  Identifiers: *North Carolina
```

You can see what happened: Asking for the two words directly adjacent but in either order pulls up false drops like this. This is to be expected in this case, because "bias test" is not the same as "test bias." However, a strategy such as BIAS(2N)TEST, which would look for "bias of a test," would also pull up documents such as the one above. Note that there are very few documents in this set.

As an aside, let us see what happens when we qualify one of these sets down to the title field alone:

```
?s S10/ti
              8870   TEST/TI
              1136   BIAS/TI  (AN IN-
    CLINATION, OR A LACK OF BALANCE
    (NOTE:...)
        S12      70   TEST(W)BIAS/TI
```

The unqualified set, S10, had over 1,700 documents; this one has 70. Obviously, the vast majority of occurrences of "test bias" as a phrase are in the abstract, descriptor, or identifier fields. Qualification can be an important tool, but at times it may be too specific.

We can narrow still further with the following:

```
?s test bias
    S13    1694   TEST BIAS  (UNFAIRNESS IN THE CONSTRUCTION, CONTENT,
                   ADM...)
?s s11 not s13
           1738   S11
           1694   S13
    S14      44   S11 NOT S13
?t 14/5/1-3
```

```
14/5/1
EJ296328   UD510634
  Beyond  IQ  Test  Bias: The National Academy Panel's Analysis of Minority
EMR Overrepresentation.
  Reschly, Daniel J.
  Educational Researcher; v13 n3 p15-19 Mar 1984
  Language: English
  Document Type: REVIEW LITERATURE (070)
  Journal Announcement: CIJJUN84
  Questions  educational  relevance  of direct measures of learning such as
the Learning Potential Assessment Device, assessment of biomedical factors,
and adaptative behavior measures. Notes increased discrepancies between EMR
and  average students in high school. Suggests a generic classification for
the  mildly  handicapped  and  the  combining  of  groups  for  educational
purposes. (CJM)
  Descriptors:   Academic   Achievement;   *Classification;   *Educational
Diagnosis;  Elementary  Secondary  Education;  *Learning  Disabilities;
Mainstreaming;  *Measurement Techniques; *Mild Mental Retardation; Minority
Group Children;  Racial Bias; Racial Composition; Research Needs; *Special
Education
  Identifiers:  Learning  Potential  Assessment  Device;  National Research
Council
```

```
14/5/2
EJ285500   EC152888
  Assessing Adaptive Behavior: Current Practices.
  Cantrell, Joan Kathryn
  Education and Training of the Mentally Retarded; v17 n2 p147-49 Apr 1982
  Available from: Reprint: UMI
  Language: English
  Document Type: JOURNAL ARTICLE (080); RESEARCH REPORT (143)
  Journal Announcement: CIJDEC83
  Twenty-nine  elementary  school  psychologists  were  interviewed  about
assessment  of  adaptive  behavior. Over 95 percent reported they routinely
assess  adaptive behavior skills, and 90 percent felt the assessment useful
in planning instruction. They rated methods of assessment (home observation
ranked  first),  cited  safeguards  against  test  bias,  discussed  school
policies, and recommended changes. (CL)
  Descriptors: *Adaptive Behavior (of Disabled); Attitudes; *Disabilities;
Elementary  Education;  Evaluation Methods; *School Psychologists; *Student
Evaluation
  14/5/3
```

EJ269692   CS706018
A Review and Critique of Procedures for Assessing Speaking and Listening Skills among Preschool through Grade Twelve Students.
  Rubin, Donald L.; And Others
  Communication Education; v31 n4 p285-303 Oct 1982
  Available from: Reprint: UMI
  Language: English
  Document Type: JOURNAL ARTICLE (080); RESEARCH REPORT (143)
  Journal Announcement: CIJFEB83
  Reviewed 45 assessment instruments with respect to content domains, response and scoring procedures, administrative feasibility, target populations, and potential sources of test bias. Identified priorities for future research and development in communication competence testing. (PD)
  Descriptors: Communication Research; *Communication Skills; *Educational Assessment; Elementary Secondary Education; Evaluation Methods; Listening Comprehension Tests; *Listening Skills; *Measurement Techniques; Preschool Education; *Speech Skills; *Test Reviews

    Interesting. The first of these documents is about "IQ test bias" among minority students, and so is marginal at best. The other two refer explicitly to "test bias" in the abstract but have not been indexed with the descriptor TEST BIAS. The indexers must have thought that this concept was marginal in these documents. We have one further step on the ladder to explore:

```
?s s13/maj
    S15      977    S13/MAJ
?s s13 not s15
           1694    S13
            977    S15
    S16      717    S13 NOT S15
?t 16/5/1-3
```

 16/5/1
EJ435542   CS742653
  Factors Influencing the English Reading Test Performance of Spanish-Speaking Hispanic Children.
  Garcia, Georgia Earnest
  Reading Research Quarterly; v26 n4 p371-92 1991
  ISSN: 0034-0553
  Available from: UMI
  Language: English
  Document Type: JOURNAL ARTICLE (080); RESEARCH REPORT (143)
  Journal Announcement: CIJAPR92
  Identifies factors that influence the English reading test performance of Hispanic children as compared with Anglo children in the same fifth and sixth grade classrooms. Suggests that Hispanic students' reading test scores seriously underestimate their reading comprehension potential. Discusses factors that adversely affect their test performance. (SR)
  Descriptors: Grade 5; Grade 6; *Hispanic Americans; Intermediate Grades; *Limited English Speaking; *Reading Achievement; *Reading Comprehension; Reading Research; *Reading Tests; Spanish Speaking; Test Bias; *Test Validity

 16/5/2
EJ435213   UD516166
  A Reconsideration of Testing for Competence Rather than for Intelligence.
  Barrett, Gerald V.; Depinet, Robert L.
  American Psychologist; v46 n10 p1012-24 Oct 1991
  ISSN: 0003-066X
  Available from: UMI
  Language: English

Document Type: JOURNAL ARTICLE (080); REVIEW LITERATURE (070)
Journal Announcement: CIJMAR92
Examines five themes in "Testing for Competence Rather than for "Intelligence" (D. C. McClelland, "American Psychologist," 1973), and reviews relevant literature. Despite wide acceptance of McClelland's views, other evidence that does not show that competency testing surpasses cognitive ability testing in predicting occupational behavior contradicts his assertions. (SLD)
  Descriptors: *Ability; Aptitude Tests; Cognitive Tests; *Intelligence; Intelligence Tests; Occupational Tests; *Prediction; Socioeconomic Status; *Success; Test Bias; Testing Problems; Test Use
  Identifiers: *Competency Based Evaluation; Occupational Behavior

  16/5/3
EJ435179   TM516009
  Gender Bias in Predicting College Academic Performance: A New Approach Using Item Response Theory.
  Young, John W.
  Journal of Educational Measurement; v28 n1 p37-47 Spr 1991
  An earlier version of this paper was presented at the Annual Meeting of the American Educational Research Association (Boston, MA, April 16-20, 1990).
  ISSN: 0022-0655
  Language: English
  Document Type: JOURNAL ARTICLE (080); RESEARCH REPORT (143); CONFERENCE PAPER (150)
  Journal Announcement: CIJMAR92
  Item response theory (IRT) is used to develop a form of adjusted cumulative grade point average (GPA) for use in predicting college academic performance appropriately for males and females. For 1,564 students at Stanford University (California), the IRT-based GPA was more predictable from preadmission measures than the cumulative GPA. (SLD)
  Descriptors: *Academic Achievement; *College Students; *Grade Point Average; Higher Education; *Item Response Theory; Mathematical Models; *Predictive Validity; Regression (Statistics); *Sex Bias; Sex Differences; Test Bias
  Identifiers: Graded Response Model; Stanford University CA

The documents above have the descriptor TEST BIAS but not as a major descriptor, and they make up fewer than half of the total number of documents that have been indexed with this term. Clearly, these documents are about test bias, but it appears that this is not a central concept in any of them. If we look at the /MAJ set, though, we see the following:

?t 15/5/1-3

  15/5/1
EJ438616   TM516192
  Content Effects on Word Problem Performance: A Possible Source of Test Bias?
  Chipman, Susan F.; And Others
  American Educational Research Journal; v28 n4 p897-915 Win 1991
  ISSN: 0002-8312
  Available from: UMI
  Language: English
  Document Type: JOURNAL ARTICLE (080); RESEARCH REPORT (143)
  Journal Announcement: CIJMAY92
  The effects of problem content on mathematics word problem performance were explored for 128 male and 128 female college students solving problems with masculine, feminine, and neutral (familiar and unfamiliar) cover stories. No effect of sex typing was found, and a small, but highly significant, effect was found for familiarity. (SLD)
  Descriptors: *College Students; Comparative Testing; Familiarity; Females;

Higher Education; Males; *Mathematics Tests; *Problem Solving; *Sex Differences; Sex Stereotypes; *Test Bias; Test Content; Test Items; *Word Problems (Mathematics)
  Identifiers: *Content Context Words

15/5/2
EJ438245   RC508610
  The Effects of Language Preference and Multitrial Presentation upon the Free Recall of Navajo Children.
  MacAvoy, Jim; Sidles, Craig
  Journal of American Indian Education; v30 n3 p33-43 May 1991
  ISSN: 0021-8731
  Available from: UMI
  Language: English
  Document Type: JOURNAL ARTICLE (080); RESEARCH REPORT (143)
  Journal Announcement: CIJMAY92
  Eighty Navajo-speaking students, aged 8-10, were administered free recall word lists in Navajo or English using a multitrial assessment format. Recall rates were higher in Trials 1 and 2 for those receiving Navajo words than for those receiving English words, but there were no differences on later trials. Contains 27 references. (SV)
  Descriptors: *American Indian Education; American Indians; *Diagnostic Tests; *Educational Diagnosis; Elementary Education; Elementary School Students; Memory; *Recall (Psychology); Second Languages; *Test Bias; *Test Format
  Identifiers: Navajo (Nation)

15/5/3
EJ436909   TM516101
  Test Bias of a Kindergarten Screening Battery: Predicting Achievement for White and Native American Elementary Students.
  Stone, Brian J.; Gridley, Betty E.
  School Psychology Review; v20 n1 p132-39 1991
  ISSN: 0279-6015
  Available from: UMI
  Language: English
  Document Type: JOURNAL ARTICLE (080); RESEARCH REPORT (143)
  Journal Announcement: CIJAPR92
  The relationship between a kindergarten screening battery (KSB) and scores on the Stanford Achievement Test was studied as a function of race for 519 white and 183 Native American students in kindergarten through grade 4. Prediction of the child's achievement test scores is more accurate when race is considered. (SLD)
  Descriptors: *Achievement Tests; *American Indians; Comparative Testing; Elementary Education; *Elementary School Students; Predictive Measurement; Racial Bias; Racial Differences; Scores; Screening Tests; Special Education; *Test Bias; *White Students
  Identifiers: *KSB Screening Battery; *Stanford Achievement Tests

We see immediately that this is a very focused set. For a real search, then, we may decide to begin with a controlled vocabulary term or even limit that to a major descriptor and then broaden out if necessary. Of course, in practice, you do not have the time or opportunity to know this kind of detail about terms, so you make your best judgment about where to begin and then move up or down the ladder as you see fit as the search progresses.

> *Your initial choice of where on the ladder to start your search depends on your expectations of search outcome. Do you expect to find a lot of material? Postings figures in the thesaurus, when available, can help you make this decision, as can personal experience and perhaps information from the user. - GW*

Search Example

The sample search we will work through here is in response to the search request form, figure 7.2. The patron is asking for documents to help her make a decision on a future career path. She has heard about "chief information officers" (CIOs), an emerging title in corporations that designates people who are in charge of all information services in the organization. She has a background in business and an interest in information issues (her mother was a librarian) and would like to know what articles have been written about the career paths taken by CIOs.

You decide to search in *ABI/Inform*, one of the databases in the general business area. The only problem is that your thesaurus for *ABI/Inform* is quite out of date (due to budget cutbacks), and this thesaurus gives very little information in any event. You check it and find no descriptor for "chief information officer" but a few for "careers," which you enter on your strategy plan. You choose to do a free-text search, reasonably broad, for "chief information officer" and see what happens. The search begins as follows:

```
DIALOG INFORMATION SERVICES
PLEASE LOGON:
  * * * * * * *
ENTER PASSWORD:
  * * * * * * *


Welcome to DIALOG
Dialog level 29.01.05B


Last logoff: 08jun92 09:23:18
Logon file001 08jun92 10:22:09
* * *  TEXTLINE is now available. Begin TXTLN or TEXTLINE * * *
* * *  File 113 is not working  * * *


File   1:ERIC   66-92/MAY.
FILE 1: Price changes will go into effect June 1, 1992.
Please see HOMEBASE Announcements for more details.

     Set   Items  Description
     ---   -----  -----------
?b 15
     08jun92 10:22:17 User007659 Session B815.1
          $0.03    0.002 Hrs File1
    $0.03   Estimated cost File1
    $0.03   Estimated cost this search
    $0.03   Estimated total session cost   0.002 Hrs.


File  15:ABI/INFORM   71-92/MAY WEEK 5
       (Copr. 1992 UMI/Data Courier)
**File 15: More full-text now available!

     Set   Items  Description
     ---   -----  -----------
?s chief()information()officer or cio
         22195   CHIEF
        103140   INFORMATION
         12594   OFFICER
           407   CHIEF(W)INFORMATION(W)OFFICER
           850   CIO
    S1    1059   CHIEF()INFORMATION()OFFICER OR CIO
```

About a thousand documents are retrieved; this appears to have been a good choice. You have a few good controlled vocabulary terms for "career plans," but you decide to expand on the word CAREER to see how many hits are involved and if any new terms have entered the vocabulary:

Fig. 7.2. Search request form.

Search Request Form

Please give a brief narrative description of your topic (use back if necessary):

I'm interested in <u>Chief information officers</u> of corporations — how do they get their jobs and what paths do their <u>careers</u> take?

Do you know of any index terms, vocabulary terms, or search terms that would be useful in searching for documents on this topic? Please list them here, or underline them in the above description.

CIO

Do you know of any authors or documents relevant to this topic? Please specify them here.

No

Type of materials of interest to you (circle):

Journal Articles	(Y) N	Conference Papers	Y (N)
Reports	Y (N)	Dissertation	Y (N)

Other (specify): News articles, magazines

Years to be covered: 1980 –

Languages of interest (list): English

Please give any other information you think might be helpful in formulating a search strategy on the back.

```
?e career

Ref    Items   Index-term
E1        10   CAREENING
E2         1   CAREENS
E3     11072  *CAREER
E4      1782   CAREER ADVANCEMENT
E5      1804   CAREER DEVELOPMENT PLANNING
E6         1   CAREERCOM
E7         4   CAREERGUARD
E8         2   CAREERING
E9         9   CAREERISM
E10       14   CAREERIST
E11       44   CAREERISTS
E12        1   CAREEROB

          Enter P or E for more
?p

Ref    Items   Index-term
E13        1   CAREERORIENTED
E14        1   CAREERPOWER
E15     3932   CAREERS
E16        1   CAREERSHIP
E17        1   CAREERSYSTEM
E18        1   CAREERSYSTEMS
E19       10   CAREERTRACK
E20        5   CAREERWATCH
E21        2   CAREERWEAR
E22        1   CAREERWISE
E23        1   CAREET
E24        1   CAREFACILITIES

          Enter P or E for more
```

The three terms you had chosen are here, and none of them seems to be overwhelmingly large. You select them all, being careful to qualify CAREERS to the descriptor field, to avoid searching it free-text. The results are as follows:

```
?s e4 or e5 or e15/de
          1782   CAREER ADVANCEMENT
          1804   CAREER DEVELOPMENT PLANNING
          1423   CAREERS/DE
    S2    4293   "CAREER ADVANCEMENT" OR "CAREER DEVELOPMENT PLANNING" OR
                 "CAREERS"/DE
?s s1 and s2
          1059   S1
          4293   S2
    S3      31   S1 AND S2
?t 3/8/1-7

 3/8/1
00610689    DIALOG FILE 15     ABI/INFORM     92-25792
                 **USE FORMAT 9 FOR FULL TEXT**
Picture  Yourself  as a CIO? Be Sure Your Image Is Current    WORD COUNT:
856
GEOGRAPHIC NAMES: US
DESCRIPTORS: Chief information officers; Changes; Career development
    planning; Recommendations
CLASSIFICATION CODES: 2130 (CN=Executives); 6200 (CN=Training &
```

development); 9190 (CN=United States)

3/8/2
00604201   DIALOG FILE 15   ABI/INFORM   92-19304
                  USE FORMAT 9 FOR FULL TEXT
Microcomputer Maven Got His Start in the Mainframe World   WORD COUNT:
1363
COMPANY NAMES: Corporate Association of Microcomputer Professionals; Simon
& Schuster Inc; I-N Tek
GEOGRAPHIC NAMES: US
DESCRIPTORS: Systems management; Qualifications; Information systems;
   Trends; Career advancement; Manycompanies; Manypeople
CLASSIFICATION CODES: 5220 (CN=Data processing management); 6200
   (CN=Training & development); 9190 (CN=United States)

3/8/3
00602737   DIALOG FILE 15   ABI/INFORM   92-17840
                  USE FORMAT 9 FOR FULL TEXT
Decentralizing Systems Is Not the Best Solution for Everyone
WORD COUNT: 1511
COMPANY NAMES: Telephone & Data Systems Inc; Plochman Inc; Perkins Coie
GEOGRAPHIC NAMES: US
DESCRIPTORS: Centralized; Information systems; Systems management; Women;
   Career advancement; Manycompanies
CLASSIFICATION CODES: 5240 (CN=Software & systems); 6100 (CN=Human resource
   planning); 9190 (CN=United States)

3/8/4
00595537   DIALOG FILE 15   ABI/INFORM   92-10710
                  USE FORMAT 9 FOR FULL TEXT
There Are Cracks, but Glass Ceiling Is Still Mostly Intact   WORD COUNT:
975
COMPANY NAMES: Mervyns; C & J Clark America Inc
GEOGRAPHIC NAMES: US
DESCRIPTORS: Women; Information systems; Departments; Career advancement;
   Sex discrimination
CLASSIFICATION CODES: 5220 (CN=Data processing management); 6200
   (CN=Training & development); 9190 (CN=United States)

3/8/5
00589303   DIALOG FILE 15   ABI/INFORM   92-04476
                  USE FORMAT 9 FOR FULL TEXT
High Achievers Retrace Their Steps   WORD COUNT: 1659
COMPANY NAMES: Avon Products Inc; Bank of Boston Corp; Dow Jones & Co Inc;
K mart Corp; Lockheed Corp
GEOGRAPHIC NAMES: US
DESCRIPTORS: Information systems; Executives; Career advancement; Skills;
   Education; Training; Manycompanies
CLASSIFICATION CODES: 5220 (CN=Data processing management); 6200
   (CN=Training & development); 9190 (CN=United States)

3/8/6
00585186   DIALOG FILE 15   ABI/INFORM   92-00359
                  USE FORMAT 9 FOR FULL TEXT
Today's Healthcare Environment: New Career Trends and Opportunities
WORD COUNT: 1097
GEOGRAPHIC NAMES: US
DESCRIPTORS: Hospitals; Executives; Career advancement; Trends; Skills;
   Industrywide conditions
CLASSIFICATION CODES: 9190 (CN=United States); 8320 (CN=Health care
   industry); 6100 (CN=Human resource planning); 2130 (CN=Executives)

```
3/8/7
00584060     DIALOG FILE 15    ABI/INFORM      91-58407
                    **USE FORMAT 9 FOR FULL TEXT**
If You Want to Manage, Start with Yourself     WORD COUNT: 791
GEOGRAPHIC NAMES: US
DESCRIPTORS: Career development planning; Recommendations; Goals;
    Information systems; Departments; Management
CLASSIFICATION CODES: 9190 (CN=United States); 5220 (CN=Data processing
    management); 6200 (CN=Training & development)
```

The first of these documents above is clearly on the right track and shows us that there is now a descriptor CHIEF INFORMATION OFFICERS, which apparently has been added to the thesaurus since the edition you used. The other documents are OK, but they look a bit further afield. We notice that these documents are all available in full text, which means that we are searching not only titles, abstracts, and indexing terms but also the full text of the documents themselves. This is very tricky business (we will talk much more about full-text searching in chapter 11), and we probably should avoid this field. But as long as we are here, let us see what a couple of these documents look like in full text, how they were retrieved, and whether or not they are useful.

```
?t 3/9/4,7

  3/9/4
  00595537     DIALOG FILE 15     ABI/INFORM     92-10710
  There Are Cracks, but Glass Ceiling Is Still Mostly Intact
  Marenghi, Catherine
  Computerworld v26n5  PP: 85  Feb 3, 1992 CODEN: CMPWAB  ISSN: 0010-4841
  JRNL CODE: COW
  DOC TYPE: Journal article  LANGUAGE: English   LENGTH: 1 Pages
  AVAILABILITY: Fulltext online. Photocopy available from ABI/INFORM 6206.00
  WORD COUNT: 975
```

ABSTRACT: For women in information systems (IS), financial services, high technology, health care, and pharmaceuticals offer the brightest prospects, while manufacturing and retailing pose the biggest hurdles. Insurance has traditionally employed large numbers of women, and many are finding their way to the top levels. Women make up roughly 45% of John Hancock Mutual Life Insurance Co.'s IS staff. The high-tech area is viewed as a boon to women because technically oriented companies emphasize capability over gender. Health care is another information-intensive business where IS talent is highly valued. Amid all this promise, however, a glass ceiling still exists for women. Even though women may run parts of IS, the top position is usually held by a man. Despite this fact, Patricia Wallington of Xerox Corp.'s US Marketing Group believes that the outlook for women IS managers in the 1990s will be bright due to their holistic style of management.

TEXT: Financial services, high technology, health care and pharmaceuticals offer the brightest prospects for women in information systems, while manufacturing and retailing pose the biggest hurdles, according to industry watchers, recruiters and women IS professionals.

In the financial services industries—insurance, banking and brokerage—women are most likely to hold senior management positions, not just in IS but across the board, according to Catalyst for Women, Inc., a not-for-profit research organization in New York. In a recent cross-industry survey, Catalyst found that 28% of financial services companies—more than any other industry—report that 11% of senior managers are women. All other industries average about 5%.

"The IS management positions I see (women) filling are in banking," says

(Text continues on page 107.)

Mary K. Hamm, a partner at the recruitment firm Romac & Associates in Phdadelphia. The reason? "Some time ago, the industry didn't pay well, and that created advancement opportunities for women and minorities in IS."

INSURANCE PLACE TO BE
Insurance, like banking, has traditionally employed large numbers of women, and many are finding their way to the top. At John Hancock Mutual Life Insurance Co. in Boston, the IS organization is "peppered at all levels" with women, according to Lee Wise, manager of employment. Women make up roughly 45% of John Hancock's IS staff, Wise estimates.

After financial services, Hamm sees pharmaceuticals as the biggest growth area for women, citing Merck & Co., McNeil Pharmaceutical and Smithkline Beecham Corp. as companies with women in IS leadership jobs.

LESS HIGH-TECH PREJUDICE

Recruiter Cissy Van Balen, president of King & Van Balen, Inc. in Research Triangle Park, N.C., sees the high-tech area as a boon to women because technically oriented companies emphasize capability over gender.

While high-tech companies have relatively few women in IS, Patricia Wallington, chief information officer at Rochester, N.Y.-based Xerox Corp.'s U.S. Marketing Group, says she believes that actually may be good. "Wherever there is a scarcity of a resource, you get evaluations based on true performance, not politics," she says.
That scarcity has hit home for Andrea Cunningham, who is president of her own public relations firm, Santa Clara, Calif.-based Cunningham Communication, Inc. In her more than four years working with one of the top electronics companies in the U.S., Cunningham has interacted with only three women. "The problem is not one of male prejudice, but the fact that too few women are interested in the field," Cunningham observes.

Health care is another information-intensive business where IS talent is highly valued, says Patricia Skarulis, vice president and CIO at Rush-Presbyterian-St. Luke's Medical Center, a $660 million academic medical center in Chicago. Because of major challenges facing health care, including political pressures to reform the system and hold down costs, "This is a particularly good field for IS people," Skarulis notes. "Women in IS can make a real contribution here."

FEMALE BARRIERS
.
.
.

[rest of the record is omitted for space]

THIS IS THE FULL-TEXT. COPYRIGHT: Copyright CW Publishing Inc 1991

COMPANY NAMES:
Mervyns (DUNS:00-796-8670)
C & J Clark America Inc (DUNS:00-300-4207)
GEOGRAPHIC NAMES: US
DESCRIPTORS: Women; Information systems; Departments; Career advancement;
   Sex discrimination
CLASSIFICATION CODES: 5220 (CN=Data processing management); 6200
   (CN=Training & development); 9190 (CN=United States)

3/9/7
00584060   DIALOG FILE 15   ABI/INFORM   91-58407
If You Want to Manage, Start with Yourself
Knight, Glen

(*Continues on page 106.*)

Computerworld v25n46   PP: 105 Nov 18, 1991 CODEN: CMPWAB   ISSN: 0010-4841
JRNL CODE: COW
DOC TYPE: Journal article LANGUAGE: English   LENGTH: 1 Pages
AVAILABILITY: Fulltext online. Photocopy available from ABI/INFORM 6206.00
WORD COUNT: 791

ABSTRACT: Those individuals who feel they have the disposition and can
achieve the skills necessary to become an information systems (IS) manager
should start grooming themselves immediately for the desired position.
There are several steps in the process: 1. Plot a path and set a target
date for reaching each stage or goal. 2. Talk to your manager after setting
your goals. 3. Find a mentor who can help you develop your management
skills. 4. Take classes in supervisory and managerial education. 5. Learn
the IS business. 6. Develop a network of contacts. 7. Work on your
attitude, emphasizing the positive and learning the value of team effort.
8. Observe the dress of other managers in the organization.

TEXT: Many IS professionals fail to make the transititon to management—not
because they wouldn't be good at it, but because they didn't think ahead.
The time to prepare for a management job is not when it's handed to you,
but while you are a technician.

Your first priority is to decide whether you actually want to be a manager.
That sounds simplistic, but it's an important consideration. Many people
are attracted to management by the challenge, personal growth, status and
money. Many fail to consider some of the downside factors—politics,
personnel problems, numerous meetings and long hours—until they are facing
them on a day-to-day basis.

If you know you are cut out to be a manager, and those challeges don't faze
you, you can start grooming yourself right now for the job you eventually
want to hold. Here's how:

Step 1. Plot your path. For example, an application programmer may decide
to reach a career goal of chief information officer by first becoming a
project leader, then a programming manager and ultimately an information
systems director.

Set a target date for reaching each stage. Putting your gals into such
concrete terms will help keep you on track and alert to the need for action
when the time is appropriate.
Plans must be flexible, of course. Real life doesn't always follow a preset
course. Review your plan occasionally and make adjustments where necessary,
always keeping the end goal in sight.

Step 2. Talk to your manager after you have set your goals. This will help
in two ways. First, you may be able to find out whether the manager has
plans to move up, which could possibly create an opening for you.

    .
    .
    .

[rest of the record is omitted for space]

GEOGRAPHIC NAMES: US
DESCRIPTORS: Career development planning; Recommendations; Goals;
    Information systems; Departments; Management
CLASSIFICATION CODES: 9190 (CN=United States); 5220 (CN=Data processing
    management); 6200 (CN=Training & development)

The above selections are not bad, but we might want to narrow this search a bit by qualifying down to fewer fields, as in the following:

```
?s (chief()information()officer? or cio or cios)/ti,ab,de
          18970   CHIEF/TI,AB,DE
          95166   INFORMATION/TI,AB,DE
          20378   OFFICER?/TI,AB,DE
            530   CHIEF/TI,AB,DE(W)INFORMATION/TI,AB,DE(W)OFFICER?/TI,AB,DE
            704   CIO/TI,AB,DE
            137   CIOS/TI,AB,DE
     S4   979   (CHIEF()INFORMATION()OFFICER? OR CIO OR CIOS)/TI,AB,DE
?s s4 and s2
            979   S4
           4293   S2
     S5    27   S4 AND S2
?t 5/8/1-7
```

```
5/8/1
00610689     DIALOG FILE 15     ABI/INFORM     92-25792
                  **USE FORMAT 9 FOR FULL TEXT**
Picture  Yourself  as a CIO? Be Sure Your Image Is Current   WORD COUNT:
856
GEOGRAPHIC NAMES: US
DESCRIPTORS: Chief information officers; Changes; Career development
   planning; Recommendations
CLASSIFICATION CODES: 2130 (CN=Executives); 6200 (CN=Training &
   development); 9190 (CN=United States)
```

```
5/8/2
00587028     DIALOG FILE 15     ABI/INFORM     92-02201
                  **USE FORMAT 9 FOR FULL TEXT**
There's a Fine Line Between Enough Variety and Too Much   WORD COUNT: 917
GEOGRAPHIC NAMES: US
DESCRIPTORS: Career development planning; Information systems; Departments;
   Career advancement; Experience
CLASSIFICATION CODES: 5220 (CN=Data processing management); 6200
   (CN=Training & development); 9190 (CN=United States)
```

```
5/8/3
00585186     DIALOG FILE 15     ABI/INFORM     92-00359
                  **USE FORMAT 9 FOR FULL TEXT**
Today's Healthcare Environment: New Career Trends and Opportunities
WORD COUNT: 1097
GEOGRAPHIC NAMES: US
DESCRIPTORS: Hospitals; Executives; Career advancement; Trends; Skills;
   Industrywide conditions
CLASSIFICATION CODES: 9190 (CN=United States); 8320 (CN=Health care
   industry); 6100 (CN=Human resource planning); 2130 (CN=Executives)
```

```
5/8/4
00555993     DIALOG FILE 15     ABI/INFORM     91-30351
Women in Communications
COMPANY NAMES: Weyerhaeuser Information Systems; Boeing Computer Services
Co; Currid & Co
GEOGRAPHIC NAMES: US
DESCRIPTORS: Women; Telecommunications industry; Careers; Manycompanies;
   Manypeople
CLASSIFICATION CODES: 9190 (CN=United States); 8330 (CN=Broadcasting &
   telecommunications)
```

(*Continues on page 108.*)

```
 5/8/5
00544171       DIALOG FILE 15      ABI/INFORM       91-18516
                     **USE FORMAT 9 FOR FULL TEXT**
CIO Careers More Lucrative, but Risky      WORD COUNT: 522
DESCRIPTORS: Chief information officers; Wages & salaries; Career
    development planning; Career advancement; Skills; Predictions
CLASSIFICATION CODES: 2130 (CN=Executives); 6200 (CN=Training &
    development)


 5/8/6
00531381       DIALOG FILE 15      ABI/INFORM       91-05725
                     **USE FORMAT 9 FOR FULL TEXT**
The Minority Void: Striving Against All Odds      WORD COUNT: 795
COMPANY NAMES: Intertechnology Group Inc; Port Authority of New York & New
Jersey
GEOGRAPHIC NAMES: US
DESCRIPTORS: Minorities; Chief information officers; Career advancement;
    Personal profiles
CLASSIFICATION CODES: 6200 (CN=Training & development); 2130
    (CN=Executives); 9190 (CN=United States); 9160 (CN=Biographical)


 5/8/7
00526155       DIALOG FILE 15      ABI/INFORM       91-00499
Life in IS: Women Under Glass
DESCRIPTORS: Information systems; Departments; Executives; Career
    advancement; Women; Career development planning; Wages & salaries;
    Statistical data
CLASSIFICATION CODES: 5220 (CN=Data processing management); 2130
    (CN=Executives); 6200 (CN=Training & development); 9140 (CN=Statistical
    data)
```

The foregoing selections appear more focused, and S5 looks like a good set. As an experiment, let us see what happens if we use just the descriptor we found:

```
?s chief information officers
     S6      310   CHIEF INFORMATION OFFICERS
?s s6 and s2
             310   S6
            4293   S2
     S7        9   S6 AND S2
?t 7/8/1-9


 7/8/1
00610689       DIALOG FILE 15      ABI/INFORM       92-25792
                     **USE FORMAT 9 FOR FULL TEXT**
Picture  Yourself  as a CIO? Be Sure Your Image Is Current     WORD COUNT:
856
GEOGRAPHIC NAMES: US
DESCRIPTORS: Chief information officers; Changes; Career development
    planning; Recommendations
CLASSIFICATION CODES: 2130 (CN=Executives); 6200 (CN=Training &
    development); 9190 (CN=United States)


 7/8/2
00544171       DIALOG FILE 15      ABI/INFORM       91-18516
                     **USE FORMAT 9 FOR FULL TEXT**
CIO Careers More Lucrative, but Risky      WORD COUNT: 522
DESCRIPTORS: Chief information officers; Wages & salaries; Career
    development planning; Career advancement; Skills; Predictions
CLASSIFICATION CODES: 2130 (CN=Executives); 6200 (CN=Training &
    development)
```

```
7/8/3
00531381      DIALOG FILE 15      ABI/INFORM      91-05725
                 **USE FORMAT 9 FOR FULL TEXT**
The Minority Void: Striving Against All Odds      WORD COUNT: 795
COMPANY NAMES: Intertechnology Group Inc; Port Authority of New York & New
Jersey
GEOGRAPHIC NAMES: US
DESCRIPTORS: Minorities; Chief information officers; Career advancement;
    Personal profiles
CLASSIFICATION CODES: 6200 (CN=Training & development); 2130
    (CN=Executives); 9190 (CN=United States); 9160 (CN=Biographical)


7/8/4
00485516      DIALOG FILE 15      ABI/INFORM      90-11273
CIO Is Starting to Stand for "Career Is Over"
DESCRIPTORS: Chief information officers; Terminations; Employment security;
    Information systems; Computer networks; Systems development; Information
    management; Career advancement
CLASSIFICATION CODES: 2130 (CN=Executives); 5220 (CN=Data processing
    management); 6100 (CN=Human resource planning); 6200 (CN=Training &
    development)


7/8/5
00463658      DIALOG FILE 15      ABI/INFORM      89-35445
Careers in Crisis
DESCRIPTORS: Chief information officers; Career advancement; Problems;
    Uncertainty; Influence; Strategy; Manycompanies
CLASSIFICATION CODES: 5220 (CN=Data processing management); 2130
    (CN=Executives); 6200 (CN=Training & development)


7/8/6
00459600      DIALOG FILE 15      ABI/INFORM      89-31387
When a Nontechie Takes Over IS
DESCRIPTORS: Information systems; Departments; Non-; Technical; Chief
    information officers; Career advancement; Advantages
CLASSIFICATION CODES: 5220 (CN=Data processing management); 2130
    (CN=Executives)


7/8/7
00397716      DIALOG FILE 15      ABI/INFORM      88-14549
Focused on Success: Kodak's Hudson Strives to Create MIS Harmony
COMPANY NAMES: Eastman Kodak Co
DESCRIPTORS: Case studies; Electronics industry; Cameras; Chief information
    officers; Personal; Profiles; Career advancement
CLASSIFICATION CODES: 9110 (CN=Company specific); 8650 (CN=Electrical &
    electronics industries); 9160 (CN=Biographical); 2130 (CN=Executives)


7/8/8
00395875      DIALOG FILE 15      ABI/INFORM      88-12708
Smith Pumps Arco's MIS, Staff's Morale
COMPANY NAMES: ARCO
DESCRIPTORS: Personal; Profiles; Chief information officers; Career
    advancement; Management styles; Case studies; Petroleum industry
CLASSIFICATION CODES: 9160 (CN=Biographical); 2130 (CN=Executives); 5220
    (CN=Data processing management); 9110 (CN=Company specific); 8510
    (CN=Petroleum industry)


7/8/9
00393609      DIALOG FILE 15      ABI/INFORM      88-10442
Courtship Rituals
```

```
DESCRIPTORS: Chief information officers; Federal employees; Air forces;
   Personal; Profiles; Implementations; Technological change; Information
   management; Career development planning; Technology transfer
CLASSIFICATION CODES: 2130 (CN=Executives); 5220 (CN=Data processing
   management); 1120 (CN=Economic policy & planning); 9160
   (CN=Biographical)
```

The foregoing examples look very nice, and there is probably relevant material in S5 and S3 as well. You might want to give all these to the user, telling her which sets you think are most likely to be what she wanted. The following is the final DS:

```
?ds

Set      Items     Description
S1       1059      CHIEF()INFORMATION()OFFICER OR CIO
S2       4293      "CAREER ADVANCEMENT" OR "CAREER DEVELOPMENT PLANNING" OR "-
                   CAREERS"/DE
S3       31        S1 AND S2
S4       979       (CHIEF()INFORMATION()OFFICER? OR CIO OR CIOS)/TI,AB,DE
S5       27        S4 AND S2
S6       310       CHIEF INFORMATION OFFICERS
S7       9         S6 AND S2
```

You see a mix of strategies in the foregoing example: starting with a free-text strategy for one concept and a controlled vocabulary term for the other, finding a good index term but searching it a bit more broadly while still qualifying it somewhat, then finally trying out the index term by itself and getting fewer but probably higher-quality documents. This illustrates once again the trade-offs between free-text and controlled vocabulary strategies, between narrower and broader, between more and fewer.

Notes

[1]At present, DIALOG allows this number to be up to 127 in most files; it's unlimited in files that provide the full text of documents. We'll talk more about this in chapter 11.

[2]Notice the hyphen in the phrase: "thirty-item" as it appears in the title. In DIALOG, all internal punctuation (hyphens, apostrophes, slashes, quotation marks, etc.) is removed and replaced by spaces. Thus, when this document was processed, the hyphen was removed, and the words "thirty" and "item" went into the inverted file next to each other.

[3]These are based on categories given in an article by Elaine Wagner (September 1986), "False Drops—How They Arise...How to Avoid Them," *Online* 10(5):93-96.

[4]Markey et al. (1980), "An Analysis of Controlled Vocabulary and Free Text Search Statements in On-Line Searches," *Online Review* 4(3):225-36.

Over the years, much has been written about the *reference interview* in the traditional library setting, and attempts to define it go back as far as 1876.[1] It is generally agreed that the reference process involves an "interaction between the librarian, the library patron, and the library's resources in order to satisfy the patron's information needs."[2] In general, the term "reference interview" refers to the conversation that takes place between a reference librarian and a library patron for the purpose of clarifying the patron's information needs. The librarian's goals are to determine exactly what information the patron needs, how much information is needed, and the form in which the information is required. This interaction differs from an ordinary conversation in that it is generally more formal and structured.

8

THE SEARCH INTERVIEW

This chapter briefly reviews the traditional view of the reference process, discusses some of the proposed models for reference interaction, and discusses their application in the online situation. Many of these strategies will also apply to the interactions between reference librarians and users who are searching on CD-ROM databases.

Traditional Reference

The earliest writers on the requirements of the reference process were in agreement that it combines the concepts of communication or interview skills with a knowledge of reference sources. Over the years lists have been developed that itemize the general attributes required for successful reference service. Unfortunately they provide little practical guidance for the aspiring practitioner.

Jennerich,[3] for example, lists 12 personal attributes of the librarian, divided between verbal and nonverbal skills. The verbal skills include remembering, paraphrasing, suggesting, encouraging, and using "open" questions (i.e., those requiring more than "yes" or "no" as an answer). It seems as if these characteristics might be summarized as "acting interested." The nonverbal skills he suggests include gestures, eye contact, facial expressions, and tone of voice, which also suggest the importance of displaying involvement. Body language such as posture, facial expressions, hand gestures, eye movements, and head nods are all indicators of approachability and have been shown to positively affect the level of user satisfaction.[4] Quint writes about body language of librarians:

Much of the interaction will be non-verbal. Body language will tell you a lot about the requestor's comfort with elements of the discussion. Remember that you send off signals as well. Be careful that the requestor does not misinterpret them. As a rule, you want clients to receive a general positive impression of your ability and willingness to solve their problems.[5]

The traditional approach to the reference interview is to try to match users to resources, based on the access points provided by the available retrieval systems—usually author, title, or Library of Congress List of Subject Headings (LCSH) in the manual situation. The typical interview is based on a series of "closed" questions, very similar to those posed on a search request form, that elicit responses from a specified range of choices.

Relatively recently, interest moved from lists of characteristics and the steps to be followed, to focus on the relationships among the four interacting elements of the reference process: the requester, the librarian, the query, and the system. A number of models of the reference interaction have been developed.

Models of the Reference Process

The development of such behavioral models of the reference process relied on theories taken from a number of other fields, including social work, psychology, journalism, and communication theory. The interaction between the requester and the librarian searcher has been described as "one of the most complex acts of human communication...(where) one person tries to describe to another person not something he knows, but rather something he does not know."[6] The inquiry is viewed as "a description of an area of doubt in which the question is open-ended, negotiable, and dynamic."[7] The emphasis is on the requester's difficulty in articulating his information need. It has also been suggested that the belief that the analyst may not understand or the system may not suit the request may lead the user to distort how he expresses it.[8]

Taylor has suggested a model that divides the information-seeking cycle into four successive levels: the visceral (unexpressed) need, the conscious (recognized) need, the formalized (expressed) need, and the compromised need. The compromised version is how the query is finally presented to the information system. The experienced information specialist has to work back through these levels in order to determine what is really required.

Remember how we started the eight-step procedure in chapter 6?

1.   Read the query.
1a.   Listen to the query.
1b.   Understand the query.

This may require quite a bit of negotiation, a lot of patience, and the use of all your skills of communication. - GW

It has been suggested that the use of "open" rather than "closed" questions improves the pace of the interchange between question and response and elicits more helpful responses from the requester.[9] Open questions begin with query words (what, when, why, etc.) and allow the respondent to answer at length, as opposed to the searcher using closed questions to control the discussion.

Dervin has suggested the idea of a "sense-making" model, focusing on "movement through time-space," which she believes underlies all information-seeking situations.[10] Information is depicted as a construct of the user, rather than having an independent existence in isolation. It is required by individuals to fill an information gap in a given real-life situation. She argues for the uniqueness of each information need and suggests that the same question may not require the same answer for different people or at different times.

Based on this idea and developing the open or closed question debate is her introduction of the idea of "neutral" questions. They are questions intended to help the librarian to learn the nature of the underlying situation, the gaps faced by the user, and the expected uses of the answers provided. This approach is also user oriented, in that it allows users to retain control over describing their needs and to identify the most important aspects for themselves. Here are some examples of neutral questions, taken from Dervin:[11]

To assess the situation:
  Tell me how this problem arose.
  What are you trying to do in this situation?
  What happened that got you stopped?

To assess the gaps:
  What would you like to know about X?
  What seems to be missing in your understanding of X?
  What are you trying to understand?

To assess the uses:
  How are you planning to use this information?
  If you could have exactly the help you wanted, what would it be?
  How will this help you? What will it help you do?

Despite extensive research, little of this theoretical base has so far been incorporated into professional training courses. Nevertheless, communication skills are obviously important for any public service professional, and all models stress that they are particularly important in the online negotiation interview, where misunderstandings are apt to be expensive.

"What transpires during this exchange affects the formulation, the search itself, and even the user's opinion of the results. The interview, then, becomes the crucial step in the overall computer search process."[12]

Explaining Online Systems

Many clients still have minimal ideas about what an online search can provide and what it cannot.

Reminds me of that undergraduate who arrived at 6:15 P.M. asking for an online search because he had to make a class presentation at 7 P.M.! He was sadly disillusioned to discover that there are no instant answers. I notice the same lack of understanding in relation to CD-ROM databases. Students are determined to use them, regardless of the fact that the most appropriate file for their particular query may be available only in print format. - GW

Library users need to be educated to the fact that they are not going to receive instantaneous information, unless it is available in full-text. In that case it is likely to be expensive and will still require synthesis and interpretation. They need to be told that in most situations the result of their search will be a list of citations that they will have to follow up in the library or elsewhere. Making this clear from the outset will prevent disappointment.

The searcher also needs to explain what types of searches can be best performed on a computer system. In general, the more complicated the question, the better it is suited to online searching, largely because it is more difficult to perform manually. The advantages of multiple access points, the ability to combine terms using logical operators, and the interactive nature of the search process all need to be explained. The limitations of online searching also need to be admitted, such as the limited time coverage of some databases and the impossibility of defining other than logical relationships. (Dog bites man versus man bites dog, for example.) It is important to confirm that an online search is appropriate for a specific query, because otherwise the request should be referred back to regular reference services.

Cost structures of the online system obviously need to be discussed, particularly when the client will be expected to pay any part of the cost. You need to explain that costs are assessed on a per record basis and that different formats are available. The option of printing citations with or without abstracts, online or offline, needs to be offered, together with an explanation of the likely time delays and cost differences. It is important to determine a rough estimate of the number of citations required and give an estimate of the likely cost of the search. The client may wish to review the choices made on the search request form in light of these explanations (see fig. 5.1).

The interview associated with CD-ROM database searching tends to be more relaxed than that for online, largely because charges will not be incurred directly during the search. Because CD-ROM searching is usually conducted by the user, most of this interaction is likely to occur during, rather than before, the search and to center on the use of the equipment and how to structure a search strategy. Less effort will, normally, be invested by the professional searcher in the analysis of the query and the choice of appropriate search terms, because the librarian's role has changed from search partner to search assistant. The elimination of the full reference interview in this situation has its unfortunate side. Examples abound of end-users scanning hundreds of citations looking for that elusive needle in the haystack, because they do not know how to reduce postings. It seems that libraries are currently committing more and more reference staff time to CD-ROM instruction and help, often employing student assistants to deal with the more mechanical tasks.[13] It is good practice for reference staff to check on first-time users while they are searching, because this is when explanations are apt to make the most sense. It will also encourage new client searchers to use CD-ROM systems again, and they will probably feel more comfortable asking for assistance when they need it in the future.

The variations in command languages and system features among competing vendors make multiple CD-ROMs a particular problem for novice searchers. (And some professionals are not too happy either. Imagine having to remember five different truncation symbols on seemingly identical systems, as our reference staff have to!) Although most CD-ROM products provide online or printed documenta-

tion or both, they are not always as helpful as they might be, and it is a fact of life that when faced with any type of technology users will turn to documentation only as a last resort.

> It is well known that many people will not use documentation at all; they prefer either to try to find online help systems, which are common but not inevitable and often not particularly helpful, or just to flail about and hope they get the idea or even just abandon ship. - JWJ

Setting Boundaries

Having established that an online search is indeed the correct way to go for a specific query, and that the patron understands the limitations and costs involved, we are ready to start discussing the search topic. The starting place is normally the written information request provided on the standardized request form. In some library situations this will be the only communication between the searcher and the requester, therefore the design of the form is crucially important. It should help the client define exactly what information is needed, how much output is required, and any limitations of time or language that exist. It should also help the searcher understand those needs. (See chapter 13 for more on the design of search request forms.)

Needless to say, most online searchers prefer to have a face-to-face interview with the requester, and most writers stress the importance of this style of negotiation. Many searchers also like to have the client present while the search is being conducted. This opportunity for the user to refine the search while it is being processed is one of the major advantages of online systems.[14] Cleverden has also stressed the importance of feedback in improving search results: "Frequently the search results will change as the user, having found some related documents, develops a clearer idea of exactly what he needs.... Alternatively, it may be that ... he will be guided to more effective search terms."[15]

It is this feedback between patron and system that minimizes the disadvantages of the delegated search process. Used in conjunction with the written request and pre-search interview these personal interactions save time and money, help to ensure that the results of the search are satisfactory, and in the long term may prevent the need for a follow-up search.

It is important for the searcher to know something about the subject field of the search topic and the relevant jargon and terminology, which may entail some background reading. It is helpful in this respect if the search request form can be made available in advance of the search appointment. It has been observed that the role of the librarian is to know how information is organized and where to find answers, rather than to know the answers directly, but it certainly seems that we need to know at least a little about almost everything. Knowing a little about your search topic, preferably in advance, is important not only in helping you with the selection of search terminology but also in communicating with your client and maintaining your professional credibility. You are not expected to be an expert in everything (indeed, many of your clients will be delighted to take that role), but you do need to be able to interact intelligently with them.

The major portion of the reference interview in the online setting is conducted prior to the search itself so as to minimize search costs. This means that it is important to establish effective communication strategies, because the role of the intermediary is "to clarify, expand, delimit, or otherwise modify the user's request so that it can be developed into an effective search strategy."[16]

There are many reasons why patrons' initial questions do not provide the librarian with accurate guidance to their real information needs. The librarian must be careful to avoid assumptions based on initial statements, past experience, or the user's appearance. The exact questions to ask cannot be specified, because every situation will be different, but neutral questions will prevent premature diagnosis. This type of clarification of the exact information need is particularly important in the online situation, where results cost money.

Negotiating Search Terms

We have talked about controlled vocabulary and free-text searching but have not really addressed the question of how to choose search terms. It has been found that allowing the user to suggest terms is not necessarily a productive strategy, and most search request forms specify a narrative statement of the information need. This may seem a strange approach, for who can know better what the user really needs than the user himself? It appears that his ability to express what he wants is inhibited by his perceptions of the system and its abilities. Talking through the whole information problem will help to expand or redefine the initial search statement. Make sure that you understand the question. The good searcher does not hesitate to consult a dictionary or to ask questions. The understanding of new ideas or concepts is often based on analogies to things that are familiar.[17]

We know that the initial search statement is a source of natural language terms, which can also provide lead-ins to the controlled vocabulary. Aside from the obvious terms, ask the user about key terminology and key sources. Oftentimes a crucial search term will not appear in the search statement or the thesaurus. It may be a new term, a colloquialism, a proper name, or an acronym.

A good example of this was a search request I received asking for information on the effect of teacher expectations on student academic performance and classroom behavior. I decided that *ERIC* was the appropriate database to search, and there were some useful thesaural terms available, such as teacher attitudes, student behavior, academic

achievement. I also decided to incorporate the term "teacher expectations" from the language of the query. This initial search turned out to be way too broad, even after it was limited to MAJor descriptors and the term "teacher attitudes" was dropped. Furthermore, the records did not look very useful. A pause for further discussion produced the term "Pygmalion effect," which had never been mentioned in the pre-search interview and was unfamiliar to me. But it turned out to be exactly what was needed.

Search terms come from many different places, and do not forget that new descriptors are being added to thesauri all the time. Word frequency lists, when available, and online EXPANDs can aid in the selection of free-text terms. Some search services have introduced their own equivalency links. These terms can include obvious linguistic matches, such as singular or plural and alternative spellings, or obvious conceptual links, such as alternative names for the same thing (e.g., U.S.S.R.=Russia=Soviet Union).[18]

You may need to explain what free-text searching means, so that the requester understands the differences between natural language and controlled vocabulary terms, and the value and limitations of each. Discuss the possibility of using truncation and select potential terms to be covered by truncating. When discussing phrases, point out that it is probably best to rely on the most essential words and allow for variant forms, rather than being exactly specific. You need to know whether you are aiming for a comprehensive search or just a few good references, as this affects the number of synonymous terms that you will include.

> When looking for search terms and preparing a search strategy I find it helpful to play a kind of game. I try to dream up titles that would make good answers to the query. (This requires a bit of imagination, but it is rather fun!) I then test my prepared strategy to check whether it would retrieve my imagined titles. If it would not, I have to do some adapting. - GW

You need to be sure that you understand the search topic thoroughly, especially the desired relationships among concepts. Ask intelligent questions about the information situation in general and how the information is to be used. Above all, act interested. Start acting as if it is a team project—talk about what WE will do. In general, "the librarian should assume a strong role in developing the search strategy."[19] This is your area of expertise, but remember that every search is a partnership affair.

Finally, anticipate possible problems that may crop up. At the very least have two alternative strategies prepared in advance. One will be used if you retrieve too few references—a broadening strategy. The other is for use if you retrieve too many postings—a restrictive strategy. Despite your best efforts, you may still find yourself having to improvise while you are online, because one of the major advantages of an online search is its interactive nature. You may need to slow down and view some titles in order to let the user provide feedback. She can identify the records that satisfy the search needs completely. Look for possible new terms in them that you might incorporate into the search. These new terms may also suggest possible alternative databases to search. It is time to stop searching when you have found enough material or have hit the cost cap. And most important, check with your user that the search results are satisfactory.

Presenting Search Results

Traditionally, the post-search role of the librarian has been to review the printout with the user, explain the search strategy, and make sure that the requester can decipher the printout and knows how to find the material. In the case of an absentee requester, the role of the searcher may be even simpler—stuff and address an envelope, or phone for a pickup.

The fact that most searchers nowadays use a microcomputer as their search terminal has provided new opportunities for enhancing the presentation of search results. Searches can be easily downloaded, reformatted on a word processor, and delivered to the client as a value-added professional end product, customized to the client's individual requirements.

The searcher can edit out confusing fields (code numbers or accession numbers, for example) and possibly add information on local holdings and interlibrary loan possibilities. The search results can be presented either as print via mail or fax, or as machine-readable data, either on disk or transmitted by E-mail. Policy decisions are needed regarding the amount of searcher time to be committed to editing and refining search results, and the question of how that time will be budgeted. There is interesting potential for improving the image of the search service overall through upgrading the presentation of the finished product. The presentation of numeric information in report or spreadsheet format, and the increased use of alternative telecommunications channels to transmit results will provide dramatic evidence of the library's use of advanced technology to enhance its user services. Such enhancements are particularly important in a situation where most searching is done by information seekers themselves using CD-ROM. It becomes vital that the professional search output should appear to be what it is—a professional product.

Notes

[1] Samuel Swett Green (October 1876), "Personal Relations Between Librarians and Readers," *Library Journal* 1:74-81.

[2] Gerald Jahoda, and Judith S. Braunagel (1980), *The Librarian and Reference Queries* (New York: Academic Press).

[3] Edward J. Jennerich, and Elaine Z. (Fall 1976), "Teaching the Reference Interview," *Journal of Education for Librarianship* 17:106-11.

[4] Helen M. Gothberg (July 1976), "Immediacy: A Study of Communication Effect on the Reference Process," *Journal of Academic Librarianship* 2(3):126-29.

[5] Barbara Quint (May 1991), "Inside a Searcher's Mind: The Seven Stages of an Online Search—Part 1," *Online* 15(3):13-18.

[6] Robert S. Taylor (May 1968), "Question-Negotiation and Information Seeking in Libraries," *College & Research Libraries* 29(3):178-94.

[7] Ibid.

[8] Sara D. Knapp (Spring 1978), "The Reference Interview in the Computer-Based Setting," *RQ* 17(3): 320-24.

[9] Marilyn Domas White (Summer 1981), "The Dimensions of the Reference Interview," *RQ* 20(4):373-81.

[10] Brenda Dervin, and Patricia Dewdney (Summer 1986), "Neutral Questioning: A New Approach to the Reference Interview," *RQ* 25(4):506-13.

[11] Ibid., 509.

[12] Stuart J. Kolner (January 1981), "Improving the MEDLARS Search Interview: A Checklist Approach," *Bulletin of the Medical Library Association* 69(1):26-33.

[13] Meta Nissley, et al. (January 1989), "Romping through ERIC: Measuring Satisfaction and Effectiveness," *Laserdisk Professional* 2(1): 93-100.

[14] Ruth T. Morris, Edwin A. Holtum, and David S. Curry (July 1982), "Being There: The Effect of the User's Presence on MEDLINE Search Results," *Bulletin of the Medical Library Association* 70(3):298-304.

[15] Cyril Cleverden (September 1972), "On the Inverse Relationship of Recall and Precision," *Journal of Documentation* 28(3):199.

[16] Carolyn K. Warden (Winter 1977), "Online Searching and Bibliographic Databases: The Role of the Intermediary," *Bookmark* 36:35-41.

[17] Knapp, "Reference Interview," 323.

[18] Barbara Quint (July 1991), "Inside the Searcher's Mind: The Seven Stages of an Online Search—Part 2," *Online* 15(4): 28-35.

[19] Arleen N. Somerville (February 1982), "The Pre-Search Reference Interview—A Step by Step Guide," *Database* 5(1):32-38.

Most search services allow searchers to view the Basic Index as a means of helping with the selection of subject search terms, and we saw in chapter 6 that this is done in DIALOG using the EXPAND command. We also learned that it is possible to reduce postings and increase specificity by limiting a search to one particular subject field through the use of suffix codes.

This chapter looks at how EXPAND can also be used with the other inverted files in order to verify the variant spelling and punctuation conventions for proper names (authors, journals, organizations, etc.) that exist in different files. You will also learn how the inverted file structure makes it possible to limit a search term not only to the subject fields but to any field of the record. Finally, this chapter explains the use of offline printing facilities and introduces some new commands that help to improve the appearance and usefulness of your search results.

9
ADDITIONAL
SEARCH FEATURES

Prefix Codes

When we looked at record structures in chapter 4 you saw that each field can be identified by a two-letter code (AU, TI, JN, etc.). We saw in chapter 6 that searches in the Basic Index can be limited to particular subject fields by using these two-letter codes as suffixes linked to the search terms (/TI or /DE, for example). Similarly, nonsubject fields can also be identified by their two-letter codes, but here the codes are used as prefixes rather than suffixes. The use of these codes makes it possible to limit a search to any individual field of the record. This device is a useful way of reducing postings and increasing specificity. As a reminder, figure 9.1

presents a listing of the Additional Index fields for a record in *PsycINFO* (file 11) taken from the bluesheets for that file.

You can specify the field to be searched by linking the appropriate prefix codes (which vary somewhat by database) to the search terms, using an equal sign. For example,

s jn=runner's world

searches only the journal inverted file, and

s au=saffady, william

searches only the author file. When you use a prefix code in your SELECT statement, the computer goes directly to the named field. Because many of these

Fig. 9.1. Additional indexes available on PsycINFO records.

FILE 11

PsycINFO®

ADDITIONAL INDEXES

SEARCH PREFIX	DISPLAY CODE	FIELD NAME	INDEXING	SELECT EXAMPLES
AG=	AG	Composite Age	Phrase	S AG=ADULT
AN=	AN	PsycINFO Accession Number	Phrase	S AN=77-03185
—	AN	DIALOG Accession Number		
AU=	AU	Author	Phrase	S AU=DOOB, ANTHONY?
CD=	CD	CODEN	Phrase	S CD=JASPBX
CS=	CS	Corporate Source	Word	S CS=(TORONTO(F)CRIMINOLOGY)
DC=	—	Descriptor Codes[2]	Word	S DC=08520
DT=	DT	Document Type	Phrase	S DT=JOURNAL ARTICLE
—	FN	File Name		
JA=	JA	Journal Announcement	Phrase	S JA=7701
JN=	JN	Journal Name	Phrase	S JN=JOURNAL OF APPLIED SOCIAL PSYCHOLOGY
LA=	LA	Language	Phrase	S LA=FRENCH
PU=	PU	Publisher	Word	S PU=(CONTINUING(W)EDUCATION)
PY=	PY	Publication Year	Phrase	S PY=1989
SF=	SF	Subfile	Phrase	S SF=DBO
SH=	SH	Section Heading	Phrase	S SH=3690
SN=	SN	International Standard Serial Number (ISSN)	Phrase	S SN=00219029
SO=	SO	Source[3]	Word	S SO=SEP
UD=	—	Update	Phrase	S UD=8901:9999

[2]Codes do not display in records.
[3]Display includes Journal Name, Volume, Issue, Pagination, and Publication Date.

fields contain proper names, the problem that you encounter when using prefix codes is that you may not be certain of the exact form of the name that you want to search. Remember that data is entered into the database in the form in which it appears in the original document. Documents come from a variety of sources, and there is no authority control of fields other than the descriptors. The fields that are phrase indexed are particularly difficult to search, because there may be variant forms of a single author's name (forename or initials, for example), in how it is punctuated (comma or space or both), or in the citing of a given journal's name (abbreviated or in full, for example).

Thus the same author may have more than one entry in the Author inverted file, due to inconsistencies in the use of initials, hyphens, Jr., Ed., or other variations in the form of entry. The same type of

variation may occur in other fields, too. Journals may be entered in full, abbreviated, or even occasionally misspelled! Proper names of organizations, products, or corporate sources may all appear in variant forms.

In addition, the way in which author names are entered varies in different databases. Surname and first name may be separated by a space, a space and a comma, or just a comma. First names may be entered in full or as initials. Initials may be separated by periods, spaces, or not separated at all. Given this variety, it is clear that database documentation is vital if online time is not to be wasted and relevant material missed.

The EXPAND command is a useful way to make sure that none of the variations in phrase indexed fields will be inadvertently overlooked. Notice the variations on the name D.J. Foskett in this example:

```
        Set   Items   Description
        ---   -----   -----------
?e au=foskett, d

Ref    Items   Index-term
E1        1    AU=FOSHEIM, ROBIN MELANIE, ED.
E2        5    AU=FOSKETT, A. C.
E3        0   *AU=FOSKETT, D
E4        1    AU=FOSKETT, D.
E5        8    AU=FOSKETT, D. J.
E6        2    AU=FOSKETT, DOUGLAS J.
E7        5    AU=FOSKETT, JOHN M.
E8        1    AU=FOSKETT, WILLIAM
E9        1    AU=FOSLER, R. SCOTT
E10       1    AU=FOSMIRE, F. R.
E11       1    AU=FOSMIRE, MONICA
E12       3    AU=FOSNOT, CATHERINE TWOMEY

        Enter P or E for more
?s e4:e6
        S1       11   AU="FOSKETT, D.":AU="FOSKETT, DOUGLAS J."
```

You will notice that the name is not entered in full in the EXPAND command. It is better not to use truncation when using EXPAND, due to the order in which the computer files the punctuation symbols.

You can similarly EXPAND search terms in all the other prefix-coded fields, though the exact fields that are available vary by database. The Corporate Source (CS=) field, which gives information on

authors' affiliations, is often particularly difficult to search effectively because it is word indexed in many files, making it necessary to use proximity operators or AND for successful retrieval.

Remember that you have to SELECT the appropriate E numbers from the EXPAND list, so that they are converted to the search terms that they represent and sets are formed.

Limiting

As an alternative to SELECTing a term using prefix codes and then ANDing the results with subject terms, some of the prefix codes can also be used as suffixes to limit previously SELECTed sets. It often proves helpful to inspect your initial postings

figures before proceeding further with your search. Adding qualifiers to previously SELECTed sets is known as post-qualification. For example, these three statements all yield the same results:

```
File 154:MEDLINE  1985-1992/AUG (9208W3)
 **FILE154:
  **See HELP NEWS 154 for Explode feature notice**

      Set   Items   Description
      ---   -----   -----------
?ss cholesterol and la=english
Processing
Processing
Processing
      S1    27136   CHOLESTEROL
      S2 2073694    LA=ENGLISH
      S3    23357   CHOLESTEROL AND LA=ENGLISH
?s s1/eng
      S4    23357   S1/ENG
?s cholesterol/eng
      S5    23357   CHOLESTEROL/ENG
```

Most databases on DIALOG offer one or more suffix codes that limit retrieval by specific criteria in addition to particular inverted files. Check the database bluesheets under "Limiting" for the codes that are applicable in a particular file. Common options include language, document type, publication year, and major descriptor. Figure 9.2 is a listing of the LIMIT options taken from the bluesheets for MEDLINE (file 154).

You may notice that many of these LIMITS are binary choices—either human or nonhuman, English or non-English. You are allowed to combine more than one qualifier for the same search term or set, separating them by commas. See the following example:

```
?ss carcinoma/human,1992
      S6    66301   CARCINOMA/HUMAN
      S7    85940   PY=1992
      S8     2606   CARCINOMA/HU-
MAN,1992
```

Here the search term "carcinoma" is LIMITed to human subjects and the publication year of 1992. You can apply these LIMITing suffix codes in a number of different ways:

- to single search terms

  s CD-ROM/pat

- to groups of terms connected by logical or proximity operators

  s (immigrant? AND worker?)/eng

- to set numbers

  s s6/maj

- in combination with other field or suffix codes or both

  s diplomacy/de,noneng,1990:92

Be particularly careful when LIMITing a set that includes a combination of search terms that have previously been ANDed. You will find that the LIMIT

Fig. 9.2. Sample *MEDLINE* Limit parameters.

MEDLINE®   **FILES 152,153,154,155**

LIMITING

Sets and terms may be limited by Basic Index suffixes. i.e., /AB, /DE, /DE*, /DF, /DF*, /GS, /ID, /IF, /NA, /TI (e.g., S S3/DE), as well as by the following features:

SUFFIX	FIELD NAME	EXAMPLES
None	Publication Year	S S3/1990
None	DIALOG Accession Number	S S3/6698000-9999999
/ABS	Records with Abstracts[1]	S S3/ABS
/NOABS	Records without Abstracts[1]	S S3/NOABS
/ENG	English-Language Records	S S4/ENG
/NONENG	Non-English-Language Records	S S5/NONENG
/HUMAN	Human Subject	S S2/HUMAN
/MAJ	Major Descriptor	S S5/MAJ

may not necessarily have been applied to every term as you probably intended. Do not LIMIT an ANDed set.

The LIMIT feature is thus a shortcut to enable certain field restrictions to apply to a search statement or even to a whole search strategy by LIMITing the final set number.

A more effective way to LIMIT an entire search is by using the command LIMITALL (abbreviated to LALL). This is usually entered at the start of a search but can also be used after reviewing postings to restrict all subsequent sets to one or more suffix codes. Enter LIMITALL followed by a slash(/) and the suffix codes desired, once again separating multiple codes with commas. Up to 40 characters, including commas and spacing, can be entered following the slash. For example, the use of LIMITALL/eng will cause every subsequent set to include only items written in English, thus being equivalent to combining AND LA=eng with each of the search sets. See the following example:

```
File   5:BIOSIS PREVIEWS   69-92/JUN BA9401:BARRM4301
       (C. BIOSIS 1992)

       Set   Items   Description
       ---   -----   -----------
?ss forest? or tree? or pine?
Processing
Processing
Processing
       S1   60996   FOREST?
       S2   52809   TREE?
       S3   32421   PINE?
       S4  125102   FOREST? OR TREE? OR PINE?
?limitall/de,ti,eng
>LIMITALL started
?ss s4 and seed()dispersal
            49744   S4
       S5   24249   SEED
       S6    5383   DISPERSAL
       S7     511   SEED(W)DISPERSAL
       S8     119   S4 AND SEED()DISPERSAL
```

Notice in this example how the postings for set 4 are reduced from 125,102 to 49,744 once the selected terms are LIMITed to descriptor or title fields and the English language. The LIMITs have also been automatically applied to sets 5, 6, and 7. This illustrates how the codes following the LIMITALL command are applied to all subsequent SELECT statements until the LIMITALL is canceled (using LIMITALL CANCEL or LIMITALL-), until a new LIMITALL command is entered, or until the search is ended with LOGOFF.

Notice that when field suffixes (e.g., /TI,DE) are used in a LIMITALL command, all subsequent search terms must be SELECTed from the Basic Index. In this situation, the use of a prefix code, such as AU=, will produce zero results. Because there is no indication in the results that the terms have been SELECTed under the LIMITALL restriction (i.e., suffix codes do not appear with the search terms), it is important to remember that LIMITALL is in operation. The codes that can be used are database-specific, but publication year is never available with LIMITALL, so it is necessary to use accession numbers in order to restrict by time periods when LIMITALL is in operation.

LIMITALL may save considerable search time during long searches involving large sets by decreasing retrieval and thus reducing the number of records that must be processed.

Offline Printing

As an alternative to viewing search results online by using the TYPE command, it is possible to have them printed offline and sent by mail from the search service. The command used to request search results through the mail is PRINT, abbreviated as PR. The format of the PRINT command will be familiar to you from your experience with TYPE:

print n/f/b-e

or

pr n/f/b-e

where n is the set number to be printed, f is the format number, and b-e are the document numbers. A system limit restricts the number of records requested by any one PRINT command to 5,000, though it seems unlikely that this will be a serious limitation. The system responds to the command by confirming the transaction and providing a transaction number and an estimated cost figure.

Because PRINT requests are processed in batches, it is possible to cancel a PRINT command within two hours of entering it. The command to do this is PRINT CANCEL or PR-, followed by the transaction number of the request. This feature is useful, for example, if the user decides that the cost quoted in the system response is too expensive. It may be preferable to print fewer citations or to use a cheaper (briefer) format, maybe dropping the abstract.

One of the options available with the PRINT command is the ability to choose what the formats will look like. Normally PRINT output is printed horizontally on the page, with two columns of records, in a format known as "landscape." (See fig. 9.3. on page 122.) The alternative format options are "portrait" (PORT) or "solo" (SOLO) layouts, which may be preferred in certain situations.

The use of the command PRINT TITLE allows you to add a title of up to 80 characters at the top of the offline prints. This can help to speed sorting in a large library where numbers of offline prints may be received at the same time. (Note that all PRINT requests following a PRINT TITLE command will be labeled with the selected title until a new BEGIN is entered.)

The VIA DIALMAIL option of the PRINT command sends the requested records to the user's DIAL-MAIL Inbox (see more on DIALMAIL on pages 128-131). The PRINT QUERY and PRINT QUERY DETAIL commands allow the searcher to keep track of all PRINT requests by viewing a log of the 60 most recent PRINT and PRINT CANCEL commands. (See fig. 9.4.) The list may include transactions from previous search sessions and previous days, but items are erased after 96 hours.

Fig. 9.3. Example of PRINT in landscape format.

```
PRINTS   User:019462  19jun92 P029: PR 8/5/2-4                              PAGE: 7
         HUMANISTS INFOSEEK                                          Item  1 of 3
```

DIALOG File 202: INFORMATION SCIENCE ABS_66-92/MAR (Copr. 1992 IFI/PLENUM DATA CO.)

0155572 9106335
Information access in the humanities: perils and pitfalls.
Walker, G. (State Univ. of New York. Albany, NY); Atkinson, S.D.
Library Hi Tech. Vol. 9. Issue 1. p. 23-34, 1991, 39
Subject relationships between the different disciplines within the field of the humanities are clearly more diverse and subtle than the behavior of information seekers might lead one to expect. These results emphasize the importance of multi-file searching and the need to use both natural language and controlled vocabulary terms. Further investigation of search vocabulary is particularly important with current developments in full-text searching and end-user access to databases. The authors discuss what their research findings imply for the future of online information retrieval in an environment where (relatively) untrained users will be needing to access a whole range of online search systems.
Descriptors: Information Systems and Applications - Social Sciences, Humanities
Identifiers: ACCESS: DESCRIPTORS; HUMANITIES; INFORMATION RETRIEVAL; NATURAL LANGUAGE; ONLINE RETRIEVAL; SEARCHING; THESAURI

the scholar, to help explain differing degrees of library use; and 3) to test a theory that personality factors are reliable indicators of information use because they effect the level of information use of scholars who work in disciplines where there are weak norms governing such behavior. Findings resulting from interviews with the twenty initial scholars was extended by mailing a questionnaire to a random sample of 250 scholars working at 38 Canadian English-language universities. The author reports findings, use of primary sources, attitudes and characteristics and summarizes the implications of his findings.
Descriptors: Information Systems and Applications - Social Sciences, Humanities
Identifiers: BEHAVIOR: END USERS: HUMANITIES: INFORMATION NEEDS: RESEARCH: SEARCHING

0216150 92-0707
Scholars seek information: information-seeking behaviour and information needs of humanities scholars.
AUTHOR(S): Loennqvist, Harriet
JOURNAL: International Journal of Information and Library Research
SOURCE: 2 (3) 1990, 195-203. 13 refs
LANGUAGES: English
ABSTRACT: Reports a NORDINFO study designed to study the information-seeking behaviour and information needs of scholars in the humanities from a holistic perspective. 64 people from Denmark, Finland, Iceland, Norway and Sweden were interviewed and results show that scholars in the humanities do not have a homogeneous information-seeking behaviour or homogeneous information needs. Compared to other information channels research libraries, as expected, turned out to be of greatest importance for scholars seeking information and printed materials for their research. The study also showed that what subject search for a scholar means, in most cases, is looking up individual names of persons. (author of a book or article, or searching for information about a person). Scholars used bibliographies only to a small extent and their bibliographical awareness was rather low. Original abstract--amended
DESCRIPTORS: Libraries; Library materials; Stock; Information use; Use; Use; User surveys; Scandinavia; Humanities
SECTION HEADINGS: USE OF LIBRARIES AND LIBRARY MATERIALS
SECTION HEADING CODES: JaHz(OO9)D48

0147010 9007126
Patterns of information seeking in the humanities.
Wiberley, S.E.; Jones, W.G.
College and Research Libraries. Vol. 50. Issue 6. p. 638-645, Nov 1989, 12
Describes an examination of the information seeking behavior of humanists in a small, interdisciplinary group. The findings include when and how these scholars employ online databases, reference librarians, archivists, and other collections, formal bibliographies, and other information sources. Further research is suggested and the implications for academic library services are discussed. (Abstract Source: ERIC)
Descriptors: Information Systems and Applications - Social Sciences, Humanities
Identifiers: DATABASES; END USERS; HUMANITIES; INFORMATION SERVICES: INFORMATION SOURCES; ONLINE RETRIEVAL; REFERENCE SERVICES: SEARCHERS: USAGE STUDIES

0146204 9006254
The information seeking behaviour of literary scholars.
Hopkins, R.
Canadian Library Journal, Vol. 46. Issue 2. p. 113-116, Apr 1989
The author outlines three objectives which were considered in the designing of a research study concerning twenty humanities scholars in order to discover more about the effectiveness of various research techniques utilized in the field of user studies. The objectives are: 1) to test long-held assumptions about the information seeking and gathering behavior of literary scholars; 2) to examine a number of variables or factors, such as the academic rank of

Fig. 9.4. Example of PRINT QUERY.

```
?  print query
P192: PR S5/5/1-4
P193: PR S2/5/ALL (items 1-28)
PRINT CANCEL P193
P196: PR S6/5/1-12
P198: PR ALL F5    (S6 items 1-12)
P199: PR            (S6 F5 items 1-12)
P200: PR F5 S7 1-4, 6-10
PRINT CANCEL P198
PRINT CANCEL P199
P204: PR 8/8/ALL   (items 1-10)
```

Sorting Output

Records are normally output in descending order of their DIALOG accession numbers, which in most databases reflects reverse input or chronological order. That is, the record most recently input has the highest accession number and is retrieved first.

In many databases, but not all, the SORT command can be used to alter the order in which records are output. The final search results can be rearranged by SORTing either alphabetically or numerically on a selected field. The SORT command creates a new set, which can then be used for output with a TYPE or PRINT command. The fields available for SORTing vary by database, so once again you will need to check the DIALOG bluesheets thoroughly. Figure 9.5 is an example from the bluesheets for the *Avery Architecture* database produced by the Avery Library at Columbia University. This shows that in this file you can sort by author, journal name, publication year, or title.

The format for the SORT command is

SORT n/all/ff,o

where n is the number of the SORTed set, all refers to the number of records in the set, ff is the field to be used for SORTing, and o is the desired order of the SORT. Output can be SORTed by fields such as author name, journal name, zip code, or sales figures, which are all identified by their two-character field codes (e.g., AU, JN, ZP, SA, etc.). SORT orders are either ascending/alphabetic (a) or descending (d), with alphabetical being the system default.

The SORT option enables the production of bibliographies in alphabetic order by author using

sort s5/all/au

or financial reports in descending order of total sales figures using

sort s5/all/sa,d

It is also possible to specify more than one field code in a SORT command, though this is not a frequently used option. When this multiple SORT option is used, codes are listed separated by either commas or slashes, and sorting precedence operates from left to right. For example, the command

sort s5/all/au,ti

sorts all items in set 5 first by author (AU) and within author by title (TI). A SORTed set cannot be used again with SELECT or SORT commands but can only be used to TYPE or PRINT results. If you want a different sequence, you need to go back to the original set that you SORTed and SORT it again.

In order to get accurate results, though, notice that the whole set must be SORTed. Even when you need only a subset of the data (e.g., the top 50 companies), you have to SORT the entire retrieved set.

A SORTed set is normally TYPEd or PRINTed straight away. However, when it is not necessary to inspect the set online, it is more efficient to combine the SORT parameters into the PRINT command. This is done by using a normal PRINT statement and adding at the end the two-letter codes of the fields to be used for SORTing following a slash (with a d if descending order is required). For example,

print s5/2/1-50/au

or

print s8/3/all/zp,d

Fig. 9.5. Sort fields available on *Avery Architecture Index*.

FILE 178

AVERY ARCHITECTURE INDEX

SORTING

SORTABLE FIELDS	EXAMPLES
Online (SORT) and offline (PRINT) AU, JN, PY, TI	SORT S13/ALL/AU/PY,D PRINT S2/5/ALL/JN

SORTing is a good first step toward providing a "value-added" output for the user. It makes it possible to provide a customized bibliography, arranged alphabetically by author, or a business report arranged in order by a chosen criterion. We will show you a SORT in action when we describe the REPORT command on page 127.

Special Formats

Downloading the search results and entering them into a word processing program is probably the most obvious way to provide a more professional-looking output for your user. Records are downloaded as ASCII (American Standard Code for Information Interchange) files, so that search results can be uploaded into nearly any standard word processor. We talked about the effort involved in editing the downloaded file in chapter 8, but this job can be greatly simplified if the citations are first SORTed online and output in the most appropriate format.

A small point: Your results are indeed downloaded in ASCII format, if you're using a DOS-based machine (an IBM PC or compatible); if you're using a Macintosh, they will be downloaded in straight text format. The thing to understand is that you'll have no formatting commands or characters in your downloaded output, and you'll have some extraneous-looking spaces and hard carriage returns, which is just how DIALOG produces it. Dump it into your word processor and reformat it. It will look fine. - JWJ

We saw in chapter 5 that DIALOG provides a choice of predefined formats that are used to control the fields that are included in your search output. Standard formats are listed on the database bluesheets, but it is also possible to design your own preferred format. Four format options are available:

- User-defined (UDF) formats
- Preset customized formats
- Keyword in context (KWIC) formats
- Report formats

One way of customizing the content of output records on some databases is through the use of a user-defined format (UDF). UDFs allow you to use the two-character field codes to select the fields you want to include in the records to be output. These formats can be specified in three different ways:

- Using *field codes* separated by commas, as in the following example where we output the title, the source, and the company name:

```
File  16:PTS PROMT  - 72-92/June 25
       (Copr. 1992 Predicasts)
  **FILE 16: New FULL TEXT titles: Europe Energy, Europe Environment,
Manufacturing Automation, Market Asia Pacific, Middle East News Network.

      Set  Items  Description
      ---  -----  -----------
?s sanka
      S1     68  SANKA
?t 1/ti,so,co/5

  1/TI,SO,CO/5
BEVERAGES: Thirst's Many Flavors

Adweek's Marketing Week Superbrands  1991   p. 62

COMPANY:
    Coca-Cola
    Pepsi-Cola
    Dr Pepper/Seven-Up
    Royal Crown Cola
```

```
            Shasta Beverages
            Cadbury Beverages
            Perrier Group America
            Sparkletts
            Eaux Minerales Evian
            Hinckley & Schmitt
            Coca-Cola Foods
            Tropicana Products
            Ocean Spray Cranberries
            Quaker Oats
            Procter & Gamble
            Kraft General Foods
            Nestle Beverage
```

- Combining a predefined format number with field codes, as in the following example:

```
File 581:AGRIBUSINESS U.S.A. 85-90/Jul 31
       Copr. 1990 Pioneer Hi-Bred Int Inc)
Not available in Onesearch as of February 1, 1992.

        Set   Items  Description
        ---   -----  -----------
?s cropping/ti
        S1     47  CROPPING/TI
?t 1/3,de/1

 1/3,DE/1
00183240
    Alley cropping to be studied by University of Hawaii staff
    Anon
    Agribusiness Worldwide v12 n3 p24 np(1) April 1990

    DESCRIPTORS:   Planting;  Fertility; Studies; Trees; Crops; Innovations;
     Research
```

- Using the SET command to store a UDF for the length of a search, as shown in the following example where we select only the title, the abstract, and the descriptors:

```
File  11:PSYCINFO   67-92/JULY
       (COPR. AM. PSYCH. ASSOC.)

        Set   Items  Description
        ---   -----  -----------
?set u1 ti,ab,de
User Defined Format 1 is set to TI AB DE.
    Type/Display Estimated Cost: $  0.30 - (File 11).
```

When you want to TYPE your output later, you can then use U1 in place of a regular format number. Nine different formats can be defined in this way by using the SET command followed by the desired display codes.

The format or formats that you set remain available for use in any database having those fields during the current search session. All UDFs are erased when the search session is terminated with a LOGOFF command. It is possible to save a UDF long-term by SETting it as a parameter of your user profile, though this may be counterproductive unless the files you normally search all use compatible field codes. Other uses of the SET command are mentioned in association with the commands with which they are most commonly used.

Another alternative format is the KWIC (Key-Word in Context) option, which is available on a number of DIALOG databases. KWIC is a format option that displays only those portions of a record that contain the SELECTed search terms, known as the "hits." It shows them in the context in which they occur, which is useful in helping you to determine the relevance of your search results. KWIC displays are generally taken from textual fields such as title, descriptors, or text, and the command is particularly useful with full-text records, where matching terms may be far apart and not related to one another at all. (Remember our search example at the end of chapter 6?)

To view only the KWIC portions of your search results, enter either KWIC or K in place of the numbered format in your TYPE command. The amount of text shown when you use KWIC consists of the search term within a 30-word window, with approximately 15 words on either side of your search term. Using the SET command it is possible to change the size of the KWIC window to anything between 2 and 50 words. For example, you can enter the command

set kwic 50

at the beginning of your search, and the KWIC window will display 25 words before and after your search term or terms. The new size will remain in operation until you LOGOFF, unless you change it with another SET KWIC command. In the following example notice how groups of three periods appear between windows to indicate that text has been omitted:

```
File 154:MEDLINE  1985-1992/AUG (9208W3)
 **FILE154:
  **See HELP NEWS 154 for Explode feature notice**

     Set  Items  Description
     ---  -----  -----------
?s self()esteem
         36191  SELF
          1299  ESTEEM
     S1   1251  SELF()ESTEEM
?t 1/kwic/1

 1/KWIC/1
  ... being  11.5  years. All subjects were given the Children's Depression
Inventory,  the  Coopersmith  Self    Esteem  Inventory and the Children's
Attributional  Style  Questionnaire. Teachers completed the Child Behaviour
Checklist  and... Scale. The results indicated that in the older subjects,
the  medicated group had lower social  self - esteem  than the nonmedicated
group and in younger subjects the medicated group had higher academic  self
-  esteem  than  the  nonmedicated  group. There  were  no  significant
differences  among  the  groups  with  respect  to...
```

Because the KWIC format used alone displays only the portions of the text that contain the hit terms, it is usual to combine it with one of the predefined formats in order to retrieve the citation itself. The following example displays the citation (format 3) and KWIC window of the second record in set 1:

```
?t 1/3,k/2

 1/3,K/2
08121915   92259915
  Sharing the memories. The value of reminiscence as a research tool.
  Newbern VB
  J  Gerontol  Nurs (UNITED  STATES)  May  1992,  18  (5)  p13-8,  ISSN
0098-9134  Journal Code: IAX
  Languages: ENGLISH
  Document type: JOURNAL ARTICLE
  ... is  a  tool  for  life review, storytelling, creation of a meaningful
myth,  and maintenance of  self - esteem  that gerontological nurses cannot
continue to neglect.
```

Another command that is particularly useful in association with KWIC is the HILIGHT (HI) command. This system feature highlights the occurrence of your search terms in the KWIC window, so that they are easier to spot. The command to implement the HILIGHT feature is

set hi on

entered at the beginning of your search. Depending on the terminal type, highlighted terms may display more brightly, in reverse video, or with a surplus character on either side (e.g., *self-esteem*) as a marker. The default HILIGHT is the asterisk (*), but it is possible to SET it to any preferred character by using the command

set hi #

where # is the character you have selected to HIGHLIGHT your hit terms. This command is helpful in drawing attention to the search terms that have caused the document to be retrieved, and the KWIC format provides a context that helps you to assess the relevance of the document. HILIGHT is canceled at LOGOFF or by entering SET HI OFF. Examine this example:

```
File  88:ACADEMIC INDEX  1976-92/JUN
      (COPR. 1992 IAC)
 **FILE088: Effective APRIL 1, 1992, there are NEW PRICES for
 hours, types and prints. See HELP RATES88 for details.


      Set   Items   Description
      ---   -----   -----------
?set hi #
HILIGHT set on as '#'
?ss inferen?(2n)statistic?
      S1     444    INFEREN?
      S2   23520    STATISTIC?
      S3      26    INFEREN?(2N)STATISTIC?
?t 3/5/1

   3/5/1
   11845066   DIALOG File 88:  ACADEMIC INDEX
Statistical reasoning in the legal setting.
Gastwirth, Joseph L.
American Statistician  v46 n1 p55(15) Feb, 1992
SOURCE FILE: AI File 88
illustration table
DESCRIPTORS:  Proof   theory—Analysis;  Discrimination  in  employment—
   Analysis; Probabilities—Analysis
AUTHOR ABSTRACT: Expert, based on #statistical# data and #inference#, has
   become a routine part of legal proceedings. This article describes the
   role of statistics as evidence in a variety of cases and how the
   relevance of statistical exhibits relates to legal standards and
   burdens of proof. KEY WORDS: Concepts of proof; Equal employment; Law;
   #Statistical# evidence; #Statistical# #inference#.  COPYRIGHT American
   Statistical Association 1992
RECORD DATE: 920502
```

Another output option available on a number of DIALOG databases, particularly files containing statistical, financial, or demographic data, is the REPORT command. It arranges selected data from a retrieved set of records into useful tables, displaying the information in columns. The extraction of selected fields of data from lengthy records in this way not only saves online time but also saves time for the user. This is definitely a value-added feature for busy managerial staff. Imagine having to read right through the long record at the end of chapter 7 (page 104) in order to gather one or two specific pieces of information!

Reports are only available online, and the results are most effective when used in combination with the SORT command, so that the data are presented in a logical order. In order to use this command you must first check the fields that are available for use with REPORT in the bluesheets of the particular database being used. Then calculate the total lengths of the fields you want to include. This is necessary because the number of characters that can be displayed readably is limited by the length of the print line. The display line is set to 75 characters, which matches the line length of most printers, but the maximum line length available on the system is 132 characters. Building a line of over 75 characters, however, will cause the data to "wrap around" and spoil the appearance of your report. (It is worth noting that data formatted using the REPORT command will often be difficult to handle when downloaded to a word processor.)

An example showing the fields available for use with REPORT on one of the *Dun & Bradstreet* databases (file 520) is presented in figure 9.6. The REPORT command has a format similar to the other output formats:

report n/ff,ff,ff/b-e

where n is the set number, ff are the field codes separated by commas, and b-e are the record numbers. You can have as many field codes in this expression as you like, so long as the resulting report can fit across the page. For example,

report s5/co,sa,ta,nt/1-10

presents a table of the first 10 records from set 5. The table will include the company name, total sales figures, total assets, and net assets, with the sequence of columns in the order in which the field codes are entered in the REPORT command. Remember to SORT before you use the REPORT command, so that the records in your REPORT are presented in a logical order. Here is an example:

```
File 100:DISCLOSURE  , Jun 22 1992
       (Copr. 1992 Disclosure (TM) Incorporated)
Use 1987 SIC codes for PC= and SC=.

       Set  Items  Description
       ---  -----  -----------
?s pc=2731
       S1     16   PC=2731
?sort s1/all/sa,d
       S2     16   Sort S1/ALL/SA,D
?report s2/co,sa,ni/1-10
Align paper;  press ENTER
?
                            Net        Net
Company                     Sales      Income
Name                        (000s)     (000s)
----------------------------  ---------  -------

HARCOURT BRACE JOVANOVICH INC  1,412,747  -80,875
WESTERN PUBLISHING GROUP INC     491,089    8,327
HOUGHTON MIFFLIN CO              466,801   25,077
SCHOLASTIC CORP                  422,893   13,800
JOHN WILEY & SONS INC            236,859   -5,985
WAVERLY INC                      147,315    3,381
THOMAS NELSON INC                 73,573    4,320
PLENUM PUBLISHING CORP            53,375   17,336
PRICE STERN SLOAN INC             36,992    1,360
WILLIAM H SADLIER INC             19,572      520
```

A useful feature of the system is the ability to eliminate records that do not contain data in essential fields before entering the REPORT command. This can be done by using Boolean NOT to link a field code such as sales (sa) equals not available (na) to the final subject set, as in

s s8 not sa=na

This removes all records that have no data in the total sales (sa) field. (It is a feature that is also useful with the SORT command in a lot of other situations.) If no range of records is given, the system defaults to TYPEing all the records in the set, so be careful!

Access to Documents

DIALOG's international electronic communication service, known as DIALMAIL, offers an electronic mail and conferencing service and can also be used to receive offline PRINTs and current awareness ALERTs via your DIALMAIL inbox. The menu-driven DIALMAIL system includes commands that allow you to READ, EDIT, FORWARD, or store your PRINTs in a DIALMAIL file folder. Figure 9.7 (on page 130) presents the DIALMAIL menu:

SCAN, READ, and CREATE are the commands that you use to send and receive mail on the system. CREATE enables you to send messages to other DIALMAIL users, either individually or through mailing lists. The conference function is an open

Fig. 9.6. Fields for use with REPORT on Canadian Dun's Market Identifiers (file 520).

FILE 520

D & B - CANADIAN DUN'S MARKET IDENTIFIERS
DIALOG FILE 520

REPORT12

FIELD NAME	FIELD ABBREVIATION	FIELD LENGTH
DIALOG Accession Number	AN	11
Street Address	A1	27
Mailing Address	A2	30
Base Employees Total	BE	12
Base Sales - Local Currency (Canadian $)	BS	17
County Name	CN	17
Company Name	CO	32
City	CY	17
D-U-N-S Headquarters Number	DH	13
D-U-N-S Number	DN	13
D-U-N-S Parent Number	DP	13
Employee Growth	EG	10
Employees Here	EH	11
Employees Total	ET	11
Headquarter City	HC	15
Headquarter State/Province	HS	13
SMSA Code	MC	7
SMSA Name	MN	22
Executive Name and Title	NA	21
Organizational Status13	OS	16
Primary SIC Code	PC	9
Primary SIC Code - Local (Canada)	PL	9
Parent State/Province	PS	8
Parent City	PY	15
Sales (U.S. $)	SA	17
Sales Growth	SG	8
Sales - Local Currency (Canadian $)	SL	17
State/Province	ST	10
Telephone Number	TE	14
Trend Employees Total	TM	12
Trend Sales - Local Currency (Canadian $)	TR	17
Year Started	YR	9
Postal Code	ZP	9

EXAMPLE
Output may be displayed in table format with the REPORT command, e.g., REPORT S2/CO,SL,ET/ALL. (Refer to Technical Note No. 7 for details.)

12When entries containing no data are not wanted, NOT out those items before using REPORT, e.g., SELECT SC=5112 NOT SL=NA.
13Entries are searchable with SF=: BRANCH, HEADQUARTERS, SINGLE.

folder that can be shared either publicly with other users or selectively with a group of specified users. Another means of disseminating messages on the DIALMAIL system is the bulletin board, on which you can post notices, either to a limited audience or to all DIALMAIL users. You can also scan the board to view messages entered by other users. Personal and public directories help you to locate any user you may wish to contact, and your inbox displays messages that other users have sent to you.

DIALMAIL is also the basis of the DIALORDER service, DIALOG's online document ordering service. DIALORDER allows users to electronically order the complete text of documents found in an online search or located through other sources. The items available include the fulltexts of documents from database suppliers and a complete range of DIALOG publications, including database chapters.

You may place your order with any of the available document suppliers and it will be stored on the

DIALOG computer in the supplier's inbox. It will be collected by the supplier when he logs-on to the system to retrieve the orders that have been placed for him. The supplier will fill the order and bill the customer directly, so that DIALOG is merely acting as an electronic mail facility.

Documents can be ordered in three ways:

- by accession number or set number during a search
- from the printout of a previous search
- by the input of a bibliographic citation not on DIALOG.

The DIALOG command to use this facility is ORDER (O), with its counterparts ORDER ITEM, ORDER CANCEL, ORDER LIST, and ORDER REVIEW. (See the sample in fig. 9.8 on page 131.)

When preparing lists for electronic ordering, the KEEP command is a useful device. KEEP is used to place selected records into an auxiliary set, numbered set zero (S0), so that you can build up the complete order from a series of searches. You can KEEP chosen records from various sets within your search, creating a single final set of search results, which you may then want to SORT.

The format of the command is KEEP (or K) followed by either

a set number
    (e.g., *keep s3*)

a set number with selected item numbers
    (e.g., *keep s6/3, 7, 10*),

which will put records 3, 7, and 10 from set 6 into set zero, or

a DIALOG accession number
    (e.g., *keep ej247653*).

You can TYPE or PRINT as well as SORT set S0, and you can use it in subsequent SELECT commands to combine it with other terms or limit it with suffix codes. When KEEP is used to prepare a DIALORDER request, the system looks for set zero and automatically places the records it finds there into the DIALORDER request. Once the order has been placed the system will delete set zero, but otherwise you can delete it yourself using the command KEEP CANCEL. The same command followed by a DIALOG accession number will delete a single record from set zero.

The use of the KEEP command to create a really nice set, which DIALOG calls S0, is a great feature to minimize the size of sets that you ask to be TYPEd or PRINTed. I must confess, though, that I don't teach it to my classes until the very end of the course. Why? Because they want to create the perfect 30-item set anyway, and this allows them to do it! It can also be a time waster, especially if you flip through the articles you've retrieved one at a time, KEEPing the ones you like and then dealing with the final S0. KEEP is certainly a valid command, but use it with some discretion. - JWJ

This chapter has covered a whole range of new commands, many of which can be used in varying combinations—SORT with PRINT, SET with UDF, SORT with ORDER, and so on. Most of them are intended to improve the appearance of your search output. The intention is to help you to provide a professional-looking, customized end product for your user. This cosmetic factor is likely to become increasingly important as users become more aware of online information resources and as they learn to perform simple searches for themselves.

Fig. 9.7. Sample DIALMAIL menu.

DIALMAIL℠
DIALOG FILE MAIL

MAIN MENU

Dialmail:
Scan	to list messages, folders . . .
Read	to read messages
Create	to create a new message, folder . . .
Answer	to answer a message
Help	for more information on any command
CLear	to clear any defaults and return to main menu
EXit	to leave DIALMAIL
	For more commands, enter Page

?PAGE
Dialmail:
Delete	to erase a message, folder . . .
COpy	to copy an item to another folder or person
Edit	to edit a message, list, or form
Join	to join a bulletin board
MAintain	to add, delete, or list members of a Bboard you host
PROfile	to modify your profile
Begin	to leave DIALMAIL and enter a DIALOG file or service
LOGOFF	to logoff

Fig. 9.8. Sample DIALORDERs in 3 forms.

- to specify certain documents:

ORDER n/items/supplier's acronym

```
?  order S4/4,8,13/ERIC

Order RD039
0394823
  RELEVENCE JUDGEMENTS OF TWINS SEPARATED AT BIRTH
Order RD039 confirmed
```

- to form S0 ("set zero"):

ORDER acronym

```
?  keep 02983487
        S0          1      02983487
?  keep 03847823
        S0          2      03847823
?  order twins

Order RD011
0394823
  RELEVANCE JUDGEMENTS OF TWINS SEPARATED AT BIRTH
Order RD2393 confirmed

Order RD012
0394823
  WHY YOU DON'T LOOK LIKE YOUR IDENTICAL TWIN
Order RD2393 confirmed
```

- to order documents which aren't records online:

ORDER ITEM title of item

```
?  order item dialog four pocket guides
Order RA032 confirmed
```

- to REVIEW your order:

```
?  order review RA027
   -------------------
Order RA027    DIALOG
Mail to:
GERALDENE WALKER
STATE UNIVERSITY OF NEW YORK
ALBANY, NY 12222
```

We have seen that databases come from many different sources and are intended for many different audiences. They vary not only in their subject content but also in the way the data are presented, the level of detail provided, and the currency of the information. With hundreds of files to choose from, selection of the most appropriate files for a given search is not always easy. This chapter explains where to find help in making this choice and discusses some of the techniques that are necessary when searching multiple databases.

10
MULTIPLE
FILE SEARCHING

When a searcher has access to a range of different search systems, the decision as to which to use in any given situation will normally depend on the databases that are available on each system. If the same file is available from more than one vendor, the deciding factor is likely to be cost. The price per hour of connect time and the cost per record are what contribute to total search costs, and both may vary, even for the same file, on different systems. In certain cases it is possible to save money by preferring one system to another.

Choosing Which System to Search

Many search topics require the use of multiple files to obtain comprehensive results, and it is common for most searches nowadays to be performed on at least two or three databases. When more than one file needs to be searched, the availability of the full range of files on one system will possibly influence the choice of search system, because it will often save time and money to complete the search on a single system.

In some small proportion of searches the availability of a particular search feature may also be a deciding factor in the choice of system, because the same file may be mounted differently and thus offer different search features on different systems. It pays to check all the available documentation with great care.

A number of sources provide information on the range of databases available across all the search services. For example, printed sources such as *Computer-Readable Databases: A Directory and Data Sourcebook*,[1] provide excellent overviews of current services and a wealth of information on databases of all types. A series of reviews by Saffady[2] offers useful comparisons among different vendors offering access to the same files.

Choosing Databases

Many of the criteria used in selecting printed reference resources are also relevant when choosing online files. The following are some points to note when considering the choice of files for searching:

- Subject scope (and how subjects are covered in the file)
- Access points (searchable fields)
- Type of material (popular, research, etc.)
- Type of data (bibliographic, numeric, etc.)
- Time period covered
- File currency (last update)

In addition to these general reference considerations, each of the online retrieval systems offers an extensive range of directories, guides, and newsletters to help choose among their own databases. For example, the *DIALOG Database Catalog* provides

- a description of each database in alphabetical order, detailing subject content, dates of coverage, publisher, and so on;
- charts indicating the type of data, special features, services, and the update frequency of each database;
- a list of database suppliers and the databases they produce; and
- the list called "DIALINDEX/OneSearch Subject Categories," with their acronyms.

DIALOG bluesheets summarize the content and list the specific search features that are available on each individual file, and other systems provide similar documentation. Each bluesheet includes a sample record, so that you can see what a typical record in the database looks like, and lists the record formats in which output can be displayed. More detailed information for each individual file, found in the whitesheets, covers each field of the record, including details of how to search it.

Despite this variety of search aids intended to assist with the choice of appropriate databases, personal experience suggests that choosing the best file or files is not an easy task for the beginning searcher. It may be important to consider factors such as the intended audience, the type of indexing used, or the fields available for searching on particular files. The type of source document required (patents or research reports, for instance) may help to narrow the choice of database. There is sometimes considerable overlap among databases, though the amount tends to vary by subject and by file. If a comprehensive search is required, it may be necessary to ignore the likelihood of overlap and accept that some records will necessarily be duplicated. They can be easily eliminated from the final output by using the REMOVE DUPLICATES or RD command.

As has been mentioned, the vendors sometimes group files by their type and coverage in some of their system documentation, and this is another useful resource to assist in database selection. But be aware that the suggested groupings should not necessarily be accepted without question, because they often include some files that will prove to be inappropriate in practice.

DIALINDEX

In order to help searchers with the task of choosing appropriate databases, each of the major vendors provides an index file, a kind of "database of databases," which is accessible online. It is a composite of all the inverted files, both Basic Indexes and Additional Indexes, of the whole range of databases available on the system. On the DIALOG system this file is called DIALINDEX (file 411), and it allows the searcher to browse selected search terms in files that look potentially useful so as to compare postings figures. In this way DIALINDEX helps you check which databases have the most information on your specific topic before you conduct your actual search in more expensive databases. It is particularly useful when there are a number of possible files for a given query, and you are unsure which of them will be the most useful. DIALINDEX allows the searcher to select up to 100 potential files to browse, though of course far fewer would normally be candidates for consideration in a given search.

It is important to remember that this is an index file. It contains no records and no sets are formed when you search it, so certain commands (such as TYPE, DISPLAY, PRINT, or EXPAND) cannot be used. In order to use this browse facility, we need a new command, usable only in DIALINDEX, to enable us to select the group of files that we think may be useful for our search. After we have selected the DIALINDEX database the first command is always going to be SET FILES or SELECT FILES (abbreviated SF) followed by a listing of files, in order to limit your search to that particular range of files. Be careful not to omit this SET FILES command, or you will get an error message!

The SET FILES command can be used with the following:

- file numbers (e.g., *SET FILES 38,56,191*)

- acronyms for database categories to select subject groups (e.g., *SF compsci, software*) (See the database catalog for details of the available categories.)

- a combination of numbers and acronyms to add files to a subject category (e.g., *SF humanit,47,111*)

- the Boolean NOT operator to exclude file numbers from a subject category (e.g., *SF chemlit not 34,87,94*)

You must enter a space after the SF command and separate file numbers and acronyms with commas. Hyphens can be used to indicate a range of file numbers. Following the selection of files the system confirms the databases chosen, and you can obtain a list of their file banners by using the command SHOW FILES.

When the system issues the next prompt, a single SELECT statement containing up to 240 characters can be entered in the usual DIALOG format. It is probably most useful to limit this SELECT to the most important concepts of your search linked by appropriate logic. Terms can be linked using Boolean or proximity operators and can be nested using parentheses. Prefix and suffix codes are also acceptable on DIALINDEX, but it is important to check their availability on all of the files selected. (You may need to OR together certain prefix codes in order to make sure that a particular feature is covered in all your selected files.) The system responds to the SELECT command by displaying the number of items retrieved from each database for the final logical statement.

Here is an example. You enter DIALINDEX as you would any other file, using BEGIN with its file number (411):

```
?b 411

  File 411:DIALINDEX(tm)

DIALINDEX(tm)
    (Copr. DIALOG Info.Ser.Inc.)

*** DIALINDEX search results display in an abbreviated ***
*** format unless you enter the SET DETAIL ON command. ***
?set files 51,79,155,164
    You have 4 files in your file list.
    (To see banners, use SHOW FILES command.)
?s low()cholesterol()diet?
 Your SELECT statement is:
    s low()cholesterol()diet?
            Items    File
            -----    ----
                5     51: FSTA_69-92/JUN
               18     79: FOODS ADLIBRA _ 74-92/APR
              169    155: MEDLINE_1966-1992/AUG (9208W1)
                1    164: COFFEELINE(SM)_73-92/MAY


    All files have one or more items; file list includes 4 files.
```

What we are interested in here are the postings figures for each file, in order to determine which database to use for our actual search. We can see in this case that file 155, the complete MEDLINE file, is going to be far and away the most useful for our search for information on low-cholesterol diets.

Here is an example of the use of DIALINDEX with one of the subject category acronyms:

```
?set files people
    You have 14 files in your file list.
    (To see banners, use SHOW FILES command.)
?s bella()abzug
 Your SELECT statement is:
    s bella()abzug
            Items    File
            -----    ----
               16     47: MAGAZINE INDEX_1959-MARCH 1970,1973-92/MAY
                6     88: ACADEMIC INDEX_1976-92/JUN
               30    111: NATIONAL NEWSPAPER INDEX _ 79-92/MAY
                9    148: TRADE AND INDUSTRY INDEX_81-92/MAY
                1    234: MARQUIS WHO'S WHO_1990-1991/OCT
                9    484: Newspaper & Periodical Abs_88-09 Jun 1992
               18    603: Newspaper Abstracts_1984-88
               45    648: TRADE AND INDUSTRY ASAP_83-92/MAY


    8 files have one or more items; file list includes 14 files.
```

The most helpful files for this search appear to be 648 (*Trade & Industry ASAP*) and 111 (*National Newspaper Index*).

The next example illustrates the use of the Boolean NOT to eliminate unsuitable files. The best files for this search on the use of intervention techniques with potential teenage suicides are clearly file 1 (*ERIC*) and 291 (*Family Resources*). This example shows how the command RANK FILES can be used to arrange files in order of postings figures, which is particularly useful when checking a large group of files:

```
?select files psych not 7
    You have 10 files in your file list.
    (To see banners, use SHOW FILES command.)
```

```
?s teenage()suicide and intervention
 Your SELECT statement is:
   s teenage()suicide and intervention
            Items    File
            -----    ----
              11       1: ERIC _ 66-92/MAY.
               4      11: PSYCINFO _ 67-92/JULY
               1      37: SOCIOLOGICAL ABSTRACTS_63-92/JUN
               1      46: A-V ONLINE_1992/MAR
               4      86: MENTAL HEALTH ABSTRACTS _ 69-92/MAY
               8     291: FAMILY RESOURCES_70-92/APR

   6 files have one or more items; file list includes 10 files.

?rank files
Your last SELECT statement was:
   S TEENAGE()SUICIDE AND INTERVENTION

Ref          Items    File
---          -----    ----
N1            11        1: ERIC _ 66-92/MAY.
N2             8      291: FAMILY RESOURCES_70-92/APR
N3             4       11: PSYCINFO _ 67-92/JULY
N4             4       86: MENTAL HEALTH ABSTRACTS _ 69-92/MAY
N5             1       37: SOCIOLOGICAL ABSTRACTS_63-92/JUN
N6             1       46: A-V ONLINE_1992/MAR
N7             0       64: CHILD ABUSE AND NEGLECT AND FAMILY VIOLENCE_1964-1
N8             0      121: BRITISH EDUCATION INDEX_1976-1992/MAR
N9             0      163: AGELINE_MAY 1992
N10            0      468: PUBLIC OPINION ONLINE_1940-92 JUN

   6 files have one or more items; file list includes 10 files.
```

NOTE: There are no records available in the DIALINDEX file. All we have learned so far is which are the best files to search. We now need to change to the appropriate databases in order to carry out the real search.

Journal Name Finder

Another useful feature provided by DIALOG to aid in database selection is the *Journal Name Finder*, file 414. Like DIALINDEX, the *Journal Name Finder* contains information from all other files in the system. In this case, that information is which files contain citations to articles from individual journals. This is particularly useful if the user knows of a good journal or two in the field, or if the subject area is interdisciplinary. Some fields of study cross several database boundaries, and material in good journals may escape your notice because it is not obvious.

Here is an example. There is no single file on DIALOG that covers the area of anthropology, and you encounter a user who is interested in urban anthropology. There is a good journal, *Urban Anthropology*, so you decide to search the *Journal Name Finder* and see which files incorporate it. We begin the search with an EXPAND command, as there may be variant forms of the journal's name in different databases:

```
?b 414
     11jun92 10:08:03 User007659 Session B817.1
           $0.03    0.002 Hrs File1
   $0.03  Estimated cost File1
   $0.03  Estimated cost this search
   $0.03  Estimated total session cost  0.002 Hrs.
```

```
File 414:DIALOG JOURNAL NAME FINDER
        (COPR. DIALOG INFORMATION SRVCS, INC.)
 **FILE414: Use /FULLTEXT to identify journals from fulltext databases.

      Set   Items  Description
      ---   -----  -----------
?e urban anthropol

Ref    Items   Index-term
E1       1    URBAN AND SOCIAL CHANGE REVIEW 1985 18 1 3
E2       2    URBAN ANTHROP
E3       0   *URBAN ANTHROPOL
E4       8    URBAN ANTHROPOLOGY
E5       1    URBAN ANTHROPOLOGY 1983 12 2 141 159
E6       1    URBAN APPALACHIAN ADVOCATE
E7       1    URBAN CLIMATES SYMPOSIUM ON URBAN CLIMATES AN
E8       1    URBAN DATA SERVICE REPORTS INTERNATIONAL CITY
E9       1    URBAN DATA SERVICE REPT
E10      1    URBAN DEMANDS ON NATURAL RESOURCES WESTERN R
E11     12    URBAN DESIGN
E12      1    URBAN DESIGN FORUM

            Enter P or E for more
```

There are variant forms, as we suspected, and we select three of them:

```
?s e2,e4,e5
                2   URBAN ANTHROP
                8   URBAN ANTHROPOLOGY
                1   URBAN ANTHROPOLOGY 1983 12 2 141 159
       S1      11   E2,E4,E5
?t 1/5/1-3

 1/5/1
 01614881
URBAN ANTHROPOLOGY   (JN=)
    DIALOG FILE    1: ERIC  66-92/MAY.
    This file contains BIBLIOGRAPHIC records.
    Number of Records for this Journal, 04 JUNE 1992:  96


  1/5/2
  01504084
URBAN ANTHROPOLOGY   (JN=)
    DIALOG FILE    7: SOCIAL SCISEARCH  1972-199205W4
                    (COPR. ISI INC.1992)
    This file contains BIBLIOGRAPHIC records.
    Number of Records for this Journal, 04 JUNE 1992:  589


  1/5/3
  01310472
URBAN ANTHROPOLOGY   (JN=)
    DIALOG FILE   37: SOCIOLOGICAL ABSTRACTS  63-92/JUN
                    (COPR. SOC. ABSTRACTS)
    This file contains BIBLIOGRAPHIC records.
    Number of Records for this Journal, 04 JUNE 1992:  234
?t 1/7/all noheader
URBAN ANTHROPOLOGY                    File:   1  BIB Recs:   96
URBAN ANTHROPOLOGY                    File:   7  BIB Recs:  589
URBAN ANTHROPOLOGY                    File:  37  BIB Recs:  234
```

```
URBAN ANTHROP                                    File:  38   BIB Recs:      3
URBAN ANTHROP                                    File:  39   BIB Recs:      1
URBAN ANTHROPOLOGY                               File:  48   BIB Recs:      1
URBAN ANTHROPOLOGY                               File:  50   BIB Recs:     11
URBAN ANTHROPOLOGY                               File:  88   BIB Recs:     59
URBAN ANTHROPOLOGY, 1983, 12, 2, 141-159 File: 291   BIB Recs:      1
URBAN ANTHROPOLOGY                               File: 291   BIB Recs:     20
URBAN ANTHROPOLOGY                               File: 292   BIB Recs:    158
```

This method of TYPEing gives a nice display, organized by file number, and we can easily identify the most useful files—7, 37, and 292.

Saving Searches

The availability of access to so many different databases and the ability to use the same search strategy on several files is an important feature of the major online systems. However, such cross-file searching is not as simple as it might seem, because files vary in content, record format, and searchable fields. It is important to realize that the search system may be inconsistent in the way in which it treats features such as prefix or suffix codes, parse rules, and limit qualifiers on different files. Extra effort is needed in planning a search that is to be run on multiple databases, and careful scrutiny of the documentation for each of the files is crucial.

The SAVE command enables the searcher to store a search strategy in the mainframe computer to use on another database or for use again at a later date. A stored strategy on DIALOG is known as a SearchSave, and there are three possible types of SearchSaves:

1. A *temporary* SearchSave, using the SAVE TEMP command, assigns a name to the search strategy and stores it for one week on the system mainframe machine. There are no storage charges for this type of SAVE, and the search will be erased automatically after seven days. This could be used to hold a search for a brief time while you consult with documentation or the user. If you will be off for only a very short

time, you might also consider the LOGOFF HOLD command. This will log you off from DIALOG, but it will preserve your sets. You can log back on within a half-hour on the same password, do a DS, and your sets will still be there.

2. A *standard* SearchSave, using the SAVE command, stores a search permanently at a cost of 15 cents per command line and 40 cents per search per month. This type of search is saved until released by the user. It is often used to store searches that may be accessed later as part of a library's current awareness service, or for "hedges" that can be used in the future as part of another search. *Hedges* are complicated blocks that include a great number of synonymous terms used to represent a single concept such as "secondary education," which the searcher may well want to use again in the future. It can save a great deal of the effort involved in search preparation to be able to store such blocks for repeat use, when they can be combined with different concept blocks.

Here is an example of the use of such a hedge. Notice that we do not have to select all the individual terms for secondary education because they have been saved previously.

```
?b 1
        11jun92 10:20:18 User007659 Session B817.10
            $0.50    0.033 Hrs File1
     $0.50   Estimated cost File1
     $0.50   Estimated cost this search
     $4.21   Estimated total session cost   0.286 Hrs.

File   1:ERIC   66-92/MAY.
FILE 1: Price changes will go into effect June 1, 1992.
Please see HOMEBASE Announcements for more details.
```

```
         Set   Items   Description
         ---   -----   -----------
?exs sasec
         S1    57845   SECONDARY EDUCATION  (EDUCATION PROVIDED IN GRADE 7, 8,
                       OR 9 THRO
         S2     8208   JUNIOR HIGH SCHOOLS  (PROVIDING FORMAL EDUCATION IN
                       GRADES 7, 8, A...)
         S3    14893   HIGH SCHOOLS  (PROVIDING FORMAL EDUCATION IN GRADES 9 OR
                       10...)
         S4     1864   GRADE 9
         S5     1290   GRADE 10
         S6     1232   GRADE 11
         S7     1403   GRADE 12
         S8     3014   SECONDARY SCHOOLS
         S9      728   HIGH SCHOOL EQUIVALENCY PROGRAMS  (ADULT EDUCATIONAL
                       ACTIVITIES CONC
         S10   83402   SECONDARY EDUCATION OR JUNIOR HIGH SCHOOLS OR HIGH
                       SCHOOLS OR GRADE 9 OR GRADE 10 OR GRADE 11 OR GRADE 12 OR
                       SECONDARY SCHOOLS OR HIGH SCHOOL EQUIVALENCY PROGRAMS
?s science fiction
         S11     360   SCIENCE FICTION
?s s10 and s11
               83402   S10
                 360   S11
         S12     114   S10 AND S11
?s s12/1989:1992
                 114   S12
               78173   PY=1989 : PY=1992
         S13      11   S12/1989:1992
?t 13/8/1-4


  13/8/1
EJ421924   SE547242
  Science Fiction Stories with Reasonable Astronomy.
  Descriptors: *Astronomy; *Bibliographies; *College Science; Earth Science;
  Educational Resources; Higher Education; Physical Sciences; Physics;
Science   Education; *Science  Fiction; *Science Materials; Secondary
Education; *Secondary School Science; Space Exploration; Space Sciences
  Identifiers: Planets; *Solar System


  13/8/2
EJ421125   CS741037
  Dragons, Dystopias,  and  Time  Travel: Fantasy and Science Fiction for
Everyone (Books for the Teenage Reader).
  Descriptors:  *Adolescent   Literature;  Adolescents;   Annotated
Bibliographies;  Book  Reviews;  *Fantasy; Reading Interests; Reading
Materials; *Science Fiction; Secondary Education


  13/8/3
EJ412339   SE546462
  Science Fiction Aids Science Teaching.
  Descriptors: *College Science;  *Films; Higher Education;  *Inservice
Teacher Education;  *Physics; Postsecondary Education; Science Education;
*Science  Fiction;  *Scientific  Concepts;  Secondary  Education; Secondary School
Science


  13/8/4
EJ406735   CS739668
  Using Film in the Humanities Classroom: The Case of "Metropolis."
  Descriptors: Class Activities; *Film Criticism; *Films; Popular Culture;
*Science Fiction; Secondary Education; Teaching Methods
  Identifiers: *Metropolis (Film); Weimar Republic
```

3. A *current awareness* or *SDI* (Selective Dissemination of Information) SearchSave, using the SAVE ALERT command, is saved and automatically called up and executed on every new collection of update records as they are added to the selected database or databases. It is stored permanently until released by the user, and the results will be sent to the searcher, either through the postal service or via DIAL-MAIL. Charges for this service vary by database, but the costs cover any number of search terms and a maximum of 25 records printed in full format per update run. This command cannot be used on all files, so once again it is important to check the documentation carefully.

The use of this SDI service means that new information is received by the user automatically as soon as it is available, without the need for the searcher to check repeatedly. This type of current awareness service is particularly useful in the business environment and can be used to

a. keep up-to-date with the latest research,
b. monitor the activities of the competition,
c. track product announcements,
d. watch for new patents, and
e. stay abreast of the market.

It is often useful to store a title or some comments using the comment feature—* (an asterisk)—as part of the SearchSave, because this simplifies the identification of the offline prints when they arrive in the mail.

Combining SAVE with the DIALINDEX feature, we can see that by using the SAVE TEMP command it is possible to enter a search once in DIALINDEX in order to discover which files will provide the highest retrieval, and then move to each file in turn in order to retrieve the actual records.

SearchSave strategies are prepared in the same way as regular searches, but only set-generating commands can be saved. Run your search online, and then enter the command SAVE after you have TYPEd your results. All SELECT, SELECT STEPS, SORT, and PRINT commands that have been entered since the last BEGIN will be saved. Notice that SAVE does not store other commands (such as EXPAND, DISPLAY SETS, or TYPE) that you may have entered during the same search, because these commands relate to file-specific data.

The response from the system will confirm that your strategy has been stored and will assign it an identifying number consisting of three digits preceded by two letters. An attractive option allows you to assign your own three- to five-character name to a SAVEd search, making it easier to identify it in the future. Note that two letters will be automatically added to the front of the name you choose in order for the system to identify it. You will need to make a note of this name for future reference. Here is an example:

```
?b 191

File 191:ART LIT. INTL. (RILA)   75-89
      (COPR.1989 J. PAUL GETTY TRUST-RILA)
 **FILE191: Records from BHA are not yet available on DIALOG

      Set  Items  Description
      ---  -----  -----------
?ss (church or churches or cathedral? ?) and byzantine and (style or architecture)
      S1    5877  CHURCH
      S2    4602  CHURCHES
      S3    3481  CATHEDRAL? ?
      S4    2070  BYZANTINE
      S5    4677  STYLE
      S6   31854  ARCHITECTURE
      S7     416  (CHURCH OR CHURCHES OR CATHEDRAL? ?) AND BYZANTINE AND
                  (STYLE OR ARCHITECTURE)
?save temp arch
Temp SearchSave "TBARCH" stored
```

Note the name to remember is TBARCH.

In order to use a search strategy that you have previously SAVEd, connect to the database in which you wish to run the search using a normal BEGIN command. Then enter the command EXECUTE (EX) or EXECUTE STEPS (EXS), followed by the serial number of the search. The search will be run as though each line of the search strategy were entered separately, with the set numbers being adjusted automatically. The command EXECUTE can also be used but only returns a single set number (S1) for the complete search strategy. This makes it impossible to modify the search, a move that may well be necessary when you are searching a different file. The use of EXECUTE STEPS is thus preferable, because it returns a set number for each command line of the stored search, enabling it to be easily modified by the use of additional SELECT commands. Note the difference in set numbers between these two examples using EX and EXS, when we EXECUTE our SAVEd result on two different databases:

```
?b 179
        11jun92 10:15:47 User007659 Session B817.6
              $0.24    0.016 Hrs File191
     $0.24   Estimated cost File191
     $0.24   Estimated cost this search
     $2.50   Estimated total session cost   0.169 Hrs.


File 179:ARCHITECTURE DATABASE  JUN 1992
        (COPR. BRITISH ARCHITECTURAL LIBRARY.)
*******************************************
* Au sorts are unavailable in file 179 *
*******************************************

        Set   Items   Description
        ---   -----   -----------
?ex tbarch
              1699   CHURCH
              1849   CHURCHES
               674   CATHEDRAL? ?
                34   BYZANTINE
               749   STYLE
             15444   ARCHITECTURE
                 7   (CHURCH OR CHURCHES OR CATHEDRAL? ?) AND BYZANTINE AND
                     (STYLE OR ARCHITECTURE)
        S1     7   Serial: TBARCH
?b 178
        11jun92 10:16:06 User007659 Session B817.7
              $0.24    0.016 Hrs File179
     $0.24   Estimated cost File179
     $0.24   Estimated cost this search
     $2.74   Estimated total session cost   0.186 Hrs.


File 178:AVERY ARCHITECTURE INDEX  1979-91
        (c.1991 J.Paul Getty Trust,A.H.I.P.)

        Set   Items   Description
        ---   -----   -----------
?exs tbarch
        S1   1276   CHURCH
        S2   2353   CHURCHES
        S3    692   CATHEDRAL? ?
        S4    183   BYZANTINE
        S5   1344   STYLE
        S6  17371   ARCHITECTURE
        S7     16   (CHURCH OR CHURCHES OR CATHEDRAL? ?) AND BYZANTINE AND
                    (STYLE OR ARCHITECTURE)
?t 7/2/1

 7/2/1
 0110446          RLINNYCA91-V1844
Paliochoro: survey of a **Byzantine** city on the island of Kythera: second
    report /G.E. Ince, et al.
 Ince, G.E
 Annual  of the British School at Athens 1989, no.84, p.[407]-416,pl.53-55,
    1989
 BIBLIOGRAPHIC NOTE(S): maps, photos., plans, secns., refs.
 LANGUAGE: English
```

```
COUNTRY OF PUBLICATION: England
NOTES: Emphasis on ecclesiastical architecture.
DESCRIPTOR(S):
    Cities and towns—Byzantine—Greece—Kythera—Paliochora; Churches—
    Byzantine—Greece—Kythera—Paliochora
```

Because a SearchSave is stored as a series of command lines, it is possible to review, it without actually running the search, through the use of the RECALL command with the search name, RECALL TBARCH in this example. It is also useful to be able to review all saved searches using the RECALL SAVE option. This will list all the serial numbers and names of searches that are stored under the password currently in use:

```
?recall temp
    Name        Date        Time      Size
    -------    --------    --------    ----

    TBARCH     11jun92     11:45:35      1
    TBPREG     11jun92     13:03:07      1
    TBSEC      11jun92     10:21:55      1
```

When a SAVEd search is no longer needed, it should be deleted from memory using the RELEASE command, because all SAVEd searches incur ongoing storage charges. As a safety measure, searches can only be EXECUTEd or RELEASEd using the same password with which they were created. So, you need to make a note of this if you have more than one password. In the following example, we are releasing the search we had previously SAVEd and EXECUTEd:

```
?release tbarch
    TBARCH released
```

The sequence of commands when saving and reusing a search is:

BEGIN file number,

SELECT search terms and logical combinations,

SAVE name (three to five characters),

BEGIN another file number,

EXECUTE STEPS search name, and

RELEASE search name.

The sequence can, of course, be repeated in as many files as necessary, without the need to SAVE the search again. Remember, it is being SAVEd automatically until it is RELEASEd.

OneSearch

The use of the SAVE TEMP command to move from file to file repeating the same search has now been superseded on the DIALOG system by the development of a new search feature known as One-Search. But SAVE TEMP is still useful when the databases to be searched differ to such an extent that searching on the additional indexes cannot be standardized and the search strategy needs to be drastically modified from file to file. It can also be used as an alternative to LOGOFF HOLD when you want to take time out to check documentation or to further develop your strategy. OneSearch enables a group of up to 40 databases to be accessed with a single BEGIN command, using both file numbers and DIALINDEX Subject Categories. The system responds with a list of the file banners for the selected databases and then the usual prompt for the search statement.

When you use the OneSearch option, the search looks exactly like a search run on a single file, though the postings figures will be those for the whole group of files together. If separate postings figures for the individual files are required, you will need to enter the SET DETAIL ON command before entering the search strategy.

Tip: OneSearch tends to provide a confusing amount of detail when used with the SELECT STEPS or EXPAND commands and DETAIL set on, so be careful!

Our previous search looks like the following when we are using OneSearch:

```
?b 56,178,179
        11jun92 10:17:14 User007659 Session B817.8
            $0.50     0.033 Hrs File178
            $0.00   1 Type(s) in Format  2
            $0.00   1 Types
    $0.50   Estimated cost File178
    $0.50   Estimated cost this search
    $3.24   Estimated total session cost   0.219 Hrs.
```

```
SYSTEM:OS  - DIALOG OneSearch
  File  56:ART MODERN   1974 THRU DEC 1991
          (Copr. ABC Clio INC.)
  File 178:AVERY ARCHITECTURE INDEX  1979-91
          (c.1991 J.Paul Getty Trust,A.H.I.P.)
  File 179:ARCHITECTURE DATABASE  JUN 1992
          (COPR. BRITISH ARCHITECTURAL LIBRARY.)
*******************************************
* Au sorts are unavailable in file 179 *
*******************************************

        Set   Items  Description
        ---   -----  -----------
?ss (church or churches or cathedral? ?) and byzantine and (style or architecture)
        S1    4063   CHURCH
        S2    4691   CHURCHES
        S3    1732   CATHEDRAL? ?
        S4     373   BYZANTINE
        S5   12127   STYLE
        S6   43830   ARCHITECTURE
        S7      32   (CHURCH OR CHURCHES OR CATHEDRAL? ?) AND BYZANTINE AND
                     (STYLE OR ARCHITECTURE)
?set detail on
DETAIL set on
?ds

Set    File    Items   Description
        56      1088
       178      1276
       179      1699
S1              4063    CHURCH
        56       489
       178      2353
       179      1849
S2              4691    CHURCHES
        56       366
       178       692
       179       674
S3              1732    CATHEDRAL? ?
        56       156
       178       183
       179        34
S4               373    BYZANTINE
        56     10034
       178      1344
       179       749
S5             12127    STYLE
        56     11015
       178     17371
       179     15444
S6             43830    ARCHITECTURE
        56         9
       178        16
       179         7
S7                32    (CHURCH OR CHURCHES OR CATHEDRAL? ?) AND BYZANTINE A-
                       ND (STYLE OR ARCHITECTURE)
```

Records retrieved using OneSearch may be TYPEd, DISPLAYed, or PRINTed in the usual manner, save that, instead of being in the usual reverse chronological order, all the records from the first file are displayed first, followed by all the records from the second file, and so on. A sampling of records from the full range of files can be viewed by using the FROM EACH option with the TYPE command.

For example, the command:
t 5/6/1-5 from each
will view the first five titles from each of the files searched and is useful to provide a flavoring of the material retrieved. The result from our previous search is as follows:

```
?t 7/3/1 from each

 7/3/1     (Item 1 from file: 56)
173445    173445
 ROBERT  WEIR SCHULTZ, ARCHITECT, AND HIS WORK FOR THE MARQUESSES OF BUTE:
AN ESSAY
 STAMP, G.
 ROTHESAY, SCOTLAND: MOUNT STUART (1981), 102PP. 38 ILLUS. BIBLIOG.

 7/3/10    (Item 1 from file: 178)
 0110446         RLINNYCA91-V1844
Paliochoro: survey of a Byzantine city on the island of Kythera: second
    report /G.E. Ince, et al.
 Ince, G.E
 Annual  of the British School at Athens 1989, no.84, p.[407]-416,pl.53-55,
    1989
 BIBLIOGRAPHIC NOTE(S): maps, photos., plans, secns., refs.

 7/3/26    (Item 1 from file: 179)
 0194760       A157071
Originality in Byzantine architecture: the case of Nea Moni. - Article by
    Robert Ousterhout -
 Society of Architectural Historians. Journal, vol. 51, no. 1, 1992 Mar.,
    p. 48-60.
 BIBLIOGRAPHIC  NOTES:  Includes  photos,  plans,  sections,  elevations,
    axonometric views, sketches -
```

It is particularly helpful when using OneSearch to use the REMOVE DUPLICATES (RD) command we mentioned earlier before TYPEing or PRINTing results because of the possible overlaps in file coverage. Using it on our previous example removes two documents (postings fall from 32 to 30):

```
?rd s7
   ...completed examining records
       S8    30  RD S7 (unique
   items)
```

OneSearch can also be used as a substitute for DIALINDEX to help with the identification of files that are likely to be the most useful for a given search, though you need to check documentation because OneSearch and RD are not available on all databases.

Using the OneSearch option incurs no additional costs and in fact is probably cheaper than searching on a file-by-file basis. DIALOG tracks the time spent in each file during a OneSearch session and charges accordingly. The search output is charged at the appropriate rate for each of the files used.

Problems of Multifile Searching

With the vast increase in the number of databases being produced today and the proliferation of full-text and nonbibliographic files, it is much more likely that almost any given topic will be covered in a range of different files. Many, perhaps most, search topics now require the use of multiple files to obtain comprehensive results, even in areas as isolated as many fields in the humanities. It has become clear that one database alone will not provide comprehensive coverage of the literature of any field.[3]

Multifile searching is something of an art in itself. It certainly necessitates additional preparation in the choice of search terms and the accurate use of prefix and suffix codes. It must be remembered that controlled vocabularies will vary among files, as will the availability of different Additional indexes. Lists of do's and don'ts that have appeared in the literature provide some useful suggestions regarding the problems that need to be addressed when searching multiple files:[4]

- Database documentation and thesauri are important as sources of terminology, but do not rely on a single controlled vocabulary.

- Prefer natural language terms linked by proximity operators, because controlled vocabularies will vary.

- Use truncation to cover variant word forms and English versus American spellings.

- Be particularly careful with classification numbers and prefix codes, as different fields may need to be ORed together to make sure that all files are covered.

- Note variations in the punctuation of authors' names in different files; use truncation if appropriate.

A couple more caveats: Remember that if you are in more than one database, your sets will probably be much bigger than if you were in only one, so do not be thrown by big sets. Use the FROM command to see what is in each file; if you find only one or two files contributing useful material, search in those only. Again, use FROM:

s madonna(1n)enthrone? from 56, 191

Also watch truncation. As we said in chapter 7, a little goes a long way, and that is especially true in a multifile search. Be especially careful truncating authors' names. There are many ways in which databases represent authors' names, and you want to get all the variant forms, but you do not want to truncate too far. For example,

s au=smith?

in five files is probably not a good idea!

Good preparation is always the key to successful searching. It is even more important when using multiple databases. Allow plenty of time for search preparation, and make full use of the available documentation.

Search Example

The following is an example of a full-blown search that makes use of many of the techniques discussed in this chapter:

```
DIALOG INFORMATION SERVICES
PLEASE LOGON:
  ********
ENTER PASSWORD:
  ********

Welcome to DIALOG
    Dialog level 29.01.05B

Last logoff: 11jun92 10:21:54
Logon file001 11jun92 12:42:44
* * * TEXTLINE is now available. Begin TXTLN or TEXTLINE * * *

File  1:ERIC   66-92/MAY.
FILE 1: Price changes will go into effect June 1, 1992.
Please see HOMEBASE Announcements for more details.

      Set  Items  Description
      ---  -----  -----------
?b 411
      11jun92 12:42:54 User007659 Session B818.1
          $0.03   0.002 Hrs File1
    $0.03  Estimated cost File1
    $0.03  Estimated cost this search
    $0.03  Estimated total session cost   0.002 Hrs.
File 411:DIALINDEX(tm)

DIALINDEX(tm)
    (Copr. DIALOG Info.Ser.Inc.)

*** DIALINDEX search results display in an abbreviated ***
*** format unless you enter the SET DETAIL ON command. ***
```

```
?sf 11,37,291,1,64
   You have 5 files in your file list.
   (To see banners, use SHOW FILES command.)
?s (premarital(n)(pregnan? or birth) or birth?(2n)(out(1w)wedlock)) and ((marital or
marriage??)(2n)(satisfact? or stable or stability or instability or well?))
   Your SELECT statement is:
   s (premarital(n)(pregnan? or birth) or birth?(2n)(out(1w)wedlock)) and
((marital or marriage? ?)(2n)(satisfact? or stable or stability or
instability or well?))
            Items   File
            -----   ----
                5   11: PSYCINFO _ 67-92/JULY
                5   37: SOCIOLOGICAL ABSTRACTS_63-92/JUN
                4  291: FAMILY RESOURCES_70-92/APR
                5    1: ERIC _ 66-92/MAY.

   4 files have one or more items; file list includes 5 files.


?save temp preg
Temp SearchSave "TBPREG" stored
?rank files
Your last SELECT statement was:
   S (PREMARITAL(N)(PREGNAN? OR BIRTH) OR BIRTH?(2N)(OUT(1W)WEDLOCK)) AND -
((MARITAL OR MARRIAGE? ?)(2N)(SATISFACT? OR STABLE OR STABILITY OR INSTABI-
LITY OR WELL?))
Ref        Items   File
---        -----   ----
N1             5   11: PSYCINFO _ 67-92/JULY
N2             5   37: SOCIOLOGICAL ABSTRACTS_63-92/JUN
N3             5    1: ERIC _ 66-92/MAY.
N4             4  291: FAMILY RESOURCES_70-92/APR
N5             0   64: CHILD ABUSE AND NEGLECT AND FAMILY VIOLENCE_1964-1

   4 files have one or more items; file list includes 5 files.


?b n1:n4
        11jun92 12:46:03 User007659 Session B818.2
            $0.99    0.066 Hrs File411
     $0.99   Estimated cost File411
     $0.99   Estimated cost this search
     $1.02   Estimated total session cost   0.069 Hrs.


SYSTEM:OS  - DIALOG OneSearch
   File  11:PSYCINFO   67-92/JULY
         (COPR. AM. PSYCH. ASSOC.)
   File  37:SOCIOLOGICAL ABSTRACTS  63-92/JUN
         (COPR. SOC. ABSTRACTS)
*
   File   1:ERIC   66-92/MAY.
FILE 1: Price changes will go into effect June 1, 1992.
Please see HOMEBASE Announcements for more details.
   File 291:FAMILY RESOURCES  70-92/APR
          (C NATL COUNCIL ON FAMILY RELATIONS 1992)
FILE 291: Price changes will go into effect June 1, 1992.
Please see HOMEBASE Announcements for more details.
```

Notice that we selected the files to BEGIN in directly from the N display of the ranked files; looks a little like SELECTing terms from an EXPANDed E or R display, doesn't it? Makes life a little easier.

Also notice that because we want to EXECUTE the last search we SAVEd, we do not really need to give the search name. EXS will do the job without a name:

```
          Set   Items   Description
          ---   -----   -----------
?exs
Executing TBPREG
               2620   PREMARITAL
              15526   PREGNAN?
              26495   BIRTH
                178   PREMARITAL(N)(PREGNAN? OR BIRTH)
              28798   BIRTH?
              68518   OUT
                279   WEDLOCK
                 88   BIRTH?(2N)OUT(1W)WEDLOCK
              29395   MARITAL
              28484   MARRIAGE? ?
              44408   SATISFACT?
              11883   STABLE
              13071   STABILITY
               3161   INSTABILITY
             110631   WELL?
               7344   (MARITAL OR MARRIAGE? ?)(2N)((((SATISFACT? OR STABLE) OR
                      STABILITY) OR INSTABILITY) OR WELL?)
          S1     19   (PREMARITAL(N)(PREGNAN? OR BIRTH) OR
                      BIRTH?(2N)(OUT(1W)WEDLOCK)) AND ((MARITAL OR MARRIAGE?
                      ?)(2N)(SATISFACT? OR STABLE OR STABILITY OR INSTABILITY
                      OR WELL?))
?rd s1
...completed examining records
          S2     13   RD S1 (unique items)
```

The foregoing is a good example of the use of REMOVE DUPLICATES. We are searching in four files here, and there are only 13 unique documents in that set of 19. Viewing the same document over and over is a waste of money, and so for reasonably sized sets (say, under 100), RD is a nice technique. It would appear that we got some good results. If we wanted to, we could pearl-grow using some of the terms from good documents here: MARITAL RELATIONS, PARENTHOOD STATUS, MARITAL INSTABILITY, PREGNANCY, DIVORCE, and so on:

```
?t 2/8/all

 2/8/1     (Item 1 from file: 11)
00829154          29-71272
  The effect of premarital pregnancy and birth on the marital well-being of
Black and White newlywed couples.
  Major Descriptors:  *PARENTHOOD STATUS;  *MARITAL RELATIONS;  *RACIAL AND
    ETHNIC DIFFERENCES;  *SPOUSES
  Minor Descriptors:  MONEY;  BLACKS;  WHITES;  ADULTHOOD
  Descriptor Codes:   36675;  29640;  42618;  49380;  31870;  06150;  56720;
    01150
  Identifiers:  premarital  pregnancy  or  birth  &  parental  or  family  of
    origin  resources  &  marital  processes,  marital  well  being,  Black  vs
    White newlywed couples
  Section Headings:  2950 -MARRIAGE & FAMILY

 2/8/2     (Item 2 from file: 11)
00822603          78-32992
  Marital  stability and changes in marital quality in newly wed couples: A
test of the contextual model.
  Major  Descriptors:  *DEMOGRAPHIC CHARACTERISTICS;  *PERSONALITY TRAITS;
    *REMARRIAGE;  *STEPCHILDREN;  *MARITAL RELATIONS
  Minor  Descriptors:  MARITAL  SATISFACTION;  MARITAL  STATUS;  SPOUSES;
    LONGITUDINAL STUDIES;  ADULTHOOD
```

Descriptor Codes: 13460; 37860; 43885; 49720; 29640; 29645; 29660; 49380; 28760; 01150
Identifiers: demographic & personality characteristics & marital history & presence of stepchildren, marital quality & stability, newlyweds, 1 yr study
Section Headings: 2950 -MARRIAGE & FAMILY

2/8/3   (Item 3 from file: 11)
00713093   77-04358
Demographic determinants of delayed divorce.
Major   Descriptors: *DIVORCE;   *MARITAL RELATIONS;   *PREDICTION; *DEMOGRAPHIC CHARACTERISTICS
Minor Descriptors: ADOLESCENCE; ADULTHOOD
Descriptor Codes: 14780; 29640; 39940; 13460; 00920; 01150
Identifiers: predictors of delayed divorce & marital stability, 15-44 yr old females
Section Headings: 2950 -MARRIAGE & FAMILY

2/8/4   (Item 4 from file: 11)
00487774   22-53213
Relationship of premarital pregnancy to marital satisfaction and personal adjustment.
Major   Descriptors: *MARITAL RELATIONS;   *EMOTIONAL ADJUSTMENT; *PREGNANCY; *HUMAN FEMALES; *PREMARITAL INTERCOURSE
Minor Descriptors: ADULTHOOD
Descriptor Codes: 29640; 16760; 40050; 23450; 40100; 01150
Identifiers: premarital pregnancy, marital satisfaction & emotional adjustment, 21-53 yr old females
Section Headings: 2950 -MARRIAGE & FAMILY

2/8/5   (Item 5 from file: 11)
00214289   56-05899
Premarital pregnancy and marital instability.
Minor Descriptors: PREMARITAL INTERCOURSE; PREGNANCY; UNWED MOTHERS; MARITAL RELATIONS; DIVORCE
Descriptor Codes: 40100; 40050; 54890; 29640; 14780
Identifiers: premarital pregnancy, marital instability
Section Headings: 2950 -MARRIAGE & FAMILY

2/8/6   (Item 1 from file: 37)
2092004   89W10729
A Study on the Stability of First Marriage for Married Women of Childbearing Age in Taiwan-An Exploration of the Relationship of Age at First Marriage, Dimensions of Premarried Pregnancy, and Marital Decision-Making
Title in Chinese
DESCRIPTORS: Taiwan (D851100); Fertility (D298200); Fecundity (D294300); Marital Relations (D490800); Stability (D828700)
IDENTIFIERS: first marriage stability, women of childbearing age, Taiwan; survey data;
SECTION HEADINGS: social welfare- marital & family problems   (6144)

2/8/7   (Item 2 from file: 37)
074110   76H7893
THE INSTABILITY OF TEENAGE MARRIAGE IN THE UNITED STATES; AN EVALUATION OF THE SOCIO-ECONOMIC STATUS HYPOTHESIS
DESCRIPTORS: Marriage, Marriages, Marital (259000); Teenage, Teenagers (456900); Instability (234976); Socioeconomic (434455)
IDENTIFIERS: SOCIOECONOMIC FACTORS OF INSTABILITY IN TEENAGE MARRIAGES;
SECTION HEADINGS: the family and socialization-adolescence & youth (1939)

```
 2/8/8       (Item 3 from file: 37)
064475   74G8263
High School Marriages: A Longitudinal Study
 DESCRIPTORS:  Family,  Families  (171600);  Adolescence,  Adolescent,
    Adolescents (014600); Marriage, Marriages, Marital (259000)
 IDENTIFIERS: A study of high-school marriages
 SECTION  HEADINGS:  the  family and socialization-sociology of the family
    (1941)

 2/8/9       (Item 1 from file: 1)
EJ355111   UD512881
  Should We Discourage Teenage Marriage?
  Descriptors:  *Adolescents;  Attitude  Change;  *Early Parenthood; Family
Characteristics;   Fathers;  *Illegitimate  Births;  *Marital  Instability;
*Marriage; Married Students; *Unwed Mothers

 2/8/10      (Item 2 from file: 1)
EJ280692   CG524249
  Early  Marriage,  Premarital  Fertility,  and Marital Dissolution: Results
for Blacks and Whites.
  Descriptors:  *Chronological  Age;  Cohort  Analysis;  Family  Problems;
Females;  *Illegitimate  Births;  *Marital  Instability; *Pregnancy; *Racial
Differences; *Spouses

 2/8/11      (Item 3 from file: 1)
ED142911   CG011645
  Household,  Family  and  Kinship  as Mechanisms of Survival in a Changing
Society: A Jamaican Example.
  Descriptors: Adjustment  (to  Environment);  Family  Life; *Family Role;
*Family  Structure;  Group  Unity;  *Marital  Instability; Marriage; *Social
Change; Social Relations; *Sociocultural Patterns; State of the Art Reviews
  Identifiers: *Jamaica; *West Indies

 2/8/12      (Item 1 from file: 291)
0232274
  MODERNIZATION AND HOUSEHOLD FORMATION ON ST. BART: CONTINUITY AND CHANGE
  Section  Headings:  FAMILY  LIFE IN FOREIGN COUNTRIES (003); DIFFERENTIAL
MARRIAGE RATES (055); FAMILY AND SOCIAL CHANGE (005); MARRIAGE SATISFACTION
AND PREDICTION STUDIES (051)
  Descriptors:   FRENCH-WEST-INDIES     MARRIAGE-RATES     SOCIAL-CHANGE
MARRIAGE-STUDIES

 2/8/13      (Item 2 from file: 291)
0206704
  JOURNAL OF MARRIAGE & THE FAMILY. VOLUME 50, NO. 2.
  Section  Headings:  MARRIAGE  SATISFACTION  AND PREDICTION STUDIES (051);
FAMILY RELATIONSHIPS (022)
  Descriptors: FAMILY-RELATIONSHIPS    MARITAL-RELATIONSHIPS
?release tbpreg
TBPREG released
?log
```

Notes

[1]Kathleen Y. Macaccio, ed. (1992), *Computer-Readable Databases: A Directory and Data Sourcebook*, 8th ed. (Detroit: Gale Research).

[2]William Saffady (January/February 1992), "Availability and Cost of Online Search Services," *Library Technology Reports* 28(1).

[3]Geraldene Walker (October 1990), "Searching the Humanities: Subject Overlap and Search Vocabulary," *Database* 13(5):37-46.

[4]Donald T. Hawkins (April 1978), "Multiple Database Searching," *Online* 2(2):9-15.

As we have said, there are many kinds of databases that may be searched online. Up to this point, we have concentrated on bibliographic databases, which provide citations to articles and other items in the published literature. The techniques we have discussed so far (controlled vocabulary searching, free-text searching, and other special features) have all been aimed at this type of retrieval.

Some of these techniques, though, can also be of use in searching other kinds of databases: files that are online versions of print reference or directory sources, files that provide information on citation patterns in the scientific literature, and files that not only give pointers to the literature but also contain the full text of the original documents. Those files are all available via the major online vendors, and each requires special techniques and tricks in order to search them effectively. In this chapter, we will look at these different files, discuss their use and usefulness, and explore some of these "tricks." Many reference sources and directories in common use are also available in online formats. As with so many of the bibliographic databases, many of these sources were produced using computer-assisted techniques, so the raw data were available in electronic form. It was thus a relatively easy matter to mount those files and provide online access to them.

11

SEARCHING OTHER KINDS OF DATABASES: REFERENCE, DIRECTORY, FULL TEXT, CITATION

Reference and Directory Files

The first question you should ask yourself when you are considering using an online system to search a reference database is: Is it worth it? If the research question is straightforward and you have the printed tool, it is probably a better idea to use print. Many of the ready reference files are among the more expensive files available on online systems, because of their wide availability and ease of use in print form, and because searching in these files tends to be rather quick. Thus, the database vendors charge more to maximize profits.

However, there are situations in which online searching of these sources may be more efficient and cost-effective: You may not have the print version, or it may be out of date. The particular query you are searching may require more in-depth work than the usual print source can readily support. Also keep in mind your time and effort as a professional. If answering a query will require 30 minutes of your time manually as opposed to five minutes online, it may be cheaper, in the long run, to go online.

Once you have made the decision to go online, you must next choose the appropriate source. In many cases, this will be much easier than choosing files for a bibliographic search. You may already be familiar with the print versions of these sources, or there may be only one potential source. In some cases, though, it may not be so clear. In that case, you will need to examine documentation or consult other staff for advice. Many of the techniques we discussed in chapter 10 for database selection (DIALINDEX, Journal Name Finder, OneSearch) probably will not work here, because they are primarily designed for use with bibliographic databases.

Searching in reference databases is often quite different from searching bibliographic databases. We are not interested as much in creating sets of potentially good documents as we are in zeroing in on the one (or more) right answer. You will find you use more special features of the databases and far less, if any, controlled vocabulary and free-text searching. In DIALOG terms, this translates into much more extensive use of prefix and suffix searching: Additional indexes, limits, qualifiers, and so on.

In reference searching, the database documentation is crucial: DIALOG bluesheets and whitesheets provide detailed information on database coverage, construction, record structure, search technique, output formats, and so on. This is even more important here than in the bibliographic files, due to the highly structured nature of the data in these files.

Let's look at a few specific examples. First, here is a search in a source you may well be familiar with in the print domain: *Books in Print* (file 470 in DIALOG). Does Stephen King have any new books coming out in the next few months? Because the online version of *BIP* also incorporates *Forthcoming Books in Print*, we can find this out. We begin by EXPANDing on his name, because we are not sure if it is Stephen or Steven:

```
File 470:BOOKS IN PRINT   THRU 1992/MAY
        (COPR R. R. BOWKER 1992)
**File 470: Price changes are effective May 1, 1992.
Please type: ?RATES 470 for new prices.

        Set   Items   Description
        ---   -----   -----------
?e au=king, ste

Ref    Items   Index-term
E1        1    AU=KING, STANLEY G.
E2        1    AU=KING, STANLEY H.
E3        0    *AU=KING, STE
E4        4    AU=KING, STELLA
E5      106    AU=KING, STEPHEN
E6        1    AU=KING, STEPHEN S.
E7        1    AU=KING, STEPHEN T.
E8        3    AU=KING, STEPHEN W.
E9        4    AU=KING, STEPHEN,PSEUD.
E10       3    AU=KING, STEVE
E11       2    AU=KING, SUSAN
E12       1    AU=KING, SUSAN E.

        Enter P or E for more
?s e5,e9
              106   AU=KING, STEPHEN
                4   AU=KING, STEPHEN,PSEUD.
     S1       110   E5,E9
?s s1 and pd>9206                              any publication dates after 6/92
              110   S1
            23059   PD>9206
     S2         3   S1 AND PD>9206
?t 2/5/all


 2/5/1
04311983   2397562XX    STATUS: Active entry
  TITLE: Gerald's Game
  AUTHOR: King, Stephen
  PUBLISHER: Viking Penguin   PUBLICATION DATE: 09/1992 (920901)
  LCCN: N/A
  BINDING: Trade - $23.00
  ISBN: 0-670-84650-3
  VOLUME(S): N/A
  ORDER NO.: N/A
  IMPRINT: Viking
  STATUS IN FILE: New (92-04)


 2/5/2
02401265   2358567XX    STATUS: Active entry
  TITLE: Honor & Glory
  AUTHOR: Shirley, Sam-Editor; Swekel, Arnie-Illustrator; King, Stephen-
Illustrator; DiZeriga, Gus-Illustrator
  SERIES: Pendragon Roleplaying Game Ser.
  PUBLISHER: Chaosium  PUBLICATION DATE: 06/1992 (920601)
  EDITION: Orig. Ed.   NO. OF PAGES: 128p.
  LCCN: N/A
  BINDING: pap. - $18.95
  ISBN: 0-933635-94-X
  VOLUME(S): N/A
  ORDER NO.: 2714
  IMPRINT: N/A
  STATUS IN FILE: New (92-01)
```

```
NOTE(S): Illustrated
INTELLECTUAL LEVEL: Juvenile
SUBFILE: PB (Paperbound Books in Print); CB (Children's Books in Print)

2/5/3
02398050   2362192XX   STATUS: Active entry
  TITLE: Needful Things
  AUTHOR: King, Stephen
  PUBLISHER: NAL-Dutton   PUBLICATION DATE: 07/1992 (920701)
  LCCN: N/A
  BINDING: Trade - $6.99
  ISBN: 0-451-17281-7
  VOLUME(S): N/A
  ORDER NO.: N/A
  IMPRINT: Sig
  STATUS IN FILE: New (92-01)
```

Records 1 and 3 answer our query.

An interesting file available since 1990 is *EVENT-LINE* (file 165), which is a database of events: trade shows, conferences, exhibitions, sporting events, and so on. Suppose a patron came in and told you she was traveling to Toronto in January 1993 and wanted to know if there would be any interesting events going on there then. A search like the following will tell you quickly:

```
File 165:EVENTLINE  1990-1992/MAY
       (COPR. ESP BV/EM 1992)

     Set  Items  Description
     ---  -----  -----------
?e cy=toronto

Ref   Items   Index-term
E1        1   CY=TORBOLE
E2        1   CY=TORINO
E3      982  *CY=TORONTO
E4       19   CY=TORQUAY
E5        3   CY=TORRANCE
E6        1   CY=TORSHAVN
E7        3   CY=TORTOLA
E8        1   CY=TORUN
E9        3   CY=TOULON
E10      56   CY=TOULOUSE
E11       1   CY=TOURNAI
E12       5   CY=TOURS

         Enter P or E for more
?s e3
     S1     982   CY="TORONTO"
?s es=9301?                        ES= for Event Start date; this will get
                                   everything starting in January 1993 (1/93)
     S2     732   ES=9301?
?s s1 and s2
            982   S1
            732   S2
     S3      11   S1 AND S2
?t 3/6/all

3/6/1
00103914
EVENT TITLE:   International Motorcycle Show
TYPE OF EVENT:   Trade Fair
```

```
3/6/2
00103913
EVENT TITLE:    Milk Marketing Board ON - Convention
TYPE OF EVENT:  Conference


3/6/3
00103912
EVENT TITLE:    Life Underwriters Association of Canada - Convention
TYPE OF EVENT:  Conference


3/6/4
00103907
EVENT TITLE:    Canadian Toy Manufacturers Association Toy Decoration Fair
TYPE OF EVENT:  Trade Fair


3/6/5
00103906
EVENT TITLE:    International Boat Show Toronto
TYPE OF EVENT:  Trade Fair


3/6/6
00103905
EVENT TITLE:    International Marine Trade Show Toronto
TYPE OF EVENT:  Trade Fair


3/6/7
00088291
EVENT TITLE:    Mode Accessories International Exposition
TYPE OF EVENT:  Trade Fair


3/6/8
00065135
EVENT TITLE:    Toronto International Marine Trade show
TYPE OF EVENT:  Trade Fair


3/6/9
00065133
EVENT TITLE:    Toronto International Boat Show
TYPE OF EVENT:  Trade Fair


3/6/10
00013509
EVENT TITLE:    Canadian Toy and Decoration Fair
TYPE OF EVENT:  Trade Fair


3/6/11
00010112
EVENT TITLE:    Convention of the World Professional Squash Association
TYPE OF EVENT:  Conference
```

She is intrigued by the boat fair, so you pull up
the full record for it.

```
?t 3/5/9


3/5/9
00065133
EVENT TITLE:    Toronto International Boat Show
TYPE OF EVENT:  Trade Fair
EVENT DATE(S):  January, 1993
```

```
HOST SITE:          Coliseum and Automotive Bldg.
EVENT CITY:         Toronto
EVENT STATE:        Ontario
EVENT COUNTRY:      Canada
REGION:             North America
NO. PARTICIPANTS:   120000
EXHIBITION:         yes
NO. EXHIBITORS:     460
EVENT FREQUENCY:    Annual
ORGANIZER:          Canadian National Sportsmen's Shows Ltd.
                    Ross Horton
                    703 Evans Avenue, #202
                    Toronto, ONT Canada M9C 5E9
TELEPHONE:          (416) 695-0311
FAX:                (416) 695-0381

DESCRIPTORS: Manufacturing (57000); Manufacturing - General (57010);
             Hobbies/Recreation (72000); Boats (72290)
RECORD INPUT DATE:     910705
```

Here is another example, closer to home. The *American Library Directory* is available online (file 460 in DIALOG). Suppose we want a sorted list of public libraries in central New York State of medium size, say between 25,000 and 40,000 volumes. We go to the documentation and find that the library type field is an additional index, so we will use LT=PUBLIC. Central New York is a bit tougher: the ST= field will capture all of New York State, but how do we get more specific? The TE= field will search by area code,

and the 315 area code covers roughly the territory we are interested in. Regarding the size of collection, there are two potential fields we could use: BK= and VO=. One says it describes the number of book titles, the other the number of book volumes. Which do we want? VO= refers to *volumes*, so we will use that. We are searching for a numeric range, so we use a colon to specify it: ?S VO=25000:40000. Notice there are no commas in the numbers.[2]

Let's execute the search and see what happens:

```
File 460:AMERICAN LIBRARY DIRECTORY 44TH EDITION
        (COPR. 1991  R.R.BOWKER)
FILE 460: Price changes will go into effect June 1, 1992.
Please see HOMEBASE Announcements for more details.

        Set   Items   Description
        ---   -----   -----------
?s tc=315
        S1     283    TE=315
?s lt=public
        S2    9861    LT=PUBLIC
?s s1 and s2
               283    S1
              9861    S2
        S3     156    S1 AND S2
?s vo=25000:40000
        S4    3072    VO=25000:40000
?s s3 and s4
               156    S3
              3072    S4
        S5      13    S3 AND S4
?sort s5/all/vo,d
        S6      13    Sort S6/ALL/VO,D
?report s6/on,cy,vo/all
Align paper;  press ENTER
?
```

| | Library | Book |
Name	City	Volumes
ILION FREE PUBLIC LIBRARY	Ilion	40,000
DUNHAM PUBLIC LIBRARY	Whitesboro	38,277
FULTON PUBLIC LIBRARY	Fulton	36,803
ONEIDA LIBRARY	Oneida	36,478
KIRKLAND TOWN LIBRARY	Clinton	31,121
HAMILTON PUBLIC LIBRARY	Hamilton	30,828
FRANK J BASLOE LIBRARY OF HERKIMER	Herkimer	30,671
WELLER PUBLIC LIBRARY	Mohawk	30,000
NORTH SYRACUSE FREE LIBRARY	North Syracuse	28,000
NEW YORK MILLS PUBLIC LIBRARY	New York Mills	27,891
SODUS FREE LIBRARY	Sodus	27,000
ONONDAGA FREE LIBRARY	Syracuse	25,217
CAZENOVIA PUBLIC LIBRARY ASSOCIATIO	Cazenovia	25,041

Here is another example: A patron wants a list of large minority-owned businesses in the United States, those with annual sales of over $50 million. Where would we search for this? There are a number of potential databases we could try: *D&B - Electronic Business Directory*, *D&B - Million Dollar Directory*, *Standard & Poor's Register - Corporate*, or *Trinet U.S. Businesses*. We notice, though, that one file, *D&B -*

Dun's Market Identifiers (file 516), has an Additional Index, SF=, for special features, and one of these features is MINORITY OWNED. We therefore choose this file and will search on SF=MINORITY OWNED. The SA= field gives annual sales, and we can search on SA>5OM to get all companies with sales over $50 million. The result set is sorted and displayed for the patron:

```
File 516:D & B - DUNS MARKET IDENTIFIERS 01/92  (COPR. 1991 D&B)
 **FILE516: Additional information on selected companies in File 519.

      Set   Items   Description
      ---   -----   -----------
?s sf=minority owned
     S1    11183    SF=MINORITY OWNED
?s s1 and sd>50m
           11183    S1
           27481    SA>50M
     S2       28    S1 AND SA>50M
?sort 2/all/sa,d
     S3       28    Sort 2/ALL/SA,D
?t 3/5/1

 3/5/1
0796826
Citizens Savings Bank & Trust Co Inc
Citizens Bank
401 Charlotte Ave
P O Box 2624
Nashville, TN  37219-1607

TELEPHONE: 615-256-6193
COUNTY: Davidson       SMSA: 388  (Nashville-Davidson,TN)

BUSINESS: State Bank

PRIMARY SIC:
 6022        State commercial banks
  60220000    State commercial banks, nsk

LATEST YEAR ORGANIZED: 1978  OWNER CHANGE DATE:        NA
```

```
STATE OF INCORPORATION:  TN    DATE OF INCORPORATION: 01/09/1904
ANNUAL SALES REVISION DATE: 01/02/1992
```

	LATEST YEAR	TREND YEAR (1990)	BASE YEAR (1988)
SALES	$ 2,982,000,000	$ 2,982,000,000	$ 2,780,000
EMPLOYEES TOTAL:	31	31	40
EMPLOYEES HERE:	20		

```
   SALES GROWTH:  2,000 %  NET WORTH: $      1,538,000
   EMPLOYMENT GROWTH:  -23 %

SQUARE FOOTAGE: 5,000  OWNED
NUMBER OF ACCOUNTS: NA

THIS IS:

     A  HEADQUARTERS LOCATION
     AN ULTIMATE LOCATION
     A  CORPORATION
     A  MINORITY OWNED BUSINESS

DUNS NUMBER:              03-635-7887
CORPORATE FAMILY DUNS:   03-635-7887
PRESIDENT:               Davidson, Rick  /Pres-Ceo
VICE-CHAIRMAN:           Hill, Henry Jr /V Chairman
EXECUTIVE VICE PRESIDENT: Ensley, Deborah S  /Exec V Pres
CHIEF EXECUTIVE OFFICER: Davidson, Rick  /Pres-Ceo
?report 3/co,st,sa,em/all
Align paper;  press ENTER
?
```

Company Name	State	Sales Dollars	Total Employees
Citizens Savings Bank & Trust	TN	2,982,000,000	31
Wang Laboratories Inc	MA	2,091,500,000	16,792
Computer Associates Internatio	NY	1,348,171,000	6,700
Kirk-Mayer Inc	CA	151,407,000	3,000
Red Man Pipe & Supply Company	OK	141,584,824	270
Prospect Enterprises, Inc	CA	100,000,000	200
Royal Contracting Co Ltd Inc	HI	96,038,289	425
Towne Realty Inc	WI	85,048,000	225
Ancira-Winton Chevrolet, Inc	TX	85,000,000	160
Ruiz Food Products, Inc	CA	85,000,000	850
Soft Sheen Products Inc Delawa	IL	81,740,249	543
Kobayashi, Albert C Inc	HI	79,009,642	250
Galicia Inc	CA	75,000,000	112
Minact, Inc	MS	72,646,790	2,000
E & G Food Co Inc	FL	70,025,837	90
Alaska Commercial Company Inc	AK	66,726,926	425
General Maintenance Co Inc	NC	63,400,000	250
Dantzler Lumber & Export Co In	FL	62,925,802	52
Azumano Travel Service Inc	OR	62,000,000	155
Network Solutions Inc	VA	61,500,000	480
R J O Enterprises Inc	MD	60,389,000	600
Pulsar Data Systems Inc	MD	60,000,000	50
Infotec Development, Incorpora	CA	60,000,000	640
Inter-Con Security Systems Inc	CA	56,400,000	5,000

Texpar Energy, Inc	WI	56,270,000	45
R T A International Inc	CA	53,727,749	45
Alvarado Construction, Inc	CO	53,700,000	250
Eastern Computers Inc	VA	53,000,000	375

The patron is quite pleased with this result but wonders why Motown Records does not appear on that list. Certainly it has annual sales that place it in that category. You try to find out why it did not come up:

```
?s motown and record?
          24   MOTOWN
       38337   RECORD?
    S4     7   MOTOWN AND RECORD?
?report 4/co,sa/all
Align paper;  press ENTER
?
```

```
Company                        Sales
Name                           Dollars
--------------------------     ----------

Motown Record Company L. P.            NA
Motown Record Company L. P.            NA
Motown Video                       64,000
J & J Motown Record Store         100,000
Motown Record Company L. P.            NA
Motown Record Company L P              NA
Motown Record Company L P      46,993,000
```

There is the answer: There are multiple listings for Motown Records, many of which have no reported sales (probably because they are branch locations) and one of which just missed our $50 million cutoff point.

Here is a final example of a search that could probably only be conducted online. Syracuse University appointed a new chancellor in late 1991, but the patron does not know his or her name. How do you find it quickly? You might be tempted to call the university and ask, but because this is an online searching textbook, we will pretend you do not think of that and choose to go online instead. Marquis *Who's Who* is file 234 in DIALOG. This is not a typical way of searching a biographical source: usually, we have a person's name and are trying to get information about them. Here, we have an official title and are trying to find the name of the person to whom it applies. This gives you some idea of the power of online versions of traditional reference sources—the ability to search them in much more flexible and effective ways.

In examining the documentation, we see fields like PO= and ON= for position held and occupation name, /CO for company name, YE= for year of employment, CY= for address city, and /DE for descriptor, which incorporates several other fields.

Putting in a variety of these, we get the following:

```
File 234:MARQUIS WHO'S WHO  1990-1991/OCT
       (COPR. MARQUIS WHO'S WHO, INC 1991)

      Set  Items  Description
      ---  -----  -----------
?s po=chancellor? or on=chancellor?
          1017   PO=CHANCELLOR?
           125   ON=CHANCELLOR?
    S1    1029   PO=CHANCELLOR? OR ON=CHANCELLOR?
?s co=syracuse?
    S2     363   CO=SYRACUSE?
?s ye=1991
    S3   64313   YE=1991
```

```
?s s1 and s2 and s3
            1029  S1
             363  S2
           64313  S3
     S4      12  S1 AND S2 AND S3
?s s4 and cy=syracuse
              12  S4
             189  CY=SYRACUSE
     S5       5  S4 AND CY=SYRACUSE
?t 5/na,ca/all
```

5/NA,CA/1
Eggers, Melvin Arnold
CAREER:
    also pres., Syracuse U.
    chancellor, Syracuse U., 1971-
    vice chancellor for acad. affairs, also provost, Syracuse U., 1970-71
    chmn. dept., Syracuse U., 1960-70
    prof. econs., Syracuse U., 1963-70
    mem. faculty, Syracuse U., 1950-70
    instr. econs., Yale, 1947-50
    Clk., Peoples Trust & Savs. Co., Ft. Wayne, 1934-38

5/NA,CA/2
Prucha, John James
CAREER:
    bd. dirs., Syracuse U. Press, 1985-90
    pres., Syracuse U. Press, 1973-85
    vice chancellor acad. affairs, Syracuse U., 1972-85
    dean Coll. Arts and Scis., Syracuse U., 1970-72
    chmn. dept., Syracuse U., 1963-70, 88-89
    prof. emeritus, Syracuse U., 1990-
    prof. geology, Syracuse U., 1963-90
    rsch. geologist, Shell Devel. Co., 1956-63
    sr. geologist, N.Y. State Geol. Survey, 1951-56
    Asst. prof. geology, Rutgers U., 1948-51

5/NA,CA/3
Shaw, Kenneth Alan
CAREER:
    chancellor, Syracuse U., 1991-
    pres., U. Wis. System, Madison, 1986-91
    chancellor, so. Ill. U. System, Edwardsville, 1979-86
    pres., So. Ill. U., Edwardsville, 1977-79
    v.p. acad. affair, dean, Towson State U., Balt., 1969-76
    asst. to pres., lectr. sociology, Ill. State U., 1966-69
    counselor, Office Dean of Men, Purdue U. (Office Student Loans),
      1965-66
    counselor, Office Dean of Men, Purdue U., 1964-65
    residence hall dir., instr. edn., Ill. State U., 1963-64
    Tchr. history, counselor, Rich Twp. High Sch., Park Forest, Ill.,
      1961-63

5/NA,CA/4
Tolley, William Pearson
CAREER:
    chmn., pres., Mohawk Airlines Inc., 1971-72
    chmn. bd., Mohawk Airlines Inc., 1970-71
    chancellor emeritus, Syracuse (N.Y.) U., 1969-
    chancellor, Syracuse (N.Y.) U., 1942-69
    pres., Allegheny Coll., 1931-42
    prof. philosophy, Drew Theol. Sem. (Brothers Coll.), 1930-31

```
dean, Drew Theol. Sem. (Brothers Coll.), 1929-31
acting dean Brothers Coll., instr. in philosophy, Drew Theol. Sem.,
  1928-29
asst. to pres., Drew Theol. Sem., 1927-28
instr. systematic theology, Drew Theol. Sem., 1926-28
alumni sec., Drew Theol. Sem., 1925-27
Ordained to ministry, Meth. Episcopal Ch., 1923
```

```
5/NA,CA/5
 Vincow, Gershon
 CAREER:
   vice chancellor for acad. affairs, Syracuse (N.Y.) U., 1985-
   dean Coll. Arts and Scis., Syracuse (N.Y.) U., 1978-85
   v.p. research and grad. affairs, Syracuse (N.Y.) U., 1977-78
   prof. chemistry, Syracuse (N.Y.) U., 1971-
   prof. chemistry, U. Wash., Seattle, 1961-71
```

We find not only the correct entry (for Kenneth Shaw) but also several false drops. You see how the false drops were retrieved—position titles that include the word "chancellor," as in vice chancellor, and even a chancellor emeritus. Some of these files are organized more effectively and consistently than others.

Quality control and update frequency are thus very important. An error in a bibliographic record (e.g., spelling error, bad index term) may eliminate one hit from a good retrieval set, but a similar error in a reference record means you do not retrieve it and the search comes up empty. Further, if the file is updated infrequently or not at all, it may be of limited use in a ready-reference environment.

What lessons have we learned? Pay attention to documentation, take advantage of special features of files and systems, and expect the unexpected.

Full-Text Databases

Full-text databases resemble bibliographic databases in a number of ways: They have a similar structure, many have abstracts, some have indexing. Indeed, some bibliographic databases now include both citations and full texts. The key difference, of course, is the full text. Many people believe that the availability of full text will solve the problems of information retrieval, but so far this has not proven to be the case. Indeed, we often find that the presence of full text serves as a distraction rather than an assistance, and that we often search more effectively in full-text files when we do not search the full text.

There are definite advantages to full-text files, of course, chiefly the availability of the text itself. Users are often understandably much more pleased when they leave an online search session with the actual texts that satisfy their requests rather than bibliographic citations to articles they must then hunt down. Full text can also provide improved access to the literature; many of the comments we made when discussing free-text searching in chapter 7 apply here. The use of a term or phrase or figure of speech in the body of a document, but not in a title or abstract, certainly will assist in retrieving it.

However, there are also disadvantages. With current technology, what we retrieve is not a facsimile of the original document but rather a copy of its text. In general, we are not able to retrieve graphics, photographs, or other images. However, systems using CD-ROM technology are being designed to allow retrieval of bit-mapped images of documents that have been scanned in. Some of these systems provide traditional title, abstract, and indexing access; some permit full-text searching as well. The quality of the output (sometimes including advertising!) is not yet as high as that of a magazine or newspaper, but it is more than adequate for almost any need.

The primary disadvantage to full-text searching is *false drops*. As we saw when discussing free-text searching, when we search on fields that include natural language, the problems of ambiguity and conflation arise. There are ways around this, but you must remember that using full-text files you could now retrieve a document based on a single, perhaps offhand use of a word buried deep in a 3,000-word text. In files with rudimentary or no indexing, like many newspaper databases, this presents us with a potentially major headache.

A word about newspaper databases. These are becoming ever more popular, and there are more of them available in full text. Most provide us with a convenient method of searching that takes advantage of the structure of a typical newspaper article. Most news articles, excluding features and other auxiliary stories, have the most important information up front, in the first paragraph or two—what journalists call the lead.

This can be very useful in searching, as the lead often serves as a kind of abstract of the story. Many news databases permit searching in just the first one or two paragraphs. Some call it /LP (lead paragraph) or even /AB or /TI.[3]

Also keep in mind the audience for newspaper stories. Written for a general readership, they are much more likely to use euphemisms and less likely to use technical terms, unless those terms are the focus of the story. These characteristics are important to bear in mind while searching newspaper files.

The inverted file (Basic Index) for a full-text database usually includes every term from the text, plus a few other fields (titles, if any, perhaps descriptors), so a simple search command will retrieve based on full text by default. If you wish to restrict a search further, you must use the appropriate prefixes or suffixes.

There are several kinds of full-text files available. We have discussed newspapers, but there are also journal articles (*Journal of School Health*, *American Demographics*, *Communications of the ACM*), newsletters (*Jane's Defense & Aerospace News*), dictionaries (*Quotations Database*), directories (*American Men & Women of Science*), other sources (*Magill's Survey of Cinema*), and my all-time favorite DIALOG file, the *Bible* (King James Version). The strategies and techniques we discuss here should help you with most of these files.

We have said that searching full-text databases resembles searching using free text, that often no controlled vocabulary is available, and that false drops are a significant problem. This might make you think of the ladder of specificity from chapter 7. The situation we have described would seem to imply that we want to be as high on that ladder as possible. AND is often just too broad to be helpful here; a strategy like AIDS AND DRUG? in a search on drug therapies for AIDS in the *Chicago Tribune* is hopeless:

```
File 632:CHICAGO TRIBUNE   1985 - 16 Jun 1992
       (c) 1992 Chicago Tribune


     Set   Items   Description
     ---   -----   -----------
?s aids and drug?
         10218   AIDS
         39459   DRUG?
     S1   3146   AIDS AND DRUG?
?t 1/5/1

 1/5/1
01979609
EVENING. People - K mart, Walgreens refuse to sell Magic's AIDS book
Chicago Tribune (CT) - FRIDAY June 12, 1992
By:  Compiled from Chicago Tribune wires
Edition:  EVENING UPDATE   Section: NEWS   Page: 2   Zone: C
Word Count:  119

LEAD PARAGRAPHS:
   Some store chains are refusing to sell Magic Johnson's book on
preventing AIDS because of its blunt language about how to avoid the
sexually transmitted disease, the book's publisher in Troy, Mich. said
Friday.

   Times Books Publisher Peter Osnos said K mart Corp. and the Walgreens
drug store chain were among retailers objecting to the book. The book,
"What You Can Do To Avoid AIDS," was written by Johnson, who retired from
professional basketball because he has the AIDS virus.

   "We're not a bookstore," said a K mart spokesman. "The book is very
informative, but it's also very graphic. It should be available to
teen-agers, . . . (but not) a 3-year-old while their mother is buying a
lawnmower."
DESCRIPTORS:  BUSINESS; DECISION; SALE; BOOK; SEX; DISEASE; CELEBRITY

           Copyright (c) 1992, Chicago Tribune
```

Because controlled vocabulary is probably not an option to begin with, we must try using proximity operators: (5N), (2W), and so on. For a specific phrase, use (W):

```
?s dead(w)sea(w)scroll?
          30360  DEAD
          13171  SEA
            570  SCROLL?
    S2        72  DEAD(W)SEA(W)SCROLL?
```

To be more specific, use qualifiers:

```
?s democratic(w)national(w)committee
          28630  DEMOCRATIC
         131158  NATIONAL
          48845  COMMITTEE
    S3       662  DEMOCRATIC(W)NATIONAL(W)COMMITTEE
?s s3/lp                                              qualifying to lead paragraph
    S4       171  S3/LP
```

Another technique for a possibly ambiguous or conflated term is to look for it twice in the same document. A search on CRACK(20W)CRACK will retrieve documents with the word "crack" twice within 20 words. Such a document is somewhat more likely to be related to the drug crack because it is less likely to be an offhand use of the word, as in "the crack of dawn," "crack of the bat," and so on.

An interesting example is searching for documents about AIDS. Clearly, a large number of articles are being published on this topic, and many of them appear in newspapers and other full-text sources. Yet the four-character sequence "aids" is also a word (e.g., "this drug aids patients' mobility"). So how do we get at documents about AIDS? The following strategy is helpful:

```
?s aids(20w)aids or acquired()immun? or hiv
          10218  AIDS
          10218  AIDS
           2764  AIDS(20W)AIDS
          15204  ACQUIRED
           6432  IMMUN?
           1300  ACQUIRED(W)IMMUN?
           1088  HIV
    S5      3833  AIDS(20W)AIDS OR ACQUIRED()IMMUN? OR HIV
```

The first of these three expressions searches for multiple adjacent occurrences of "AIDS," the second searches for "acquired immune deficiency syndrome" or "acquired immunodeficiency syndrome," and the final one will search for "HIV," the abbreviation for human immunodeficiency virus. (Don't truncate on this: you will retrieve HIVE, HIVES, etc.)

There is another proximity operator that is often useful in full-text searching: (S), which specifies that two words occur in the same subfield. In full-text databases, this corresponds to paragraphs or

sentences (check the whitesheets to determine which). This operator takes advantage of the natural structure in the document. Rather than guessing with (W)s, you can ask for AIDS(S)AIDS or NBA(S)PLAY-OFF? and get documents in which the author uses these words in a natural language unit.

You can also take advantage of /LP or /TI or /AB fields. If you are searching for a relatively broad topic or one that you think will retrieve a large number of documents, you might decide to search in these more restrictive fields:

```
?s (higher()education or college? ? or universit?)/lp
           7841  HIGHER/LP
          10234  EDUCATION/LP
            565  HIGHER/LP(W)EDUCATION/LP
          16775  COLLEGE? ?/LP
          26058  UNIVERSIT?/LP
    S6     38852  (HIGHER()EDUCATION OR COLLEGE? ? OR UNIVERSIT?)/LP
```

```
?s president?(1n)election
          160931   PRESIDENT?
           31527   ELECTION
      S7    2267   PRESIDENT?(1N)ELECTION
?s s7/ti
      S8      18   S7/TI
?s s7/lp
      S9     768   S7/LP
```

However, you might choose to search narrower or less popular topics in full text (i.e., unqualified):

```
?s minh()city
             317   MINH
          132571   CITY
     S10     147   MINH()CITY
?s science()fiction
           16580   SCIENCE
            5187   FICTION
     S11    1193   SCIENCE()FICTION
```

The first of these examples above deserves a comment: If you were searching for documents about Ho Chi Minh City, Viet Nam, you might be tempted to search HO(W)CHI(W)MINH(W)CITY, but what

documents would satisfy MINH(W)CITY but not the longer expression? None. So you might as well save a bit of search time and use the shorter strategy. Here's proof:

```
?s ho()chi()minh()city
            1938   HO
            1402   CHI
             317   MINH
          132571   CITY
     S12     147   HO()CHI()MINH()CITY
```

The above example is also an illustration of a good technique to use in searching full text: Get a "hook," some very definite piece of strategy that will effectively reduce the size of the database you have to search in. It could be a personal name, geographic location, company name, data, organization, anything, but if you can get a subset of only several thousand, hundred, or even dozen records to search through, and you are reasonably certain that the ones you want are in there, it makes your job considerably easier.

In many cases, the database will help you. There may be Additional Indexes for some of these proper names, the data field is almost always there, and use of these special features will make searching easier.

Here is an example: A patron recalls seeing an article in a trade magazine about attempts by Lipton to buy Celestial Seasonings, the herbal tea company. You decide to search in *Trade and Industry ASAP* (file 648), which covers a number of business-oriented magazines. It has a CO= field for company names, so you EXPAND on "Celestial" and get the following:

```
File 648:TRADE AND INDUSTRY ASAP  83-92/MAY
        (COPR. IAC 1992)
  **FILE648: Effective APRIL 1, 1992, there are NEW PRICES for
 hours, types and prints.  See HELP RATES648 for details.

     Set  Items  Description
     ---  -----  -----------
?e co=celestial

Ref  Items  Index-term
E1       1  CO=CELESTE COMPANY INC.
```

(Text continues on page 164.)

```
E2      1   CO=CELESTE UPHOLSTERING INC.
E3      0  *CO=CELESTIAL
E4      1   CO=CELESTIAL ARTS PUBLISHING CO.
E5      1   CO=CELESTIAL FARMS INC.
E6      1   CO=CELESTIAL REALTY GROUP INC.
E7      1   CO=CELESTIAL SEASONING INC.
E8      9   CO=CELESTIAL SEASONINGS INC.
E9      1   CO=CELESTION INDUSTRIES PLC
E10     1   CO=CELETTE
E11     1   CO=CELETTE-CHURCHILL
E12     1   CO=CELEX GROUP INC.


           Enter P or E for more
?s e7-e8
               1   CO=CELESTIAL SEASONING INC.
               9   CO=CELESTIAL SEASONINGS INC.
       S1     10   E7-E8
?s s1 and lipton
              10   S1
            1296   LIPTON
       S2      5   S1 AND LIPTON
?t 2/8/all


  2/8/1
11916478  DIALOG File 648: TRADE & INDUSTRY ASAP
          *Use Format 9 for FULL TEXT*
TITLE:  Perrier, Celestial  join iced tea party. (Perrier Group of America
    Inc. and Celestial Seasonings Inc. team to produce packaged iced teas)
 AVAILABILITY: FULL TEXT Online  LINE COUNT: 00049  WORD COUNT: 581
 COMPANY:  Perrier  Group  of  America Inc.—Product development; Celestial
    Seasonings Inc.—Product development
 SIC CODE: 5149  Groceries and related products, not elsewhere classified
           2099  Food preparations, not elsewhere classified
           2086  Bottled and canned soft drinks
 DESCRIPTORS:  Beverages—Product    development;   Tea   industry— Product
    development; Mineral water industry—Product development


  2/8/2
11759639  DIALOG File 648: TRADE & INDUSTRY ASAP
          *Use Format 9 for FULL TEXT*
TITLE:  Return  of  the  red  zinger.  (Mo  Siegel,  founder  of  Celestial
    Seasonings Inc., returns to company after five-year absence)
 AVAILABILITY: FULL TEXT Online  LINE COUNT: 00090  WORD COUNT: 1,283
 COMPANY: Celestial Seasonings Inc.—Management
 SIC CODE: 2099  Food preparations, not elsewhere classified
           2833  Medicinals and botanicals
 NAMED PERSON: Siegel, Mo—Management
 DESCRIPTORS: Tea industry—Management; Herb industry—Management


  2/8/3
08802901  DIALOG File 648: TRADE & INDUSTRY ASAP
          *Use Format 9 for FULL TEXT*
TITLE: C/D/M  sips  a  soothing  cuppa:  the  $5-mil.  Celestial  Tea  biz.
    (Chiat/Day/Mojo)
 AVAILABILITY: FULL TEXT Online  LINE COUNT: 00050  WORD COUNT: 659
 COMPANY:  Chiat/Day/Mojo  Inc.—contracts;  Celestial  Seasonings  Inc.—
    advertising
 SIC CODE: 7311  Advertising agencies
           2099  Food preparations, not elsewhere classified
 DESCRIPTORS: Advertising agencies—contracts; Tea industry—advertising
```

```
2/8/4
08121409   DIALOG File 648: TRADE & INDUSTRY ASAP
           *Use Format 9 for FULL TEXT*
TITLE:  Victory  at  tea II. (R.C. Bigelow sues to prevent Thomas J. Lipton
     takeover of herbal tea market)
 AVAILABILITY: FULL TEXT Online  LINE COUNT: 00024  WORD COUNT: 277
 COMPANY: R.C. Bigelow Inc.—cases; Thomas J. Lipton Inc.—cases; Celestial
     Seasonings Inc.—cases
 SIC CODE: 2099  Food preparations, not elsewhere classified
          2086  Bottled and canned soft drinks
 DESCRIPTORS: Tea industry—cases; Beverage industry—cases

 2/8/5
07726140   DIALOG File 648: TRADE & INDUSTRY ASAP
           *Use Format 9 for FULL TEXT*
TITLE:  U.S.  Supreme  Court  refuses  hearing for Lipton appeal on Bigelow
     antitrust decision. (Thomas J. Lipton Inc., R.C. Bigelow Inc.)
 AVAILABILITY: FULL TEXT Online  LINE COUNT: 00043  WORD COUNT: 558
 COMPANY:  Thomas  J.  Lipton  Inc.—Acquisitions,  mergers,  divestments;
     Celestial  Seasonings  Inc.—Acquisitions,  mergers,  divestments; R.C.
     Bigelow Inc.—cases
 SIC CODE: 2099  Food preparations, not elsewhere classified
 DESCRIPTORS: Tea industry—cases
?t 2/9/4

 2/9/4
08121409   DIALOG File 648: TRADE & INDUSTRY ASAP
           *FULL TEXT RECORD*
TITLE:  Victory  at  tea II. (R.C. Bigelow sues to prevent Thomas J. Lipton
     takeover of herbal tea market)
 JOURNAL: Food & Beverage Marketing
 VOL: v8  ISSUE: n11  PG: p8(1)
 PUB DATE: Nov, 1989
 ISSN: 0731-3799
 AVAILABILITY: FULL TEXT Online  LINE COUNT: 00024  WORD COUNT: 277
 SOURCE FILE: TI File 148
 SUBFILE:  ADV  Advertising, Marketing and Public Relations
           FOOD  Food, Beverages and Nutrition
 COMPANY: R.C. Bigelow Inc.—cases; Thomas J. Lipton Inc.—cases; Celestial
     Seasonings Inc.—cases
 SIC CODE: 2099  Food preparations, not elsewhere classified
          2086  Bottled and canned soft drinks
 DESCRIPTORS: Tea industry—cases; Beverage industry—cases
 FULL TEXT:


    Victory At Tea II

    Food industry legal eagles may remember R.C. Bigelow's antitrust
lawsuit against Thomas J. Lipton last year. Bigelow sued to prevent the
purchase of Celestial Seasonings by Lipton, which would have given Lipton
84% of the herbal tea market.

    The lawsuit was dismissed by a federal judge in May of 1988, but
Bigelow appealed, and in June of '88 won a Federal Appeals Court ruling,
temporarily blocking the sale until the court reached a decision.

    Celestial Seasonings' parent company, Kraft, apparently didn't feel it
was worth the wait, and sold the herbal tea unit to Vestar Capital
Partners, a private investment firm in New York City in September of 1988.
However, Bigelow, seeking to avoid similar future confrontations, proceeded
with the lawsuit.
```

(Continues on page 164.)

       In January, the Federal Appeals Court sided with Bigelow. Lipton
appealed to the Supreme Court, which last month declined to hear the case.

       Praising the decision, attorneys for Bigelow say that the January
Court of Appeals ruling specifically declined to follow the previous
standard, set in the 1987 Phototron Corp. vs. Eastman Kodak case, which did
not allow competitors to sue under antitrust laws. Furthermore, the
decision shifts the burden of proof from plaintiff to defendant. Now the
company sued must prove there will not be a monopoly, instead of the suing
company having to prove the merger does constitute a monopoly.

 COPYRIGHT Capital University 1989
 RECORD DATE: 910914

   It is also possible to pearl-grow in full-text files
or at least in those that have indexing. In many files,
this indexing is rudimentary at best, but in full text
you need all the advantages you can get. An example
from *Health Periodicals Database* (file 149) illustrates

this. The following is a search for information about
the decision by the U.S. Centers for Disease Control
to change the definition of what it means to have
AIDS:

```
File 149:HEALTH PERIODICALS DATABASE   1976-92/WEEK 24
        (COPR. IAC 1992)

     Set  Items  Description
     ---  -----  -----------
?s aids(20w)aids or acquired()immun? or hiv
Processing
          24273  AIDS
          24273  AIDS
           6539  AIDS(20W)AIDS
           6090  ACQUIRED
          23094  IMMUN?
           2907  ACQUIRED(W)IMMUN?
          10949  HIV
     S1   14336  AIDS(20W)AIDS OR ACQUIRED()IMMUN? OR HIV
```

   That is very large; let's limit it to the abstract
field:

```
?s s1/ab
     S2   2224  S1/AB
?s s2(10n)(define or definition or defined or diagnose or diagnosis)
           2224  S2
           4162  DEFINE
           4698  DEFINITION
          10144  DEFINED
           2822  DIAGNOSE
          24514  DIAGNOSIS
     S3    224  S2(10N)(DEFINE OR DEFINITION OR DEFINED OR DIAGNOSE OR
                DIAGNOSIS)
?t 3/8/1-5

 3/8/1
 12318337  Dialog File 149: Health Periodicals Database
  TITLE: AIDS guidelines: why were they postponed? (includes related
     article)
 DESCRIPTORS: United States. Centers for Disease Control - Standards; AIDS
    (Disease) - Diagnosis
```

```
3/8/2
12293819  Dialog File 149: Health Periodicals Database
 TITLE:  Study  shows  impact  of  HIV-related  illnesses.  (National  Public
     Health  and  Hospital  Institute  study  reported  in  the  Journal  of  the
     American Medical Association)
DESCRIPTORS:  United  States.  Centers  for  Disease  Control  -  Standards;  HIV
     patients - Care and treatment; Hospitals - Statistics


3/8/3
12177140  Dialog File 149: Health Periodicals Database
 TITLE:  HIV-infected  professionals,  patient  rights,  and  the  'switching
     dilemma'.  (new  Centers  for  Disease  Control  guidelines  for  HIV-infected
     health professionals)
DESCRIPTORS:  Medical  personnel  -  Diseases;  HIV  infection  -  Moral  and
     ethical aspects


3/8/4
12167043  Dialog File 149: Health Periodicals Database
  TITLE:  The  new  tuberculosis.  (resurgence  of  tuberculosis  in  the
     US)(Editorials)
DESCRIPTORS: Tuberculosis - Evaluation


3/8/5
12160547  Dialog File 149: Health Periodicals Database
        *Use Format 9 for FULL TEXT*
 TITLE:  Longitudinal  patterns  of  California  Medicaid  recipients  with
     acquired immunodeficiency syndrome.
DESCRIPTORS: Medi-Cal - Economic aspects; AIDS patients - Economic aspects
     ; Medicaid - Usage
```

There are some good hits here, especially documents one and two. We notice a good descriptor, which includes the word "standards," so try that:

```
?s standards/de
     S4    3551    STANDARDS/DE
?s s1 and s4
          14336  S1
           3551  S4
     S5     164  S1 AND S4
?t 5/8/3-4


5/8/3
12208461  Dialog File 149: Health Periodicals Database
        *Use Format 9 for FULL TEXT*
 TITLE:  CDC's  expanded AIDS case definition sparks controversy. (Centers
    for Disease Control) (AIDS advocates call for national meeting)
DESCRIPTORS:  United States. Centers for Disease Control - Standards; AIDS
    (Disease) - Reporting


5/8/4
12202165  Dialog File 149: Health Periodicals Database
        *Use Format 9 for FULL TEXT*
 TITLE:  Prevention  tries  to break into medicine's mainstream. (includes
    related  article  on the Physician-based Assessment and Counseling for
    Exercise program)
DESCRIPTORS:  Association  of  American  Medical  Colleges  -  Standards;
    American  College  of  Preventive Medicine - Management; Association of
    Teachers  of  Preventive  Medicine  -  Management;  Preventive medicine
    physicians - Training; Medical colleges - Curricula
```

We were a little broad there; let's go instead for
CENTERS and STANDARDS in the same descriptor
field and also search for AIDS in the same field:


```
?s aids/de and centers(f)standards/de
           16204   AIDS/DE
            4356   CENTERS/DE
            3551   STANDARDS/DE
             129   CENTERS/DE(F)STANDARDS/DE
     S6       51   AIDS/DE AND CENTERS(F)STANDARDS/DE
?t 6/8/1-6

 6/8/1
 12318337  Dialog File 149: Health Periodicals Database
  TITLE: AIDS  guidelines:  why  were  they  postponed?  (includes related
     article)
 DESCRIPTORS:  United States. Centers for Disease Control - Standards; AIDS
    (Disease) - Diagnosis


 6/8/2
 12208461  Dialog File 149: Health Periodicals Database
           *Use Format 9 for FULL TEXT*
  TITLE:  CDC's  expanded AIDS case definition sparks controversy. (Centers
     for Disease Control) (AIDS advocates call for national meeting)
 DESCRIPTORS:  United States. Centers for Disease Control - Standards; AIDS
    (Disease) - Reporting


 6/8/3
 11969121  Dialog File 149: Health Periodicals Database
  TITLE: What's in a name? The policy implications of the CDC definition of
     AIDS.  (Research on  Human  Populations:  National  and International
     Ethical Guidelines)
 DESCRIPTORS:  United States. Centers for Disease Control - Standards; AIDS
    (Disease) - Diagnosis; Medical research - Standards


 6/8/4
 11947026  Dialog File 149: Health Periodicals Database
  TITLE:  CDC  surrenders  to  health groups on AIDS strategy. (Centers for
     Disease  Control  abandons  plan  to  publish  list  of exposure-prone
     healthcare procedures)
 DESCRIPTORS:  United States. Centers for Disease Control - Standards; AIDS
    (Disease) - Prevention; HIV infection - Risk factors


 6/8/5
 11719702  Dialog File 149: Health Periodicals Database
           *Use Format 9 for FULL TEXT*
  TITLE:  Agency delays final action on new case definition for AIDS. (U.S.
     Centers for Disease Control)
 DESCRIPTORS:  United States. Centers for Disease Control - Standards; AIDS
    (Disease) - Terminology; Nosology - Standards


 6/8/6
 11706643  Dialog File 149: Health Periodicals Database
 TITLE: Experts differ on effects of definition change. (medical definition
    of HIV disease)
 DESCRIPTORS: AIDS (Disease) - Laws, regulations, etc.; United States.
    Centers for Disease Control - Standards; United States. Social Security
    Administration - Standards; HIV patients - Laws, regulations, etc.
```

A final, obvious, but nonetheless worthwhile point: Do not TYPE or PRINT these documents in full format without first checking their relevance. First of all, you will incur larger charges if you display records in format 9 (full text), but if you are TYPEing, remember that some of these records are documents of considerable length. Get an indication (using format 3 or 8, usually) of how long the document is in words or lines. Often these fields are also searchable, so you could ask for documents of, say, less than 1,500 words. Typically, however, you are more concerned with the lengths of the documents that you have already retrieved for display purposes.

Full-text databases are an exciting development that offers great potential, but they must be searched with additional care and preparation.

> Joe is right about being particularly careful when TYPEing these full-text documents. It is sometimes sufficient to type only the KWIC sections where the hits actually occur. Particularly if you are dealing with a ready reference question, the client may not need the entire article. - GW

Citation Databases

This category of databases is quite different from the others we have discussed so far. In fact, searching citation databases is almost backward from searching "normal" bibliographic files. Citation databases were developed in the 1970's to provide access to documents in a new and different way—not by subject, words in titles or abstracts, or index terms, but by how the documents had been cited as references by other authors in the scientific literature. This could easily be confusing; we have been using the word *citation* throughout this book to refer to the bibliographic representations of documents we found in databases. In citation databases, "citation" is used in a quite different way.

Let's take, as an example, the journal article "A Re-Examination of Relevance: Toward a Dynamic, Situational Definition," which appeared in *Information Processing & Management (IP&M)* in 1990.[4] This was a review article, written by three good friends of the authors, Linda Schamber, Michael Eisenberg, and Mike Nilan, which summarized the research literature on relevance up to that date and presented a new framework for thinking about such research. As it was a review article, it contained a large number of citations or references to existing literature. This reference list, or bibliography, appeared at the end of the article.

One of the articles in this reference list is by Michael Eisenberg and is entitled "Measuring Relevance Judgments." It, too, appeared in *IP&M*, in 1988.[5] This is a report of his doctoral dissertation and is really a seminal work on the measurement of relevance judgments. As a researcher in the area of relevance and user evaluation, this author would like to know who else has cited this paper specifically, and the rest of Eisenberg's work as well. Anyone who has read this material and found it worthy of citation is probably working in a similar area, and it would be useful to know who they are and what they are doing.

> Just a word about citations: Don't always assume that because an author is citing another author's work, he or she believes that work to be any good. One does run across negative citations: "As Smith (1978) quite incorrectly stated...." But at least they are in the same subject area. - JWJ

This kind of searching is possible using citation databases. The Institute for Scientific Information (ISI) has been compiling these databases since 1972, scanning the scientific, social science, and, later, the arts and humanities literature, and collating the citations to other works. These databases are available in manual format (a true pain to search) as well as online and on CD-ROM.

What we are searching in citation databases, then, is who has cited whom. The original article (in this case Eisenberg 1988) is the *cited work*. The article that refers to it (Schamber et al. 1990) is the *citing work*, and the link between them is the *citation*, as shown in figure 11.1.

Fig. 11.1. A citation.

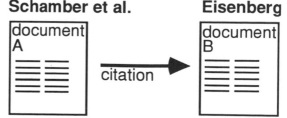

Fig. 11.2. A simple citation web.

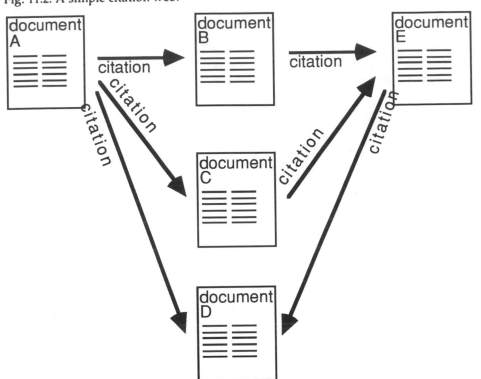

As you can see in figure 11.2, Schamber and the others have cited quite a number of works, and there are many works that cite Eisenberg 1988, so we really have a complex web of citations at work here.

In fact, there is an entire body of research on citation patterns themselves, falling under the general heading of *bibliometrics* and including work on scientific communication, citation patterns, co-citation patterns, self-citation, and so on.

This kind of searching presupposes that you have a good "seed" article to begin with. This is often the case with researchers or faculty who have a reasonably good idea of the field and want to see material that has recently appeared. This author did a lot of manual citation searching for a doctoral dissertation: there were two good books and four or five seminal articles. The objective was to find anything written by anyone who had cited those works, and indeed this turned out to be a more efficient method of searching that literature than straightforward topic searches attempted in *Mathsci*.

Citation databases can also be a good way to search topics that cross disciplinary boundaries. More and more interdisciplinary and multidisciplinary

research is being conducted, and finding literature that reports on it can be difficult at times. Because there are only three citation databases covering very broad subject areas (science, social science, and arts and humanities), they can be a good source for broad or cross-disciplinary work. Until recently, those searches could be only rudimentary, as the only subject access was via titles of citing works, but ISI has now started adding indexing terms and even some abstracts, so more recent articles will be easier to retrieve in the future.

However, we still primarily search these databases using rather specialized techniques. The citation databases have highly structured records, and there is very little to go on for searching. You must remember that the database is composed of records corresponding to *citing works*, not necessarily *cited works*, although many of them will also appear as citing works themselves. It can be very convoluted: You want to find everyone who has cited an article by Armstrong, but you are not searching for Armstrong. Let's look at our sample record as it appears in *Social SciSearch* (file 7):[6]

```
1/5/5
02180966    Genuine Article#: EK779    Number of References: 64
Title: A REEXAMINATION OF RELEVANCE - TOWARD A DYNAMIC, SITUATIONAL
    DEFINITION
Author(s): SCHAMBER L; EISENBERG MB; NILAN MS
Corporate Source: SYRACUSE UNIV,SCH INFORMAT STUDIES/SYRACUSE//NY/13244
```

Journal: INFORMATION PROCESSING & MANAGEMENT, 1990, V26, N6, P755-776
Language: ENGLISH   Document Type: ARTICLE
Subfile: SocSearch; SciSearch; Scisearch; CC ENGI—Current Contents,
    Engineering, Technology & Applied Sciences; CC SOCS—Current Contents,
    Social & Behavioral Sciences
Journal Subject Category: INFORMATION SCIENCE & LIBRARY SCIENCE
Cited References:

ALLEN TJ, 1969, V4, P3, ANN REV INFORMATION
BARHILLEL Y, 1960, P42, AD236772
BARHILLEL Y, 1960, PB161547
BEGHTOL C, 1986, V42, P84, J DOC
BELKIN NJ, 1982, V38, P61, J DOC
BELKIN NJ, 1982, V38, P145, J DOC
BELKIN NJ, 1980, P187, THEORY APPLICATION I
BOOKSTEIN A, 1979, V30, P269, J AM SOC INFORM SCI
BOYCE BR, 1985, V20, P153, ANNU REV INFORM SCI
BRITTAIN JM, 1982, V2, P139, SOC SCI INFORM
COOPER WS, 1971, V7, P19, INFORMATION STORAGE
COOPER WS, 1973, V24, P87, J AM SOC INFORM SCI
COOPER WS, 1978, V25, P67, J ASSOC COMPUT MACH
CUADRA CA, 1967, V23, P291, J DOC
CUADRA CA, 1967, NSF TM352000100 SYST
DERR RL, 1985, V21, P489, INFORM PROCESS MANAG
DERVIN B, 1986, V21, P3, ANNU REV INFORM SCI
DERVIN B, 1983, INT COMMUNICATION AS
DERVIN B, 1983, P153, KNOWLEDGE STRUCTURE
EISENBERG M, 1986, V23, P80, P AM SOC INFORM SCI
EISENBERG MB, 1988, V24, P373, INFORM PROCESS MANAG
ELLIS D, 1984, V8, P25, J INFORM SCI
FAIRTHORNE RA, 1963, P109, INFORMATION RETRIEVA
FOSKETT DJ, 1972, V8, P77, INFORMATION STORAGE
GARDNER H, 1987, MINDS NEW SCI
HALPERN D, 1988, V25, P169, P ASIS ANNU MEET
INGWERSEN P, 1984, V4, P83, SOC SCI INFORM STUD
KATZER J, 1987, V12, P15, CANADIAN J INFORMATI
KEMP DA, 1974, V10, P37, INFORMATION STORAGE
KOCHEN M, 1974, PRINCIPLES INFORMATI
LANCASTER FW, 1979, INFORMATION RETRIEVA
MACCAFFERTY M, 1977, V1, P121, J INFORMATICS
MACMULLIN SE, 1984, V3, P91, INFORMATION SOC
MARON ME, 1977, V28, P38, J AM SOC INFORM SCI
NILAN MS, 1987, V24, P186, P ASIS ANNU MEET
NILAN MS, 1988, V25, P152, P ASIS ANNU MEET
NILAN MS, 1989, V26, P104, P ASIS ANNU MEET
OCONNOR J, 1968, V19, P200, AM DOC
PAISLEY WJ, 1968, V3, P1, ANN REV INFORMATION
REES AM, 1966, V18, P316, ASLIB P
REES AM, 1967, V1, FIELD EXPT APPROACH
REGAZZI JJ, 1988, V39, P235, J AM SOC INFORM SCI
ROBERTSON SE, 1979, P202, ANAL MEANING
ROBERTSON SE, 1979, 3RD INT RES FOR INF
RORVIG ME, IN PRESS J AM SOC IN
ROUSE WB, 1984, V20, P129, INFORM PROCESS MANAG
SALTON G, 1983, INTRO MODERN INFORMA
SARACEVIC T, 1970, P111, INTRO INFORMATION SC
SARACEVIC T, 1975, V26, P321, J AM SOC INFORM SCI
SARACEVIC T, 1988, V39, P197, J AM SOC INFORM SCI
SIMON HA, 1981, V32, P364, J AM SOC INFORM SCI
SWANSON DR, 1977, V47, P128, LIBRARY Q
TAYLOR RS, 1986, VALUE ADDED PROCESSE
TESSIER J, 1977, V68, P383, SPEC LIBR
TESSIER JA, 1981, THESIS SYRACUSE U

```
TIAMIYU MA, 1988, V24, P391, INFORM PROCESS MANAG
VICKERY BC, 1959, V2, P1275, 1958 P INT C SCI INF
VICKERY BC, 1959, V2, P855, 1958 P INT C SCI INF
WALKER DE, 1981, V32, P347, J AM SOC INFORM SCI
WERSIG G, 1985, V5, P11, SOC SCI INFORM STUD
WILSON P, 1973, V9, P457, INFORMATION STORAGE
WILSON P, 1968, P45, 2 KINDS POWER
WILSON TD, 1984, V4, P197, SOC SCI INFORM STUD
WINOGRAD T, 1986, UNDERSTANDING COMPUT
```

You see how little information we have here about the subject content of this document: title, authors, authors' affiliations, bibliographic citation, some rudimentary subject information, and a list of cryptic references. These references are the heart of the citation databases and are the major access point when searching them. These are the 64 articles that the authors cite in the body of this particular paper. The one we were interested in is presented in figure 11.3.

These references are contained in an additional index, CR=, and are *phrase indexed*, so you cannot search by individual words or parts of the field. That is not entirely true—in addition to having the whole thing available as a cited reference, there are three parts of the field that are also separately available: CA= (the cited author's name), CY= (the year of the cited work), and CW= (the name of the cited work). As you will see, it is probably a better idea to stick with CR= for citations to a specific work.

Fig. 11.3. Sample cited reference.

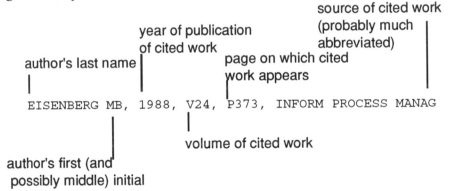

This figure shows the structure of reference fields in citation databases. We strongly advise you to read the bluesheets very carefully before you attempt a citation search, as this is only one example of how such a field is structured; you can see immediately that there are many more kinds of structures corresponding to books, conference papers, reports, doctoral dissertations, and so on than we have been searching previously.

Let's look at a couple of sample citation searches. We will start with the search for articles that cite Eisenberg's 1988 paper. We begin the search by EXPANDing on the CR= field, looking for citations to articles by Eisenberg. We use his middle initial, B, because we know it; if we did not, or if he did not use it, we would have to try CR=EISENBERG M instead. Be sure not to truncate on this EXPAND request!

```
File   7:SOCIAL SCISEARCH  1972-199205W5
        (COPR. ISI INC.1992)
  **FILE007:    --- Abstracts are available as of January 1992 ---
  ** Author Keywords (/DE) and KeyWords Plus (/ID) added as of March 1991


      Set  Items  Description
      ---  -----  -----------
?e cr=eisenberg mb


Ref   Items  Index-term
E1       1  CR=EISENBERG MA, 1989, V89, P1497, COLUMBIA LAW R
E2       1  CR=EISENBERG MA, 1991, UNPUB PRINCIPLE HADL
E3       0 *CR=EISENBERG MB
```

```
E4        1   CR=EISENBERG MB, IN PRESS J AM SOC IN
E5        1   CR=EISENBERG MB, 1979, P32, MEDIA METHODS MAR
E6        1   CR=EISENBERG MB, 1986, MAGNITUDE ESTIMATION
E7        1   CR=EISENBERG MB, 1986, THESIS SURACUSE U SY
E8        2   CR=EISENBERG MB, 1986, THESIS SYRACUSE U
E9        1   CR=EISENBERG MB, 1986, THESIS SYRACUSE U SY
E10       1   CR=EISENBERG MB, 1986, 49TH P AM SOC INF SC
E11       1   CR=EISENBERG MB, 1987, P66, 50TH P AM SOC INF SC
E12       1   CR=EISENBERG MB, 1987, V24, P66, 50TH P AM SOC IN

          Enter P or E for more
?p

Ref    Items   Index-term
E13       1   CR=EISENBERG MB, 1987, 50TH P AM SOC INF SC
E14       1   CR=EISENBERG MB, 1988, CURRICULUM INITIATIV
E15       3   CR=EISENBERG MB, 1988, V24, P373, INFORM PROCESS
E16       3   CR=EISENBERG MB, 1988, V24, P373, INFORMATION PRO
E17       1   CR=EISENBERG MB, 1988, V39, P293, J AM SOC INFORM
E18       2   CR=EISENBERG MB, 1990, INFORMATION PROBLEM
E19       1   CR=EISENBERG MB, 1990, V18, P139, SCH LIBRARY MED
E20       1   CR=EISENBERG MB, 1990, V18, SCH LIBRARY MEDIA Q
E21       1   CR=EISENBERG ME, 1986, THESIS SYRACUSE U SY
E22       1   CR=EISENBERG ME, 1986, V23, P360, 49TH P ANN M AS
E23       1   CR=EISENBERG ME, 1986, V64, P907, TAXES
E24       1   CR=EISENBERG MF, 1965, V7, P41, P ALLIANCE ENG ME

          Enter P or E for more
```

We see two items that look like the 1988 *IP&M* article: E15 and E16. Notice the two variant forms of the journal name for *Information Processing & Manage-* *ment*; we must select both of these to get all the citations to this work:

```
?s e15-e16
             3   CR=EISENBERG MB, 1988, V24, P373, INFORM PROCESS
             3   CR=EISENBERG MB, 1988, V24, P373, INFORMATION PRO
     S1      6   E15-E16
?t 1/3/all

  1/3/1
02356218   Genuine Article#: HR435   No. References: 17
Title: RELEVANCE JUDGMENTS OF ACTUAL USERS AND SECONDARY JUDGES - A
    COMPARATIVE-STUDY
Author(s): JANES JW; MCKINNEY R
Corporate Source: UNIV MICHIGAN,SCH INFORMAT & LIB STUDIES,550 E UNIV,304 W
    ENGN/ANN ARBOR//MI/48109; OHIO STATE UNIV,DEPT HIST/COLUMBUS//OH/43210
Journal: LIBRARY QUARTERLY, 1992, V62, N2 (APR), P150-168
Language: ENGLISH   Document Type: ARTICLE   (Abstract Available)

  1/3/2
02301895   Genuine Article#: GR501   No. References: 13
Title: RELEVANCE JUDGMENTS AND THE INCREMENTAL PRESENTATION OF DOCUMENT
    REPRESENTATIONS
Author(s): JANES JW
Corporate Source: UNIV MICHIGAN,SCH INFORMAT & LIB STUDIES,550 E UNIV,304 W
    ENGN/ANN ARBOR//MI/48109
Journal: INFORMATION PROCESSING & MANAGEMENT, 1991, V27, N6, P629-646
Language: ENGLISH   Document Type: ARTICLE
```

```
1/3/3
02299518   Genuine Article#: GP789   No. References: 7
Title: AN ALTERNATIVE TO PRECISION
Author(s): JANES JW
Corporate Source: UNIV MICHIGAN,SCH LIB & INFORMAT SCI/ANN ARBOR//MI/48109
Journal: PROCEEDINGS OF THE ASIS ANNUAL MEETING, 1991, V28, P102-105
Language: ENGLISH   Document Type: ARTICLE


1/3/4
02205563   Genuine Article#: EX755   No. References: 36
Title: AN ANALYTIC MEASURE PREDICTING INFORMATION-RETRIEVAL SYSTEM
     PERFORMANCE
Author(s): LOSEE RM
Corporate Source: UNIV N CAROLINA/CHAPEL HILL//NC/27599
Journal: INFORMATION PROCESSING & MANAGEMENT, 1991, V27, N1, P1-13
Language: ENGLISH   Document Type: ARTICLE


1/3/5
02180966   Genuine Article#: EK779   No. References: 64
Title: A REEXAMINATION OF RELEVANCE - TOWARD A DYNAMIC, SITUATIONAL
     DEFINITION
Author(s): SCHAMBER L; EISENBERG MB; NILAN MS
Corporate Source: SYRACUSE UNIV,SCH INFORMAT STUDIES/SYRACUSE//NY/13244
Journal: INFORMATION PROCESSING & MANAGEMENT, 1990, V26, N6, P755-776
Language: ENGLISH   Document Type: ARTICLE


1/3/6
02148784   Genuine Article#: DV900   No. References: 27
Title: RELEVANCE AS AN AID TO EVALUATION IN OPACS
Author(s): OBRIEN A
Corporate Source: LOUGHBOROUGH UNIV TECHNOL,DEPT LIB & INFORMAT
     STUDIES/LOUGHBOROUGH LE11 3TU/LEICS/ENGLAND/
Journal: JOURNAL OF INFORMATION SCIENCE, 1990, V16, N4, P265-271
Language: ENGLISH   Document Type: ARTICLE
```

You may also notice a number of other variations in this display. E7, E8, and E9 are all citations to Eisenberg's dissertation but with subtle differences; E11-E13 are all variations on a conference paper he presented at the 1987 American Society for Information Science (ASIS) conference; some of these have page numbers, some do not; and E21 and E22 are errors, giving his middle initial as E, not B. Further, not every citation uses his middle initial, so we also need to EXPAND on his name without the B:

```
?e cr=eisenberg m, 1986

Ref   Items   Index-term
E1       1   CR=EISENBERG M, 1985, UNPUB THEORY ADJUDIC
E2       1   CR=EISENBERG M, 1985, V33, P1, AM ARCH REHABILITA
E3       0  *CR=EISENBERG M, 1986
E4       1   CR=EISENBERG M, 1986, THESIS SYRACUSE U SY
E5       1   CR=EISENBERG M, 1986, V114, P31, MED TIMES
E6       1   CR=EISENBERG M, 1986, V23, P80, ASIS 86
E7       3   CR=EISENBERG M, 1986, V23, P80, P AM SOC INFORM S
E8       1   CR=EISENBERG M, 1987, P66, 50TH P AM SOC INF SC
E9       1   CR=EISENBERG M, 1987, UNPUB FINANCIAL SERV
E10      1   CR=EISENBERG M, 1987, UNPUB ISP DRUG TESTI
E11      1   CR=EISENBERG M, 1987, V51, P28, FED PROBAT
E12      2   CR=EISENBERG M, 1987, 50TH P AM SOC INF SC

          Enter P or E for more
?p
```

```
Ref     Items   Index-term
E13       14    CR=EISENBERG M, 1988, NATURE COMMON LAW
E14        1    CR=EISENBERG M, 1988, PROGRAMMING SCHEME
E15        2    CR=EISENBERG M, 1988, P1, NATURE COMMON LAW
E16        1    CR=EISENBERG M, 1988, P104, NATURE COMMON LAW
E17        1    CR=EISENBERG M, 1988, P135, NATURE COMMON LAW
E18        2    CR=EISENBERG M, 1988, P14, NATURE COMMON LAW
E19        1    CR=EISENBERG M, 1988, P15, NATURE COMMON LAW
E20        1    CR=EISENBERG M, 1988, P156, NATURE COMMON LAW
E21        1    CR=EISENBERG M, 1988, P2, NATURE COMMON LAW
E22        1    CR=EISENBERG M, 1988, P209, CORPORATIONS
E23        1    CR=EISENBERG M, 1988, P58, NATURE COMMONLAW
E24        1    CR=EISENBERG M, 1988, P83, NATURE COMMON LAW

            Enter P or E for more
?p

Ref     Items   Index-term
E25        1    CR=EISENBERG M, 1988, R7, NATURE COMMON LAW
E26        3    CR=EISENBERG M, 1988, V25, P164, P ASIS ANNU MEET
E27        4    CR=EISENBERG M, 1988, V39, P293, J AM SOC INFORM
E28        1    CR=EISENBERG M, 1990, PROBLEM SOLVING BIG
E29        1    CR=EISENBERG MA, 1963, V86, P673, J BACTERIOL
E30        1    CR=EISENBERG MA, 1969, V57, P50, CALIF LAW REV
E31        1    CR=EISENBERG MA, 1969, V57, P50, CALIFORNIA LAW R
E32        1    CR=EISENBERG MA, 1969, V57, P84, CALIF LAW REV
E33        1    CR=EISENBERG MA, 1972, NOV C CONC BUS STUD
E34        1    CR=EISENBERG MA, 1972, V15, P999, COMM ACM
E35        1    CR=EISENBERG MA, 1972, V15, P999, COMMUN ACM
E36        1    CR=EISENBERG MA, 1975, P375, CALIFORNIA LAW R MAR

            Enter P or E for more
```

Several of these are citations to Eisenberg's work: E4, E6-E8, E12, E26-E27. How do we know this? We have to figure it out from very abbreviated titles and a general knowledge of the field and his work. In practice, it may be very difficult to disambiguate these. We see also that another M. Eisenberg is rather prolific in legal research. Separating the two Eisenbergs' citations could be tricky, because we have no further information, such as where they are located, to help us. Citation searching can be challenging, but it can also be most rewarding if you can find the right strategies. Notice that although citations are entered as they appear in the citing article, including any errors, there is a strict format to entries. The order of elements and the punctuation and spacing have to be entered exactly:

?S CR=EISENBMAN GR, 1957, V126, P831

Let us examine a more straightforward example, now, a search for citations to the work of Elfreda Chatman, who has done some superb research on the information needs of groups of people who have not been much studied, such as older women, janitors, and so on. We begin by expanding on her name in the CA= (cited author) field:

```
?e ca=chatman e

Ref     Items    Index-term
E1         1     CA=CHATMAN D
E2         5     CA=CHATMAN DL
E3         0    *CA=CHATMAN E
E4         7     CA=CHATMAN EA
E5         6     CA=CHATMAN J
E6        23     CA=CHATMAN JA
E7         1     CA=CHATMAN JE
E8       101     CA=CHATMAN S
E9         1     CA=CHATMAN SB
E10       11     CA=CHATMAN SP
E11        5     CA=CHATMAN T
E12        1     CA=CHATOFF
```

```
         Enter P or E for more
?s e4
    S2       7  CA="CHATMAN EA"
?t 2/6/all

2/6/1
02327031   Genuine Article#: HD038   Number of References: 52
Title: CHANNELS TO A LARGER SOCIAL WORLD - OLDER WOMEN STAYING IN CONTACT
    WITH THE GREAT SOCIETY  (Abstract Available)

2/6/2
02326960   Genuine Article#: HD039   Number of References: 80
Title: INFORMATION-SEEKING BEHAVIOR OF GATEKEEPERS IN ETHNOLINGUISTIC
    COMMUNITIES - OVERVIEW OF A TAXONOMY  (Abstract Available)

2/6/3
02226679   Genuine Article#: FG046   Number of References: 95
Title: INFORMATION TECHNOLOGIES AND SOCIAL EQUITY - CONFRONTING THE
    REVOLUTION

2/6/4
02098739   Genuine Article#: CW845   Number of References: 32
Title: ALIENATION THEORY - APPLICATION OF A CONCEPTUAL-FRAMEWORK TO A STUDY
    OF INFORMATION AMONG JANITORS

2/6/5
01877264   Genuine Article#: N4010   Number of References: 51
Title: THE INFORMATION WORLD OF LOW-SKILLED WORKERS

2/6/6
01654902   Genuine Article#: E7191   Number of References: 68
Title: DIFFUSION-THEORY - A REVIEW AND TEST OF A CONCEPTUAL-MODEL IN
    INFORMATION DIFFUSION

2/6/7
01590147   Genuine Article#: C1025   Number of References: 74
Title: THE DIALECTIC OF DEFEAT - ANTIMONIES IN RESEARCH IN LIBRARY AND
    INFORMATION-SCIENCE
```

These all look correct; there is only one E. Chatman, and because all these citing works seem to be in the general area, it appears that we have the right one.

Another interesting and useful feature of the citation databases is that you can also find most[7] of the works by a particular author. We expand on the AU= field to find Chatman's work:

```
?e au=chatman e

Ref   Items   Index-term
E1      7   AU=CHATLOSH DL
E2      1   AU=CHATMAN DL
E3      0  *AU=CHATMAN E
E4      9   AU=CHATMAN EA
E5      4   AU=CHATMAN J
E6      4   AU=CHATMAN JA
E7      1   AU=CHATMAN JE
E8      1   AU=CHATMAN L
E9      4   AU=CHATMAN S
E10    10   AU=CHATMAN SP
E11     1   AU=CHATO F
E12     1   AU=CHATOFF M
```

```
          Enter P or E for more
?s e4
     S3        9  AU="CHATMAN EA"
?t 3/6/all


 3/6/1
02350780   Genuine Article#: HP254   Number of References: 51
Title: THE ROLE OF MENTORSHIP IN SHAPING PUBLIC-LIBRARY LEADERS  (Abstract
    Available)


 3/6/2
02327031   Genuine Article#: HD038   Number of References: 52
Title: CHANNELS TO A LARGER SOCIAL WORLD - OLDER WOMEN STAYING IN CONTACT
    WITH THE GREAT SOCIETY  (Abstract Available)


 3/6/3
02253985   Genuine Article#: FU468   Number of References: 96
Title: LIFE IN A SMALL WORLD - APPLICABILITY OF GRATIFICATION THEORY TO
    INFORMATION-SEEKING BEHAVIOR


 3/6/4
02098739   Genuine Article#: CW845   Number of References: 32
Title: ALIENATION THEORY - APPLICATION OF A CONCEPTUAL-FRAMEWORK TO A STUDY
    OF INFORMATION AMONG JANITORS


 3/6/5
01877264   Genuine Article#: N4010   Number of References: 51
Title: THE INFORMATION WORLD OF LOW-SKILLED WORKERS


 3/6/6
01756551   Genuine Article#: H6694   Number of References: 47
Title: OPINION LEADERSHIP, POVERTY, AND INFORMATION SHARING


 3/6/7
01654902   Genuine Article#: E7191   Number of References: 68
Title: DIFFUSION-THEORY - A REVIEW AND TEST OF A CONCEPTUAL-MODEL IN
    INFORMATION DIFFUSION


 3/6/8
01485865   Genuine Article#: ALL55   Number of References: 25
Title: INFORMATION, MASS-MEDIA USE AND THE WORKING POOR


 3/6/9
01423754   Genuine Article#: TY822   Number of References: 38
Title: FIELD-RESEARCH - METHODOLOGICAL THEMES
```

If we were to look at a full record for any of these, we would see what works Chatman has cited. You begin to envision the network of citations that is encompassed by this file. It is a fascinating, but as we have said, potentially perilous area, not the least because these files are *very* expensive to search, so speed and careful preparation are again most important.

Finally, it is also possible to conduct a rudimentary topic search in these files. A search for review articles on information needs in the information science and library science area can be quickly done. SC= is the Additional Index for subject codes, one of which is "Information Science and Library Science;" it is word-indexed so we search just on SC= INFORMATION:

```
?s information(1n)need?/ti
          30138  INFORMATION/TI
          12297  NEED?/TI
     S4     301  INFORMATION(1N)NEED?/TI
?s s4 and sc=information
```

```
           301   S4
         72014   SC=INFORMATION
    S5      182   S4 AND SC=INFORMATION
?t 5/8/1-5
```

```
  5/8/1
02353928    Genuine Article#: HQ645    Number of References: 17
Title: COMMUNITY INFORMATION NEEDS - THE CASE OF WIFE ASSAULT  (Abstract
    Available)
Journal Subject Category: INFORMATION SCIENCE & LIBRARY SCIENCE
```

```
  5/8/2
02344358    Genuine Article#: HL544    Number of References: 5
Title: INFORMATION NEEDS IN THE SOCIAL-SCIENCES - AN ASSESSMENT - GOULD,CC,
    HANDLER,M
Journal Subject Category: INFORMATION SCIENCE & LIBRARY SCIENCE
```

```
  5/8/3
02299614    Genuine Article#: GP789    Number of References: 0
Title: AN EMPIRICAL-STUDY OF MANAGEMENT PROBLEM SITUATIONS AND INFORMATION
    NEEDS - A USER DERIVED MODEL
Journal Subject Category: INFORMATION SCIENCE & LIBRARY SCIENCE; COMPUTER
    APPLICATIONS & CYBERNETICS
```

```
  5/8/4
02299532    Genuine Article#: GP789    Number of References: 18
Title: CLIENT NEEDS WITHOUT CLIENTS - CAN WE UNDERSTAND INFORMATION NEEDS
    WITHOUT CLIENTS PRESENT TO EXPLAIN THEM
Journal Subject Category: INFORMATION SCIENCE & LIBRARY SCIENCE; COMPUTER
    APPLICATIONS & CYBERNETICS
Identifiers—KeyWords Plus: RETRIEVAL
```

```
  5/8/5
02292641    Genuine Article#: GM399    Number of References: 14
Title: USERS INFORMATION NEEDS IN THE PROCESS OF LEARNING WORD-PROCESSING -
    A USER-BASED APPROACH LOOKING AT SOURCE USE
Journal Subject Category: INFORMATION SCIENCE & LIBRARY SCIENCE; COMPUTER
    APPLICATIONS & CYBERNETICS
?s s5/review
    S6      6   S5/REVIEW
?t 6/8/all
```

```
  6/8/1
01645355    Genuine Article#: E2565    Number of References: 136
Title: INFORMATION NEEDS AND USES
Journal Subject Category: INFORMATION SCIENCE & LIBRARY SCIENCE
```

```
  6/8/2
01398228    Genuine Article#: TN709    Number of References: 24
Title: THE INFORMATION NEEDS AND USES OF SCHOLARS IN THE HUMANITIES - A
    REVIEWING OF STUDIES IN THE HUMANITIES
Journal Subject Category: INFORMATION SCIENCE & LIBRARY SCIENCE
```

```
  6/8/3
01172683    Genuine Article#: PW511    Number of References: 86
Title: HUMANITIES SCHOLARS - INFORMATION NEEDS AND USES
Journal Subject Category: INFORMATION SCIENCE & LIBRARY SCIENCE
```

```
  6/8/4
00658757    Genuine Article#: FT055    Number of References: 107
Title: INFORMATION NEEDS AND USES
Journal Subject Category: INFORMATION SCIENCE & LIBRARY SCIENCE
```

```
6/8/5
00401662   Genuine Article#: CG627   Number of References: 1
Title: INFORMATION NEEDS OF SOCIAL-SCIENTISTS - REVIEW ARTICLE
Journal Subject Category: INFORMATION SCIENCE & LIBRARY SCIENCE

6/8/6
00222374   Genuine Article#: V6856   Number of References: 35
Title: INFORMATION NEEDS AND USES
Journal Subject Category: INFORMATION SCIENCE & LIBRARY SCIENCE
```

As you can see, we searched this file primarily using the EXPAND command, then SELECTing from the E-display. You certainly do not have to do this: AU=CHATMAN E? or CR=EISENBERG MB? will work. Note the truncation operators, though—these are phrase indexed fields. However, you should also have a sense now of the inconsistencies in this file. Citations are entered into the database *exactly* as they appear in the citing work, abbreviations, errors, and all. Because there is no authority control, working with an E-display allows you to identify variant forms and gives you more confidence in your searching. As with full-text searching, citation databases are powerful but require thorough preparation and some advanced skills.

> These are particularly difficult files to search because of all the inconsistencies. Nevertheless, they are worth the effort required to learn to search them efficiently, largely because the manual files are even more difficult to use, in their own way. Not only is the type so small it is practically illegible without a magnifying glass, but it is also very easy to miss relevant material. - GW

Notes

[1] Don't be fooled, though, into believing that all online files are more up-to-date than print versions. Some reference databases are updated infrequently, intermittently, or not at all. Always check the documentation before you log on and the database banner as you BEGIN to search the file to see when the last update was.

[2] Searching on numeric ranges is not difficult, as you can see, but there are several shortcuts and special features you should know about. Check whitesheets for numeric fields or system documentation to get complete details.

[3] Why /TI? Headlines, which you might think of as titles, are often of little use in searching, because their stilted style and cryptic wording make them unreliable subject indicators.

[4] Linda Schamber, Michael B. Eisenberg, and Michael S. Nilan (1990), "A Re-Examination of Relevance: Toward a Dynamic, Situational Definition," *Information Processing & Management* 26(6):755-76.

[5] Michael B. Eisenberg (1988), "Measuring Relevance Judgments," *Information Processing & Management* 24(4):373-89.

[6] The other two citation databases are *SciSearch* (file 34) and *Arts & Humanities Search* (file 439).

[7] Not everything goes into the citation databases, but most of the good journals and conferences are indexed, along with a selection of monographs, technical reports, and other sources.

W hen discussing evaluation in the context of online searching and information retrieval, we really need to talk about it from two different perspectives: the practical and the theoretical. The practical kinds of evaluation are those used in day-to-day, real-life online searching settings. The theoretical kinds are used in research into online and information retrieval issues and in design of online systems.

12

EVALUATION

These two perspectives are related, but there are important differences as well. Ideally, they should feed off each other, with practical work providing grist for the mill of theory and research, and research better informing the practice of searching. This is not always the case, unfortunately, but in this chapter we will examine evaluation from both points of view and see how they can better relate in the future.

The Basic Measures: Precision and Recall

B efore we can go very far in discussing evaluation and the issues that surround it, we must begin with the basics. There are two evaluative measures that have been used for decades in this area. They are used both in practical settings and in virtually all information retrieval research and design. As you will see, they are quite simple to compute and understand, but there are some problems with their use and interpretation. Both are expressed as ratios (or sometimes percentages) and attempt to tell us how effective or efficient a particular search or system is.

The first is *precision*, and this is defined as the proportion of documents retrieved in a given search that are relevant.[1] In formula form, it is

$$\text{precision} = \frac{\text{\# of relevant documents retrieved}}{\text{\# of documents retrieved}}$$

If a given search retrieves 50 documents, 17 of which are relevant, that search gets a precision rating of 17/50, which is 0.34 or 34 percent. A search that retrieves nothing but relevant documents would have a precision rating of 1.00, the maximum; a search retrieving no relevant documents gets a precision rating of 0.00, the minimum.

The other measure used is *recall*, and this is defined as the proportion of relevant documents in the database that are retrieved by a particular search. Its formula is

$$\text{recall} = \frac{\text{\# of relevant documents retrieved}}{\text{\# of relevant documents in database}}$$

Our search above netted 17 documents; if there were in fact 72 relevant documents in the database, we have a recall rating of 17/72, which is 0.236 or 23.6 percent. If a search retrieves all relevant documents available, it gets a recall rating of 1.00; if it retrieves no relevant documents, it gets a recall rating of 0.

A couple of things may strike you immediately. First of all, how can we know, in practice, how many relevant documents there are in the database? If we knew that, couldn't we retrieve them all? That's a good observation, and in fact recall is impossible to calculate in real life. An attempt to calculate something like it has been developed, which is called *normalized recall*. In this procedure, several searchers perform searches on a particular topic, determine how many relevant documents are in the big merged set, then calculate recall figures for each individual search. This is better than recall, but not by much. As an estimate, however, it will suffice.

In research settings, testing different search modules or improvements, searchers may actually know all the relevant documents, enabling them to calculate real recall. However, this type of research typically is done with very small document collections of several hundred to a few thousand. Systems that perform well on small collections do not always work so well on big ones of millions of documents. The bottom line is that recall is at best a metaphysical measure; it is not used much or taken seriously in practical situations.

Also, this notion of using numbers of documents, relevant and otherwise, to measure effectiveness is easy and straightforward but perhaps also simpleminded. A number of researchers (most notably Bertram Brookes[2]) have contended that it is not possible to add up "relevance" the way one would add up bricks. If one has a pile of 25 bricks and adds one more, the result is 26 bricks. This will be the same operation no matter how many bricks one starts with. With information, it is not so easy. Does a user have the same amount of additional information with the retrieval of the 54th relevant document as she did with the fourth? And does the result not also depend on the quantity and quality of the information in those documents? Some of them may be "relevant" (more problems with the definition of this word) but not contain much that is new, yet others may absolutely answer all of a user's questions and satisfy her needs.

It is not as simple as it seems at first. Recall and precision are gross measures that we can use to get a very rough idea of the performance of systems and searchers, but they cannot give us very detailed information. True, they are easy to calculate, but they mask some serious and deep theoretical questions that are as yet unresolved. Nonetheless, they are used constantly, both in research and in everyday settings.

The Recall-Precision Trade-Off

If recall and precision are not of much use as fine measurement tools, they can be helpful in establishing a mindset for a particular search. If we take them literally, then the ideal search would be one in which recall and precision both equal 1.00—a search that retrieves all the relevant documents in the database and no others. In practical terms, this is virtually impossible (except when one is searching for a single known item or doing a search to demonstrate that there are no relevant documents), but it is often perceived as the goal for which we shoot in searching.

These mindsets are often discussed in the online searching literature and practice in terms of planning a *high-recall search* or a *high-precision search*. These mindsets come not only from experiences and conversations with users, but also from the perception that there is a trade-off between the two—that it is very difficult to do a search, that is both high-recall and high-precision, so we must choose between them.

That may be true in the current situation, but we can always hope that better-designed systems and a better understanding of some of the fundamental concepts underlying information retrieval can improve our chances. But that is another story. The recall-precision trade-off is widely discussed and accepted, both for particular searches and for system design. In many cases it can be useful in planning searches.

High-precision searches: Conventional wisdom tells us that high-precision searches are best for users who are looking for a few good documents in a smallish set without a lot of garbage to wade through. The stereotypical user here is a senior researcher, faculty member, businessperson, or other person who is familiar with the field in question and only wants to pick up a few good citations. Other high-precision users might include people who cannot afford extensive, comprehensive searches, people who do not have the time or energy to wade through a long list of potentially good documents, or people for whom only a few good documents will be necessary, such as high school students with term paper assignments.

To conduct a high-precision search, we often use highly specific strategies that seek to produce small, high-quality sets. This is a perfect opportunity to use controlled vocabulary or very narrow free-text techniques, limiting to major descriptors, articles from only the last few years and in English, and so on. Perhaps the user knows of potentially good authors or journals that could be used in focusing the search— ANDing them in with bigger result sets.

High-recall searches: The other side of the coin— the quintessential high-recall user is the doctoral student doing a literature review. She wants *everything* ever written that even remotely relates to the topic, so a big, high-recall set will make her very happy. She will not mind getting junk, so long as she senses that most of the good documents have been retrieved. Getting everything is unrealistic, but the searcher can cast the net pretty wide.

High-recall searches often use lots of terms ORed together, may use free-text as well as controlled vocabulary techniques (and broader free-text strategies at that), and probably do not use year limits very extensively. Knowledge of authors or journals helps in broadening the search through pearl-growing techniques.

Beware, though, the notions that 1) these two are the only kinds of searches, and 2) that the two are mutually exclusive. A user who says he wants a high-precision search may really want more than just a few good things; another user may want a search high in both recall and precision; and the doctoral student may quickly decide she needs a more focused set. Be flexible and open and listen to the user.

We have discussed the necessity of broadening and narrowing search strategies already; figure 12.1 presents a collection of techniques we have found to be useful:

Fig. 12.1. Refining a search.

To Narrow a Search Strategy:	To Broaden a Search Strategy:
AND in a new concept set.	Stop using a concept set, especially the one *least* crucial to the query.
Use *fewer* terms in concept sets.	OR in *more* terms in concept sets.
Move *up* the ladder of specificity: Use narrower proximity operators, go from free-text to controlled vocabulary, limit to major descriptors.	Move *down* the ladder of specificity: Stop using major descriptors, go to free text, use broader proximity operators.
Truncate further to the *right*.	Truncate further to the *left*.
Use *narrower* controlled vocabulary terms.	Use *broader* controlled vocabulary terms.
Qualify search strategies to titles, descriptors, abstract.	Remove qualifiers; search in full-text field if available.
Limit by language, publication year, publication type, age group, and so on.	Remove limitations.

Other Measures of Performance

Recall and precision are fine as far as they go, but in the big bad world, other factors often intrude. For instance, a library may have policies in place that restrict searches to a particular length of time, number of citations retrieved, or total cost. In these circumstances, searching will be constrained. One can still do high-quality searching in an environment such as this, but there are added considerations.

You may not be able to do much pearl-growing, so your initial strategy for a high-recall search may have to be broader than you would like. Such a search may even not be possible, if the search is limited to 10 or 15 citations. In a high-precision search, you may not be able to focus it quite as effectively, but these constraints are usually less of a problem because this kind of search lends itself more to this setting.

A search may also be evaluated using cost or time measures. Because the system provides detailed information at the end of each search and on monthly invoices, it becomes an easy matter for management to see how long searches are taking and how much they cost. This could be good or bad: Using this information alone may give a misleading impression of search performance, but taking users' evaluations of retrievals into account as well can form a better picture of what is going on.

This also leads to another interesting question: when should a search be ended? Beginning searchers often ask this, and there is really no good answer. However, it is a good question: There has been a line of research on this matter for a number of years.[3]

There are a few rules of thumb that a searcher can use here. The first is the easiest: If the user is happy, the search can be ended. If, upon later reflection, the user decides there might be more to be retrieved, one can always try again. If the user is not present during the search, the searcher will have to rely on his own impressions of how the search is going. It will depend on whether the user wanted a high-precision, a high-recall, or some other kind of search, and on the searcher's or the user's perception of how many documents would constitute an ideal set. If one is limited by policies on length or cost, those will certainly affect the decision on when to stop. Also, one may get a sense, after searching for a while, that there is just nothing more or nothing at all to be found. One may also feel that the search is simply not going well. In such a circumstance, it may be best to save the search, get off, regroup, and try again rather than staying online and flailing around.

So far, we have discussed ways and measures used to evaluate searches from a neutral perspective. Recall, precision, time, cost—these are all objective measures used to evaluate searches, systems, and searchers, but there are other possibilities, too.

As a beginning searcher, you may feel unsure of yourself as you search. You are still learning the commands and techniques of searching, and you are probably not comfortable with the process yet. (If you are, that's great—you are one of the lucky ones.) As you gain experience, though, you will start to feel more comfortable and more confident, and this will lead you to be a better searcher. If you employ some simple self-evaluation tactics, that process will happen more quickly and more easily. Ask yourself the following questions as you review searches that you have conducted:

- *What were your best sets?* Look for sets you are particularly pleased with. Be honest—even if your search did not go particularly well, there has to be at least one set you think was pretty good. How did you get it? What techniques or strategies did you use? Is there any way you could improve on it?

> A major temptation is to "fall in love" with your results, so be strict with yourself. I find students selecting citations as "relevant" when they really have minimal usefulness. OK, I know you feel good when you complete your first few searches, but let's get real with the results. - GW

- *What sets caused you trouble?* It is easy to create a set that does not work and be unaware of it as you are doing it. Often, beginning searchers make spelling or typing errors and get sets with no items or the wrong items. When combining sets, neglecting an S in a set number can result in searching on a number rather than a set. Notice the difference between sets S4 and S5 in this example:

```
File   1:ERIC   66-92/JUN.
FILE 1: Price changes will go into effect June 1, 1992.
Please see HOMEBASE Announcements for more details.

       Set  Items  Description
       ---  -----  -----------
?ss stress variables or stress management
       S1   4143   STRESS VARIABLES  (CAUSES AND CONSEQUENCES OF
                   PSYCHOLOGICAL AN
       S2   1054   STRESS MANAGEMENT  (TECHNIQUES TO HANDLE PSYCHOLOGICAL
                   AND/OR
       S3   4762   STRESS VARIABLES OR STRESS MANAGEMENT
?s 3 and beginning teacher induction
     121807  3
        315  BEGINNING TEACHER INDUCTION  (STRUCTURED PROCESSES OR
             PROGRAMS DESIGNED T
       S4   107  3 AND BEGINNING TEACHER INDUCTION
?s s3 and beginning teacher induction
      4762  S3
       315  BEGINNING TEACHER INDUCTION  (STRUCTURED PROCESSES OR
            PROGRAMS DESIGNED T
       S5    1  S3 AND BEGINNING TEACHER INDUCTION
```

The second search statement searched on the digit 3 rather than set S3; therefore finding all documents that have the number 3 in Basic Index fields. S4 will have very little of use, while S5 is a very focused result set. An error like this can be very hard to notice online.

These technique difficulties are easier to see once the search is over and you have a chance to review the printout. Don't despair and fret about them—just make notes to yourself and try not to repeat the things that did not work. Also look for terms that are too broad or narrow and sets that are too big or too small (too many or too few terms, or search expressions at the wrong level the ladder of specificity).

- *What did you learn through this search?* Did you use any new techniques or system features? How did they work? Would you use them again, and in what situations?

- *How will you improve as a result of this search?* It sounds like a cliché, but you should aim to be a better searcher with each search that you undertake. Explicitly thinking about what you learned and how you will improve can help you to see that process and thus feel better about your searching in general.

The Other Side: Research and Theoretical Notions of Evaluation

Recall and precision are common practical methods of evaluation, but they also are used in a wide variety of research into system design, search and searcher performance, and other topics in information retrieval and online searching. Underlying these methods, though, are the central questions of evaluation: What are people looking for, and how can we measure this? This part of the chapter will give you an idea of how these questions have been addressed over the last few decades.

When we talked about recall and precision earlier, in both cases we defined them in terms of the number of relevant documents retrieved. What exactly do we mean by relevant? You probably have a pretty good idea right now of what you think relevant means. That is the problem—so does everybody else. The definition of relevance has occupied many researchers in the area of evaluation. Many possible alternate terms, expressions, and ideas have been offered over the years: topicality (documents that are on the same topic as the search request), satisfaction (documents that the user or someone else says satisfy the request), utility (documents that are useful to the user), pertinence (related to topicality and aboutness), and on and on. One of the best definitions comes from Saracevic, who in 1975 called relevance "a primitive y'know concept."[4]

> Speaking of user satisfaction, at least in a business environment it would seem that **accuracy** and **timeliness** would be considered important. For example, you can have a rough guesstimate within the hour, but an accurate answer will take a day or more. It is worth pointing out that these requirements may be in conflict, and it is necessary to establish priorities. - GW

Each of these terms seems to have some applicability and some relationship to the others. Most "relevant" documents are on the topic of the request, satisfy, and are useful to the user. Yet we have all probably had the experience of running across a "rogue" document that is way off the topic yet brings a new insight or point of view, so we pursue it, use it, and eventually are satisfied with it. Conversely, we may retrieve a beautiful document, spot on the topic—yet we have already seen it, perhaps even violently disagreeing with it, so it will never be used. Is this document "relevant" to the question at hand?

Your initial response to that question may well be that it depends—on the information about the document that we have, the query, the situation, the time and place in which that judgment is made, the user's state of mind, other documents which we have seen, and, probably most important, who is doing the judging.

All of these and more have been identified as variables that affect or influence the processes of relevance judgment. Some experimental research has been conducted to examine these issues, but there is a great deal more to be learned. We do know, for example, that relevance can be measured in much the same ways as other physical or psychological stimuli,[5] that the order in which documents are presented affects the judgments people make,[6] that judgments change in many different ways as people get more information about documents,[7] and that librarians and students make rather different judgments than do users—typically overestimating relevance but with some other interesting patterns.[8]

Schamber and others, in an excellent article reviewing more than three decades of work on relevance and related issues, end with the following conclusions about the nature of relevance and its role in information behavior:

1. Relevance is a multidimensional cognitive concept that's meaning is largely dependent on users' perceptions of information and their own information need situations.

2. Relevance is a dynamic concept that depends on users' judgments of the quality of the relationship between information and information needs at a certain point in time.

3. Relevance is a complex but systematic and measurable concept if approached

conceptually and operationally from the user's perspective.[9]

Note the words *multidimensional, dynamic, complex, systematic,* and *measurable.* Note also the heavy emphasis on the user.

What does all this mean to you as a searcher? Outside of the intellectual interest of trying to find out how and why people make the judgments they do about documents, evaluation research can offer you the following information and assistance for your searching:

- *Have the user with you during searching.* The practical online searching literature has been suggesting this for years, since research tells us that the judgments we as professionals make are sometimes quite different from those of users. Having the user there relieves you of this burden and will probably lead to better searches as you utilize feedback from the user about good documents to retrieve even more good ones.

- *If you cannot have the user with you, be liberal in judgment.* This is probably not a problem—many of us seem to do this naturally, and we are trained to do it as well. Research shows us that some information professionals and students are conservative in judgment, which may exclude potentially good documents or lead the search down a less productive path.

- *You'll get better at judgment.* Your ability to approximate users' judgments will probably improve as you gain experience in the

profession—although it will probably plateau within a few years.

- *Give the users as much information as you can about documents,* but ask them what kinds of information they will find most helpful. Titles and abstracts also help, as does information about authors and sources, especially if the user is experienced in the area. Experienced users tend to make less use of index terms in decision making; less experienced users may find them more helpful. We as professionals also seem to use subject information.

- *Do not ask yes or no questions about relevance.* Ask how good the citations are and why. Find out what features are important and whether the "good" documents are *really* good or just OK. It is more than a black or white decision, or should be.

- *Be sensitive to the dynamism of the process.* Users may actually change what they are looking for as the search progresses but might not actually say so or even realize it themselves. Also, be aware that seemingly marginal, or worse, documents may pique a user's interest for reasons we could only guess at.

As you can see, there is considerable overlap between these two perspectives on evaluation. A recent renaissance in interest and research into these issues is encouraging, because if we better understand how users make judgments about information items, we may gain insight into their information needs and help in designing systems, interfaces, and document representations to assist in answering those needs.

Notes

[1]This is, in my mind at least, the crux of the whole evaluation issue: What is "relevant" anyway, and is relevance the best measure to use to evaluate searching? We'll discuss this further in this chapter; in the meantime, rely on your intuitive notion of "relevance" for the rest of this discussion.

[2]See, for example, B. C. Brookes (1980), "Measurement in Information Science: Objective and Subjective Metrical Space," *Journal of the American Society for Information Science* 31:248-55.

[3]An older but somewhat more accessible article on this topic is D. H. Kraft and T. Lee (1979), "Stopping Rules and Their Effect on Expected Search Length," *Information Processing & Management* 15:47-58.

[4]Tefko Saracevic (1975), "Relevance: A Review of and a Framework for the Thinking on the Notion in Information Science," *Journal of the American Society for Information Science* 26(6):321-43.

[5]Michael B. Eisenberg (1988), "Measuring Relevance Judgments," *Information Processing & Management* 24(4):373-89.

[6]Michael B. Eisenberg and Carol Barry (1986), "Order Effects: A Preliminary Study of the Possible Influence of Presentation Order on User Judgments of Document Relevance," *Proceedings of the 49th Annual Meeting of the American Society for Information Science* (Medford, NJ: Learned Information), 80-86.

[7]Joseph W. Janes (1991), "Relevance Judgments and the Incremental Presentation of Document Representations," *Information Processing & Management* 27(6):629-46.

[8]Joseph W. Janes and Reneé McKinney (1992), "Relevance Judgments of Actual Users and Secondary Judges: A Comparative Study," *Library Quarterly* 62(2):150-68.

[9]Linda Schamber, Michael B. Eisenberg, and Michael S. Nilan (1990), "A Re-Examination of Relevance: Toward a Dynamic, Situational Definition," *Information Processing & Management* 26(6):755-76.

We have seen that the earliest users of online information retrieval services were professional librarians in special information agencies. But over the years the use of online systems has become increasingly common in all types of libraries. This chapter examines some of the issues involved in the setting up and management of such online search services.

Decisions regarding the allocation of available resources in libraries have become increasingly complicated over the years, involving not only the choice between different formats in which the same information may be available, but also the often conflicting claims of direct user access versus the provision of a service using trained search professionals. Funding is likely to be a crucial factor in such decision making,

13
MANAGEMENT ISSUES

and all library services have to demonstrate their efficiency and cost-effectiveness.

The following discussion is concerned with four aspects of the establishment of a search service: (1) Starting a search service, (2) Formulating policies and procedures, (3) Administering a search service, (4) Selecting and training searchers.

Many of the management issues discussed here in regard to intermediary online searching are also relevant to similar decisions that are being made by libraries considering the introduction of end-user online searching, mounting files in-house, or subscribing to databases in CD-ROM format. Some of the points discussed will also provide useful suggestions for end-users who are considering taking out an individual subscription to an online service in order to do their own searching.

Setting Up a Search Service

The first consideration when contemplating the introduction of any new library service is likely to be funding. This unpleasant fact of life is particularly relevant in the case of online searching, where the costs are highly visible. With the budgetary restrictions facing library managers today, the suggested introduction of an online search service will probably come under close scrutiny, so it is important for a proposal to be properly prepared. A process of data gathering and analysis is essential in order to determine

- whether a need exists for such a service and

- how funds can be found to implement and operate it.

One of the first problems will be to estimate the volume of usage that can be expected. Many users will probably be quite unaware of the advantages of online access to information, so that initial use is likely to depend on how effectively the service is promoted. Users will need to be told exactly what the service has to offer them and the advantages of its use. Bahr[1] recommends the development of a promotional program using marketing concepts such as market segmentation and product design in order to concentrate on the user groups that are most likely to benefit from such a service. She suggests that the best way to reach a particular market segment is to speak its language and to devise materials that focus on its particular information needs. The online vendors, too, have employed this strategy and over the years

have focused specialized services toward health-care and business users as "high benefit" groups. Some public libraries have also developed this type of specialized service geared to local industry. One objective of an online search service in an academic environment will presumably be its gradual integration into selected areas of coursework, though the exact areas are likely to depend on faculty with some personal experience and enthusiasm for online information resources.

Conversely, it may be that the implementation plan is to allow usage to grow gradually in parallel with the expertise of the searchers, rather than face the possibility of promotion leading to the service being overwhelmed in the early stages. Fliers, brochures, demonstrations, and even free searches have all been used as publicity in different situations. But overall, recommendations from satisfied customers have generally been found to be the most effective means of promoting the use of an online search service, and levels of repeat use are usually high. (See page 189 for further discussion of promotion and advertising.)

Meanwhile, the initial step to getting started will have to be an educational campaign geared toward those who will be actively involved. The education of upper management, library staff, and potential users of the service are all important. The spread of online catalogs and the more recent introduction of CD-ROM systems have both gone a good way toward convincing all these groups of the usefulness of information resources available in computerized form.

184

Perhaps the most obvious advantages to be stressed are

- the speed of searching,
- the access to a broader range of material, and
- the ability to undertake complex searches that would be impractical in a manual situation.

It is certainly very satisfying to obtain in minutes an extensive bibliography that would have required hours or even days of manual searching. The speed and apparent ease of access are particularly impressive to first-time users.

However, the costs of a search service are likely to represent a significant part of the ongoing library budget, so it is necessary to have the appropriate facts and figures at hand from the start. Start-up funding, in particular, is often difficult to acquire, and costs will probably need to be amortized over a period of years. Using purely hypothetical figures, a fixed-costs budget might look something like the following:

Hardware (computer, modem, printer)	$2,000 - $3,000 & up
Software (for telecommunications, etc.)	$100 - $600 & up
Site Preparation (power, phone line, furniture)	$0 - $4,000
Supplies (paper, forms, documentation, etc.)	$500 - $1,500 & up
Searcher Training	$0 - $1,500
TOTAL	$2,600 - ?

> And boy, are these rough numbers. Where you fall on these scales depends on so many things: Are you buying IBM-compatible or Macintosh computers? Are you getting a dot-matrix or a laser printer? Do you already have some of this equipment or software on hand? Do you need a new phone line or furniture? How extensive and intensive will your searcher training be? How strong a commitment to the online endeavor are you making? Please don't go by these as gospel; your experience may be unusual or unique—if it is, let us know! - JWJ

Regardless of the size of the intended operation, the basic costs of a microcomputer with modem and printer, the essential system documentation, and the training of search staff cannot be avoided. Sometimes it is possible to acquire this initial funding through a special start-up grant, which will cover at least the hardware and software costs. Other times it may be possible to minimize costs by negotiating the part-time use of a machine already available in the library, though this is obviously not the ideal solution and may require some sophisticated scheduling! When this departmental sharing has to be accepted, it is important that policies regarding the allocation and use of the machine be developed from the beginning.

Aside from start-up costs, the service will also need ongoing operational funds, unless it is intended to be entirely self-supporting. In reality, very few services are completely self-supporting, because even those that charge users do not normally calculate their charges to cover all overhead costs, such as staff training and time, maintenance of equipment, purchase of necessary documentation, and so on. Estimates for annual ongoing costs might look something like the following:

Equipment maintenance contract	$0 - $2,000
Additional search aids	$0 - $500
Continuing searcher training	$0 - $1,000
Stationery, etc.	$0 - $500
TOTAL	$0 - $4,000

> Same comment as above: If you choose to try to do this on the cheap, you can, but you will get a cheap service (in all senses of that word). That may or may not be the best way to go. Keeping up to date with documentation, both system-specific like bluesheets and whitesheets and database-specific like thesauri, is expensive but very valuable in terms of time and money spent online, as well as continuing training. Again, keep in mind that these are rough figures. - JWJ

It is probable that most libraries will face some additional costs as a result of introducing an online search service, and initial decisions have to be made regarding the source of the additional money that is required. Other areas of the library will not be happy to hear that their budgets are to be cut in order to finance the new service! Will online funding be part of the reference budget, because it is an extension of the normal reference service? Will that mean that the purchase of printed reference materials will be reduced, and will some items be discontinued altogether? It is clear that there are hidden ramifications here.

It is also important to recognize that areas of the library outside reference may be affected by the introduction of an online service in ways other than the purely financial. For example, it is common for libraries to experience a considerable increase in interlibrary loan requests as a direct result of offering a new online search service.

But money is merely the starting point in terms of what is required to get the service up and running. It will be essential that the search service have its own space in which to operate—space for the hardware, for administrative work, and to store the system documentation. Most libraries offering a search service do so from a single centralized site in order to minimize these space requirements. The site should be easily accessible to clients, and a highly visible location is an asset for promotional purposes. But the space also needs to offer some degree of privacy in order to conduct a confidential reference interview and provide a quiet atmosphere conducive to efficient searching. Security for expensive equipment may also need to be considered, so that the ideal choice may not be easy. The floor area should be large enough to allow room for the equipment, the searcher, at least two clients, and bookshelves for the storage of the system documentation.

It is also essential to have commitment from management in terms of staff time for searching. It is not possible to search efficiently at odd moments between other jobs. One needs dedicated time not only for the searching itself but for search preparation and practice in order to maintain search efficiency. In the University Libraries at the State University of New York at Albany, for example, almost all subject bibliographers have been trained to search and are responsible for the searches requested in their special subject fields. They have search periods built into their regular work schedules.

This raises another point for consideration. How many of the staff will be doing searching? Will searching be performed by subject specialists or will it be regarded as part of the normal reference service, seen as just an alternative resource? It seems likely that the latter will become the more general approach in the future, and it is certainly important to avoid the development of a "them versus us" mindset. It is also important that all searchers get enough practice to maintain effective search skills. This suggests that the size of the team of searchers will depend on the number of searches to be performed, which may be difficult to assess initially but will no doubt increase over time. If there are only 20 searches a month and little prospect of increasing that number, it is a waste of time and money to train a large team of searchers. But you need to recognize that fewer searches mean that the cost of each search is higher, because overhead has to be divided among fewer clients. Consider the following example:

A library spent $6,000 setting up the service and expects to amortize that amount over three years. That's $2,000 a year. Further, annual ongoing costs come to about $2,500 a year, for a total of $4,500 a year. If the average search costs $25 in online costs, and 100 searches are conducted in the first year, that's $2,500. So $7,000 ($2,500 + $4,500) has been spent to do 100 searches, for an average cost of $70 each. But if 1,000 searches are conducted in the first year at $25 each, total costs are $29,500 ($25,000 + $4,500), for an average cost of $29.50 per search. You see the difference that scale can make, and your estimates of scale may have an impact on the kind of service you plan to implement.

After all this preparatory data has been gathered, the planner will often be required to prepare a formal proposal recommending the implementation of an online search service. There are a number of useful sources in the literature, such as Wax,[2] to assist with the assessment of needs and the preparation of such a proposal. The amount of detail to be included will probably vary, depending on personalities and on the management structure of the organization involved. The basic essentials should include the plan for the service, the expected benefits, and the costing data.

Deciding Search Policies

All decisions regarding how the new search service will operate need to be implemented through the design of appropriate policies. In addition to the points already discussed, decisions will need to be made regarding the following matters:

- *What service vendor or vendors will be used?* The use of a single system and only a few databases makes it possible to keep overheads to a minimum. Complete flexibility through providing access to a variety of different search services is likely to be much more expensive. The factors affecting this decision will involve

subject coverage, the expected number of search requests and the availability of important files on particular search systems.

- *Who will do the searching?* In some organizations a single searcher will suffice, but in others a number of staff may be required to search as part of their normal duties. This decision tends to be linked to the degree to which online access is integrated into the general organizational structure of the library. Whichever policy is adopted—treating online reference as special or as a regular part of the general reference service of the library—there are related consequences. More searchers will probably mean the immediate availability of the service to users on a request basis and the promotion of team spirit and sharing of experience. But it will also require the scheduling of all searches and may lead to a reduction in the quality of searches for difficult requests, because each searcher will have more limited experience. It also appears to be a fact of life that some people are less effective and less comfortable with computers than others, so that all reference staff may not wish to become involved with online searching.

- *Who will be allowed to use the search service?* Will it focus on selected user groups? Is it intended to serve only internal users, or will outsiders be able to request searches, too? Some libraries operate on a differential policy, with different user categories being treated differently in terms of both access and costs. For example, searches may be available only to faculty or graduate students in some academic libraries, or they may be free for certain groups of privileged users. Some public libraries may charge businesses, but give free or discounted searches to individuals.

- *How will searches be paid for?* Many libraries see this "fee versus free" debate as an important ethical issue. Traditionally most libraries funded from public money have supported the professional ideal of free access to information of all types for all users. Their rationale is that information obtained from a computer is no different from information obtained from any other reference source, because all information has to be paid for in some way. It is also assumed that charging for information will inhibit its use, at least for certain user groups. In fact, it has been demonstrated that search requests are less common in those libraries that charge the user more than 10 percent of the actual search cost than in those where it is free.[3]

The fee versus free argument sometimes goes like this: Many of these sources are available in print or CD-ROM format, which are free for use. If a patron wanted to, he could go to these sources and get the same information, although admittedly it would take a long time and he might miss good things. (Who knows? He might actually do better.) If he chooses to have an online search done or do it himself, that's an extra service that we provide, but he should be willing to pay for that service. OK.

The other side goes like this: True, but some files are **only** available online or searching them manually is extremely cumbersome, and aren't we supposed to be providing service to all patrons regardless of format?

This argument goes on from there. You can fill in the details. - JWJ

Conversely, many libraries today would be unable to offer an online search service at all without recouping some of the costs involved. One partial solution is differential pricing for different groups of users. Faculty versus students, insiders versus outsiders, individuals versus businesses, all those groups are used as the basis for differentiated charging. The exact way in which charges are calculated will often vary, too. A flat rate per search (easy to calculate), a percentage of the search costs (complicated to compute), the actual online costs (available on the printout), and the displayed costs plus a profit have all been used in different situations.

Most search vendors currently charge for use of their services by a combination of connect time per hour plus charges for each individual record retrieved. Typically, connect time charges range from $15 to $120 per hour, with certain chemical and patent files going as high as $300 per connect hour. Charges for bibliographic records range from 10 cents to $10 per record, though records from some of the highly valued business files and those in full text may cost as much as $120 each.

Some services offer reduced charges as incentives to frequent customers, such as libraries, that will pay in advance for a stipulated amount of search time. The advantage to the customer is more searches for the money and simplified budgeting. The advantage to the vendor is money paid up front at the beginning of the financial year.

- *What do we do if a search is not successful?* The cause of search failure is often difficult to determine, and sometimes searches are unproductive through no failure of the searcher. Many users find it difficult to express their information needs very exactly. There is also a well-documented tendency for users to mistakenly ask for a topic broader than the topic they actually require, though this kind of misunderstanding should of course be remedied during the reference interview. On occasion the searcher may be at fault through failure to clarify the search topic, inexperience on a particular system or database, or lack of subject knowledge. Regardless of the cause for a search failure, it is probably politic in terms of maintaining good customer relations to have an official policy of offering a free search if a user is seriously dissatisfied. (The budget should allow money to cover "extras" like these.)

> Just to be difficult—some patrons **want** a zero-hit search. I call these "disconfirmatory" searches; others have called them "negative" searches. The most common type are patent searches, where the user really wants to find nothing (meaning he has a better chance at patenting his new, improved onion peeler). Other researchers, though, especially doctoral students, may want to be reassured that no one has done or reported a particular study, so the way is clear for them to do so. Zero-hit searches are not always failures, and should be paid for somehow. - JWJ

Every organization starting an online search service should consider compiling a policy and procedures manual in order to simplify these kinds of decisions. It could take the form of either a separate online searching manual or a separate chapter within the existing staff manual. It should explain which search services are available and list searcher expertise, as well as clarifying the points discussed here.

Finally, it is important to have some mechanism in place for the regular review of the operation of the online search service and its role within the general reference service. It is necessary to review the use and cost of different systems, because the advantages or disadvantages of a particular service may alter over time. New services and additional training options should be monitored for possible adoption when they are appropriate to the needs of the organization. The views of users can also be a helpful source of information in assessing the effectiveness of the search service and suggesting ways in which it can be improved.

Administration of the Search Service

A clear set of policy statements, such as those recommended here, provides a sound framework for the administration of the search service. In addition, it is advisable to design a set of forms to facilitate the task of record keeping. One of the major tasks will be keeping a search log in order to track all the searches that are performed. Such a log should include details of the searcher, search service, and database or databases used; the date and time of the search; and a record of the costs involved. These elements are important for checking the accuracy of the monthly bills as they come from the different vendors, and it is probably most convenient to enter them in the log at the time that the search is performed.

Fig. 13.1. Search Service Log.

Date	Time	System	Database(s)	Cost	Searcher

Each organization will have its own record-keeping requirements, but a chart like figure 13.1 will probably suit most situations.

It is important that all searchers be conscientious about keeping this log, because discrepancies will have to be resolved before bills can be passed to the accounts department for payment. Most host systems have mechanisms for automatically chasing unpaid accounts and may resort to threats to terminate the service when payments are unduly delayed.

> Some specialized searching software (I'm thinking here about examples like DIALOGLINK or ProSearch) will create automatic search logs that have billing and invoice modules, so if you elect to use software like this, some of this may be done for you. It could be a big time saver and also increase your confidence in the accuracy of your logs. - JWJ

Some procedure will also need to be devised in order to organize the matching of users with searchers and machine time. When searchers are allocated particular search times within their work schedules, it is necessary for users to be scheduled, too, using some kind of reservation system. This can usually be easily incorporated into the regular reference desk duties, but forms will need to be designed to facilitate booking. A great deal of the administration of the service will revolve around forms, so it is worth expending considerable thought on their initial design. A search request form is the obvious starting point, but exactly what questions should be asked? It has been found that a search request expressed in narrative form and natural language is likely to produce better results than a list of potential search terms. A known citation that can be used for pearl growing is also a useful starting point, and it is helpful to know if there are any limitations of time period or language to be imposed on the search. Is the aim of the search to be high recall or high precision? In addition to information about the search topic itself, most libraries also collect demographic data about the user for their own use—user status, academic department, previous searches, and so on. Figure 13.2 is an example of such a form:

If the user fills out a search request at the time he books a search, it will allow adequate time for the searcher to prepare the search topic in advance. (Undergraduate users in particular have been found to have difficulty expressing their exact needs, probably as a result of lack of familiarity with the subject field.)

A different type of form that will also be needed is the publicity flier intended to bring the search service to the attention of potential users. When starting a new service from scratch, one is in the contradictory position of wanting to show management how popular and well-used the service is, and yet not wanting to get deluged with more requests than one can handle! Posters, brochures, and press releases all take time to design and produce. Luckily, most libraries are willing to share their promotional materials, which are rarely copyrighted. Online service vendors also supply promotional materials, which can be adapted for local use. Figures 13.3, 13.4, and 13.5 are examples of publicity fliers, but the possibilities are obviously limited only by one's originality and, possibly, the intended audience.

Advertising is not merely a one-off operation at the time of start-up but an ongoing necessity, because the user population and user needs are continuously changing. Despite one's best efforts, people often do not seem to notice things that they do not understand or do not immediately need. Despite aggressive advertising, most use seems to come in practice as a result of previous use or personal recommendations, rather than from advertising.

Strict internal administration will often require the keeping of additional records. It will probably be necessary to collect data about the number of searches performed, the searchers who did them, the systems and databases used, the types of searches, and so on for insertion into the annual report of the unit's work. This information will be available from the search logbook, but time can be saved if it is periodically inserted into a microcomputer database system, so as to simplify the final printing and analysis. In some libraries it may also be necessary to keep forms listing the allocation of tasks and the criteria by which searchers are to be evaluated, because many organizations require formal staff evaluations on an annual basis.

Selection and Training of Searchers

Much has been written about the role of the online searcher and the characteristics that are required for success in the field.[4] Online searching is an area that requires an unusual combination of considerable system knowledge with quite complicated mechanical and analytical skills. The mechanics of searching are not difficult to master, and the necessary factual information can be learned, although there is a great deal of detail to absorb and much of it is changing rapidly. The analytical skills are much harder to acquire, because they involve what could almost be described as an individual cognitive "style." Certain characteristics have been cited as conducive to good searching—self-confidence, a logical mind, flexibility, and good communication skills, for example—but researchers have been unable to link successful searching to either intelligence[5] or personality traits.[6] It has even been suggested that a "suspicious mind" may be useful![7]

This strange set of characteristics means that most good searchers are born and self-selected rather than trained. It is clear that you cannot force people to search if they do not want to, especially if they do not accept it as part of their job description. However, some members of staff will be eager to practice their search skills whenever possible. But how does the manager evaluate the effectiveness of their searching? The following division of the search process into stages provides some criteria that may help with the evaluation of search personnel:

- A primary requirement is *knowledge of both printed and online reference sources*, possibly within a particular subject field or on a particular system. The emphasis is on practice and keeping up-to-date.

- The *reference interview* tests the searcher's ability to listen effectively, to clarify the search request, and to establish limiting parameters of language, dates, and so on. The emphasis is on communication skills.

Fig. 13.2. Sample request form from SUNY Albany Libraries.

CONTROL/REQUEST NO.

```
                         SUNY ALBANY LIBRARIES
                       COMPUTER SEARCH SERVICE
                            REQUEST FORM
```

LAST NAME_____FIRST_____PHONE: DAY_____
                                                     EVE._____

ADDRESS_____

       _____   A.   Have you done a CSS search here
                                            before?
       _____   PLEASE CIRCLE ONE (YES/NO)

B.   Please circle categories which apply and check (C) the appropriate
box/boxes. Users _must_ sign and date agreement.

ACTIVE SUNYA   NON-SUNYA (Y)
SUNYA DEPT. OR MAJOR   SUNYA STATUS   (includes SUNYA Alumni
                                                     and other SUNY units)

Business. . . . . . . .B   Faculty. . . . . . . .F   For-Profit Business. . B
Criminal Justice. . . .C   Graduate Student. . . G   Non-Profit Organiz. . .P
Education. . . . . . . E   Undergraduate. . . . .U   Other SUNY Unit. . . . N
Humanities. . . . . . .H   Staff. . . . . .S   Academic (non-SUNY). . A
Library & Info Sci. . .L   Other. . . . . .O   Empire State Coll. . . E
Natural Science/Math. .N   Other. . . . . O
Public Affairs. . . . .P
Soc/Behavioral Sci. . .S   C. ☐ I agree to pay 50% (SUNYA), or 100% plus $6
SUNYA Resrch Ctr/Inst. R   for (non-SUNYA), of cost of the online time
Univ. Admin. . . . . . A   required for this search and 100% of the
Univ. Libraries. . . . V   cost of such printing as I designate at the
Univ. Lib.-Lib. Wk. . J   time of the search.
College of Gen Study. .G
Social Welfare. . . . .W   Signature_____Date_____
Undeclared Major. . . .M   OR
Other. . . . . .O   ☐ I have arranged for this search to be
                              charged to a valid account.
                              Account #_____

                              Signature_____Date_____
```

| D. PURPOSE OF SEARCH | LANGUAGE SPECIFICATIONS | SEARCH RESTRICTION |
|---|---|---|
| _____ Term Paper | _____ English Only | Please indicate search |
| _____ Thesis or Diss | _____ Other (Specify) | limitations such as: |
| _____ Research |  | human; animal; plant; |
| _____ Other (Specify) |  | age; female; male; grade |
|  |  | level; time period; |
|  |  | racial or ethnic group; |
|  |  | geographic area. |

E.   Please give a narrative description* of the information you seek and
titles of relevant citations, if you have them.

* Search topics are confidential and, except for necessary library faculty consulta-
tion, will not be shared with others without patron consent.  If confidentiality is
of concern, please write the description of the information you seek on a separate
sheet and request to retain the sheet and your search strategy.
```

- The *design of efficient search strategies* requires the identification of key concepts, the understanding of Boolean logic, and the effective use of controlled vocabulary and natural language. The emphasis is on analytical skills.

- Performing the search efficiently requires *familiarity with the equipment*, knowledge of the features of different systems, and the ability to recognize cost-effective strategies. The emphasis is on mechanical skills.

- *Post-search tasks* involve assisting the patron with understanding the search results and explaining how to find the materials both within and outside the library. The emphasis is once again on communication skills.

These criteria suggest that the education and training of all searchers is a continuous process. There are new systems, new databases, and system refinements appearing all the time. In a one-searcher organization it is probably more efficient to limit the number of systems that are used, merely in order to limit inefficiencies that might be due to intellectual overload. In a larger organization with a team of searchers, some degree of specialization is probably appropriate. In an academic library organized on a subject specialist basis, searching can be allocated effectively by specialty. In a public library it may be easier to specialize by system.

Fig. 13.3. Publicity flier from Gallaudet College Library.

.......GIRS, GIRS*

˙GALLAUDET
Information Retrieval Service

The very diversity of available online systems may pose considerable problems for training a team of searchers, because cost is likely to be a major consideration. Rather than sending all searchers for vendor training on all systems, it is more efficient to let one searcher have "official" training on each system and use in-house workshops to transfer the knowledge they acquire to the other members of the searching team. Once all searchers have basic training, vendor workshops can be best utilized to learn details of specialized databases or new search features.

The expense of online use has led to the development of a wide range of aids and techniques to assist in the training of online searchers. DIALOG's first response to this need was the mounting of a number of mini-sized, reduced-price training files—the ON-TAP databases—to provide cheap-rate ($15 per connect hour) access for practice searching. The number of such files has increased over the years, and today such sample files are available for nearly 50 of the databases.

Most professional searchers receive their initial training within university schools of information and library science. DIALOG's classroom instruction program, available only to educational institutions, offers cheap access to almost all DIALOG files for training purposes. It has recently been enhanced and expanded to offer multiple passwords, CD-ROM files for offline practice, and student sets of documentation and sample searches for use by library school trainers.

Originally, schools had to rely on a range of noninteractive aids, such as tape-slides and videos, which are suitable for use with a wide audience. The major vendors have produced their own videos giving general overviews of their systems, and some of the schools have also produced more specialized training packages. Unfortunately, all such "static" materials tend to date rapidly.

These teaching aids can be divided into three types:

- Computer-assisted instruction packages, which merely test the students' understanding of the command language and the correct use of Boolean logic. They are helpful at a very basic level to assist rote learning of factual data.

- Simulations, which guide the trainee through a prerecorded search and correct student errors. Here the learner must follow the predefined search path without the interactive capability that is one of the most challenging aspects of online searching.

- Emulations, which are software packages incorporating a subset of the command language and a miniature database and search engine. They make it possible to perform real searches in an interactive mode, though the topics searchable are limited by the subject coverage, the small size of the database, and the limited commands available.

Emulations and simulations offer students the opportunity to gain keyboard experience, to become familiar with the command language, and, best of all, to try different features of the system at their own pace. The fact that experience is gained without incurring the expense of connect time makes for a more relaxed learning atmosphere. Similar experience is now available using CD-ROM databases, and many instructors are using them as a nonstressful way to get over the initial trauma of online!

And they work, too. For students, though, it can still be a bit of a shock to go from CD-ROM searching to online. The sets often get much bigger online, because many CDs don't go as far back as online files, and often small differences in interfaces or system operation can throw people off. I've had several students tell me they did great searches on CD-ROM—and then got very different and poorer results online. - JWJ

The increasing availability of text retrieval software, some of it used by the search services themselves (for example, BRS/Search) has encouraged some larger organizations to mount and search databases using their own mainframe machines. Widely used packages of this type are STAIRS or SIRE and

Fig. 13.4. Publicity flier from the Free Library of Philadelphia.

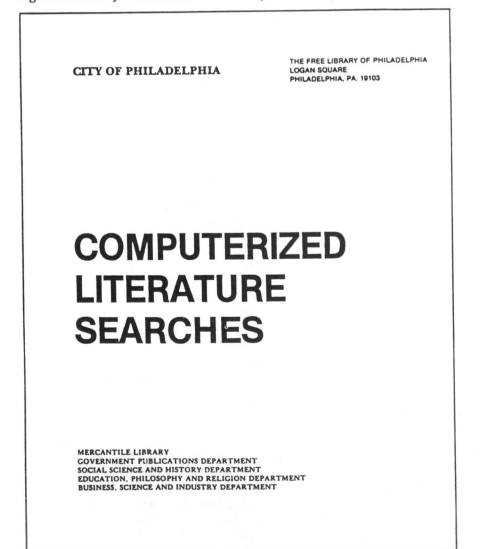

CITY OF PHILADELPHIA

THE FREE LIBRARY OF PHILADELPHIA
LOGAN SQUARE
PHILADELPHIA, PA. 19103

COMPUTERIZED LITERATURE SEARCHES

MERCANTILE LIBRARY
GOVERNMENT PUBLICATIONS DEPARTMENT
SOCIAL SCIENCE AND HISTORY DEPARTMENT
EDUCATION, PHILOSOPHY AND RELIGION DEPARTMENT
BUSINESS, SCIENCE AND INDUSTRY DEPARTMENT

Fig. 13.5. Publicity flier from the University of California.

Customized Bibliographies in the Current Literature of Education

Computer Searches
of
RESOURCES IN EDUCATION *and*
CURRENT INDEX TO JOURNALS IN EDUCATION

Here's an easy way for you to stay up to date on the literature in your field of education. Computerized Information Services (CIS) of the University of California can offer you an annual subscription to monthly searches of *Resources in Education (RIE)* and *Current Index to Journals in Education (CIJE)* prepared by the National Institute of Education, and published by the Educational Resources Information Center (ERIC). CIS automatically searches for you the computer tape versions of each issue of *RIE* and *CIJE*, which precede the printed issues by several weeks due to the time required to print, bind, and distribute the hard copy.

Resources in Education contains references to research and report literature in education, including all Office of Education-funded projects. *Current Index to Journals in Education* indexes over 600 key periodicals in education. Both indexes also include references to the literature of languages, library science, counseling and personnel service, etc.

How
CURRENT AWARENESS SEARCHING
works

This service which provides periodic searches of pertinent educational information to researchers with an on-going information need is called "current awareness" searching. Information analysts who are librarians and specialists in various subject disciplines are available throughout the CIS system to work with you in formulating search questions into a satisfactory "profile" of subject terms, codes, author names, journals, etc. Each time CIS receives a new issue of *RIE* or *CIJE*, the user's profile is matched against that issue to provide a tailor-made list of bibliographic citations which alert the user to current information in his/her area of interest.

Each computer search produces a bibliography, printed on 8½ x 11 inch paper, of retrieved citations or "alerts." Each alert contains standard bibliographic information, such as journal title, author, indexing terms, etc. In addition, *RIE* includes abstracts. For UC users the call number and UC library location of the journal in which the cited article appears will also be given.

University of California

Computerized Information Services

their microcomputer versions, such as Micro-QUESTEL. Most of these systems are based on inverted file structures and use a command-driven interface similar to those of the major vendors. The files they search may be either publicly available databases or files created within the organization itself. These in-house systems are particularly attractive for files of confidential data.

Conclusion

Broad, generalized recommendations regarding the introduction of an online search service are difficult to formulate and can be misleading. There are too many factors that can vary widely from place to place. For instance, librarians in some organizations have a high degree of autonomy and can allocate funds to provide any new service they deem appropriate, without outside consultation. Others may be able to take advantage of subsidies from

particular vendors or database producers. Yet others may have to persuade several levels of a bureaucratic hierarchy before they will be permitted to start a new service. In the latter case, the library manager will find that a well-prepared proposal based on the points discussed in this chapter will be helpful in convincing top management that online searching can provide a valuable extension to traditional reference services.

A final word from me: I would hate to have people in school media settings feel as though they have been excluded from this discussion, but the truth is that they have not figured largely in the literature. There have been a number of good articles about online in the schools, and DIALOG's Classmate program, aimed directly at the schools, is the fastest-growing segment of their service today. The school library community, for a variety of possible reasons, did not originally embrace online searching in the same numbers or depth as special, academic, or even public libraries. I understand many of the reasons why that's the case, but I also think there's some real potential here that has not yet been realized. On the bright side, though, we both think that the widespread adoption of CD-ROM systems in school settings, along with the use of E-mail networks, will lead to a larger role for online systems as well. - JWJ

Notes

[1] Alice H. Bahr (1986), "Promotion of Online Services," in *Managing Online Reference Services*, ed. Ethel Auster (New York: Neal-Schuman), 137-57.

[2] David M. Wax (1976), *A Handbook for the Introduction of Online Bibliographic Search Services into Academic Libraries* (Washington, DC: Association of Research Libraries, Office of University Library Management Studies).

[3] I. R. M. Mowat and S. E. Cannell (July 1986), "Charges for Online Searches in University Libraries: Follow-up to 1981 Survey," *Journal of Librarianship* 18(3):193-211.

[4] W. M. Henry et al. (1980), *Online Searching: An Introduction* (London: Butterworths), 98-99.

[5] Trudi Bellardo (July 1985), "An Investigation of Online Searcher Traits and Their Relationship to Search Outcome," *Journal of the American Society for Information Science* 36(4):241-50.

[6] Nancy Wolfel (1984), "Individual Differences in Online Search Behavior: The Effect of Learning Styles and Cognitive Abilities on Process and Outcome" (Ph.D. diss., Case Western Reserve University).

[7] D. R. Dolan and M. C. Kremin (April 1979), "The Quality Control of Search Analysts," *Online* 3(2):8-16.

[8] See, for example, a series of articles under the banner "Planting the Seed: Online in Schools," *Online* 11(3). These articles include Elizabeth Aversa and Jacqueline Mancall, "Online Users in Schools: A Status Report" (15-19), a collection of experiential reports from a variety of schools, and a good bibliography by Ann Lathrop (33-36). See also Lathrop's 1989 *Online and CD-ROM Databases in School Libraries: Readings* (Englewood, CO: Libraries Unlimited).

The designers of the original online bibliographic retrieval systems expected that their customers would be users seeking information to resolve their own research needs. But it soon became apparent that these early systems were too complex for casual users, who were not prepared to take the time necessary to become efficient searchers. Over the years, a general pattern of delegated searching emerged, based on libraries and other information agencies, where trained searchers acted as intemediaries between the users and the information they needed.

This chapter reviews how this pattern has changed over the last 10 years, so that today the greatest amount of computer searching is being conducted by the information users themselves. A variety of new, easy-to-use systems geared to the end-user market have been developed, which have transformed the whole environment of computerized access to information.

14
END-USER SEARCH SERVICES

Online Public Access Catalogs

The first interaction with computer search systems for most ordinary information-seekers comes through the use of an automated library catalog, which we often call an *online public access catalog*, or *OPAC*. These online catalogs started appearing in libraries in the early 1970s, usually based on the shared cataloging services offered by vendors such as OCLC. Both card-based and automated catalogs offer access to the same information; the crucial differences lie in the speed of retrieval and the interactive nature of the new online systems. The user is connected directly in "real time" to the data, which enables search requests to be modified dynamically during the progress of the search.

The new online catalogs thus offer the user expanded and more convenient access to bibliographic records, while at the same time providing functional capabilities far more diverse and powerful than their printed counterparts. They have created a problem-solving environment that supports and encourages new methods of information retrieval. The telling difference between an online catalog and a card catalog does not lie in the information accessed, but in the way that the user interacts with the system. The online catalog has not only increased the speed of searching but raised user expectations regarding what can be retrieved and also provided basic experience in the use of interactive searching that proves to be useful on other systems.

> It is worth remembering that many of these OPAC systems in academic and research institutions are now also loading external databases for in-house searching using OPAC software. Though this approach may eliminate search keys, it certainly simplifies access to a range of different types of material.[1] - JWJ

Meanwhile, as library users have become familiar with the OPAC search systems, the librarian intermediaries have remained the experts in the use of the remote search services. They have retained a kind of professional monopoly on access to certain information resources that may be available only through them. Until the early 1980s all parties to this arrangement—system vendors, intermediaries, and users— appeared to be happy with the status quo. The intermediaries provided a close-knit and well-defined market for the system vendors, and most new search features and system enhancements were targeted to their requirements. But gradually it became clear to the vendors that new markets would have to be found in order to expand their customer base.

The Market for Online End-User Systems

The microcomputer revolution provided the catalyst from which the myth of unlimited markets for online search services emerged, and over the last decade the term *end-user* has become commonplace in the online industry. The widespread availability of microcomputers that could function as dial-up terminals and the increase in general levels of computer literacy, including experience with OPACs, have changed the environment for online searching and provided a potential new market for the system vendors.

At the same time, it was also accepted that the currently available systems were too difficult for effective searching by untrained casual users, and that simplified systems would be necessary in order to develop a mass market. The impetus toward the design and development of "user-friendly" search systems was based on the assumption that the potential market for information had previously been discouraged by the complexity of the early systems. The new systems were advertised much like a new piece of household equipment, as something that no home could afford to be without.

With hindsight, this was obviously a misconception. Most people do not think in terms of formal, let alone computerized, information retrieval systems when they need to resolve a problem situation. It has since become apparent that even easy-to-use systems are of interest to only a limited market of educated users, believed to consist mainly of professional, technical, and managerial people and students. Ojala has suggested that such users are "reasonably affluent, relatively young, and computer literate,"[2] although they currently appear to be a fairly diverse group. Many of them are not regular library users, and some have never even seen a search performed. But they do have two things in common: They are all interested in searching as a new technique, and they are all experienced computer users whose initial interest was probably aroused by a spate of articles that appeared in the popular computer press during the mid-1980s.

Although the adoption of these systems has been unexpectedly slow, it seems reasonable to expect that the numbers of end-user searchers will increase as personal computers become more widely available and as greater numbers of scientists are exposed to online systems during their formative years. At the same time, it is also clear that online information access is unlikely to achieve the mass acceptance that was initially expected.

Simplified Online Systems

All computer information retrieval systems consist of three separate elements:

- the database or databases
- the search engine
- the user-system interface

The original search systems incorporated all three into the software of the vendor's mainframe machine. When the hunt for ways to popularize the systems started, attention focused on the third element—the *user interface*. The interface can best be described as the point at which the user and the system interact on both a functional and a cognitive level. It serves as a kind of filter that helps the user to exploit the system's capabilities. Without affecting the power of the search engine or the content of the databases, the interface can make the system easier or more difficult to use. It therefore became the focus for the development of simpler systems.

A number of different approaches to the problem of simplifying the interface were developed during the early 1980s. There was almost unanimous agreement that menus were the best way to enhance user-friendliness, but it gradually became clear that on occasion menus can have problems of their own. For example, individual screens must not offer too many options and the menu levels must not be nested too deeply, or users lose their conceptual picture of the logic of the system. The objective is to make the interaction as intuitive as possible, with the computer anticipating the user's next move. It is well known that computer users at all levels rarely refer to system documentation, so the system needs to be self-explanatory, and the more complicated of its operations need to be transparent to the user. It soon became clear that criteria such as these were easier to define than to implement.

A second problem to emerge in the design of new systems was that the features desired by novice searchers were found to be counterproductive for trained intermediaries. For example, a wish list of ideal features for libraries would probably include support for multiple communication protocols and autodial functions, reasonable price structures, and a reporting facility to assist administration and management decision making.[3] Conversely, features attractive to the user might include personalized distributed access, the automation of as much as possible of the search process, and some sort of information regarding likely potential costs.[4] Database selection and the development of search strategies using Boolean logic have been found to be particular problem areas for naive searchers.[5] These divergent requirements have meant that most of the new systems have developed a choice of two search modes: novice and expert. It has also become clear that providing a product to a diverse market of end-users has raised a variety of problems that were never encountered when formal information agencies provided a relatively cohesive user population.[6]

The changes involved in these moves to provide systems for end-user access have led to a major shake-down in the online marketplace, involving drastic adaptation by the original system vendors, extensive takeovers by international information conglomerates, and the entry of new groups of information entrepreneurs onto the scene. In this situation, it is hardly surprising that a number of different approaches to simplified searching have developed:

- new multipurpose systems developed specifically for end-users

- gateway systems providing a single interface to a range of different services

- simplified versions of the traditional systems, using a menu-based front-end interface

- software packages providing a similar front-end interface at the user end

- single databases on compact disk for in-house searching.

All five of these approaches are aimed at making the search process easier for untrained users by providing a user-friendly interface. Let's look at the different ways that these ends can be accomplished and how they affect the search process.

Multipurpose Systems

Systems like Prodigy and CompuServe are geared toward personal and individual information needs. They were designed from the beginning to provide a service to the end-user microcomputer market, and the original users were probably computer hackers playing with communications software. They are simple-to-use, menu-driven systems that provide access to many different types of popular information.

On these systems, an initial menu comes up automatically when the user logs-on and offers a series of options. The example shown in figure 14.1 illustrates the range of services available. These multipurpose systems concentrated at first on services such as electronic mail, bulletin boards, and timeshared use of the mainframe machine for large-scale computer processing and storage. They have gradually expanded to include databases that provide quick reference and news information, home shopping and banking, video games, education, travel, and entertainment. For example, the bulletin board menu offers the options shown in figure 14.2.

Their business sections provide up-to-date stock market data, investment advice, and financial analysis, and some of these systems can also be used to access the major bibliographic search services, such as DIALOG. The data they provide come from a variety of sources and are very varied in terms of intention and accuracy. These services are trying to provide a one-stop information and entertainment center for the widest spectrum of casual information seekers.

Fig. 14.1. Sample menu from CompuServe.

```
  CompuServe Top Menu          TOP
 1 Instructions/User Information
 2 Find a Topic
 3 Communications/Bulletin Bds.
 4 News/Weather/Sports
 5 Travel
 6 The Electronic MALL/Shopping
 7 Money Matters & Markets
 8 Entertainment/Games
 9 Home/Health/Family
10 Reference/Education
11 Computers and Technology
12 Business/Other Interests
Enter choice number :
```

Fig. 14.2. Sample bulletin board from CompuServe.

```
NATIONAL BULLETIN   Main Menu
1 BROWSE through bulletins
2 SCAN bulletins
3 KEYWORD list
4 READ a bulletin
5 COMPOSE a bulletin
```

Gateway Systems

Gateway systems are designed to provide access to a range of other online systems—a kind of one-stop supermarket for the more serious novice information-seeker. They simplify access through the use of a single password, one set of log-on protocols, and one command language. They provide links to other, usually bibliographic, search systems, rather than providing their own information resources. In effect, the gateway is the middleman between a range of online search services and its own customers, via a standardized interface provided by its gateway software.

This kind of information supermarket eliminates the problems involved in accessing a variety of systems with a range of different protocols and search languages. After an initial menu-based interaction to narrow the search request, the gateway selects an appropriate vendor and database, translates the request into a search strategy in the required command language, and downloads the retrieved citations.

The switching and translation are transparent to the user, who merely inputs the query in natural language. The big advantage of a gateway, such as Easynet, is the access it provides to a great number of online services and databases without the need for multiple passwords, protocols, and search languages.

> These gateways have proved particularly popular within school library media settings, and their menu-driven approach undoubtedly simplifies the online search negotiation for the uninitiated. A service such as IQuest or Einstein does not assume much in the way of online search skills, but the search results are obviously limited. - GW

Most of these gateways have a subscription pricing structure and online costs based on the number of documents retrieved. Input is often limited to a single search line, and the system downloads a subset of the most recent citations from those retrieved. The user receives a notification of potential costs before charges are incurred, so it is simple to control the amount of money being spent.

> Einstein, for example, offers a fixed price of $4.50 per search (or $3.50 plus $0.12 per minute telecommunications charge) to retrieve up to eight citations plus one full-text article, where available. The service can also be ordered by schools in sets of 50 single-search passwords for $225. - GW

The major disadvantage of this type of simplification is that it eliminates the interactive nature of the search, which is one of the most attractive features of the online search process.

Simplified Bibliographic Systems

These are adaptations of the traditional research-type search services we have been discussing that are provided by the major online vendors. The first of these new services was BRS/After Dark, which appeared in 1982, closely followed by DIALOG's Knowledge Index (KI). Both offered a subset of their most popular databases at reduced rates during off-peak hours, usually 6 P.M. to 6 A.M. and all day on weekends. These services were an attempt by the vendors to attract a wider searching population from among personal computer users and also to make more efficient use of slack time on their mainframe machines.

The initial response from microcomputer users in general was disappointing, though a number of libraries transferred part of their online searching to evening hours in order to take advantage of the reduced costs. It seemed that most users were unaware of the advantages of online information retrieval, despite considerable advertising in the popular computer press. It gradually emerged that most of the nonlibrary use was concentrated among small professional groups, such as doctors and lawyers, who were willing to pay for speedy access to work-related information. Both DIALOG and BRS quickly adapted their end-user services to target these specialist user populations in the medical and business fields (Colleague and Brkthru from BRS, and the Business Connection and the Medical Connection from DIALOG). DIALOG also offers a special version of KI, known as CLASSMATE, for instructional use in educational institutions.

Each service offers a group of related subject files, which can be accessed via a menu-based front end mounted on the vendor's mainframe or in command mode. The front end assists with database selection by offering a listing of subject-grouped files from which the searcher makes a choice. For example, see a sample database selection from KI in figure 14.3.

KI also helps to modify a search by offering a series of alternative strategies but does not assist with the actual selection of search terms. (See figure 14.4.)

Even with this type of help, users generally appear to be inefficient searchers in terms of speed and the comprehensiveness of their retrieval, and the numbers of those using these adapted systems have remained small. For instance, although 71 percent of physicians in a recent survey admitted that they considered it desirable to be able to search online, only 8 percent were currently using one of the systems.[7]

Although these systems do allow untrained people to perform searches and offer very attractive connect hour costs, the menu interface often limits the power of the search engine and slows the search process, so that connect time is considerably increased. In addition, menus tend to be particularly irritating for anyone who is not a complete novice, so it is now common to offer a "fast track" alternative for more experienced searchers.

Fig. 14.3. Sample database selection from KI.

```
                        Knowledge Index
                           Sections

  1  Agriculture & Nutrition          8  Law & Government
  2  Bibliography--Books & Monographs  9  Medicine & Drug Information
  3  Business Information             10  News & Current Affairs
  4  Chemistry                        11  Popular Information
  5  Computers & Electronics          12  Science & Technology
  6  Directories & Reference          13  Social Sciences & Humanities
  7  Education


Enter option NUMBER and press ENTER to continue.  Enter D for a list
of databases in each subject category of D<option number> (e.g., D2)
for specific section descriptions.


/H = Help              /L = Logoff          /Nomenu = Command Mode
? 3
```

Fig. 14.4. Sample search screen from KI.

```
                         ABI/Inform
                        Modify Search

 **   336  **  records were found

 Concept 1:GENETIC? AND TECHNOLOG?

 1.  Narrow subject concepts (logical AND)
 2.  Widen subject concepts (logical OR)
 3.  Replace subject concepts
 4.  Select limits
 5.  Select author
 6.  Select journal

 Enter option NUMBER and press ENTER to continue.
 /H = Help         /L = Logoff      /M = Previous Menu   /MM = Main Menu
 ? 2
```

Search Software

Another approach to simplifying searching provides a similar front-end interface in the form of a software package, mounted on the user's microcomputer rather than on the vendor's mainframe. This type of software is available at varying levels of sophistication:

- communications only

- single systems or databases

- multiple systems

The most basic type of communications software package merely simplifies the connection to the telecommunication network used to provide a link between remote computers. Such packages normally permit automatic log-on and facilitate uploading and downloading of files. They can sometimes be customized to perform frequently used functions via a single keystroke and may also be linked to related spreadsheet programs. Some of these packages are system-specific, others may be limited to a particular group of systems. The more sophisticated of them can be customized via a menu to assist access to a selection of online services chosen by the user. Among the best known of them are Procomm Plus, Smartcom, Xtalk, and PFS Access. They are designed to assist with the communications protocols, but have no effect on the search process at all.

The more complex packages add some limited assistance with the search process to the standard communications software. Their limitations are that they work only on a single database or a group of similar files from a single producer. For example, Wilsearch provides simple access to all the Wilson databases; MicroDISCLOSURE searches only the Disclosure databases on DIALOG. GRATEFUL MED is the most widely used of these specialized software packages. It is produced by the National Library of Medicine for use with the MEDLARS range of databases. Notice that this software is designed to recognize particular record structures available on products from individual database producers and cannot be used on other files that are constructed differently.

The general-purpose packages are the most powerful and sophisticated of the communications software packages. They can be used to access a variety of search systems and can cope with variant database formats. Not only do such programs facilitate the communications process and permit uploading and downloading, but also they can assist with tasks such as database selection, the selection and combination of search terms, and the choice of print formats.

A package such as ProSearch uses these menus and windowing (see figs. 14.5 and 14.6) to assist untrained searchers, but the upload and download features and the fast-track option also help experienced searchers. This particular package can also translate between the BRS and DIALOG command languages, collects cost data, and can be linked to related software for the manipulation and reformatting of the downloaded data.

Fig. 14.5. Sample ProSearch database selection.

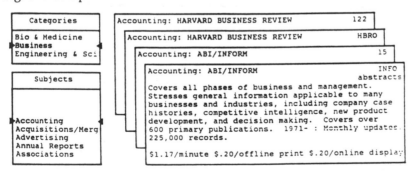

Fig. 14.6. Sample ProSearch input.

Set #	FIND/SVP REPORTS & STUDIES INDEX 196 Search Keywords and Phrases	Index Selected	Hits Found
S1	food packaging or packaged food	DESCRIPTOR	
S2	market/industry study	DOCUMENT TYPE	
S3	1982 to 1985	PUBLICATION YR	
S4	s1 and s2 and s3		
S5			
S6			
S7			
S8			
S9			
S10			
S11			
S12			
S13			
S14			

CD-ROM Search Systems

Although databases on CD-ROM (compact disk read-only memory) are not strictly online searchable files, because the user is not connected to the search system by a telecommunications link, they access many of the same databases and provide very similar search capabilities to those available o line. The first of these databases appeared in January 1985, and by 1992 there were over 2,000 disk products available from a wide range of producers (see fig. 14.7). Their big advantage for information storage is their capacity to hold very large files of information—currently about 540 megabytes. For example, the *SilverPlatter* version of the *ERIC* database, covering the years 1966 through 1992 and containing over 600,000 records, is contained on two compact disks.

CD-ROM software is characterized by its great variety and rapid change, with 80 percent of programs being used on only two or three CD-ROM titles.[9] This means that the same file is often available from different vendors with an alternative interface and different search capabilities. Many organizations in the online industry, including online search services such as DIALOG and H.W. Wilson, database producers such as Bowker and OCLC, and software producers such as Meridian Data and Lotus are all marketing databases on CD-ROM as by-products of their other services. Although the majority of these disk products use some type of menu to facilitate access, there has been no standardization of menu design.

Libraries are the major market for these new products, which are increasingly being used as substitutes for online access. The proliferating market has raised new problems for libraries regarding the most appropriate choice of disks and the most efficient methods for training users. Most libraries are now offering a variety of databases on CD-ROM for direct user searching, and it has been found that considerable training and a certain amount of professional help are necessary for the smooth operation of a library-based CD-ROM search service. In an attempt to cope with the problem of variant interfaces, some libraries have standardized on a single family of disk products. Although this lowers training costs and makes for a more efficient service, it also limits the choice of possible databases.

Originally databases on CD-ROM could only be searched by a single user at a time and required changing disks in order to change files, but multiplatter workstations are now available to enable a bank of disks to be networked for simultaneous searching and automatic switching between files. Although this is more efficient, it also makes the problems of incompatibility and the confusion of multiple interfaces more obvious. Just as many libraries now offer dial-up access to their online catalogs, some are also allowing remote use of their networked CD-ROM databases. This encourages unassisted user access from a variety of convenient locations, such as home, office, dorm, and so on.

The major disadvantage of this new search device relates to its static nature—as its name implies, CD-ROM is read only. That is, once the disk has been produced, it cannot be updated, and to incorporate the most recent data requires production of an entirely new disk. Because the mastering process is expensive and multiple copies are cheap, prices are high at present, though they have been decreasing as

Fig. 14.7. Commercially available CD-ROM titles.[8]

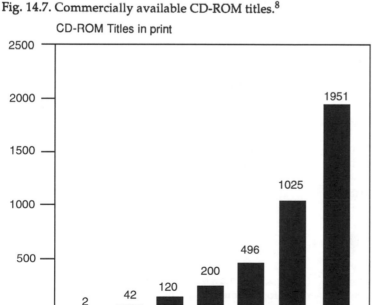

the market grows. Most CD-ROM producers offer their product on a serial basis with quarterly updates, and libraries have been attracted by this one-time cost structure, which enables tighter control over search expenditures. Increased searching no longer means increased costs; in fact, it means better value for money.

Libraries tend to select their disks based on previous patterns of frequent online use and continue to provide online service via an intermediary for access to less frequently used files.

The most noticeable development in information access in academic research libraries today is the variety of available options—print, online, CD-ROM, and locally mounted files from both in-house and external sources—used either individually, in parallel, or in combination. The very success of these new search options has meant increased activity at the reference desk in most libraries, and Tenopir has suggested that reference desks have responded by improving the level of service provided.[10] - GW

It should be noted that access to databases in CD-ROM format is likely to be particularly attractive for information agencies in the developing world, where air contamination, lack of reliable communications infrastructures, and high costs of long-distance telephone connections may limit access to remote online services. The availability of full-text information is also important for these less fortunate information users.

Future Developments

The development of all these new search options in recent years should have provided a solution to the problems of search complexity, but unfortunately initial reports suggest that this is not true. Online providers have found that "end-users are not able to use the machines easily and effectively" and that "supporting a product or service to an end-user requires a different set of skills."[11] As we have seen, the market is very fragmented, with a range of differing user requirements, and vendors have responded by concentrating on specialized services for the more easily identifiable and homogeneous user groups.

Overall, the literature tends to suggest that these new user groups are not as different from the early scientist-researchers as one might expect. It appears that their searches are usually relatively simple (low recall), they use few of the system commands, and they make minimal use of the system's interactive capabilities. Despite this, user reaction to CD-ROM databases has been overwhelmingly positive, with most libraries having to limit the length of search sessions and many having to establish reservation systems and even express lines.

A number of writers have suggested that certain situations are more appropriate for the introduction of end-user searching than others, for example, to provide immediate information, when using a single database, or when only a few articles are required. It seems fair to conclude that, despite the popularity of CD-ROM, end-user searching will never be to everyone's taste, and the role of the librarian as intermediary will continue to be preferred by some users, particularly for complicated or comprehensive searches.

To date, end-user searchers are still a very small minority, but their numbers, at least on CD-ROM databases, are growing rapidly. Under these conditions the role of the intermediary has changed from that of provider of a mediated search service to manager of a variety of search options and trainer and adviser to end-user searchers. Evidence suggests that eventually the greatest numbers of end-users will probably be outside libraries, untrained and unsupervised, using personal computers in their own homes and offices. It has been suggested that system enhancements that incorporate artificial intelligence techniques into the search interface will be needed to help these users with the choice of search terms[12] and the use of Boolean logic[13] if they are to perform effective searches.

Over the past 10 years the online industry's search for the elusive end-user market has led to the investment of enormous efforts in the design and implementation of new human-system interfaces. Whether these moves will provide the looked-for upturn in the market remains to be seen, for progress has been slow. It may be that popular acceptance is not merely a question of facilitating use but of changing long-established and ingrained behavior patterns and recognizing the value of information and information products. The wider availability of CD-ROM products may be the catalyst that will transform the information-seeking behavior of users and lead to the wider, more generalized use of online information retrieval systems in the future.

This situation is strange and somewhat disturbing. Here we are, in the midst of the Information Age (a term I find less appealing every day), and end-user searching is still a novelty to the majority of people. The technological impediments are few; there just simply does not seem to be an interest or desire to use these systems. Part of it is marketing and lack of awareness, and the fact that home computing is not as widespread as, say, VCRs, but I think a lot of it is lack of perceived value—for most people it just doesn't appear to be worth it to look for information this way.

The part that disturbs me is the same old song: Who's doing end-user searching? Business, lawyers, and doctors—the information "haves," who can afford and are willing to pay for the infrastructure and the searching costs. The rest of the population, who can't, have to have their searching done for them by intermediaries (we hope in libraries that are subsidizing the searches), or rely on other, largely print media, which are not as current. That is, provided there **is** a manual equivalent, in this era of increasingly electronic information resources.

However, because we know that the end-users aren't doing such hot searches, maybe this isn't such a bad scenario after all. - JWJ

Notes

[1] Carol Tenopir and Ralf Neufang (March 1992), "Electronic Reference Options: How They Stack Up in Research Libraries," *Online* 16(2):22-28.

[2] Marydee Ojala (1986), "Views on End-User Searching," *Journal of the American Society for Information Science* 37(4):197-203.

[3] J. Santosuosso (1986), "Requirements for Gateway Software for Libraries," *Proceedings of the Seventh National Online Meeting* (Medford, NJ: Learned Information), 409-13.

[4] Phil W. Williams (1985), "How Do We Help the End User?" *Proceedings of the Sixth National Online Meeting* (Medford, NJ: Learned Information), 495-505.

[5] Raya Fidel (1986), "Towards Expert Systems for the Selection of Search Keys," *Journal of the American Society for Information Science* 37(1):37-44.

[6] Stephen E. Arnold (1987), "End Users: Dreams or Dollars?" *Online* 11(1):71-81.

[7] Paul Nicholls et al. (1990), "A Framework for Evaluating CD-ROM Retrieval Software," *Laserdisk Professional* 3(2):41-46.

[8] Paul Nicholls and Trish Sutherland (February 1992), "CD-ROM Databases: A Survey of Commercial Publishing Activity," *Database* 15(1):36-41.

[9] Nicholls et al., "A Framework for Evaluating," 41-46.

[10] Carol Tenopir and Ralf Neufang (May 1992), "The Impact of Electronic Reference on Reference Librarians," *Online* 16(3):54-56, 58, 60.

[11] Steve Arnold (1986), "End Users: Old Myths and New Realities," *Proceedings of the Seventh National Online Meeting* (Medford, NJ: Learned Information), 5-10.

[12] Fidel, "Towards Expert Systems," 37-44.

[13] M. H. Heine (1988), "A Logic Assistant for the Database Searcher," *Information Processing & Management* 24(3):323-29.

In this final chapter, we make a bit of a departure. Up to now, we have been discussing databases that are available through traditional electronic means (if anything this recent can be considered traditional): what has come to be known, generically, as online. It encompasses systems like DIALOG, Lexis/Nexis, BRS, EPIC, and so on, also CD-ROM and other end-user-focused systems.

In the last few years, though, another mode of searching for information electronically has arisen, and it could well change the way librarians and other information professionals do their business. We are referring to information resources that are available over wide-area, high-speed, distributed networks such as the Internet.

This chapter will briefly describe what the Internet is, a bit of its history and background, what kinds of resources are available, the tools we currently use to search for them, how to get at them, how to learn more, and, finally, what it holds for the future.

15
THE INTERNET

The most important thing to remember here is that, due to the nature of this new setting, things change very quickly. It may well be that by the time you read this, some of this discussion will be out of date or simply wrong. This is not intended to be a definitive or complete description of the Internet and the resources available there. Rather, we are just trying to give you a short introduction and, we hope, intrigue you and encourage you to learn more. There are some suggestions on page 211 for books or journals you can read, but the best way to know what is going on with the network is to get onto the network and see for yourself.

We include this chapter for two reasons: First, this is a rapidly emerging area of interest for the information and library world, and it clearly relates to online searching as we have typically thought about it. More broadly, though, the development of these high-speed networks may well produce a sea change in the way we do our jobs, and so the more we know about the Internet, the better off we are.

What is the Internet?

One of the most important points to remember about the Internet is that it is not a single-minded, monolithic, centralized creature; there is no Internet czar, no InternetCorp board of directors, no U.S. Department of Internet. Rather, the Internet is really the sum of many individual, distinct parts that share certain common protocols that allow them to work together. These parts are the regional, statewide, and local area networks that tie together mainframe computers, workstations, and personal computers. These networks are able to be interconnected because they share the TCP/IP (Transmission Control Protocol/Internet Protocol) suite of protocols, standard programs that allow users to move data across disparate networks to the benefit of all. Tools like Telnet, FTP, and electronic mail, described in this chapter, can be used by almost anyone to access and provide information on the Internet, regardless of the specifics of his local network connections.

I like to think of the Internet as a network of networks, which, like Topsy, "just growed." It is a simple idea (the sharing of expensive resources and speedy communication between users) that is made very complex in implementation. It has been described using a variety of metaphors:

as a highway—**cruising the Internet**
as an ocean—**navigating the Internet**
as a place—**crossing the Internet threshold**

All of them seem appropriate. - GW

Yet although the Internet provides an array of common tools for communication and data transmission, the standards end there. There are now hundreds of thousands of computers of almost every imaginable type (IBM computers, Macintoshes, UNIX workstations, mainframes, supercomputers, etc.) connected via the Internet, with an international user community of millions from academia, government, the military, and increasingly, from business.

According to John Markoff, writing in the **New York Times** (24 January 1993, Business p. 1.6), in January 1993 there were 10 million people from 102 countries connected to the 9,000-plus networks that comprise the Internet. The number of people is continuing to double annually. - GW

As the Internet grows, there is a diminishing chance that universal standards for selecting, describing, organizing, maintaining, and weeding information can arise. No bluesheets are ever likely to exist to describe the wide array of resources available to users of the Internet. And so, those who seek information on the Internet must learn to be comfortable with an environment of widely distributed resources and decentralized control or, put simply, chaos—at least for now.

The Internet got its start back in the late 1960s, when the U.S. Department of Defense created ARPAnet, an experimental network that connected expensive supercomputers at a few military sites. Some universities and colleges owned similar mainframes and borrowed the ARPAnet protocols to share their computing resources. While these networks of mainframes were developing, the computing market itself underwent an epic upheaval with the advent of cheap, powerful microcomputers. As these proliferated, they in turn were networked using the same protocols in order to allow users to access the more powerful mainframes. As access and demand grew in the 1980s, a loose infrastructure of regional networks and national superhighways, like the NSFnet backbone, was created by government and academia to meet the increased needs of the Internet community.

Although levels of performance vary greatly at each Internet node, the current trend is toward increased data transmission speed at each site. In the mid-1980s, the maximum rate was two pages of text per second; this will soon be eclipsed by rates 800 times faster, allowing the transmission of images, audio, and real-time video, as well as text. Faster network speeds and improved software design now allow programs to be modularized, so that front ends (*clients*) can be custom designed to conform to the interface of a specific computing platform while accessing data stored on *servers* on other platforms. The continuing revolution of cheaper and ever more ubiquitously networked computers is also causing an exponential expansion of the Internet community. Those millions of academic users are accustomed to the luxury of Internet connectivity on their desktops. When they graduate, they take the Internet with them to jobs in industry, spawning more commercial nodes. The growth of commercialization calls into question whether the free (i.e., tax-funded) nature of the Internet will survive the 1990s. And yet, this decade has witnessed an explosion of resources available for no charge, thanks to democratizing technologies like Gopher, WAIS, and WorldWideWeb, as discussed on pages 209-210.

Resources Available on the Internet

If you have had some experience on the Internet, you may know of some of the resources that are available there. In this section, we will describe several different kinds of resources on the network. Some of these are very common and widely known; others less so. This is by no means an exhaustive list, but it will give you an idea of what is going on out there and how it might be useful to you.

Sources of Information

This type of resource is the closest to what we have been discussing in the online environment, but there is a much greater variety of kinds of sources on the network.

The information and library community is most familiar with *online catalogs* made available by libraries around the world. These are, today, almost exclu-

sively catalogs of research or academic libraries, because these institutions typically have better connectivity than public, school, or special libraries, most of which have poor or no connections to wide-area networks. We hope this situation may change as networking becomes more common and cheaper.

These catalogs are the same ones that are available in the owning libraries, but they have also been made available for searching over the network. This can be a boon to interlibrary loan, reference, and cataloging departments in smaller or more remote libraries. The difficulty, of course, is getting the items once they have been found. Librarians, especially in academic libraries, may find, once their campus has been connected to the Internet, that they get many more and more specific interlibrary loan requests. Why? Their patrons are exploring the network and finding items on catalogs of other institutions.

A tip for aspiring information professionals: If you are applying for a job in an academic or research library, it pays to check and see if their catalog is available over the network or if they have any other networked resources (Gophers, etc.). If they do, get on the network and play with them so that you will be able to discuss these resources intelligently during your interview. A year or so ago, that was really impressive to prospective employers; by the time you read this, it may well be expected. - JWJ

There are other information resources available. Some of the *bibliographic databases* that can be searched via DIALOG or one of the commercial vendors are also on the net. In many cases, libraries have paid license fees to the database producers and put these files up with their catalogs. In such situations, you probably will not be able to access them over the network unless you have some authorization code (e.g., valid student or staff ID number) because license agreements block access to off-campus users. Public domain databases, such as *ERIC*, may be more easily accessed.

Then there is *everything else*. There are so many different sources and kinds of sources out there that it is difficult to even give you an idea. Here are a few of our favorites; just keep in mind our caveat that they may be gone or moved or radically changed by the time you read this:

Dartmouth Dante Database
telnet to library.dartmouth.edu
login: library
This database, which uses the BRS/Search interface, provides access to the full texts of many

well-known critical texts on the works of Dante Alighieri in their original languages (English, Latin, Italian) and can be searched using free-text and other techniques.

Weather Underground
telnet to madlab.sprl.umich.edu 3000
This source provides up-to-the-minute weather forecasts for cities around the United States and abroad. It also includes fun weather information such as tornado statistics, severe weather statements, ski conditions, and so on.

Spacelink
telnet to spacelink.msfc.nasa.gov
Spacelink is a bulletin board sponsored by the National Aeronautics and Space Administration (NASA) Marshall Space Flight Center in Alabama. Primarily geared to kindergarten through 12th-grade educators and students, it contains information about shuttle launches (menu 3, option 15), astronauts' biographies, and NASA publications.

Recently PACS-L (a LISTSERV for library and information science) ran a contest to find various things through the Internet. These included the results of a Supreme Court case, newspaper stories, song lyrics, public domain computer programs, personal directories, bibliographic databases not available on DIALOG, international demographic data, and reviews of recent movies. This gives you a flavor of what is available! - GW

Files

There are many repositories of files on the network. Although it is possible to download these files in their entirety, they are not the same as full-text databases. Some of these files are not even text; they contain images. These are simply the data themselves—imagine wanting a particular article from *Magazine ASAP* or *Health Periodicals Database* and only being able to search on a 12-character title, and you get an idea what these are like. There is no database in front of these files, no controlled vocabulary or keywords to describe them, no search system to use to find what you are looking for. There is a tool called Archie, described below, which can help some-

what in looking for files, but it is extremely crude compared to DIALOG, for example.

Again, there are so many files and sites that it is daunting to even think about characterizing them in general. Here are two samples:

LIBSOFT (LIBrary SOFTware Archive)
ftp to hydra.uwo.ca
login: anonymous
password: (your E-mail address)
LIBSOFT contains programs of interest to librarians. File descriptions are in the file INDEX. TXT, which you should read before transferring files. This site does not contain any general software (word processors,

databases, etc.) as they are easily obtainable from the archives at simtel or its mirrors such as wuarchive.wustl.edu. LIBSOFT also has files to help librarians make use of the Internet. Moderator is Gord Nickerson.

Recipe Archive
ftp to gatekeeper.dec.com
login: anonymous
password: (your E-mail address)
This archive contains hundreds of recipes submitted by subscribers to the rec.food.cooking Usenet newsgroup.

You may have noticed that the LIBSOFT archive contains software in addition to text files. Often these collections, sometimes called archives, contain software that can be downloaded in a way similar to text files. This software is usually *public domain* (i.e., not copyrighted), sometimes called *freeware* or *shareware*. Shareware is software that has been written without the intent to sell it through commercial vendors, but rather to distribute it widely, via networks, cooperatives, and other methods, and ask for small donations. Surprisingly enough, it works, and shareware sites can be quite a useful method of getting cheap software. If you use shareware, send in the money. It is the right thing to do.

People: Electronic Mail, Bulletin Boards, Usenet

One of the less obvious but potentially most valuable resources available in cyberspace (a term used to describe the Internet environment) is people. Millions of people (and more all the time) are linked via the network through electronic mail systems, bulletin boards, and the Usenet. We will discuss each of these briefly:

Electronic mail (E-mail, email, Email) is arguably the simplest way to use the network, provided you have someone to send mail to. Its closest analogy is probably the telegram—you can use E-mail to send brief (sometimes not so brief) messages to other people. A sort of shorthand similar to that of the telegram has arisen in E-mail; abbreviations are common, and a variety of symbols, called *emoticons*, are used to express emotions and other nonverbal aspects. Here are a few. (Turn the page 90 degrees to the right to see them more clearly.):

:-) smile :-(frown   :-| no comment

;-) wink :-O amazement   8-O real amazement

This gives you a sense of the uniqueness of electronic mail as a communication medium. It allows a freer, more informal way of communicating; the person you are sending a message to will get it the next time he checks his mail, even at 3 in the morning; and many people find it easier to send E-mail than to call

or speak to someone face to face because it is a bit less personal.

As a way of getting information, though, E-mail can be very powerful. After reading an article or other printed version of an author's thoughts, if you can get the author's address you can E-mail her directly and ask questions. Many people on E-mail are quite amenable to this, and it can be a quick and easy way to find out otherwise unavailable information.

Bulletin boards are semi-organized chat sessions, often sponsored by a group that shares a common interest (IBM PC users' groups, role-playing game groups, bird watchers, etc.). Although a sizable proportion of the activity on such bulletin boards is back-and-forth chatter among the participants and discussions on particular topics, many allow users to ask questions and get responses from whomever is interested in replying. Bulletin boards may also provide access to commonly sought-after information that is pertinent to the topic at hand, like conference announcements, calendars, and policies. Many bulletin boards are run out of people's homes, using phone lines; others are available through the commercial, non-Internet information utilities such as CompuServe, America Online, GEnie, and Prodigy.

Usenet is a tangle of bulletin boards run wild. Available through a variety of means via wide-area networks, there are thousands of Usenet newsgroups, organized by subject, that provide an avenue for discussion, announcements, and question posting. If your institution has access to Usenet, you may have already discovered that it can be a very effective method of getting a quick answer to a question, finding an expert in a particular field, learning about new resources and sites on the Internet, or just listening in on some fascinating conversation. Here are some sample Usenet newsgroups:

talk.abortion

soc.culture.korean

rec.sport.football.college

sci.physics.fusion

comp.sys.ibm.pc.hardware

LISTSERVs

LISTSERVs are related to both electronic mail and bulletin boards. Like bulletin boards, they are organized around specific interests, yet they are not as interactive. Rather, the postings to a LISTSERV are mailed to subscribers via E-mail. There are now many hundreds of LISTSERVs, and more are organized all the time. Some are moderated, which means that the organizers read submissions, which come in via E-mail, and do some editing or selection before sending them across the network to the subscribers; others are not, and so everything received is sent. Some people find subscribing to a LISTSERV to be an exhausting proposition—one can quickly be overwhelmed by E-mail, which takes quite a while to wade through every morning.

Electronic Journals

Electronic journals are perceived by some people as the next logical step in the wide dissemination of scholarly information. Authors can submit manuscripts in electronic versions, editors send them to referees who read, evaluate, and comment on them via E-mail, and the accepted revised versions are distributed via LISTSERVs, bulletin boards, and so on. This whole process can take place much more quickly than in the print domain and may reduce costs somewhat. However, there are other potential problems with intellectual property and copyright, acceptance, and intellectual rigor. A number of such journals currently exist: *Postmodern Culture*, *Psycoloquy*, and the *International Journal of Current Clinical Trials* are some examples.

Tools

To a large extent, this section and the previous one go hand in glove. The tools described here are the ones used to access or use the resources listed above. Indeed, a few of these have been mentioned already.

The simplest tool is electronic mail, which is used to send messages to people and access and post to LISTSERVs. There are two main wide-area networks that support E-mail: BITNET, available to academic and research institutions, and Internet, available to anyone who can get on. (See pages 204-205.) There are a large number of E-mail software packages, some used with mainframe computers, others with networked microcomputers, and almost any of them can be used for the purposes discussed here. They will be unique to your institution, as will most of these tools.

The following tools are specifically for use with resources available on the Internet.

Connecting to Hosts: Telnet

When we wish to use one of the information resources somewhere on the network, we often use a standard tool known as telnet. Telnet allows you to connect directly to a remote machine; once you have made that connection, you can run programs just as if you were sitting in front of that actual machine, provided it has been made accessible to you. But you do not have to be there. You can telnet to machines anywhere—next door, in the next state, or around the world. This is how you can access library catalogs, the Dante database, Spacelink, or thousands of other information resources.

To connect to a host, you must have its address. This is not a geographic location but rather the host machine's address on the network, sometimes referred to as its IP address. Once you know this, you can connect immediately, but there is no central index of addresses. Finding out what kinds of resources are out there and what their IP addresses are is one of the great challenges of life on the networks. A lot of informal sharing of addresses goes on.

A couple of notes: Sometimes, you may attempt to telnet to a host and you will not be able to connect. This is probably because the host machine is down for some reason, or all the available network ports are filled. If the latter is the case, another port could open up quickly; just try again. If you do not get in after two or three attempts, the machine may well be down. Try again a little later.

Also, you may find that when you get to a host computer, it asks you for a login name or a password or both. It is customary when describing a system to tell people what these logins and passwords are; it is no fun to get to the front door and not know how to open it. So you often will get this information when a host is announced, say over a LISTSERV or bulletin board, or when a friend tells you about it. If you find, though, that you do not have a login or password and you need one, try some of these common ones:

For logins: login, guest, library, help, public

For passwords: guest, or just nothing at all (hit return)

If these do not work, see if you can find the person responsible for the system and send him an E-mail asking how to log on. Or try sending a message to **postmaster@xyz** where xyz is the name of the system you are trying to connect to.

Finding and Downloading Files: Archie and FTP

To grab one of those files out there (of text, software, etc.), you must use the File Transfer Protocol, usually referred to as FTP. To find out what is available, you can use a companion program called Archie.

Archie allows you to search through file names in FTP archives for particular keywords or character strings. As we mentioned earlier, this is a bare-bones kind of search; there is almost no sense of a controlled vocabulary, although some software archives have adopted index terms to describe available programs. You either have to know what you are looking for or have a really good idea what the file is likely to be called to be able to use Archie effectively. Technologically, it is a terrific tool; intellectually, it leaves a lot to be desired.

Once you have found a file you want and its path and host, either through Archie or some other way, getting a copy is very straightforward. Using FTP, you work your way through the directory structure of the host machine (these directories look a lot like DOS trees on IBM-compatible machines) until you find the subdirectory containing the file or files you want. Then, you just give the command to get the file, and it will be downloaded to your computer.

You will often hear people refer to anonymous FTP. Some files in FTP archives are freely available; others require passwords to get at them. When you use FTP to get a file, it will ask you for a login name and password. To get a freely available file, you really do not have to give a login and password; login as **anonymous** and type in your E-mail address as a password. This custom allows the system administrators to know who is using their files and to contact then if necessary.

Bringing a Little Order to Chaos: Gopher and Veronica

Telnet and FTP are fine, but they do assume that you know where you are going. You could try randomly entering addresses, but that gets boring after a while. An alternative is available in many places that makes roaming, exploring, searching, and downloading resources easier, without having to know addresses. It is called Gopher, and it was developed at the University of Minnesota (home of the Golden Gophers, hence the name). Gopher provides a hierarchical menu-driven way to move to information resources, that is, interactive resources as well as files and FTP archives.

You will have to telnet to a gopher, and once you are in, you can work through the menus. It does not much matter which gopher you start with; they are richly connected and you can move from one to another easily. The following are addresses of some public gophers:

consultant.micro.umn.edu or telnet 134.84.132.4
gopher.virginia.edu or 128.143.22.36 (logn: gwis)
panda.uiowa.edu or 128.255.40.201
grits.valdosta.peachnet.edu or 131.144.8.206
gopher.uiuc.edu or 128.174.33.160
wsuaix.csc.wsu.edu or 134.121.1.40(Logn: wsuinfo)
fatty.law.cornell.edu or 132.236.108.5
cat.ohiolink.edu or 130.108.120.25
gopher.ora.com or 140.186.65.25
finfo.tu-graz.ac.at or 129.27.2.4 (Login: info)
info.anu.edu.au or 150.203.84.20 (Aussie)
nstn.ns.ca or 137.186.128.11 (login: fred)
tolten.puc.cl or 146.155.1.16   (Chile)
gopher.denet.dk or 129.142.6.66 (Denmark)
gopher.th-darmstadt.de or 130.83.55.75
ecnet.ec or 157.100.45.2
gopher.isnet.is or 130.208.165.63
siam.mi.cnr.it or 155.253.1.40   (Italy)
sunic.sunet.se or 192.36.125.2   (Sweden)
gopher.chalmers.se or 129.16.221.40   (Sweden)
info.brad.ac.uk or 143.53.2.5 (login: info)

You must remember that although gophers are menu-driven and thus very easy to begin using, there are no standards for how these menus are organized. It is really just a matter of how the gopher organizers decided they want to do it. Often, the organization makes sense. Sometimes, it does not. You only have one-line descriptions of each menu choice, and that does not provide a lot of opportunity for elaboration. Some gophers are mounted by libraries, so they at least have some notion about how people search for information and how to organize it. Others are not, though, and some of them can be a bit cryptic. Also, as the menu structures become more elaborate and add more levels, it can become easy to get lost in the menus.

All of these difficulties notwithstanding, gophers are a major help in finding and using networked resources. They serve as islands of calm in an otherwise turbulent sea, although they do change themselves to reflect the changing nature of the information resources they cover.

As this is being written, a new tool called Veronica is just becoming available. Veronica is to Gopher as Archie is to FTP. (Get it? Archie and Veronica? Can Jughead be far behind?) It allows you to search for free-text words in menu titles of a variety of gophers. This is an admittedly cumbersome and clumsy procedure, but it can be of some use. At the moment it is rather slow and not terribly usable, but it is a good idea and may well become faster and more widely used.

Searching: WAIS

Another attempt to make these resources more accessible by providing a way to search them is Wide Area Information Servers, or WAIS (rhymes with maze). So far in discussing life in cyberspace, we have said that the tools are rather crude and not as powerful as those in online searching. With WAIS, the reverse may be true. In fact, at least one producer of online databases, Dow Jones Information Service, makes its products available via WAIS, probably because Dow Jones helped to fund the start-up of WAIS.

WAIS is an attempt to provide an interface that takes queries in natural language and performs them against a potentially large number of distributed databases. One can use a traditional Boolean approach, but the real power of WAIS comes from its use of probabilistic retrieval techniques.

Documents added to a WAIS server are indexed first. (A type of inverted file is created; documents are not indexed in the sense of using a controlled vocabulary.) When it searches documents, WAIS calculates a score based on how frequently words in the query occur in parts of the documents. It then produces a ranked list of the top documents, which then can be examined by the user. If the user finds a document that is useful, that document itself can be used as a query to find other documents like it.

It sounds great, and it is a good idea, but at present the system is still a bit primitive. It cannot deal with negation in documents, field searching, or the use of NOT; it has no stop words; and because searching is all free-text of full texts, it is vulnerable to all the problems of both free-text searching and full-text searching. Furthermore, the documents included in many of these servers are not of the same type, so users may get the apples and oranges effect. One can get some rather spectacular false drops with WAIS, but also some very good hits.

There are a number of versions of WAIS. One can get a WAIS client for a Macintosh, UNIX workstation, DOS machine, and so on, or just Telnet to quake.think.com and use the command-line interface. Login as wais and type a ? to get help.

WorldWideWeb

WorldWideWeb (WWW) uses a radically different approach to searching called hypertext. WWW allows the creation of hypertext pointers within and between documents on the Internet. These pointers can be linked to other documents or to parts of the same document. For example, a user may encounter the name Clifford Stoll in the text of a document and may wish to learn more about Stoll. In WWW, the user could select the numbered pointer beside the phrase (or in the case of a Macintosh client, the user could double-click on the phrase itself) and instantly be presented with the appropriate entry from a *Who's Who* document residing elsewhere on the Internet.

This of course assumes that someone has created the links between the two documents. It also begs the question of what actually is being linked. Perhaps the user would have preferred a bibliography of Stoll's works, his E-mail address, or his image. WWW links are based on what can be very personal associations; this could be detrimental to WWW's success as an Internet navigation tool that is usable by large-scale communities. And because the user navigates information primarily document by document, there is potential danger that the user may forget the forest for the trees. A document usually occurs within a collection or archive of related documents; this gives the information found in the document a contextual value that is less likely to be found in WWW documents.

Perhaps WWW's greatest promise lies in the possibility that it will be integrated with gopher. As one system is designed to navigate among documents, while the other moves among groups or archives of documents, the two together would seem to be complementary.

WWW was created at CERN, the European Particle Physics Laboratory in Geneva, Switzerland. To try out WWW, type info.cern.ch after accessing CERN through Telnet.

Finding People

Because the Internet community is so widely distributed and is growing so quickly, there is no single authoritative set of white pages that keeps track of everyone. Instead, there are a number of tools that offer differing levels of authority and ease of use. It is often necessary to use more than one of these tools to find an E-mail address. We will mention just a few.

One of the easiest methods is to use Gopher. Many institutions have made available their campus directories via Gopher. Chances are that if the person you wish to reach is a college student at an institution that maintains a Gopher, you will find her E-mail address there.

NETFIND is another fairly easy-to-use tool. If you query NETFIND with your friend's last name and the name of the institution that provides her an Internet account, you will often get an acceptable answer. Sometimes NETFIND may ask you to be more specific, for example, is your friend in the computer science or electrical engineering department? You can install NETFIND on your networked workstation or access the public NETFIND client software by telnetting to bruno.cs.colorado.edu

FINGER can be used if you already have a good idea of the person's domain address. You simply type finger smith@domain (e.g., smith@umich.edu) to see if there is a Smith at that domain address. If there is more than one Smith, you will be presented with a list to help you narrow your choice.

There are a lot of other approaches. You can search a WAIS source for Internet addresses of people who have submitted postings to Usenet. Or try the WHOIS databases, maintained at nic.ddn.mil and some other sites, which are especially useful for tracking down the addresses of military personnel. The X.500 directory service is an Internet-wide attempt at linking and sharing directory information among institutions, but is not yet firmly established; still it is worth a look. If you think the person you are looking for subscribes to a particular LISTSERV, you can send a message to the LISTSERV@host with the text review list-name to receive a list of its subscribers and their E-mail addresses. Or consider the radical idea of picking up the phone and calling the person, or sending him a letter instead.

Getting On

It is almost impossible to give a simple recipe for getting connected to the Internet. Much depends on your situation: Are you affiliated with a university or college, or some other institution that provides access to the Internet? If so, chances are that your institution can provide you with an account with at least minimal services, such as E-mail and FTP. If your institution does not provide Internet access, can you become affiliated fairly painlessly with one that does?

If not, you may consider applying for an account on a local bulletin board system or perhaps a FreeNet; these often provide some level of Internet access for little or no charge. Commercial Internet companies and regional networks can also provide varying arrays of Internet services for a fee.

Another important consideration is the technology available to you; that is, can you physically access your Internet account at the providing institution, or will you need to have access from your home? If the latter is the case, much will depend upon the quality of your personal computer, telecommunications software, and, especially, telecommunications hardware and connectivity. Most people access the Internet via modem and phone lines that, due to their slow transmission speeds, can support only a limited number of Internet services and software packages. However, new protocols for high-speed data transmission over phone lines, such as ISDN (Integrated Services Data Network), offer promise for the future.

Getting Going

There is not nearly enough detail here to give you a real sense of what is happening on the network. What we hope we have done is give you the briefest taste and intrigue you enough that you will explore on your own. Keep in mind that anything we have said here could be dead wrong by the time you read it, because things change so fast on the Internet. Do not be put off by that; think of it as a challenge. The best way to learn more is to read a bit more and get on the network yourself.

There are a number of books available that describe the Internet in various levels of detail and for various audiences. We can recommend that you consult one or more of these and hope that by the time you get to them, they still will be helpful to you:

> *Zen and the Art of the Internet*, by Brendan Kehoe (New York: Prentice-Hall) 1993.[1]

> *The Whole Internet*, by Ed Krol (Sebastopol, CA: O'Reilly & Assoc.) 1992.

> *The Internet Companion*, by Tracy LaQuey with Jeanne C. Ryer (Reading, MA: Addison-Wesley) 1992.

> *Crossing The Internet Threshold: An Instructional Handbook*, by Roy Tennant, John Ober, and Anne G. Lipow (Berkeley, CA: Library Solutions Press) 1993.

There are also occasional tidbits in some of the professional literature of information and library science. *Computers in Libraries* often has some good, basic material on Internet resources and the network in general; there have also been articles in *Online* and *Database*.

The best way to stay current, though, is to get on the network. Subscribe to LISTSERVs like PACS-L, read Usenet newsgroups, find bulletin board systems in your area, and ask lots of questions of everybody. Once you are on the network and feel comfortable there, which might take a bit of time, you will find yourself exploring more and more things. It is a fascinating world out there.

Comparison with Traditional Online Searching

Let us look more closely at the relationship between the networked information resources discussed in this chapter and the online databases and search techniques described in the rest of the book. The following perspectives are important:

Interface: One of the advantages of using the systems provided by large online vendors such as DIALOG is that you get a consistent interface. Whether you are searching in the *Philosopher's Index* or *MEDLINE* or *World Patents Index*, you see the same prompt, you can use the same commands, and the same command will do the same thing in each database. Now, it is true that the command-line interface of native-mode DIALOG is not the most sophisticated ever invented, and a graphical interface could certainly simplify things, especially for end-users and beginning searchers, but at least you do not have to try to remember 20 or 30 different command languages.

Because there is no central control or standardization of networked resources, you never know what kind of interface you will encounter: command-line, graphical, object-oriented, UNIX-based, DOS-based. And because many of these sources change over time, you may find new commands appearing and old ones going away.

Many of these interfaces, though, are superior in many ways to those of traditional online systems. The Macintosh and UNIX clients for WAIS are quite nice, and the Macintosh Gopher client is intuitive and easy to use for novices.

Searching: Beyond the interface, though, there is the issue of how one searches in these sources, specifically the interactive resources that one accesses through telnet or gopher. In most cases, these systems have been designed by people who have little or no background in working with large-scale textual information systems. The fact that there are now hundreds of such independent efforts complicates matters even further. As a result, these systems often provide only keyword (i.e., free-text) searching capabilities. In addition, the commands available typically are not as sophisticated as those in the online systems, not allowing, for example, proximity searching, field qualification, or limiting by document characteristics such as language and year. This can be very frustrating for the professional searcher experienced in the use of DIALOG or some other system, because retrieval will not be as effective or efficient. In many of these systems, the best a searcher can do is to go for a high-recall approach and deal with the potentially massive results afterward. Provided, of course, that one can find the resource or database in the first place.

Cost: The reason we can adopt the perspective described above is that networked information resources are, for the time being, free. That certainly removes the pressure of searching in databases that cost up to $5 a minute with extra charges for every document viewed or printed in its entirety. Yet they might not be free forever. Funding of the Internet (or what makes it run) is an open and unaddressed question, as of this writing.

Documentation: There is little documentation with networked resources. Certainly, there is nothing centrally produced that is comparable to bluesheets or whitesheets, and many of these systems have little or no online help facility.

Having said that, let us hasten to point out that in many cases, that kind of help really is not necessary—gophers, for example, are self-explanatory. However, if you use a gopher to telnet to a remote host that you have no idea how to search, you may have problems. But the people who design and implement these networked systems want you to use them, so often the greeting screen will give you introductory instructions, and many systems will lead you by the hand to help you in working through them. This is a two-way street: those instructions are nice, but, like menu-driven CD-ROM systems, you cannot do anything they did not think you would want to do or ought to do, and so you are stuck with the designer's ideas of how you will search.

Consistency, Authority, and Dynamism: We have discussed the fact that interfaces found in networked information resources are inconsistent; so are the sources themselves. Again, because of the lack of central control, almost anyone who has the technical capabilities to mount a resource can do it, whether or not the data they have to provide are accurate, up-to-date, or worthwhile. This is a real problem for searchers. One can deal with bad interfaces, no documentation, and a poor search capability, but if the information itself is unreliable that is another matter entirely.

Dynamism is an issue in two ways: First, with networked resources, new sources appear and old ones go away all the time. Certainly, the same situation occurs in the traditional online systems, but users generally receive advance notice. When DIALOG adds or removes databases, there are notices in the *Chronolog* and in the messages that appear at log-on. However, on the net, you may try to telnet to a source you have been using for months and find that it simply is not there any more. Either it has been taken down by its provider, or the address has changed. If you do not have some way to find out what happened (sending E-mail to the provider, for example—always a good idea to have these addresses handy), you may have lost that source forever. Furthermore, an absolutely perfect system may come up, and you may never know about it.

Second, the data in the sources themselves are dynamic. Within gophers, FTP archives, or interactive sources such as library catalogs, the kinds of information available may change over time, again with little or no warning. Institutionally sponsored resources such as library catalogs or gophers produced by colleges or libraries are less guilty of this, and they are more likely to notify you of any change. The major difficulty is not when new features are added but when old features go away.

End-User Versus Mediated Searching: Librarians experienced this before, when CD-ROMs became really popular. Like CD-ROMs, networked resources have been designed with untrained users in mind, so they are much simpler to learn and use. Menu-driven systems are very common. Compare this with the traditional systems with quite sophisticated command structures. As we said before, this can frustrate experienced searchers, but there seems to be little that can be done about it.

Access: One of the major concerns that have been expressed about the proliferation of networked information resources is that of access. To log-on to a traditional online service, one needs a computer, a modem, a phone line or other connectivity, telecommunications software, and an account with the vendor. These are considerable requirements, but by no means out of the reach of most libraries.

To connect to the Internet, though, one must also have access to a regional network or other service provider, which will probably mean an extra cost beyond the cost of one of the telecommunications providers used for online searching. Why? Because of bandwidth. It would be at best cumbersome, at worst impossible, to access some of these resources using a conventional 2400 baud modem over a phone line. To download a large text or software file using FTP would take forever; some of the interactive hosts simply would not work.

At the moment, academic and research libraries have the best levels of access to the network because their institutions are connected. What about public, special, and school libraries? There have been proposals to ease connections to the backbone network for these institutions, but until then, these libraries will have to pay for better connections or do without.

The Future

Trying to speculate on the future of the network environment is risky business at best; because it changes very rapidly and since no one is in charge almost anything can happen. What we will attempt to do in this final section is ponder some of the issues that are likely to be important in the next few years.

It is difficult to know what will happen to costs. If commercial activity becomes more prevalent on the Internet, you may find some providers of networked resources charging for their use. In that case, the community of users has a perfect right to demand that some of the issues discussed here, such as interface, searching power, and documentation, be addressed and resolved.

In December 1991 Congress passed and President Bush signed the $3 billion High-Performance Computing Act. The money is to be used to develop and install computer hardware and fiber optic cables and to bring some formal organization to the existing Internet. So far, not very much has happened, but change is definitely in the air. - GW

Proposals for a National Research and Education Network (NREN) have been floating around Washington, D.C., for some time. The purpose of the NREN would be to make the information superhighway of the Internet available much more easily to institutions such as schools, businesses, and, we can only hope, libraries. At this writing, the status and future of the NREN are uncertain, but it is inevitable that access to the network will increase. How it will be accomplished, and with how much equity and fairness are perhaps the most important issues.

No single entity runs the Internet. This tends to result in a lack of coordination and organization of efforts and resources. However, most network people see the lack of central control as a strength, allowing for flexibility, experimentation, and freedom. Will this ever change? Probably not. There are too many forces at work to keep things the way they are. However, if funding becomes critical, if governmental and institutional funds to support the infrastructure of the nets start to dry up and commercial funding starts to dominate, there may be greater impetus for a more centralized structure.

This impetus could also come from end-users. We think it likely that as more and more people get on the Internet and start to use these resources, they will create a demand for standardization, especially if some of these resources require payment for use. They will want more regular and predictable ways of knowing where resources are, how the information in these resources is organized, how to search them, and so on. At present, there are a few de facto standards: FTP and telnet are the basic tools but they have serious drawbacks; Gopher is extremely popular and easy to use but very limiting; WAIS makes searching easier but only of certain sources, and it remains at base a keyword approach.

The fact that most systems available here are designed for naive users does not mean that the Internet is an end-users' paradise. The kinds of complex searching techniques required for online searching may not be of great help on the network, but certainly no one will claim that there is no place on the network for people who so far have been thought of as online searchers.

In the near term, knowledge of organizational schemes of different kinds, such as controlled vocabularies, record structures, inverted files, and so on will help in searching these networked resources, as will skills, instincts, and intuitions developed in the online arena. Here is a brief sample of the specialized skills of online searchers:

- an understanding of the importance of controlled vocabulary and the difficulties of representing information and information needs in natural language

- knowledge of how to broaden or narrow searches

- the ability to find out what users really want and translate that into likely terms or keyword combinations

- experience in using the techniques available in a given system

In the longer run, though, these skills will be invaluable in the design and maintenance of networked systems. Should not people who have been trained in methods of organizing and accessing information be involved in the development of these systems? It is unclear whether traditional systems such as DIALOG will persist in an increasingly networked environment; they probably will, but new interfaces, organizational schemes, and tools will likely arise to join them, and we believe that the knowledge, skills, and experiences of present-day online searchers are an absolutely necessary component of their development.

These changes will not happen overnight. The development of organizational structures in the print world, things we now take for granted like titles, authorial credits, back-of-the-book indexes, tables of contents, section headings, and subject headings, took hundreds of years to develop. It is likely that whatever methods of organizing (one is tempted here to say humanizing) networked resources arise, they will come more quickly, but we should not expect the old ways to work that well or the new ones to fall in our laps tomorrow.

A final thought: In the past, a library could only provide access to materials that it owned—items that were physically located in the building—or that it could obtain some other way. Interlibrary loan and other sharing arrangements are examples of how libraries have dealt with the ownership problem. Access and ownership have always been inextricably tied.

Now, though, they can be separated. High-speed wide-area networks such as the Internet will make it possible to access materials immediately, regardless of where they are. Of course, ownership is still an issue, as the discussions in the literature about intellectual property and its protection in the electronic environment demonstrate only too well. If, however, the networks become ubiquitous and the resources available there become manageable or managed, this will enable librarians to do efficiently what they have always wanted to do: provide access to information quickly, economically, and freely.

We leave you with a vision of the future perhaps more uncertain than anyone could have anticipated even a few years ago. Will networked information resources mean the death of online searching as we have known it? Time will tell. What is certain, however, is that the community of people who deal with information leads and provision and the making of connections between them must be educated about these developments and must take on the responsibility of helping to shape the future that they will produce.

Note

[1]*Zen and the Art of the Internet* can, in fact, be downloaded from Project Gutenberg on the net using the FTP. Try it, and get your copy free!

Index

(). *See* (W)
(F) operator, 83, 90
(N) operator, 83, 90
(nN). *See* (N)
(nW). *See* (W)
(S) operator, 160
(W) operator, 80-83, 90, 159-160
/DF, 64
/MAJ, 64-65, 90, 97-98
/MIN, 65
? (DIALOG Truncation operator). *See* Truncation

ABI/INFORM, 33, 89, 89, 100
Abstract, 28, 63, 88, 90, 180, 183
Abstracting, 10
Academic Index, 127
Access points, 11, 113, 132
Accession number, 27
Accuracy, of searching, 182
Acquisitions, 26
Acronyms, 89, 115
Additional indexes (DIALOG), 117-18, 141, 143,
    149, 161, 170
Administration of search service, 188-89
Advertising of a search service, 189
Advice to beginning searchers, 44, 61, 69, 81, 115,
    183
Agribusiness U.S.A., 125
AIDS, 160
AIDSLINE, 1
ALERT, 128
Ambiguity, or terms, 158, 160
America Online, 207
American Library Directory, 153
American Psychological Association, 19
Analog, 22
AND (Boolean operator), 34, 43, 45, 67, 78-80, 90,
    118, 179-80
Anonymous FTP, 209
Appropriateness, of an online search, 38, 67, 113,
    149
Archie, 206, 208
Architecture Database, 140, 142
Archives (on Internet), 207, 209
Armed Services Technical Information Agency, 18
ARPANet, 17, 205
Array term, 62
Artbibliographies Modern, 142
Arthur D. Little/Online, 1
Artificial Intelligence, 202
ASCII (American Standard Code for Information
    Interchange), 124
ASK (Anomalous States of Knowledge), 12
Author, 27, 67, 88, 117, 179

Author, corporate, 28
Authority control, 118, 177
Availability (field), 28
Avery Architecture Database, 123, 140, 142

B. *See* BEGIN
Basic Index (DIALOG), 28, 43, 57, 58, 60, 63-64, 117,
    120, 159
Batch searching, 16, 198
Baud rate, 23, 25
BEGIN, 40-43, 133, 139, 141, 145
Beginning searches. *See* Advice to beginning
    searchers
Belkin, Nicholas, 12
Bias, Leonard, 58
Bibliographic citations, 1-2, 12, 18, 47, 113, 158, 195
Bibliographic networks, 11
Bibliometrics, 167
BIOSOS Previews, 3-4, 120
Bit-mapped images, 158
BITNET, 23, 208
Bits (binary digits), 22, 36
Bits per second (bps), 23
BLAISE, 23
Bluesheets, 65, 117, 119, 123-24, 127, 132, 149, 170,
    205, 212. *See also* Documentation
Books in Print, 2, 63, 149
Boole, George, 32
Boolean logic, 32, 36, 191, 202
Boolean operators, 32-35, 43, 113, 133
Boolean searching, 32-35, 197, 209
Bound descriptors. *See* Descriptors, bound
Bowker Corporation, 201
Brkthru (BRS service), 199
Broadening searches, 65, 69, 87, 89-99, 115, 179-80,
    213
Broader term, 61, 65, 69, 90
Brochures. *See* Promotional materials
Brookes, Bertram, 178
BRS, 36, 83, 198
BRS/After Dark, 198
BRS/Search, 192
Budget, for search service, 185
Buffer, 25
Building blocks. *See* Concept blocks
Bulletin boards, electronic, 19, 129, 197, 207-8, 211
Business Connection (DIALOG service), 199
Business users, 184, 187
Bytes, 22

CA Search, 1
Card catalogs. *See* Library catalogs
Card-based systems, 15